the Cultural Study of Music
a critical introduction

edited by Martin Clayton
Trevor Herbert
Richard Middleton

Routledge
New York and London

Published in 2003 by
Routledge
29 West 35th Street
New York, NY 10001
www.routledge-ny.com

Published in Great Britain by
Routledge
11 New Fetter Lane
London EC4P 4EE
www.routledge.co.uk

10 9 8 7 6 5 4

Library of Congress Cataloging-in-Publication Data

The cultural study of music : a critical introduction / edited by Martin Clayton,
Trevor Herbert, Richard Middleton.
    p.   cm.
   Includes bibliographical references and index.
     ISBN 0-415-93844-9 (hardcover : alk. paper) — ISBN 0-415-93845-7
(pbk. : alk paper)
     1. Music—Philosophy and aesthetics. 2. Music—Social aspects. I. Clayton,
Martin. II. Herbert, Trevor. III. Middleton, Richard.
     ML3845 .C85 2002
     306.4'84—dc21

                                                        2002152031

Contents

v

PART II *Issues and Debates*

Music Studies and the Idea of Culture

RICHARD MIDDLETON

In recent years we have, one might suppose, seen the publication of more than enough navel-gazing collections exploring the current state of the disciplines of music studies. Why another? The idea for this book arose in a quite specific moment. Members of the newly formed Musics and Cultures Research Group at The Open University in Britain found that, although their work as individuals stemmed from a variety of disciplinary positions, they shared a sense that, to quote the book proposal:

> A tendency towards increasing concern with "culture" has been manifested in music scholarship for some time, and in a variety of ways. It would be too much to say that the various trajectories are converging, let alone that all will crystallize into a single field of "cultural musicology." Nonetheless, different approaches are interacting, and with increasing intensity, such that it is clear that a new paradigm may well be on the horizon. All the disciplines involved in the study of music will continue to be changed by this process, and some form of reconfiguration seems inevitable.

It is more than five years since the original discussions, and the degree of programmatic clarity signaled, however hesitantly, in that statement already looks premature. The contents of this book could certainly not be taken to justify the announcement of any new paradigm (even though they do map many of the trajectories, approaches, and changes that we had in mind); but that was to be expected. More disappointing is the fact

I

that, in the discipline at large, the process of reconfiguration seems to have slowed markedly. This alone would justify engagement with the questions that initially exercised us, especially when so many other essays in intradisciplinary reassessment concentrate on one perspective alone (gender, the canon, history, musical analysis, or whatever the case may be).

To look across the full range of disciplinary perspectives is important. Indeed, the parallelism of the different histories of engagement with "musics and cultures" research, together with their varied dialogues, seems to be integral to its problematic. The cultural turn in ethnomusicology associated above all with Alan Merriam's *The Anthropology of Music* (1964) and carried forward subsequently by Blacking, Feld, and many others; the maturing (from Howard Becker to Antoine Hennion and Tia DeNora) of a cultural sociology interested in music; the emergence of Anglophone cultural studies in the 1970s, its work on music partly overlapping with the equally new area of popular music studies (Frith, Hebdige, Grossberg, Tagg); the development of a "new" or "critical musicology," its birth conventionally dated from Joseph Kerman's *Musicology* (1985), and most influentially represented in the work of such authors as McClary, Tomlinson, and Kramer: the concurrence of these histories, roughly through the final three decades of the twentieth century, following distinctive but often mutually affecting routes, marks a historical node in thinking about music that demands attention. This story, of course, is a story of the Western, particularly the Anglophone, academy. But then, notwithstanding the fruits of a multitude of ethnographic fieldwork projects, that academy has been conspicuously poor at learning from other intellectual traditions, or recognizing its impact in the outside world.

It is hard to delineate with precision all that these various trajectories have in common, beyond a position against pure musical autonomy: "Music is more than *notes*" represents the bottom line, an idea whose seeming banality today perhaps signals its triumph. But this idea would hardly have come as a surprise to Baroque theorists of *Affektenlehre*, or medieval thinkers about music and theology, or even Plato (not to mention classical Indian or Chinese music theorists). What was new in the late twentieth century, however, was precisely the concept of *culture*, in a specific sense associated with the post-Enlightenment world. We will return to the ramifications of this concept; for now, it is enough to note the political thrust of its usages in late modernity, which, within musical studies, has generated a whole range of characteristic impulses: attacks on "the canon," on "great composer history," and on "transcendental" aesthetics;

critiques of "positivistic" historiographies and analytical methods; deconstructions of patriarchal, ethnocentric and other "ideological" interpretations; valorization of popular music cultures; the relativizing of differences between musical systems; and so on. On this level, the new approaches all stand for the proposition that *culture matters,* and that therefore any attempts to study music without situating it culturally are illegitimate (and probably self-interested).

Still, even on this level, some might be tempted to ask what all the fuss is about. Surely this battle has been won. Does anyone still believe that musicology is the study of the scores of the great masters and nothing more? Aren't we all, to a greater or lesser extent, culturalists now? Well actually, the buzz of the new apparent at conferences, in journals and publishers' lists, and in certain university departments masks a rather slow rate of change, together with innumerable tactical adjustments in the academy at large designed to mask conservatism with the minimal accommodation possible. There is still plenty to fight for. Indeed, not only is the small proportion of academic posts allocated to specialists in ethnomusicology or popular music indicative of this conservatism, it is all too clear that the pace of this accommodation is much slower than the speed with which these disciplines are transforming themselves.

But in any case, to locate the battle on this terrain is to succumb to the parochialism of much of the old musicology itself. A tendency to treat the category of "culture" as transparent and universal, and therefore its accommodation as purely pragmatic, needs to be brought up against its historicity: as Francis Mulhern (2000, xiii) has pointed out, "culture" is a *topic,* and, as one of the most successful topics of late-modern discourse, has assumed the status of a commonplace—one of "those places in discourse in which an entire group meets and recognises itself" (Bourdieu 1993b, 168). It is this dimension of the commonsensical that explains how culture can so often still be taken for granted; to advance the debate, to win the battle, eventually perhaps to reconfigure the field, demands as a minimum the recognition that an introduction to the cultural study of music should be *critical*—and a useful starting point is the awareness that the concepts of both "culture" and "critique," in their recognizable modern meanings, emerged concurrently in the moment of the European Enlightenment.

Previously, the discourse of culture had metaphorically linked the cultivation of mind and of ground: the culturing of inner and outer nature, through education on the one hand and by farmers on the other, formed a coherent conceptual field. But, while many ramifications of this metaphor have survived, in the late eighteenth century—in England and especially in Germany—the idea of "culture" took on a more politicized edge: it assumed the role of critique (*Kulturkritik*, as the Germans put it), posed against the contemporary concept (typically French) of *civilization*. "Culture" now stood for inward, spiritual qualities, a wholeness of life, as against the apparently external, mechanical, alienating characteristics of Enlightenment democracy, in the emergent phase of industrial capitalism. This new culture concept soon split into divergent tendencies. The humanistic proposition of a universal measure of value ("the best which has been thought and said in the world . . . the study of perfection," in Matthew Arnold's words of 1869 [1993, 6, 11]) was one, and it possessed a distinct moral dimension: right thinking led to right living. But this perspective could be narrowed to a focus on culture as art—the best art, naturally, the art of an elite—or, in a later variant, to the sphere of meaning as such, the symbolic order. A third tendency—the *völkisch* turn—began with Herder's equation of cultures (plural rather than singular) with distinctive ways of life, each embodying a national soul; in this approach, a people "has a culture," and its value is incommensurate with any other. It is easy to recognize the influence of this view on the development of the discipline of cultural anthropology and on early ethnomusicology, but it also fed into many strands of cultural studies.

These three tendencies have competed, interacted, and mutated. That story has been told many times, classically by Raymond Williams (1961, 1965, 1981), and in recent books by (among others), Adam Kuper (1999), Terry Eagleton (2000), and Francis Mulhern (2000). It does not need repeating here. It is worth drawing attention, though, to a few of the most important features; these take the form of continuities on the one hand, and contradictions on the other.

The continuities arise precisely from the culture concept's historicity. Culture may, in one sense, be a universal attribute of humankind, but we cannot escape the specific provenance of culture theory and its historical development. In the tradition this development represents, culture always has a political force (even when it is posed as antipolitical); indeed, it often threatens to absorb or displace the sphere of politics as more conventionally understood. In part this is because culture functions as an other: it "is always defined in opposition to something else" (Kuper 1999, 14)—economics, society, psychology, biology—and its representations have their roots elsewhere: in a golden past, in a utopian future, in the captivating unfamiliarity of "primitive" societies, of the "folk," the "people," the anthropologically *different*. It is defined, too, in opposition to Nature: Culture is what is learned, what is cultivated; it is just what is not in the genes, and culture theories have figured in a long-standing critical relationship not only with raciologies of various sorts but also with more reputable disciplines of evolutionist anthropology, social Darwinism and, today, evolutionary psychology. At the same time, culture can seem "natural"; and indeed, the organic metaphor—good culture as wholeness and health—has a strong presence in much of the theory. Terry Eagleton has worked hard to close this gap: "If culture really does go all the way down, then it seems to play just the same role as nature, and feels just as natural to us"; but this coherence is deceptive: "what is peculiar about a symbol-making creature is that it is of its nature to transcend itself. . . . It is not that culture is our nature, but that it is *of* our nature, which makes our life difficult. . . . Culture is the 'supplement' which plugs a gap at the heart of our nature, and our material needs are then reinflected in its terms. . . . Human nature is naturally unnatural, overflowing the measure simply by virtue of what it is." (Eagleton 2000, 94, 97, 99, 101) The gap, then, is inescapable—indeed "natural." But its representations, in such formulations as these, are historically specific—part of the history of the theory; and the tension between nature and culture is part of a broader crisis of knowledge. If the culture idea—from Vico through Marx, Nietzsche, and Freud to Sartre, Williams, and Habermas—is a secular theory of man's self-making, then it carries along with it an inevitable strand of reflexivity that ensures that it will always fall short of what it claims. Eagleton again: "What is it that connects culture as utopian critique, culture as way of life and culture as artistic creation?" (20). The answer is that all are responses to "the failure of culture as actual civilisation—as the grand narrative of human self-development" (23); "culture in this sense arises when civilisation begins to seem self-contradictory. . . . Our very notion of culture thus rests on a peculiarly modern alienation of the social from the economic, meaning from material life. . . . It [culture] is itself the illness to which it proposes a cure" (31).

To even glance at the continuities within culture theories is thus to find the contradictions also flooding out. There is a strong strand right across the theories emphasizing culture as the sphere of meaning, of collective symbolic discourse, webs of significance, processes of signification; culture in this view is the dimension in which humans interpret their activities, institutions, and beliefs to themselves. Yet an equally strong tradition emphasizes that, far from being just a commentary, culture is *everything*. Thus, Raymond Williams, who talked often of culture in terms that focused on signifying practices, "meaning-bearing activity in all its forms" (Mulhern 2000, xiii), nevertheless offered as his considered formula for a theory of culture "a theory of relations between elements in a whole way of life" (Williams 1961, 12). In a reciprocal tension, cultural anthropology, while never forgetting Tylor's classic definition—"the complex whole" (1871, 1)—has also, particularly since the 1950s, followed Talcott Parsons's narrower perspective in claiming the study of collective consciousness as the specific province for the discipline, alongside and by contrast with the different arenas policed by sociology, economics, and psychology; and indeed the "hermeneutic turn" evident in the work of many of Parsons's successors in American anthropology—from Geertz to Clifford—further extends the idea of culture as a "text," and sidelines these other arenas almost completely. There are many variants of this tension. It can be written in terms of a distinction between culture as *practice* (e.g., Bourdieu 1977) and culture as the sphere of *subjectivity*, of identity formation (e.g., Bhabha 1994; Morley and Chen 1996). Or it can be figured through the picture of culture as a specific sector or subsystem in a complex set of relationships with other systems—this is Parsons's view, but an even more influential theory is of course that associated with Marx, in contrast with the idea that culture is more of a register, a level of thought and discourse applicable to all social spheres: this is the thrust of the later Williams's cultural materialism, neatly encapsulated by Stuart Hall—"Culture is not *a* practice. . . . It is threaded through *all* social practices, and is the sum of their interrelationship" (Hall 1980, 59).

Other significant contradictions within the nexus of culture theories often relate to, but sometimes cut across, this one. Is culture a human universal, and if so, is it ethically or aesthetically normative or merely a capacity that is ontologically given? Alternatively, can culture only be thought of relative to history, place, and context, and if so, are cultures radically noncomparable? If the latter is the case, judgment across boundaries—which, in today's fragmented, fluid societies, can be quite localized—would seem to be ruled out, let alone general projects of human emancipation. But if culture is taken to be a putative substantive universal, it is hard to avoid the elitism of Arnold, T. S. Eliot, and other proponents of traditional *Kulturkritik*. Should culture be seen, then, as making any sort of claim to special or specialist value or ambition, or is it, in Williams's telling word, radically *ordinary*, the property of everyman (and woman)? A final question (final for now) might be this: If culture is learned, and if, especially, it is seen as providing in today's world the mechanisms for ever-mutable self-identifications, does this mean that it is entirely "performative"? Or is there, still, any sense in which culture can be regarded as authentic (or not)—as "true (or not) to . . . (something)"? Part of the price paid for the seeming triumph of the culture idea is the difficulty this leaves in specifying that "something."

With these questions, the political dimension of the culture idea emerges clearly. Mulhern has, intriguingly, connected the apparently different traditions of European (initially German) *Kulturkritik* and Anglophone cultural studies, the leftist, relativistic populism of the second acting, it would seem, as a radical critique of the elitist universalism of the first. What links them, he argues, is their displacement or absorption of "real" politics: they offer an alternative locus of authority, which acts as "a 'magical solution' to the poverty of politics in bourgeois society" (2000, 168), providing "a symbolic metapolitical resolution of the contradictions of capitalist modernity" (169). From distinct viewpoints, both Eagleton (2000) and Kuper (1999) also note the overweening status of culture in contemporary understanding and explanation, attacking the tendency to reduce issues to a purely cultural level, and often an especially localist, relativistic cultural level at that. All three writers call for a greater modesty on the part of culture theorists, a recognition that culture is not all there is. For Kuper, "unless we separate out the various processes that are lumped together under the heading of culture, and then look beyond the field of culture to other processes, we will not get far in understanding any of it" (1999, 247).

Such issues are particularly pressing at the present moment. "Identity politics" have inscribed cultural claims and sufferings as primary weapons of struggle, in ways that can as easily have reactionary as progressive outcomes. The culture wars in the academy, especially in the United States, have positioned elitists against populists. But, as Eagleton points out (2000, chapter 3), they function as a rather provincial proxy for broader conflicts: between concepts of culture as civility, as identity, and as commerce; and on the global level, between a singular culture standing, in mystificatory fashion, for a hegemonic new world order and a host of threatened little worlds and neglected or threatening outlooks and problems. After September 11, 2001, Samuel Huntington's prophecy that henceforth "the great divisions among humankind and the dominating source of conflict will be cultural" (quoted, Kuper 1999, 3) took on a particularly terrifying quality as the reduction of political, economic, and social difference (not to say injustice) to culture tout court assumed official status. To resist such facile culturalism is a *political* imperative; lives depend on it. And even if, heeding the call for modesty, we acknowledge the limited power of music scholars to change the world, it remains important to note the degree of congruence between the writers I have cited, which suggests that an important turn in conceptions of the culture idea may be in progress. If we take a fresh look at the cultural inscription of music—where necessary, "disaggregating" spheres, to use Kuper's word, and reconfiguring relationships—we may both improve our understanding of culture, and clear some room for politics, both "real" and "cultural" politics. We may also, who knows, happen upon a new paradigm for the cultural study of music.

The contents of this book could in one sense certainly be seen as congruent with a policy of disaggregation. The editors proposed no particular concept of culture and no line was laid down. Our strongest suggestion to authors was that they write polemical essays, placing the stress at least as much on where music studies might (or ought to) be heading as on summaries of work done on their topic to date.

Part I addresses the music–culture question but by circling around it, from a variety of perspectives involving a range of disciplinary standpoints, intersections, and themes. Tellingly perhaps, we did initially plan a chapter that would consider the question head on (music and culture, music in culture, music as culture, etc.) but failed to recruit an author willing to take it on; we eventually accepted the point that this might be a gap worth leaving. This part of the book takes the shape, then, of a debate between different concepts not only of music and culture but also of society and history, and their possible interrelationships. In Part II the treatment becomes even more specific, each component chapter being oriented around a key issue or debate; the list makes no claim to comprehensiveness, but rather is generated by topical urgency.

The choice of chapter subjects was not just pragmatic, however. They emerged out of our own understandings of where the key issues are currently located. And indeed, a striking quality in the completed book is the extent to which a cluster of overarching themes, many of them already identified in this Introduction, appears.

This is of course not to prescribe any particular reading strategy. Part of the condition of writing or editing any book is that, happily enough, one has no control over the ways in which it will be read and discussed. In preparing this volume, nonetheless, we had it in mind to facilitate certain kinds of usage. Thus, it should be suitable for use not only in university teaching at master's or final-year undergraduate level, but also accessible to readers outside the academic establishment (hence, for instance, the almost complete absence of footnotes and the inclusion of a list of further reading at the end of each chapter); and it should be accessible not only to musicians, but also to anyone interested in the ways in which cultural approaches have been, and can be, applied to music (no author relies on music notation in developing his or her argument). The simplicity of the two-part structure is partly in recognition of the fact that it can be read other than cover-to-cover: In fact, for many purposes (including, but not limited to, university seminars) readers will find it useful to read, successively, two or more chapters dealing with closely related topics (such as the clusters mentioned below). The arguments will sometimes be mutually reinforcing and sometimes contradictory—they do not serve some overbearing model of the relationship between music and culture so much as reveal a patchwork of distinct, but also overlapping and complementary, conceptions of that relationship.

Many contributors are concerned with the central cultural theory category of *meaning*. This is of course particularly true of Lawrence Kramer's chapter on hermeneutics, in which he emphasizes the inescapability of music's discursive construction, a topic approached from a different angle by Martin Clayton; but the issue appears in a variety of forms elsewhere, from discussions (and critiques) of homology theories by John Shepherd and Ian Biddle to Kevin Dawe's account of musical instruments as sites of meaning production, from Ruth Finnegan's emphasis on the role of emotion to the wider-ranging theory of "affordance" utilized by Eric Clarke and Nicola Dibben. Jason Toynbee puts forward, and Richard Middleton exemplifies, a notion of musical meaning as produced by "ensembles of coded voices"; but otherwise, it is striking that rigorous semiotic theories popular some years ago have become much less central. More visible—and indeed more urgently discussed currently—is an interest in the connection of meaning construction with the production of *subjectivity* and *identity*. Simon Frith's description of how users employ music as a "technology of self," balanced by Nicholas Cook's account of how identity emerges through performance, should be mentioned here, in addition to authors already named, and we should note the suggestion that identity is often not unitary but fragmented, as emphasized, for instance, by psychoanalytic theorists such as Jacques Lacan, drawn upon by both Middleton and Biddle. The domain of *listening*, or, to use the language of cultural studies, *consumption*, is often a privileged sphere for that discipline, and receives considerable attention here. Frith, Clarke, Dibben, and Finnegan all lay stress on the importance of "ordinary," "everyday" listening and vernacular interpretation, but there is more emphasis on perceptual and affective levels of response than is often the case; Clayton addresses the relationship between such vernacular interpretation and "expert" discourses. The other side of this debate, of course, is constituted by *text* and/or *performance*. Jeff Todd Titon carries Geertz's textualism and his strategy of "thick description" even further than its originator, arguing for the multivoiced quality of all cultural texts, while Kramer construes musical texts, more conventionally defined, as always sites for discursive elaboration—or "constructive description," as he terms it. Cook presents performances not as texts but as scripts, which structure social contexts and meanings; Ian Cross sees the human infant as primed for interactive musical behavior, a state with adaptive evolutionary value; and Ian Biddle describes the "performativity" of music and of our representations of it as offering important cultural resources through which other dimensions of subjectivity, such as gender and sexuality, can be performed out. Both Cook and Kramer, and also Antoine Hennion, regard the apparent *autonomy* of musical works making up the Western musical canon, and the disengaged listening practices recommended for their appreciation, as atypical and highly historically contingent cases. Gary Tomlinson suggests that the emergence of the category of autonomous instrumental music was responsible for the discipline split between music anthropology and music history, previously part of a relatively holistic focus on the semantically rich, culturally embedded category of song. But Hennion insists that the specificity of aesthetic experience is irreducible, and similarly, David Clarke, while by no means blind to the contingent and ideological claims of autonomy, argues for a sense of its variegated dispersal across a range of repertories, and the utopian potential of this dispersal, not least in the context of the means–end rationality to which musical meaning is often reduced in commodity culture.

A characteristic figure in contemporary discussions of musical repertoires, identities, and meaning effects is that of dialogue or alterity: musical subjects are defined in relation to their *Others*. For Tomlinson, as we have seen, autonomous art music arose as a subject of history, in contrast to the allegedly timeless exotic "others" who were the subjects of anthropology. Rob Wegman presents the past itself as the other with which the historian, guiltily aware of his narcissistic subjectivism, struggles for objectivity. Philip Bohlman presents colonial, racial, and national encounters as figures of alterity, constructing historical knots of music–culture disjuncture. For Richard Middleton, the figure of "the people" functions in a similar way, while Ian Biddle locates boundaries of gender and sexuality (masculine/feminine; hetero/homo) in relation to analogous distinctions within musical practice. Understandings of such musical categories as "art" music, "world" music (Martin Stokes, Dawe), and "popular" music (Middleton, Frith, Trevor Herbert) are readily interpreted this way. So too is the interplay of *"local" and "global,"* a key trope in the present turn-of-the-century mood. It underpins Bohlman's culturalist historiography, and generates the ceaseless movement depicted in Kevin Dawe's organological essay and especially in Mark Slobin's study of diaspora, grounded as this is in multileveled "intercultural traffic." What is striking here too is the degree of hard-headed reference to institutional specifics; for Stokes's account of "world music," in particular, the pious ecstasies of so much globalization discourse have no place, alongside the harsh realities of national state policies, music industry agendas, and ethnic and gender conflicts. Much of the background, indeed, lies in the pervasiveness (but also the variable forms) of the idea of the market, as Dave Laing points out. For all these writers, also, the present cannot be understood outside of *historical explanation.* Indeed, Tomlinson, Middleton, and David Clarke all set their narratives in relation to the *longue durée* of "modernity," with its point of departure sometime in the eighteenth century. Bohlman's story starts there as well. And, while Herbert responds to postmodernism's challenge to grand narrative with an emphasis on the fruitfulness of microhistory, Wegman's acknowledgement that history cannot avoid being the mirror for the historian's own desires and fantasies leads him not into a fashionable rejection of the whole idea of historical truth but into an embrace of its necessary if risky heuristic value.

As these broader canvases suggest, for many writers included here, music can only be grasped properly as a *social practice.* Although several distinct perspectives are exemplified—Kramer stresses the social contingency of musical meaning; Hennion the way that music mediates social variables; Middleton, Shepherd, and David Brackett the many mechanisms through which different musics mediate and produce representations of social categories such as class, gender, and ethnicity—there is agreement throughout the book that music cannot be other than something that is constructed by and in, and that constructs, social activity. For Finnegan, one of music's roles is the construction of *communitas*; for Frith, it is thoroughly embedded in the diverse spaces and time-tables inhabited by its users; for Toynbee, it is always socially (rather than individually) produced. In the chapters by these writers too, as in several other chapters, what emerges strongly is the proper *materiality* of music—a materiality of the body and also of institutional and collective practices. Finnegan, for example, stresses the bodily setting of musical emotions, Dawe the potentials for bodily disciplines and representations contained within instrument specifications, and Eric Clarke the physical givens that limit semantic "affordances." There is no naturalism here: Musical resources, including the body, are seen as always socially constructed and historically variable. Similarly, while in these discourses *nature*, in its obligatory dance with culture, can hardly help but appear—as it does most explicitly in Cross's discussion of evolutionary theory—it is always through the lens of history. Cultural practices of music are grounded in biology, according to Cross, but they are not "cleanly dissociated."

Some contributors push these tendencies to a point that, cutting rather against the grain of much recent work in cultural theory, could perhaps be described as *system thinking*. Good examples are Lucy Green, who sets her account of music education in the context of class, gender, and ethnicity formations and of the institutions and ideologies of educational reproduction; Brackett, who roots his account of African-American musical difference in the specifics of music industry practice and of demographic change; and Stokes, who, similarly, grounds his essay on the often nebulous topic of "world music" in the hard facts of political economy. Some writers, while less systematic in this sense, nevertheless couch their argument against a large-scale geographical or historical backdrop. In Middleton's case, this even warrants a hint of "universalism." Tomlinson allows his world-history perspective to generate a program of neocomparativism; Clayton focuses his attention on this comparative dimension, addressing both the inescapability of comparison and its proper specification. This does not mean that the *fluidity, fragmentation,* and *eclecticism* typical of so much contemporary musical practice, and so remarked on by postmodernist commentators, go unnoticed. These tendencies are central to Slobin's account of diaspora, and are important points in the chapters by Shepherd, Stokes, and David Clarke. But they do not seem to have inhibited the interest in systematic thought. Similarly, two chapters explicitly address the Holy Grail of postmodernist polemic, *cultural differ-ence.* Yet Brackett, although insisting on the reality of African-American difference, roots this firmly in historical contingency, as we have seen, while Kofi Agawu goes further, contesting altogether the power politics that he sees as intrinsic to ascriptions of difference, and proposing, on eth-ical grounds, a methodological presumption of sameness.

There is no chapter on technology. But this is because its importance is taken for granted. Technological dimensions are of course central to Dawe's discussion, and an awareness of the role of technological change is strongly in evidence elsewhere; for example, in the chapters by Hennion, Frith, and Laing. There is also no chapter on politics. But, as will be clear by now, many of the essays reveal political dimensions of varied sorts. For political work, some conception of *agency* is required. This is a notion that has taken a battering at the hands of poststructural-ism. It survives in Hennion's account, albeit dispersed through the circuits of mediation. Toynbee grounds creativity in collaborative pro-duction, a "social authorship." Stokes finds scope for the work of several actors in the production and circulation of world music, situated in a range of "sites of agency." Laing, while emphasizing the ubiquity of market processes, not only reveals some of the failures and problems of market theories and systems but also celebrates their incompleteness in the face of an "aesthetico-musical unconscious that overflows the eco-nomic." Finally—and perhaps most important in a critical introduction to the cultural study of music—we should note the agency of the *researcher*, in particular the importance of *scholarly self-reflexivity.* Slobin recommends that students of diaspora should query their own possible diasporic status; Cook suggests that the analyst or fieldworker is always partial; Kramer argues that the interpreter's own subject-position is part of the field of interpretation. Agawu notes the difficulties of speaking for the African, Wegman those of representing historical subjects, Titon those of reporting on ethnographic actors, Middleton those involved in speaking for the people. But these are problems, not disablements, call-ing not for self-effacement but for self-knowledge.

And in that spirit, the authorial name at the head of this Introduction is meant to signal an awareness of both the responsibilities and the inade-quacies of such markers of individual agency. My editorial colleagues are certainly not guilty of any intellectual crimes committed here; but at the same time their central role in the planning and production of this book, not to mention the part played by every single contributor, should be taken as symptoms of what, in any enterprise of this sort, can only be, indeed, an exercise in social authorship of the happiest kind.

This survey of the book contents, partial as it is, reveals processes not only of disaggregation but also of a certain mood of reaggregation, or at least a reconfiguring, a search for connections. (Of course, one might, in a further gesture of self-reflexivity, confess that the story could easily have been told differently.) At the very least, the fear of many recent writers—Eagleton, Mulhern, Kuper—that culturalism rampant and reductive, in its most relativistic but also imperialist mode, might signal a triumph of the culture concept that was altogether reactionary, is not borne out. Is this because music studies, as normal, are behind the game? Or, unusually, ahead? Or is it the effect of the bewitching idiosyncrasy of music itself, its specificity so hard to ignore, its dependency on economic, social, technological, and political processes equally irreducible? So intricate, heterogeneous, and incommensurate are the assembled arguments in the book, so relatively autonomous in many cases, that one might easily end up asking whether the culture concept is necessary to them at all.

As culture commodifies more and more, these questions take on increasing urgency. Manchester's museum of the modern city, Urbis—at the time of writing, soon to open—will narcissistically reflect to people their own urban lifestyle. "'There was a buzz about the urban renaissance,'" said the director of the Manchester Institute for Popular Culture (part of the Urbis team). "'The two sides were looking for each other. The city wanted a landmark project and the people on the popular culture scene wanted to do something for the city'" (*The Guardian*, February 23, 2002, 12) What exactly is "culture" in this scene? In the same issue of *The Guardian*, writer, academic, and media pundit Tom Paulin, raised in Belfast, plugged the city's case in the competition to be European City of Culture in 2008, citing the vibrancy of its intellectual, industrial, and popular-cultural history. Other contenders—including Newcastle/Gateshead with my own university fully on board—will no doubt make equally compelling cases. And success certainly brings a fistful of euros. In an ironic sense, the arguments for cultural materialism and cultural determinacy come home to roost here.

It is not hard to agree with both the sentiment and the tone of James Clifford's rumination: "Culture is a deeply compromised idea I cannot yet do without" (quoted, Kuper 1999, 212). Just as some Marxists have suggested that the primacy of economics in Marxism might be specific to the historical stage of capitalism (hence Marx's theory really represented a cultural self-diagnosis), so we might do well to regard the concept of culture (and especially its apparent hegemony) as a staging post: full of important leads, still indispensable to thinking, but always overambitious, never fully identical to its objects, part of a moment that we need to push past, while retaining what is valuable in its patrimony, most particularly the challenging proposition that it remains worthwhile to think about the possibility of living life as a whole.

PART I

Music and Culture

CHAPTER 1

Music and Biocultural Evolution

IAN CROSS

How should we understand music? The ways in which we can answer this question are conditioned by the status that we are willing to grant to music. If music is a universal human behavior, part of "human nature," then it should be possible to understand music by identifying and applying general principles of the type found within formal and scientific theories. And music has been claimed as a human universal. Alan Merriam (1964, 227) bluntly asserts that music "is a universal behavior," while Blacking (1995, 224) states more circumspectly that "every known human society has what trained musicologists would recognize as 'music'."

But this view is difficult to square with more recent scholarship, which would replace music with musics, holding that musics are musics only in their cultural contexts. Musics only make sense as musics if we can resonate with the histories, values, conventions, institutions, and technologies that enfold them; musics can only be approached through culturally situated acts of interpretation. Such interpretive acts, as Bohlman (1999) makes clear, unveil a multiplicity of musical ontologies, some or most of which may be mutually irreconcilable: hence a multiplicity of musics.

In the first view, there is a singular phenomenon called music, which has a knowable relationship to human biology, mind, and behavior. In the second view, music exists as musics, diverse, multiple, and unknowable within a single unitary framework. But in this second view music seems to have lost much of its materiality, and while the materialities of musics may be heterogeneous and heteronomous, they are irrefutably grounded in human behaviors.

From a materialist perspective, underlying human behaviors are minds, and underlying minds are embodied human brains. Underlying embodied human brains are human biologies, and underlying human biologies are the processes of evolution. Musics as culturally situated, minded human behaviors—musics as material phenomena—thus stand in some to-be-determined relationship to human evolution. Of course it might be the case that the cultural dynamics of music owe little or nothing to the evolutionary processes that underlie our biologies. But this position is only tenable if our biological being can be cleanly dissociated from our cultural lives, and given that our cultural lives are mainly evidenced in material behaviors and their traces, a clean dissociation between culture and biology—or between music and evolution—is unfeasible. To state this is not to argue that musics are reducible to—are knowable wholly in terms of—an understanding of evolution, merely that the relation between musics and evolution needs to be explored and specified.

Current theories of evolution are concerned with the ways in which the operation of processes of random variation, natural selection, and differential reproduction within a population leads to changes in the state and makeup of that population. Random variation leads to the emergence of entities with different attributes or capacities; natural selection, operating through ecological pressures, leads to the preferential survival of those types of entities whose capacities are best adapted to immediately prevailing sets of circumstances; and those entities that are best adapted have a better chance of reproducing and passing on their genes than do less-well-adapted entities. It is important to note that the entities referred to above might be genes themselves, organisms, groups of organisms, or individual or group behaviors (Sober and Wilson, 1998; Sperber 1999). An evolutionary approach will tend to focus on the attributes that allow a gene, a behavior, an organism, or a specific intra- or intergroup dynamic to be functional in the processes of evolution, that is, to be adaptive in contributing to the differential success in survival and reproduction of the entities that make up the population.

Hence an evolutionary perspective seems to offer an integrated framework that has explanatory power with respect to individuals' biological components and behaviors, as well as with respect to groups of individuals (and the existence of groups of individuals is a necessary though not sufficient premise for the existence of culture). So evolutionary thinking may provide a means of exploring relationships between human biology, behavior, and culture. There are, however, very good reasons why anthropologists and psychologists have been wary of applying an evolutionary perspective to human behaviors and culture. The genetic determinism and racist stereotyping that the evolutionary thinking of the first half of the twentieth century appeared to sanction led to some of the worst barbarities in recorded history.

But contemporary evolutionary thinking offers comfort neither to genetic determinists nor to racists. Evolution is currently seen as impacting on human mind and behavior not by shaping or determining complex behaviors directly but by providing general constraints on how minds interact with their environments. And modern genetics has shown that two gorillas five miles apart in a central African rain forest are likely to differ more in their genetic makeup than are a Basque inhabitant of San Sebastian and an Australian aborigine from the Northern Territories. Humans are one single, recently emerged species, biologically fairly uniform though culturally diverse.

Bearing this diversity in mind, are there reasons to expect that musics, as culturally situated human behaviors, have anything other than a contingent relationship to evolutionary processes? In the first place, a hint of a more than contingent relationship can be found in music's ancient provenance as a human behavior. The earliest unambiguously musical artifact identified to date is a bone pipe dated to around 36,000 BP found near Württemberg in southern Germany, which was uncovered in a context that associates it with modern *Homo sapiens sapiens*. The pipe predates almost all known visual art, and in any case a capacity for musicality (most likely vocal) would predate the construction of a sophisticated musical artifact such as a pipe, probably by a considerable period. Archaeology suggests that human musicality is ancient; the fact that music appears about as early as possible in the traces of *Homo sapiens sapiens* in Europe, together with the fact that musicality is an attribute of both the peoples of the pre-Hispanic Americas and of the aboriginal people of precolonial Australia, provides good grounds for believing that music accompanied *Homo sapiens sapiens* out of Africa.

And not only is music ancient, but musicality may be universal for all members of the human species; it has been claimed that "musical ability [is] a general characteristic of the human species rather than a rare talent" (Blacking 1995, 236). Of course, there are societies within which the term *music* does not seem to offer a good fit to any discretely identifiable set of cultural practices. But this does not seem to connote an absence of activities that might be interpretable as "musical." This lack of fit might arise because such "musical" behaviors are so embedded in broader categories of cultural practice as to be inextricable from them (as is the case in many African societies); or it may arise because "music" is a proscribed activity (as in the case of the Taliban regime in Afghanistan). Even in this latter case, behaviors interpretable as "musical" may be manifested in contexts such as devotional song, though unacknowledged as music by the participants.

But both music's ancient provenance and apparent universality are more suggestive than conclusive. It may be that musics are contingently human. Perhaps they are human behaviors that are not adaptive (in the evolutionary sense), which have arisen simply because humans have evolved other capacities that music can parasitically exploit; or they might be behaviors that have specifiable functions but that have neither played a role in, nor been impacted upon by, processes of human evolution.

The most widely disseminated theory of music from an evolutionary context is undoubtedly that of Pinker (1997), who is committed to an attempt to reevaluate the entire repertoire of human behaviors in light of the adaptive value of those behaviors in evolution. For Pinker, music scores low; in his words "music could vanish from our species and the rest of our lifestyle would be virtually unchanged." He claims that music is related to evolution only contingently, being a form of "auditory cheesecake," a technology or "spandrel," a human behavior that has arisen not because of its adaptive value but because other adaptive human capacities enable it and allow its perpetuation. Music, for Pinker, simply tickles faculties (such as those for language, auditory scene analysis, motor control, etc.) that have evolved for other purposes.

But Pinker's view of music is not without competition. Miller (2000) conceives of music as being evolutionarily adaptive, suggesting that what we regard as music is an instance of a display of protean or unpredictable behavior inherited from our (male) primate ancestors and intended to attract mates. For Miller, music is operational in evolutionary processes of sexual selection; in effect, his theory might be summed up as "tunes help you breed more easily." In this view musicality is a genetically conditioned behavior, and degrees of musicality are expressions of different genetic endowments for protean behavior.

However, both these views can be largely discounted. The notions of music employed by both Pinker and Miller are circumscribed and superficial, treating music solely as it might be conceived of within contemporary Western culture: patterned sound employed primarily for hedonic ends, whose production constitutes a specialized, commodified, and technologized activity. This concept of music is minimally representative of what music is and has been at other times and in other cultures. Of course, to argue against Pinker's and Miller's theories is not to argue that they are unequivocally mistaken. At some times, for some people, in some cultures, music might be as insignificant as Pinker claims, or it might be functional in processes of sexual selection as Miller maintains. But neither offers compelling evidence to support these views; the culture specificity of the attributes in terms of which they choose to characterize music—the attributes of being wholly aural and being efficacious only in the hedonic responses it evokes—militates against accepting either of these two accounts as adequate.

Given the limits of Pinker's and Miller's musical horizons, are there any attributes of musics that are general enough to allow music to be considered as being rooted in the dynamics of evolution? To start with, music involves action; this is self-evident when we look at and listen to musics that are beyond the bounds of contemporary Western culture. For most of the times and cultures that we know of, their mature musics overtly involve not just sound, but also action (Kubik 1979; Stobart and Cross 2000). Any attempt to find general attributes in music must acknowledge the embodied nature of music, the indivisibility of movement and sound in characterizing music across histories and societies.

Moreover, a cross-cultural perspective on music suggests that it also involves multiplicity of reference and meaning; a piece or performance is simultaneously capable of bearing many different meanings. Music can function as a medium for communication with the dead for the Kaluli of Papua New Guinea (Feld 1990), binding birds, souls, places, and people at a time of transformation; music can be a mechanism for restructuring social relations, as in the *domba* initiation of the Venda (Blacking 1973), or in the remaking of cultural narratives, as in klezmer (Slobin 1993). In all these very different circumstances, music's meaning is rarely if ever explicit. Music is about something, but its aboutness—its intentionality—can vary from context to context, within a context, and from individual to individual.

Finally, music appears to have no obvious survival value, no immediate and specifiable physical efficacy. Music can neither provide sustenance nor kill enemies, nor can it enjoin others—explicitly and unambiguously—to do so. In itself music does not seem capable of being a material cause of anything other than a transient emotional encounter. It seems to be ineffi-cacious. Something that might be identified as music, then, appears to have some general attributes—roots in sound and movement, heterogene-ity of meaning, a grounding in social interaction, and a personalized sig-nificance, together with an apparent inefficacy. Music embodies, entrains, and transposably intentionalizes time in sound and action.

But is there any reason, other than their generality, to believe that these attributes should be considered from an evolutionary perspective? If the focus of inquiry is shifted away from consideration of mature music to musicality as manifested in infancy, the answer is "yes." As we shall see, the effects of evolution are most evident in infant rather than in mature, encultured behaviors. And there is increasing evidence that infants engage in behaviors with just the general attributes of music iden-tified above.

Music in Evolution and Development

The theories of music's role in evolution outlined above attempt to account for the mature expression of music in evolutionary terms. In doing so they can be interpreted as subscribing to a level of genetic deter-minism that appears to leave little space for cultural processes to effect any great divergences in mature adult behaviors. As noted above, to adopt an evolutionary perspective is not to buy into a view that behavior is determined by our genes; a more rounded account interprets mature adult behaviors as shaped by both biology and culture. The interactions with other human beings, and with the products of those others, that we are involved in throughout our infancy, childhood, and adolescence, con-stitute a major component of the ecology of the human mind and behav-ior, though while the types of interactions might be constrained by evolutionary forces they are not solely determined by them. Interaction with other humans leads to shared ways of understanding the world and each other (the latter predicated on a capacity to know others as ourselves rather than as the world), aspects of which may be transmitted and con-served by nongenetic means, and those shared ways of understanding those cultures play a significant role in shaping mature perceptions and cognitions. If there is an impact of our evolutionary past on our present behaviors, this is likely to be manifested in a quite general way; as Foley (1995, 199) suggests, "genes for behaviour occur at a very low level of specificity . . . in the course of the evolution of human behaviour it is not specific behaviours that have been selected for but the ability to respond appropriately to specific conditions."

In fact, the clearest traces of the impact of evolutionary processes on the mind are evident not in encultured adult behaviors but in the capacities of the infant mind. Recent research has yielded a vast amount of evidence (e.g., Keil 1994; Spelke 1999) that very young infants develop certain competences too quickly to be explained as the outcome of learning processes that involve interaction with the environment over relatively short time scales. Very young infants quickly cue in to behavior that can be interpreted as "goal directed"; they react with surprise to events that they experience as violating the laws of physics; and they respond appropriately to different facial expressions. All this suggests that they are primed for a sort of intuitive biology, physics, and psychology. And all human infants acquire language quickly and expertly; they seem to come into the world primed for language, though they require continuous linguistic interaction with other humans in order for their language capacity to be fully expressed (Pinker 1994).

Evolution can be thought of as acting on the mind in terms of shaping infant predispositions; infants and children are primed to deal with certain types of information rapidly and expertly without being taught to do so. Culture, in the form of human interactions that are shaped by common ways of understanding, particularizes the developmental trajectory of those predispositions; so, for example, in the case of language, human interactions lead to the acquisition of mature competence in a particular language with a specific syntactic structure, lexicon, and so on. If evolution has shaped the human mind, it has most likely selected at the level of infant predispositions, and culture can be thought of as shaping into specific and distinct forms the expression of those predispositions. In Sperber's words (1999, cxv), "Today, with a few undistinguished exceptions, it is generally agreed among cognitive and social scientists that cultural variation is the effect, not of biological variation, but of a common biological, and more specifically cognitive endowment that, given different historical and ecological conditions, makes this variability possible."

It has been suggested that music constitutes an element in this common cognitive endowment; infants appear to be primed for music. Sandra Trehub and her collaborators (e.g., Trehub, Schellenberg, and Hill 1997) have demonstrated that at six months infants are "rather capable listeners"; for example, they are sensitive to melodic contoural constancy, experiencing as "the same" melodies that share the same contour or pattern of ups and downs, even though the pitches might have changed. Even younger infants show a capacity for music; the work of Mechthild Papousek (1996) shows that infants display a range of "proto-musical behaviours" in their interactions with their caregivers, using rhythm and pitch in a musical way. These protomusical behaviors consist not only of listening to sounds but also of producing them and actively moving while doing so; as she puts it (1996, 100), "regular synchronization of vocal and kinaesthetic patterns provides the infant with multimodal sensory information including tactile, kinaesthetic and visual information."

So it would appear more appropriate to understand the human predisposition to be musical, rather than the expressions of that musicality shown by mature individuals in particular cultures, as being a product of evolutionary forces. And that predisposition to be musical is more than just a tendency to be a competent listener; infant protomusicality involves not just listening to but also producing patterns of sound in time, incorporates not just sound but also action, and serves a range of functions that are critical in an infant's development.

Colwyn Trevarthen's work (Trevarthen 1999) suggests that these protomusical infant–caregiver interactions are crucially important for the infant in allowing the development of "primary intersubjectivity" based on the "sharing of emotional states" between caregiver and child; the temporal, patterned, and embodied nature of the protomusical behaviors evidenced in the infants' interactions enables the sharing of patterned time with others, and facilitates harmony of affective state and interaction. Interestingly, in one of the few cross-cultural studies to have been conducted in this area, Gratier (1999) has shown that musical attributes of mother–infant interactions differ little from culture to culture, but that the coherence of interactions is severely affected by the degree of rootedness in a specific cultural context of the parent–infant dyad. Ellen Dissanayake (2000) supports Trevarthen's view in proposing that the musical characteristics of mother–infant interaction are of critical importance in the acquisition of capacities for "social regulation and emotional bonding." The importance of protomusical behavior is not limited to young infants; Hanus Papousek (1996) sees childhood musical behaviors as constituting forms of play that involve higher-level integrative processes that act to nurture the child's "exploratory competence."

Cross (1999; 2001) suggests that protomusical activities provide mechanisms for acquiring cognitive flexibility as well as consequence-free means of exploring and achieving competence in social interaction. Children appear to have early-developing competences in discrete domains of cognition and behavior, and protomusical behaviors help in the integration of these different domains. Protomusical behaviors are not about any specific thing (in the way that a declarative sentence may be about one thing, having a specifiable sense and reference), but the same protomusical behavior may be experienced as being about different things at different times, and might even be experienced as being about more than one thing at the same time. In other words, protomusical activities have a sort of "floating intentionality," a transposable and possibly multiple aboutness. The floating intentionality of protomusical behaviors may be exploited in infancy as a means of forming connections between different domains of infant competence such as the psychological, the biological, and the mechanical. Music, in the guise of protomusical activity, can sustain the emergence of a *metaphorical* domain, acting to create and to maintain the cognitive flexibility that appears to be the hallmark of our species.

Furthermore, protomusical activities are specifically suited to the exploration of social interaction because of their nonefficaciousness and their multiple potential meanings. For example, each child in a group involved in a cooperative musical activity may interpret that activity as something different yet the collective musical activity is not threatened by the existence of potentially conflicting meanings. And indeed it can be suggested that music's embodied status, and the temporal constraints linked to voluntary and preattentively controlled movement that its production and reception thus incorporate (Pöppel and Wittmann 1999), makes it a unique means of communicating and perhaps humanly sharing emotional body-states. Music, or protomusical activity, provides for a child a medium for the gestation of a capacity for social interaction, a risk-free space for the exploration of social behavior that can sustain otherwise potentially risky action and transaction.

In this view, the mature musical competences exhibited by members of a culture are grounded in infant protomusical capacities. Culture, in the form of specific modes of interaction conditioned by shared ways of understanding, shapes and particularizes protomusical behaviors and propensities into specific forms for specific functions. The potential for multiplicity of meaning embodied in protomusical activity is likely to underwrite though not to direct or determine a culture's musical ontologies.

Given that infants are primed for music, and that protomusicality is functional for individuals in processes of cognitive and social development, it is possible to suggest how protomusical behaviors might have been adaptive in the course of human evolution, perhaps even in the very emergence of our species, *Homo sapiens sapiens*. The principal feature that seems to distinguish us from our predecessors is flexibility in confronting the problems of survival; as a species, we appear to have been much more versatile than our predecessors in dealing with habitat selection, tool manufacture and choice, exploitation of natural resources, and management of complex social relations.

For many cognitive archaeologists (e.g., Mithen 1996) this suggests that a fundamental change in the nature of the hominid mind occurred in the transition to *Homo sapiens sapiens*; while some of our predecessor species had very highly developed skills in discrete domains of life (such as tool manufacture), we appear able to transfer expertise between domains, or to develop expertise that is independent of any particular domain. Moreover, it has been suggested that such flexible cognitive capacities are linked to coping with the complexities of social living, and *Homo sapiens sapiens* appears to have exhibited, from our earliest significant appearance in the archaeological record, a substantial and flexible proficiency in social interaction. In other words, the modern human mind is characterized by immense cognitive flexibility, and modern cultures can involve extremely complex social structures. And given that music appears to play a role in the development of cognitive and social flexibility for modern human infants, it seems likely that the emergence of protomusical behaviors and their cultural actualization as music were crucial in precipitating the emergence of the cognitive and social flexibility that marks the appearance of *Homo sapiens sapiens*.

The view of evolution followed here proposes that processes of human evolution are operational across the integrated realm of human biology and culture; music is a product of complex processes of gene-culture coevolution (Sober and Wilson 1998). But the dynamics of music conceived of solely as a cultural phenomenon cannot be articulated by the dynamics of evolutionary processes, as would be the case, for instance, in an account of human culture expressed in terms of the propagation and transmission of "memes," such as that of Blackmore (1999). To account for human culture in terms of evolutionary processes acting on memes is to apply an interpretive model that might be informative about the context of its application but that cannot adequately account for music as a process in and product of the embodied human interactions that constitute culture. The dynamics of culture are not reducible to the dynamics of evolution.

It should be evident that this chapter does not seek to reduce music to something that can be understood only in scientific, evolutionary, and "natural" terms, but rather tries to explore one way of expressing a scientific understanding of music that can be situated within an understanding of music as an aspect of culture. The dichotomy posited by some (Scruton 1983), between scientific and other modes of understanding, is more apparent than real; there is an inevitable societal dimension to science at any one time that will determine and circumscribe its scope, applicability, and explanatory powers. The only necessary reductive attribute of science is epistemological rather than ontological. But science, in its commitment to "the metaphysical thesis that all the facts supervene on the facts of basic science" (Fodor 1998), provides discourses that can complement the culturally particular musicological stories that can be told about music; after all, an understanding of the types of stories that may be told, of the manner of the telling, and of the ways in which they are understood is at least as informative about the cultural dynamics that give rise to these stories as cultural artifacts as are the subject matters of the stories themselves. Music in contemporary Western society, despite its tendencies towards global homogeneity, is sustained by and sustains not just interacting individuals but also interacting subcultures and microcultures—it would be remarkable if the stories to be told of these are not more complex and surprising than any that have so far been told, including this one.

Further Reading

Blacking, John. 1995. *Music, culture and experience*. London: Univ. of Chicago Press.

Cook, Nicholas, and Mark Everist, eds. 1999. *Rethinking music*. Oxford: Oxford Univ. Press.

Cross, Ian. 1999. Is music the most important thing we ever did? Music, development and evolution. Pp. 10–39 in *Music, mind and science*. Edited by Suk Won Yi. Seoul: Seoul National Univ. Press. see: http://www.mus.cam.ac.uk/~cross/MMS/

MIT Encyclopedia of the Cognitive Sciences (MITECS). Edited by Robert A. Wilson and Frank C. Keil. Cambridge, Mass.: MIT Press, 1999. In particular, see introductory chapter on "Culture, cognition and evolution" by Sperber, and entries on "Infant cognition" by Spelke and "Time in the mind" by Pöppel and Wittmann.

Mithen, Steven J. 1996. *The prehistory of the mind.* London: Thames and Hudson.

Musicae Scientiae Special Issue. 1999. For papers by Trevarthen and by Gratier.

Wallin, Nils, Björn Merker, and Steven Brown, eds. 2000. *The origins of music.* Cambridge, Mass.: MIT Press.

CHAPTER 2

Musicology, Anthropology, History

GARY TOMLINSON

In their present-day forms, ethnography and historiography are twins, born of the same parentage at the same moment in the eighteenth-century dawn of Western modernity. They have most often seemed, however, to be nonidentical, even antithetical twins, each trait of the one answering to a corresponding but converse trait in the other. This complementary relation has been remarked on and analyzed almost since the eighteenth century itself. One recent summary, offered by Michel de Certeau in the wake of Lévi-Straussian structuralism, puts it this way: Where ethnography has taken as its object *orality*, historiography scrutinizes *written* traces; where the one has wanted to describe an atemporal *space* of culture, the other follows change through *time;* the one starts from a gesture of radical estrangement and *alterity*, the other from an assumption of transparent *identity;* the first analyzes collective phenomena of a cultural *unconscious*, the second the *consciousness* of historical self-knowledge (de Certeau 1988, 209–10).

These contrasts have certainly been blurred, revised, and rearranged over the two centuries of development of anthropology and history as modern disciplines. In much recent work we witness anthropology gauging informants' consciousness of change through time, and weighing written

This essay is a revised and abridged version of one published under the same title in *Il Saggiatore musicale* (8.1, 2001, pp. 21–37).

documents from an otherwise irretrievable past (e.g., Sahlins 1985; Comaroff and Comaroff 1992), or, conversely, history setting itself to recover an unwritten legacy and discover the distant otherness of its once-familiarized actors (Ginzburg 1985; Burke 1987; de Certeau 1988). Such moves must broach a basic doubt whether any substantive differences separate the two disciplines—any differences, that is, other than those sanctioned by time-worn ideologies or ethnographers' fond hopes for the survival of lived experience in their written accounts.

Nevertheless, the disciplinary differences of history and anthropology have never been effaced altogether. These distinct endeavors continue to elaborate, if tacitly or, often these days, in a climate of explicit self-critique, an ideology that limns a historical, alphabetic, conscious Western self and opposes to it a static, unlettered, un-self-conscious other.

The relation, over more than two centuries, of musicology to this set of disciplinary distinctions and their equivocation must be a complex one. Music scholarship assays a performative mode akin to the anthropologist's orality; at the same time it moves in the medium of writing naturalized in historiography but uneasily wedded, as a means at odds with its sources, to ethnography. Moreover, music itself was at the moment of musicology's appearance being refashioned in a manner that set it in opposition to the voices behind ethnography. It was assuming a place in European ideology that would eventually exalt it, ally it more tightly with the written than ever before, and distance it from related non-European activities that an earlier, more ecumenical designation had embraced.

*Music*ology—the very name incorporates a word that came, across the European eighteenth century, to betoken a "fine" art at the center of new aesthetic concerns and that designated, by the midnineteenth century, the *finest* art, the art to whose transcendental, spiritual capacities all others looked with envy. Across the century from 1750 to 1850, music lodged itself at the heart of a discourse that pried Europe and its histories apart from non-European lives and cultures. Perched at the apex of the new aesthetics, it came to function as a kind of limit-case of European uniqueness in world history and an affirmation of the gap, within the cultural formation of modernity, between history and anthropology. Music, in this sense, silenced many non-European activities that it might instead have attended to.

There is another side, however, to musicology's connection with the twins ethnography and historiography. If, on the one hand, the new aesthetics of music and the musicology to which it gave rise widened the distance between history and anthropology, on the other hand, an older ideology of singing worked to emphasize their affinities and draw them together. The commonplace conception of musicology as a discipline invented after the full emergence of Romantic views of music—invented even in the late nineteenth century, with a *fons et origo* in Guido Adler's famous manifesto of 1885 (Adler 1885; Mugglestone 1981)—cannot replace this earlier formation. It not only forgets the large literature on music history produced in the eighteenth century but also ignores a fact of subtler, deeper import: the presence of singing at the heart of eighteenth-century accounts of the history of European society, of Europe's relation to other societies, and indeed of the origins of all societies.

The central position of song in writings offering generalized theories of the origins of language and society tended to unite rather than distinguish European and non-European musical experiences. This position, solidified across the 1700s in writings of Vico, Condillac, Rousseau, Herder, and others, situated singing at the nexus of the emergent disciplines of ethnography and historiography. It could even offer song as the nexus itself—as a vanishing point, so to speak, of distinctions of European from other societies. Musicology, then, is not solely the nineteenth- and twentieth-century grandchild of an anthropology and a historiography long since sundered. An earlier musicological impulse (or *cantological*, as I have called it elsewhere, half seriously, to distinguish it from later developments) precedes the full emergence of modern historiography and ethnography; forms, even, a part of their parentage; and resists, at the moment of their birth, their too-clear separation.

Song, not music, is the fundamental category here. It is characteristic of a period when a full-blown modern conception of music had not yet taken hold so that song could still pose itself as an expressive mode shared by Europe with the rest of the world. This is the general role it played in the protoethnographic accounts of European travelers, explorers, and missionaries through the sixteenth and seventeenth centuries. Here the singing of non-Europeans was not differentiated in any categorical way from European song, but rather was assimilated into it, gauged against it, at times celebrated in comparison with it, and set with it at different points along the same spectrum of metaphysical expressive functions (usually extending from the divine to the demonic).

Later, in writings such as Rousseau's *Essay on the Origins of Language* and Vico's *New Science*, an element of historicity, in some measure novel, entered into European views. Now non-European singing was conceived not as equivalent (in whatever manner) to contemporary European practices but as a survival in far-off places of practices Europe had long since outgrown. This perceiving of historical distance in geographical and cultural difference hinted at later distinctions of historiography and ethnography while still resisting them in the commonality of song itself. Non-European singing was still *commensurable* with European singing, though it was *displaced* from it along a historical axis.

Song, in this dispensation, presented authors such as Vico and Rousseau with the conundrum of Derrida's supplement (Tomlinson 1995, 346–51). At once envisaged as the earliest and most immediate of utterances—the form in which language first emerged—and as a passionate but modulated art of the present day, song was endowed with expressive features both primitive and modern, brutally direct and delicately metaphorical, barbarously non-European and of consummate (European) refinement. The conundrum points forward to later developments in European ideology while at the same time affirming for us the proximity, at this moment, of historical and anthropological perspectives. Around 1750, song offered a category, at once conceptual and perceptual, in which anthropology and historiography began to assume their modern outlines while resisting the oppositions that would later separate them.

The *music* that came to counter such *song* in the decades before 1800 was not conceived as a European version of worldwide activities but instead as a European métier opposed to practices elsewhere, however much it might superficially resemble them. It was sanctioned within views novel in the late eighteenth century: new conceptions of the nonmimetic expressive capacities of music and of music's transcendence of the sensible world (Dahlhaus 1989a), a novel discreteness and fixity of the musical work itself (Goehr 1992), even a revising of the human subject that perceived all these things (Tomlinson 1999). It was represented above all by the burgeoning genres, institutions, and traditions of instrumental music. If around 1700 song had offered a conceptual umbrella under which the world's musical activities, non-European and European, might gather (if uneasily), now instrumental music—music without words, *nonsong*—posed a new, exclusionary category redolent of European spiritual superiority. Such a category could not help but carry deep implications for both anthropology and historiography.

An early marking of this new category is Kant's positioning of instrumental music in his analysis of beauty in his *Critique of Judgment* (Kant

[1790] 2000 pt.1, bk.1, section 16: "The Judgment of Taste, by Which an Object is Declared to Be Beautiful Under the Condition of a Definite Concept, Is Not Pure"). The free or unattached, hence pure, beauty Kant finds in such music—in "music fantasies (i.e., pieces without any topic [*Thema*]) and in fact all music without words"—is foreign to most other human products, such as the human body itself, buildings, even horses (seemingly conceived only, by Kant, as livestock). The beauty of these human products depends on the concepts of the ends or purposes envisaged for them; it therefore emerges from a human moral and rational order. The beauty of instrumental music, instead, manifests a kind of errancy, an independence from such humanist moral orders that likens it to the meaningless beauty of flowers, exotic birds, and seashells.

The converse of Kant's example is implicit but clear: Song, music with words, must manifest a dependent beauty. Kant considers song only *in absentia*, so to speak, by specifying that free beauty is restricted to instrumental music; but this restriction poses, in effect, a deep-seated differentiation of the two. In this distinction (though he certainly would not have relished the consequence), Kant prepared the ground for the ennoblement of instrumental music throughout the nineteenth century that would take forms as different as the complexities of Wagner's relation to Beethoven or Hanslick's ([1885] 1974) resolute separation of music from speech and musical from other beauty. In its own time the effect of Kant's differentiation was to mark off, within a solidifying conception of aesthetics considered the philosophy of beauty, one precinct for singing, a different one for playing.

Kant's assignment of categorically differing modes of beauty to non-song and song punctuated a period when instrumental practices in elite Europe—the ascendancy of symphony, concerto, and sonata, the challenging of the supremacy of opera by public concerts featuring instrumental virtuosity, and so on—called forth a sense of European musical accomplishment and uniqueness that could not easily square with the global ubiquity of singing. In the years after Kant, indeed, the achievements of recent European instrumental music could be viewed as the culmination of a progressive world history. In 1800 Herder, writing in *Kalligone*, his response to Kant's *Critique*, described "the slow progress of music's history" toward the moment, in his own Europe, when it "developed into a self-sufficient art, *sui-generis*, dispensing with words" (Le Huray and Day 1981, 257; Goehr 1992, 155). It was a very short step, soon taken, from the Kantian distinction of instrumental and vocal musics to the assertion of Europe as the privileged endpoint of music history.

If in this way Kant's remark on instrumental music points toward a Eurocentric separation of music history from music anthropology, Johann Nikolaus Forkel's *Allgemeine Geschichte der Musik* ([1788] 1967), from the same years, spins out a full-fledged narrative of their divorce. The novel force of Forkel's account lies neither in its frankly progressive tone, common enough in his predecessors, nor even in its less commonplace linkage of the advancement of music to the evolution of language. Instead the crucial, innovative move by which Forkel pries music history apart from music anthropology is his insistence that music progresses not only in tandem with language but also with *writing*.

Forkel asserts first that music and language develop in parallel ways from their earliest origins to their "highest perfection" (Forkel [1788] 1967; trans. Allanbrook 1998, 280). But "Language and writing always proceeded at an equal pace in their development; therefore music and notation can be presumed to have done the same." Peoples who use imperfect music notations can, then, attain only "imperfect, extremely unordered" musics (p. 288). A perfect music depends on a perfected music writing. In language writing, Forkel reasons (echoing many eighteenth-century predecessors), the approach to perfection moves from pictographic through ideographic to alphabetic stages. Alphabetic writing emerges only after a people's attainment of a level of intellectual sophistication in which writing can be abstracted from the things it represents; ideographic writing shows a less-developed mode of abstraction, pictographs no abstraction at all. Since music writing is the inscribing of airy, invisible bodies, it requires, like alphabetism, a high degree of abstraction. Therefore, Forkel sweepingly concludes, "No people could arrive at any method at all for translating its melodies into signs before the invention of alphabetical writing" (p. 287).

Forkel's specific inferences concerning the history of music notation are complex. After the invention of the alphabet this history reverses, in a way, the evolution of language writing, moving from an incipient, alphabetic mode toward something akin to pictography in its perfected state. But we need not follow these particulars to be staggered by the blunt force of Forkel's syllogism: *Musical perfection is dependent on notational perfection; notational perfection follows alphabetism; therefore musical perfection follows alphabetism.* Forkel subsumes the evolution of musics worldwide under a history pointing toward the circum-Mediterranean achievement of the alphabet. In doing so he creates for music both a *course* of history and a *space* of anthropology, separating the two in their specific domains:

the first traversed by alphabetic societies and their precursors, the second inhabited by analphabetic peoples. Societies with the alphabet can move closer to a perfect musical art; those without must move elsewhere or not move at all. "How long a people can tolerate [the] first crude state of music cannot be precisely determined," Forkel writes. "We still find it today, however, among many Asiatic, African, and American peoples, whom we also know to have made no progress for millennia in other branches of culture" (p. 285).

In the service of a music history and anthropology thus clearly distinguished, Forkel has deployed oppositions closely related to those described by de Certeau (1988) in separating general historiography and ethnography. European music history will evolve from writing, while music anthropology encounters a space of orality. Europe's writing will enable a progressive evolution contrasting with the cultural stasis of others ("We still find it today . . ."). The alphabetic writing that enables musical perfection, finally, will arise from a mode of consciousness—the capability for abstraction—not attained by others. By 1788, the date of the introductory volume of Forkel's work, the history of European musical development could be plotted as a story of the progress of writing, the anthropology of non-European musics as the trackless space of writing's absence.

The exemplary instances of Forkel and Kant may seem at first glance to touch on each other only tangentially. The one offers a differentiation of beauty in song from beauty in instrumental music that militated toward a Eurocentric music history, the other an emphasis on alphabetism that could separate music history from music anthropology. The two cases are, however, connected at a deep level. Each is predicated on a mode of abstraction: for Forkel, the capacity that leads to alphabetic writing and then to music notation and musical perfection; for Kant a humanly created instance of beauty somehow loosed from all human ends.

Each of these abstractions, in turn, represents a separation of the musical materials involved from their human creative matrices—a manner, that is, of *decontextualization.* The beauty of instrumental music is, for Kant, like that of tulips and parrots. In drawing this similarity, however, he detached (mysteriously) instrumental music from the human means and ends of its production, dissemination, and consumption. Forkel's move away from context is less self-evident than this but no less basic to his thought. For him alphabetism represents an attainment of human consciousness whereby a system of writing looses itself from the

conditions of visual perception, a detachment signally absent from pictography; in general alphabetism amounts to a mark of the separation in
advanced peoples of concepts from sense stimuli. Music writing follows as
a related (if obverse) detaching of sense from intellect. The attainment of
a sophisticated music notation yields something like a pictographic representation of invisible, disembodied aural perceptions. In notation invisible
sounds take on visible form, marking the soul's conceptual ability to discern, finally, the subtlest differences among them (Allanbrook 1998, 282).
This increased conceptual power of the soul, not some change in sense
perception, enables the perfection of music. The whole advancement of
music is idealist, relying on the conceptual abstraction manifested in
music notation. The progress of *situated* musical practice follows from the
possibility music writing offers of its *detachment* from its situation.

It is not hard to recognize in Forkel's and Kant's modes of decontextualization ingredients of the novel conception of musical autonomy that
would take strong root in nineteenth-century Europe. From thinking
related both directly and indirectly to Kant's detached musical beauty
sprang, as I have already suggested, the ideology of absolute music: the
view that special capabilities and privileges adhere to music without text
or program, "that instrumental music purely and clearly expresses the
true nature of music by its very lack of concept, object, and purpose"
(Dahlhaus 1989a, 7). The separation itself of such music from its context,
in the views of its proponents, marked its transcending of history and the
material world.

Viewed against the backdrop of the cantological intuitions of a slightly
earlier European moment, this conception of musical autonomy appears
as a powerful philosophical assertion by elite Europe of its own unique
achievement and status. In historical terms—the terms already set forth by
Herder in 1800, as we have seen—it presumes the European instrumental traditions of its time as the telos of all musical progress. In doing this
it simultaneously posits for territories beyond Europe a set of anthropological limitations. These locales are, now more than before, spaces of
primitive (that is, static or ahistorical) or regressive (historically failed)
musical practices. In coming to seem a marker of European distinction,
instrumentalism is now set off in complex ideological opposition to non-
European *vocalism*. The singing that Rousseau could still offer as a trait
shared across all humanity is now instead an index of human difference.
(Later, near the end of the era of European colonialism, this view of instrumental music found its reflection in European or European-influenced

conceptualizations of other elite musics. Bruno Nettl has argued that European instrumentalism had a profound impact on the emergence, around 1900, of the instrumental *radif* basic to the theory and pedagogy of modern Persian classical music [Nettl 1987, 133–37]. Indian classical traditions have also felt the impact of modern Western instrumentalism since the late nineteenth century.)

The example of Forkel, for its part, shows us how this European cooptation of musical (hence artistic, creative, imaginative) history is allied from the start with conceptions of writing. From the early nineteenth century on, conceptions of absolute music ran together with views related to Forkel's of the determining importance of notation in music history. The result was another crystallizing of ideological forms and new practices reflecting them.

The idea of instrumental music as an autonomous, nonmimetic expressive means, together with the emergent formation of the modern conception of the discrete musical work, invested new and substantial powers in the written form of the work. The notated music came to be viewed less as a preliminary script for performance than as the locus of the truest revelation of the composer's intent, the unique and full inscription of the composer's expressive spirit which was elsewhere—in any one performance—only partially revealed. Music writing itself seemed an inscriptive means endowed with nonsemantic, mysterious, even transcendent significance. It was now conceivable, to a degree that it had not been before, that the work as embodied in music writing, divorced from its contexts of production, performance, and reception, could become the avatar of the transcendent spaces absolute music could attain and inhabit. The notated work took on almost magical characteristics, projecting spirit outward in legible form, and traversing the distance between musical exegete and composer. The search for the secrets of this written work could in large degree ignore and thus conceal the social interactions of performers and audience at the scene itself of music making. (The language here hints intentionally at Marx: By 1900 the musical score shows many of the hallmarks of the fetishized commodity of late capitalism; see also Tomlinson 1999, 81.)

The ability for abstraction that Forkel had seen as a prerequisite for musical notation and hence musical advancement has here posed itself in the European mind as a new, quintessentially musical ability: the ability to comprehend an unperformed work from its writing alone. The idealism behind this proposition is a direct outgrowth of the idealism attendant on notions of absolute music all told; but this variant of the general idealism relies on the fixed inscription of the work. The music writing that Forkel had held up as a sine qua non of an advanced musical tradition has exerted its full prerogatives.

The two primary activities that mark the emergence of modern musicology in the late nineteenth century grew up in the shadow of this conception of music writing. Fist, the huge projects of establishing "critical" editions for Bach, Handel, and other composers, which arose in these years and continued at an accelerating pace across the early twentieth century, mark the new faith in the work fixed in music writing; in the possibility of representing it as a stable, authoritative text; and in the belief that this text can bring us closer to the singular expressive intent that motivated the composer.

The search for the expressive secrets of the score, meanwhile, blossomed from descriptive beginnings, in writings such as those of E. T. A. Hoffmann, into modern music analysis ([1810] 1989). Analysis, in this light, can be seen to be the interpretive praxis that arose from the absolution of instrumental music from its context at the moment of the apotheosis of music writing as manifestation of transcendent spirit. Moreover, as an outgrowth of Eurocentric conceptions of music, writing analysis was linked to Europe's positing of its own musical (and other) uniqueness in world history. In a profound tautology it was positioned so as to confirm a Hegelian culmination of world musical history in the very absolute music that helped define it. In this confirmation, analysis offered criteria constructed on a foundation of European views, including an ideology of writing, as a universal gauge of musical worth.

We can sense here the colonial dilemma, as we might call it, that conditioned from the start the kind of musicology that attends mostly to discrete works fixed in music writing. Such musicology starts from a historically local and recent mode of musical self-awareness and projects it outward from Europe toward the rest of the world. As long as this gesture is clearly understood, it is not inevitably a bad thing. In itself it only points up the general role of musicology in a Eurocentric self-scrutiny that characterizes in varying degrees all the modern humanities—considers literature, for instance, as a category in many ways similar to music (Eagleton 1983, chap.1). It locates music in the modern university's pedagogical effort of humanistic *Bildung*, itself in some measure circular. The posing of such self-knowledge becomes problematic when it is not accompanied by more or less strenuous attempts to gain *other*-knowledge—when, to paraphrase Paul Ricoeur's famous aphorism, knowledge of the self is thought to be meaningful without detour through knowledge of relatively distant others.

We can also predict from these discourses the difficulty ethnomusicology would face as it emerged, in the midtwentieth century, from a Eurocentric musicology to offer itself as the alternative to self-knowledge. Preordained as the study of de Certeau's oral, ahistorical, unwritten cultures in a disciplinary matrix that was from the first defined by European powers of writing, it was unable simply to ignore the discourses that shaped its sibling discipline. It reacted against them, instead, from a position still partially within them. Ethnomusicology's deep, even constitutive ambivalence, at once fascinated and wary, in the face of music analysis, the score, and the inscription of unwritten traditions and practices shows this as clearly as any other feature. Modern ethnomusicology and musicology, like modern historiography and ethnography before them, arose as antithetical twins; but they arose as a single, dualistic function of the emergence of music from song.

The disciplinary genealogy that is here no more than sketched encourages some general observations about the relations of musical study to anthropology and history. First, it shows the opposition of modern musicology and ethnomusicology for what it originally was: a disciplinary artifact arising in musical thought from a new stage, attained not much before 1800, in the evolution of European conceptions of self and others. In this light, modern musicology itself, and not only ethnomusicology, appears as a discipline erected on propositions of cultural difference, European versus non-European. In founding itself on such propositions, it was from the start ethnographic through and through—though the conditions of its local culture led it to found itself in such a way as to conceal its sources. Meanwhile ethnomusicology arose, ambivalently, as a reaction to musicology's concealment of the truth that it was always already a particular instance of ethnomusicology.

Second, an anamnesis is needed to foster alternatives to the conceptual categories that created and still sustain these disciplinary constructs. This might assume a number of different forms: a commemoration of the fact that European musical thought preceded Europe's modern distinction of anthropology from history; a recognition of the ways this earlier musical thought gathered together human activities that would be categorically separated by the impact of later discourses; and a revisiting of European conceptions of writing—of its own and others', musical and nonmusical—as they changed across the eighteenth century. It might take the form of a realization that the powers of voice have come to pose themselves in our musical culture as a powerful (and in some measure suspect) "other" of instrumentalism. The anamnesis might even take the form, finally, of a meditation on how a musicology might constitute itself from a conceptual frame of sufficient breadth to see that song, the universal corollary of the human propensity toward language, is not so much a musical thing as music is *songish*.

All this suggests that a reelaborated musicology needs to embrace the fact of its position within a more general ethnomusicology. This would not involve a repudiation of musicology's canons—of its canon of works, with common-practice instrumental pieces at its heart, or of its methodological canons, revolving around close scrutiny of these works—but rather a relocation of these canons in the broader disciplinary and historical panorama. It would, at the same time, ensure that their deployment was accompanied by an ideological critique of the sort sketched above—by an awareness of the circumscribed conceptual structures and political interests that helped sponsor such canons in the first place.

The usefulness of such a critique lies in its clearing the way for meaningful comparison of the urges to make music and modes of music making across large stretches of human history and culture—ultimately, perhaps, across the whole stretch of human history and culture available to us. I mean here to espouse, in our disciplinary ruminations and pedagogical practices, a sweeping *neocomparativism* that could explore the broadest questions about the place of musical activities in human experience, aspiration, and achievement: What is the significance of the ubiquitous relation between speech and song, activities at once proximate and distinct in all cultures? Why are song and religion or song and drama constantly linked? How is the body in musical motion extended into the material world through technologies of instrument making, and how are these related to other technologies? What is the nature of the peculiar powers of repetitive musical structures, and how are they differently deployed in different situations? How are musical traditions altered by modes of music writing? How have recorded sound and sound storage reshaped the nature of song cultures? How, in different societal structures, does political power accrue to musical acts? And so forth.

This neocomparativism would take off from the particularism that has marked most musical ethnography and, certainly, most Eurocentric music history and criticism. It would not avoid situated, detailed study of musical matters but rather transform them by making the means of their situating and the definition of their detail objects of its own scrutiny. This approach would also differ from earlier comparativisms in its critical dismemberment of the hegemonic, Europe-first strategies on which they rested. In such a neocomparativist approach, ethnomusicology and popular music studies might also find a new footing. Both might cast off their lingering defensiveness in the face of the European canon by coming to regard it as a set of practices comparable to, perhaps subsumed within, and in any case usually standing in complex relation with the musics they customarily examine.

Such comparisons of, and realignments of relations between, repertories scrutinized in various branches of musical study cast a wide net. In doing so they bring a deep historical consciousness to ethnomusicological areas not usually conceived in this way and, at the same time, grant a cross-cultural perspective on European musics too often walled off from the rest of the world. In doing so, in other words, they enact the exchange I noted at the outset of this essay of conventional historiographic and ethnographic values. They confound the differences European ideologies have for two hundred years presumed between historical and anthropological approaches.

In the end, then, at a moment when musicology is emerging from a period of strenuous attempts to clarify the differences among various modes of musical study, the affinities of all our efforts instead need to be emphasized. At the dawn of the twenty-first century the challenge facing musical scholarship is to feel its way toward a set of intuitions about music making that preceded and has always surrounded the opposition of history and ethnography.

Further Reading

Burnham, Scott. 1995. *Beethoven hero.* Princeton, N.J.: Princeton Univ. Press.

Chakrabarty, Dipesh. 2000. *Provincializing Europe: Postcolonial thought and historical difference.* Princeton, N.J.: Princeton Univ. Press.

Chua, Daniel K. L. 1999. *Absolute music and the construction of meaning.* Cambridge, U.K.: Cambridge Univ. Press.

Clifford, James. 1983. On ethnographic authority. *Representations* 2: 118–46.

——— and George E. Marcus, eds. 1986. *Writing culture: The poetics and politics of ethnography.* Berkeley: Univ. of California Press.

De Certeau, Michel. 1988. *The writing of history.* Translated by Tom Conley. New York: Columbia Univ. Press.

Derrida, Jacques. 1976. *Of grammatology.* Translated by Gayatri Chakravorty Spivak. Baltimore: Johns Hopkins Univ. Press.

Marcus, George E., and Michael M. J. Fisher. 1986. *Anthropology as cultural critique: An experimental moment in the human sciences.* Chicago: Univ. of Chicago Press.

Tomlinson, Gary. 1999. Vico's songs: Detours at the origins of (ethno)musicology. *The Musical Quarterly* 83: 344–77.

CHAPTER 3

Music and Culture
Historiographies of Disjuncture

PHILIP V. BOHLMAN

It is not easy to talk about music and culture together, much less define them in ways that draw them together. Definitions of music that we might extract from widely used dictionaries neither include the word *culture* nor refer to any intrinsic or extrinsic property of the "arranging of sounds in time" or "a musical composition" (*American Heritage Dictionary*) that has anything to do with culture. Definitions of culture, it goes without saying, also do not refer to music in any explicit way. Music and culture, broadly or narrowly defined, are not convenient discursive fits. When we do try to fit them together—and at base, this is what the authors contributing to the present volume are committed to doing—not everyone is happy. We have all had music teachers who have insisted that "music is music," and that it "doesn't need to be about culture." We have all known social scientists who have kept music at arm's length from culture because it is so many "notes on a page," a technical language spoken by specialists and not the generalists who want culture to be an umbrella for all human activity.

I take the difficulty with which we formulate definitions of music and culture that fit together as my point of departure in this essay. I am not concerned here with finding definitional compromises or forging discursive methods that will repair the bad fit. I do not propose that we look for the widespread presence of music in culture, nor do I take an ameliorative position urging us to recognize traces of culture everywhere in music. The bad fit, instead, results from what I call *disjuncture* in this essay. That disjuncture has been with us for a very long period of history, and it shows no signs of disappearing, even as the authors in this volume and the many other scholars concerned with the cultural study of music draw our attention to the critical importance of understanding the relation between music and culture.

In this essay, I take as a given that disjuncture itself is one of the historically most critical reasons to study music and culture. Employing an approach that is primarily historiographical, in other words, concerned with the history of ideas about music and culture, this essay strikes out in a direction that is different from others in the book. First, I should suggest that, historically, there is far greater acceptance that music and culture are related, if not inextricably so, than many commonly assume. Second, the question that concerns me here is why so many theories and aesthetics of music resist that acceptance. Above all, why does the historiography of Western art music, which includes historical musicology, music theory, ethnomusicology, and popular-music studies, cling to the counterintuitive assumption that music and culture are separate? Third, I wish to suggest that one reason there is resistance to accepting the relatedness of music and culture results from the paradoxical unwillingness to admit to the full range of cultural work that music accomplishes. Finally, I turn in this essay to a series of historical moments of disjuncture between music and culture, examining the points at which the cultural work of music is most powerful and unsettling.

The historiography of music and culture for which this essay is a first stage does not and could not unfold chronologically. The intersections between music and culture exposed by these historiographical moments reveal not so much the alternative side of their relation as the nature of power generated through their embeddedness. Recognition of that power, the destructiveness of which is undeniable, raises the stakes considerably for an historiography that interpellates the cultural study of music.

Historiographical Moment 1—Colonial Encounter

The historiography of music and culture begins with the moment of encounter. Intensifying encounter is the awareness of difference, and that awareness engenders wonder and awe, which, however, lie precariously close to fear and danger. Music marks the moment of encounter, for it stands out as the form of communication that is at once most familiar and most incomprehensible. Even more than language, music is the key to understanding and to the power that will turn initial encounter into prolonged dominance. To music, then, accrues the potential to articulate colonial power, and that potential was never lost on those most eager to colonize and missionize the worlds of the others they encountered (see, e.g., Pagden 1993).

Encounter transformed music into a resource that fired the engines of modernity, first in the Early Modern era that followed on the heels of the Age of Discovery, and then the modernity that accompanied the Enlightenment. Music and, by extension, music history underwent an ontological transformation of revolutionary proportions when they were mustered to intervene during encounter. Music represented culture in two ways, as a form of expression common to humanity, and as one of the most extreme manifestations of difference. On the one hand, the essence of a universal culture was borne by music; that is, the commonness that the colonizer and the colonized shared. On the other hand, the fact that music might embody profound differences accounted for the ways it was totally incompatible with the culture of the colonizer. Missionaries and colonial officials were quick to recognize such contradictions, which were exaggerated by the incongruities that marked moments of encounter.

Among the first missionaries to write a travel account that formed one of the earliest treatises of early modern historiography was the Calvinist Jean de Léry, whose descriptions of Tupinamba song, dance, and ritual from a 1557 to 1558 sojourn near the Bay of Rio de Janeiro were reproduced by European writers such as Montaigne in his celebrated essay, "Des Cannibales" (cf. de Léry 1578; Montaigne [1580] 1952). The musical and the cultural differ from each other in such accounts, sometimes radically so. For de Léry and Montaigne the possibility that music could accompany seemingly horrific cultural acts, especially cannibalism, made it most unfamiliar, while songs seemingly consonant with European repertories nonetheless accounted for familiarity (Greenblatt 1991, 14–19). Jesuit missionaries, charged with the obligation to convert, frequently found music to be their most effective weapon, transcribing and recomposing music from the cultures they encountered into a new global language that would allow them to "sing salvation" (Aracena 1999). New practices of inscription and transcription, therefore, were crucial to the acts of possession that transformed colonial encounter into forms of domination, for they allowed the colonizer to map unknown cultural terrains by expanding music's cartographic power.

The nature of encounter is highly contested in the debates about the relation between music and culture in modern musical scholarship.

Anthropologists urging a move away from comparative musicology in the 1950s elevated encounter to a position of primacy. Until music was encountered in its cultural contexts, so the slogan went, there could be no comparison. Effectively, such anthropological claims on encounter undercut the privileged position that music had enjoyed in comparative musicology. Still, the political implications of encounter remained relatively unremarked, thus exacerbating the disjuncture between music and culture at the moment of encounter.

With the expansion of postcolonial studies in the 1980s and 1990s criticism turned more sharply toward the moment of encounter. Culture, once the privileged site of social sciences, was no longer a safe haven for study. Everything about encounter was questioned, stripping culture of its former privilege, even in the eyes of many anthropologists. Concomitantly, forms of representation, the arts, and performance—and, of course, music—rose in significance, as if they had been immune to the exercise of power all along. Although there was a greater willingness to include music, at least tangentially, in cultural studies, the disjuncture between culture and music in many ways widened. Few scholars in cultural studies, for example, heeded calls to address music less obliquely by engaging in some form of ethnographic study that would recognize the power produced by encounter. From an historiographical standpoint the vital question is not that such contradictory issues of music and culture accrue to encounter, but why musical scholarship and the cultural study of music persist in their failure to close the gap that encounter continues to expose.

Historiographical Moment 2—Racism

The most remarkable thing about the use of music to formulate a sweeping vocabulary of racism in German-language musical scholarship during the first half of the twentieth century is that racist musicology took shape so unremarkably at the very core of musical and cultural study. As a link shared by music and culture, race was simply a given. So unremarkable was the presence of racism in German-language musicology from the 1920s through World War II and the Holocaust that it was only in the 1990s that scholars began to unravel the full extent to which modern musicology failed to extricate itself from an earlier musicology that was itself a racist response to modernism. In particular, Pamela Potter's study of Nazi musicology has uncovered the step-by-step acquiescence of German musicologists to the steady racialization of German thought in both the public and scientific spheres (Potter 1998).

Discovering racism in the musical discourse of the public sphere should hardly have been unexpected, but identifying an extraordinary presence of racial language in the scientific discourse of musicology was. It is not simply the use of music to justify a cultural ideology of racial exclusion that implicates racial theories of music in an alternative historiography of music and culture. The question of racism in the scientific study of music is far more deeply and historically located in the disjuncture between music and culture than we wish to admit.

The musicological language of racism forged by Nazi scholars became convincing for a number of different reasons, but I concentrate here on only one: The racial traits of music were immanent in nature. Racism grows from the impulse to witness music in nature, one of the original uses of "culture" in the interpretation of music. Nature in two forms, human biology and the human transformation of natural landscapes, could explain not only cultural difference but also cultural dominance. Basic intervallic structure in music and the scales that formed around it, for example, were based in the measurements of skull shape, which in turn formed global patterns based on racial groups (e.g., Metzler 1938). The differentiation of musical structure according to biological structure required collaboration across several disciplines, with historical and comparative musicologists at one end of a disciplinary continuum and physical anthropologists and folklorists at the other. It was furthermore significant for the use of nature to justify racial differences in music that these differences were not limited to Central Europe or even to Europe, but rather stretched across the entire globe (see, e.g., a 1938 map of racial differences, translated into English, that appears in Bohlman 2000, 658).

Maps of racial traits in music were not simply representations of racist fantasies, for they were used to justify cultural work of the most extreme kind, above all, the German military expansion. One of the central projects of German folk song scholarship during the Weimar, Nazi, and Cold War periods, for example, was the publication of a series of anthologies—a total of forty-seven appeared in print—that charted "German folksong landscapes" (*deutsche Volksliedlandschaften*) across Europe, musically claiming the continent as German through repertories that would show how German folk song grew from the soil of Poland and Ukraine or was fundamental to the Christianity of Alsace-Lorraine (see Bohlman 2002a for a study of individual volumes). German folk song, thus, was imbued with the meaning of *Blut und Boden* ("blood and soil"), nature in its most German essence.

Stereotypes of race exacerbate the disjuncture between music and culture. So common are such stereotypes that it is only when they are most brutally misused that they attract our attention. The several subdisciplines of musical scholarship have all relied to greater or lesser degrees on stereotypes of race to explain local distinctiveness and to construct global theory. The boundary between terminology that is racial and language that is racist, as Stephen Blum (1991) has demonstrated in his thorough examination of European discourse about African music, is at best blurred and often entirely indistinguishable. Even as ethnomusicologists at the end of the twentieth century increasingly questioned the reliance on racialized and racist stereotypes in the study of the music of Africa and the African diaspora, there remained resistance to abandoning biological and natural explanations for music's distinctiveness (e.g., Blacking 1995).

The contradiction that ethnomusicologists were unable to resolve in their examination of differences that so critically characterized the gap between music and culture resulted from the inability to separate the racial from the racist in music. The "racial" was regarded positively, as an explanation for difference. The "racist" was regarded negatively, as a perversion of difference. To eliminate one or the other would also eliminate difference in music itself, which by the end of the twentieth century had been elevated to the common ground shared by all the subdisciplines of musical scholarship (e.g., Solie 1993; Radano and Bohlman 2000).

Historiographical Moment 3—Nationalism

More than any other form of identity, nationalism closes the gap between music and culture. In so doing, it heightens the disjuncture created by conflicting musical processes for constructing the nation. The nation that emerges from the intersecting domain shared by music and culture is remarkable for both its vastness and the detail of its landscapes, and it is for this reason that nationalists so eagerly reach toward music, and that so much power accrues to music when it is enlisted for nationalist ends. As the twentieth century gives way to the twenty-first, there is no music that is as often celebrated and maligned as that which represents the cultural identities to which we ascribe the label *national*.

In the post-Enlightenment era of nationalism, music acquired the potential to articulate nationalism by representing place. The nation grew as an amalgamation of places, for example, from the welter of dialects that nineteenth-century nationalists identified in folk song. There was an expansion of folk song repertories in concentric patterns as local songs constituted regional repertories, which in turn stretched across a national repertory. The nationalist model of the nineteenth century was anchored to its core, and the music that fulfilled the conditions of the core functioned like a national canon. Following the rhetorical model of Herder, who affixed national labels to folk musics in relatively democratic fashion, proclaiming the possibility that national "peoples" (*Völker*) without politically independent nations gave "voice" to the nation through songs (Herder 1778–1779), nineteenth-century nationalists constructed enormous canons of folk song from the collective endeavors of folklorists, linguists, ethnologists, philologists, and musicologists. The landscapes of the nation and its songs were isomorphic.

The problem of musical nationalism emerged when that relation between music and culture was disturbed; when, for example, the landscape of national song was imagined to extend beyond a nation's borders. European nationalists were especially adept at discovering national songs beyond their borders and mustering those songs to imperialist ends. German "speech islands" (*Sprachinseln*)—linguistically bounded regions, especially in eastern and southeastern Europe, where German was spoken by a minority population—were one of the primary justifications for German expansionism in the late nineteenth century. Hungarian nationalists, among them Béla Bartók, were no less willing to point to the presence of regions where Hungarian songs were still sung, especially in Romania and Slovakia, and to encourage the mobilization of national forces, including national armies, to unite the periphery to the center, thus reinforcing the national musical repertory (e.g., Trumpener 1996).

The nationalist expansion of the nineteenth century culminated in the implosion of the European nation in the twentieth, particularly in the global tragedies of the two world wars. Among those symbols of the nation demonstrating the greatest resilience to the implosion was national music. Within years after the realignment of national borders following World War I, national song projects took shape, more often than not challenging the very validity of the new national borders. As former colonial and imperial holdings beyond Europe began to construct national myths and to transform these into national histories, national music quickly became invested with the power to serve as international political capital, mapping the rest of the world according to European musical geographies (e.g., Chakrabarty 2000; cf. the essays in Stokes 1994).

At the beginning of the twentieth century, many predicted that the potential of music to do the cultural work of nationalism would diminish as music's historical trajectory pulled it toward increasing complexity and aesthetic autonomy. At the end of the twentieth century, there were predictions that music would lose the functions of nationalism because its movement across national borders would erase those borders. The predictions that framed the past century, however, have not come to pass. Quite the contrary, during a century in which the destructive force of nationalism was almost unimaginably extreme, new nationalist ontologies accrued to music. National music was liberated from the soil, that is, from the bounded landscape and geography of the nation. The emerging technologies of the period between the world wars, particularly the growing availability of radio and recordings, invested music with the possibility of creating what Brian Currid calls a "national publicity," whereby a national public experiences the nation through regularly listening to its musical broadcasts (see Currid 1998). National publics experience the nation in even more complex ways than the populations that gather at specific moments to perform the nation in the phenomenon Benedict Anderson calls "unisonality" (Anderson 1991).

The technological revolutions in the closing decades of the twentieth century similarly failed to erase the traces of the nation in music but instead intensified their nationalist functions on a global plane, creating the new nexus between nationalism and cosmopolitanism. It is hardly surprising, then, that the most scholarly and most popular compendia devoted to world music, for example, the *Garland Encyclopedia of World Music* (Nettl et al. 1998–2002), or global popular music, for example, *The Rough Guides* to world music (Broughton et al. 1999–2000), remain, at base, organized according to national categories. We could not shake music of its nationalist potential even if we wanted to. As nations rise and fall, and the claims to national identity go unresolved, music will continue to problematize the gap separating the image of the nation from its political reality.

Historiographical Moment 4—Eschatology

At the turn of the present century, music and culture crowd in upon each other in their common domain of disjuncture. As they draw nearer, there is a price to be paid and a sacrifice to be made. The place previously allowed for history becomes increasingly small, heightening premonitions that history itself will come—or indeed has come—to an end (Fukuyama 1992). If history underwent a radical acceleration in the earliest colonial encounters, it had reached a point of eschatological disintegration at the end of the twentieth century, when encounter had become so thoroughly globalized as to become meaningless. The anxiety of history's closure is immanent in postmodernism, in which culture is privileged over all else, in other words, in which the possibility of constructing histories according to one's own needs with rapidly changing technologies at one's disposal empowers one to negate history and rise beyond it (Lyotard 1991).

The twentieth century witnessed unprecedented levels of human destruction and death, and music, too, was present in unprecedented ways at moments of massive violence and death. Music, too, was a participant in the cultural work of persecution and genocide. Eschatological meaning has long been recognized in musical practices, particularly those accompanying religion and ritual. As the end of the twentieth century and the beginning of a new millennium approached, eschatological meaning itself intensified, and with it music was implicated in the imminent end of history. The eschatological power of music results from both its cultural and musical sides. The former is evident in the overt use of music to mark moments of death; for example, in the concentration camps of the Holocaust. The latter resides in the temporal phenomena that shape the ontologies of music, in other words, the power of music to calibrate and shape—as well as negate—time.

Music inscribes eschatology on culture, all the more so on the culture of globalization and postmodernity. World music in its many globalized and postmodern forms, too, mixes and remixes its historical contexts, negating them and exiting from history to move along new paths of endism (Bohlman 2002b). The world-music mix blurs the borders between text and context, in so doing rendering the borders between music and culture meaningless. Any music can function within any cultural context, if, of course, it is in the interests of producers and consumers to make it do so. The question remains, nonetheless, just where does the cultural work of history end and that of eschatology begin?

The question is hardly rhetorical, for a welter of answers rushes in to expose the sites cohabited by music and the culture of death. The Holocaust in which World War II was grounded is the most immediate site to pose and answer the question. The very horror of the Holocaust is amplified by the recognition that music was, in fact, omnipresent. Music mobilized the fascism and racism of the Nazis. And music afforded the victims thereof, for example, Jews and Roma in concentration camps, a last chance to express their cultural and religious identities in new ways.

Since the Holocaust, moreover, music has served as one of the most contested areas of memory work. Many survivors have insisted that the music of Wagner memorializes the death and genocide of the concentration camps. In attempts to reckon with the history of genocide, revival of repertories erased during the Holocaust itself—the folk, popular, and art music of the era at the end of European Jewish history—serves not so much to construct past history as to reimagine it as a virtual monument in the present.

Music serves entirely different eschatological ends for the radical right, especially in the era of the New Europe that began with the fall of the Berlin Wall in 1989. A disenfranchised youth subculture coming of age in that culture turned to musics that explicitly recall the images of death and genocide. "Skinhead music" and "Oi" thrived in the subculture of the radical right during the 1990s, not simply providing texts for complaints about minorities competing for employment, but also instigating violence and memorializing it in forms eerily consistent with the century of unimaginable destruction (Schwarz 1997).

In the course of the twentieth century, as modernity yielded its hold on history and gave way to postmodernity, the musical competition for place, history, and culture accelerated, and in extreme cases could no longer be checked. As war and ethnic strife entrenched themselves deeper in the Balkans, to take one of the most extreme cases, the use of music to wage cultural war slid toward an extreme, to a level of cultural crisis referred to by Tomislav Longinovic as "music wars" (Longinovic 2000). The "music wars" that Longinovic locates at the "end of Yugoslavia" are by no means simply metaphorical or rhetorical. Their stakes are considerable, as folk songs, those imagined to be traditional, and those "newly composed" as popular music, strip away layer upon layer of history to unearth the racial core that precedes all political claims to southeastern Europe. The music wars, aided and abetted by technological developments in all areas of musical production, ensure that the battle for cultural domination will never run out of fuel. The region's pasts proliferate in the music wars, and the culture of the present constantly takes on new identities that lay new claims on the ownership of the future.

The paradox remains that music and culture draw ever nearer to each other, while the disjuncture in the domain they share heightens a sense of crisis at the end of history. The music wars in the Balkans may be but one example for the crisis at the end of history, but they serve as an example that is frighteningly familiar.

Music's Embeddedness in Culture

It is hardly new to make a case that music and culture relate to each other, even that one is inseparable from the other. When Guido Adler inscribed the tablets for a modern science of *Musikwissenschaft* in 1885, culture was there, all over the place, and it accompanied the many sub-disciplinary branches that constituted Adler's vision for a comprehensive study of music (Adler 1885). Later comprehensive models for the study of music continued the methodological practice of connecting music and culture (see, e.g., C. Seeger 1977). While most ethnomusicologists concerned themselves with the appropriate prepositional connective between the two—music *in* culture, music *as* culture—historical musicologists and music theorists, at least the progressive ones who looked beyond canonic art-music repertories, wrestled with ways of interpreting text in relation to context.

It would seem that the battle was won long ago. And yet, the debates that fill the pages of this volume remind us that the matter is no closer to being settled than it ever was. The "musicological juncture" for which Charles Seeger famously called continues to elude us, and the nagging question that stimulates the polemics argued by the authors whose essays fill this volume is, Why? If the fact that there is a relation between music and culture is not at issue, what, then, is?

At issue, of course, is why that relation is skewed, why there is imbalance, which in turn destabilizes the ways in which we understand the presence of music in culture and vice versa. Metaphysically, musicological juncture—or any other kind of juncture in the study of music—may well be inherently impossible, for music and culture occupy two fundamentally different phenomenological domains. Rather than juncture, it is disjuncture that makes for a very specific kind of embeddedness. That embeddedness results not from an attraction based on similarity but instead from an affiliation predicated on difference. And this in turn produces the anxiety of disjuncture.

Culture allows for the domestication and possession of music, but it also allows for forms of domination. Music is well fitted to do cultural work, but the more we engage it in cultural work, the more its ontology as an aesthetic object is sullied. This is how it has always been. Any music historiography that would ignore that, by seeking to establish neat interrelations between music and culture, would necessarily also ignore the power that emerges when music interacts with culture in ways we do not want. Our hopefulness notwithstanding, music may be so embedded in and tangled with culture that it cannot rise above culture. Accordingly, historiographies of disjuncture might well reveal that music's relation to culture is not what we have thought it was, and that music itself is not what we imagine it to be.

Further Reading

Blacking, John. 1995. *Music, culture, and experience: Selected papers of John Blacking.* Chicago: Univ. of Chicago Press.

Blum, Stephen. 1991. European musical terminology and the music of Africa. Pp. 3–36 in *Comparative musicology and anthropology of music: Essays in the history of ethnomusicology.* Edited by Bruno Nettl and Philip V. Bohlman. Chicago: Univ. of Chicago Press.

Bohlman, Philip V. 2002a. Landscape-Region-Nation-Reich: German folk song in the nexus of national identity. Pp. 105–27 in *Music and German national identity.* Edited by Celia Applegate and Pamela M. Potter. Chicago: Univ. of Chicago Press.

———. 2002b. World music at the "end of history." *Ethnomusicology* 46 (1): 1–32.

Pagden, Anthony. 1993. *European encounters with the new world: From Renaissance to romanticism.* New Haven, Conn.: Yale Univ. Press.

Potter, Pamela M. 1998. *Most German of the arts: Musicology and society from the Weimar Republic to the end of Hitler's Reich.* New Haven, Conn.: Yale Univ. Press.

Radano, Ronald, and Philip V. Bohlman, eds. 2000. *Music and the racial imagination.* Chicago: Univ. of Chicago Press.

Schwarz, David. 1997. Oi: Music, politics and violence. Pp. 100–32 in *Listening subjects: Music, psychoanalysis, culture.* Durham, N.C.: Duke Univ. Press.

Seeger, Charles. 1977. *Studies in musicology 1935–1975.* Berkeley: Univ. of California Press.

Solie, Ruth A., ed. 1993. *Musicology and difference: Gender and sexuality in music scholarship.* Berkeley: Univ. of California Press.

Stokes, Martin, ed. 1994. *Ethnicity, identity and music: The musical construction of place.* Oxford: Berg.

Trumpener, Katie. 1996. Imperial marches and mouse singers: Nationalist mythology in central European modernity. Pp. 67–90 in *Text and nation: Cross-disciplinary essays on cultural and national identities,* ed. Laura García-Moreno and Peter C. Pfeiffer. Rochester, N.Y.: Camden House.

CHAPTER 4

Comparing Music, Comparing Musicology

MARTIN CLAYTON

My aim in this chapter is to offer some observations on the past, present, and future of comparison in musicology. These comments concern the necessity of comparison, but also the profound difficulties it presents: Understanding both the importance and problems of comparison is an important part of any cultural study of music. In order to introduce and to illustrate these observations, I make reference to a couple of quite different examples, both of which include an autobiographical element. The first of these concerns a particular performance event and my experience of and reaction to it. The second example refers to my own research on the temporal organization in North Indian classical music, which I published in the book *Time in Indian Music* (2000).

The rationale for introducing such different examples is precisely in order to ask to what extent they may be compared: in fact my concern is not only how *music* can be compared, but also how far *modes of describing music* can be compared. I move from the description and comparison of my own examples to a more general discussion of comparison in musicology, and in particular the legacy of the academic field known between about 1880 and 1950 as "comparative musicology." I begin my argument with a musical performance as experienced, and a discussion of the relationship between such experiences and musical discourse.

London, December 16, 2001

The event I alluded to above was the Icelandic pop singer Björk's performance at the Royal Opera House in London, England, in December 2001. I do not present a review of the concert here, still less do I burden you with an account of the emotional roller-coaster that my co-celebrants and I enjoyed over the course of the evening. On the contrary, I would argue that much of what I consider important in the event could not be adequately expressed in words. Suffice it to say, as we stumbled out into the chilly London night my companions and I were all but speechless. We tried, with little success, to share our reactions to the evening's performance, until—abandoning the attempt—we digressed into a comparison of "all-time top five live performances," as if transformed into characters from Nick Hornby's novel *High Fidelity* ([1995] 2000). Fascinated by our inability to even attempt a verbal account of the evening's experience, the next day I checked Björk's website (www.bjork.com/unity) for the reviews which I knew our fellow concertgoers would soon be posting. Somehow, although the challenge of transforming the experience into words had defeated me, it seemed important that someone should at least *try*, and perhaps delay the dissipation of our memories.

At the heart of any musicological work, comparative or otherwise, lies the relationship between our experiences, and the discourse we generate around those experiences (and through which we explain and interpret them). Musicology cannot enter the domain of unmediated experience, since the academic discipline is by its very nature discursive. This is an essential condition of the musicological enterprise, a condition that becomes problematic only when we confuse that discourse with a true or sufficient account of music, rather than recognizing it as an adjunct to experience.

In 1885 Guido Adler began a famous and influential article defining the scope and aims of musicology by suggesting that the experiences of singing, playing, and listening were not in themselves sufficient for the operation of "tonal art," which required self-conscious reflection. As he put it, from the top:

> Musicology originated simultaneously with the art of organising tones. As long as natural song breaks forth from the throat freely and without reflection; as long as the tonal products well up, unclear and unorganised, so long also there can be no question of a tonal art. Only in that moment

when a tone is compared and measured according to its pitch ... only then can one speak of a musical knowledge as well as an art of working with tonal material. (Mugglestone 1981, 5)

While I would express the relationship between music and discourse somewhat differently, I think Adler's observation on the importance of this relationship remains valuable. For a century or more after Adler's article, most musicologists fell shy of discussing the epistemological basis of music-theoretical discourse. Yet, as the music theorist Benjamin Boretz has suggested, such questions are actually crucial to our endeavors. For Boretz theoretical description was not so much a necessary condition of music as a description erroneously taken for the experience, which in the process became simplified and impoverished (1992). I argue (with acknowledgment to both Adler and Boretz) that musicology needs to resist this error, something I characterize as the collapse of experience into discourse.

Musicology, while it cannot *contain* unmediated experience, can at least enact a sense of its own complex relationship with the material fact of people experiencing music. I call this relationship "complex" because musicological discourse does not only comment on practice and experience; it is not merely parasitical. It also influences that very practice and experience, insofar as musicians and listeners are aware of it. Verbal and graphical discourse can describe, interpret, or otherwise account for musical experience; at the same time, the music we make or choose to listen to is inevitably influenced by this paramusical activity; thus, each feeds off the other.

Time in Indian Music as Comparative Musicology

A decade or so back I was preparing a doctoral thesis on rhythm in North Indian classical music. Through a combination of tuition, practice, informal ethnography, and reading, I felt that I was well on the way to acquiring an understanding of the matter at hand—the system of temporal organization operating in this repertory—and would in due course distill something I might usefully share with others. When I did so my readership would be made up of people expecting me to tell them something comprehensible about Indian music: in particular, how does it work, and how does it relate to Indian culture in general? (Perhaps also, how does it differ from Western music?)

In order to meet this challenge I needed a language; a body of terminology, and of the concepts and ideas to which those terms refer. There was no shortage there, since I had two sets of terms and concepts: one Indian, which I imagined would be useful in explaining how the music works, and the other English, which I assumed my readers would understand.[1] Naturally then, my task seemed to comprise the translation of Indian musicological discourse into English.

So far so good? Well, not exactly. I had understood my task as the translation of a set of repertory-specific and culture-bound concepts (tala, laya, laykari, and so on) into a general, ahistorical, and culturally neutral set of concepts (rhythm, meter, anacrusis, etc.). But as I also knew, these concepts are anything but culturally neutral, general terms, but have their own history, tied up with a long tradition of Western musical thought. What I was doing, in fact, was implicitly comparing Indian rhythmic organization to Western rhythmic organization. But I didn't want to write a comparative study, but rather to write about Indian music on its own terms, so for a while I neglected to resolve this contradiction.

Ultimately I took on the comparative challenge somewhat more explicitly, acknowledging at the same time the problematic nature of the English concepts and terms when applied cross-culturally. Bitten by the comparativist bug, I also tried some comparison within the tradition, examining the relationships not only between different genres, but also between what musicians' discourse was telling me and what I could observe empirically in the music. I became convinced of the need in ethnomusicological analysis to examine both musical sound and discourse, and to interpret the relationships between the two.

Ethnomusicological orthodoxy at the time, to which I subscribed no less than any of my contemporaries, held (as Bruno Nettl put it) that one must "study each music in terms of the theoretical system that its own culture provides for it" (1973, 151). I came to believe that this model was too simplistic, and that any theoretical system must itself be considered critically, *alongside* the music with which it is associated. In the case of North Indian classical music, the relationship between the two proved to be rather complex: I have no doubt that the same would be true elsewhere, and is equally true of the relationship between European music theory (of whatever period) and the music it describes. It can hardly be otherwise.

---

1. The use of the adjective *Indian* here for musical terminology is a shorthand for "in various Indian languages, such as Sanskrit, Hindi, and Urdu."

So much for studying Indian music on its own terms. First, those terms can only belong to the discursive field that surrounds music. Second, musical discourse does not have its own terms: on the contrary, the terms of musical discourse are precisely those that metaphorically link sound to other domains of experience. This is a significant problem with discussing the connections between music and culture: the language we use to construct music is language that already embodies metaphorical links to other domains of culture and experience—the high and low, large and small, balanced and symmetrical, all of the materiality and structure we impute to music (Lakoff and Johnson 1980).

The implication of this line of argument is that notions of musical text, structure, and system are exposed as problematic. Each (text, structure, system) inheres in discourse: but what ontological status do they have as part of a musical experience? Does sonata form exist in music as experienced, or only in music as discussed? Does raga exist as a system in our preverbal musical percepts and memories, or only in our internalizations of paramusical discourse? Such questions have rarely been considered in mainstream musicology, although they are touched on in psychological studies of topics such as categorization and schema formation—in other words, studies attempting to clarify what kind of cognitive structures or processes are implicated in an individual's experience of music (e.g., Krumhansl 1990; Leman 1995; Zbikowski 2002). Given the present state of the field, these questions do not dispose themselves to easy answers.

Attention to the distinctions and relationships among sound, experience, and discourse (such as I am proposing above) does not simplify the business of musicology. This attention does, however, help us to face some problems we have generally avoided. It also opens an important space for empirical work: What features of the sound energy can be specified in a way that permits meaningful comparison? More productive than a retreat from comparison (or indeed a headlong rush toward it) would be an acknowledgment of comparison's inevitability, and a concerted attempt to deal with the epistemological and ontological questions that inevitably arise (what kind of things are we comparing, and how do we know?).

Comparing Music, Comparing Discourse

What, if anything, does this have to do with my experience of Björk's performance at the Royal Opera House? I speculated above that the impulse to discuss and interpret this experience might be linked to an urge to fix my memory of that moment—my angst at the slow evaporation of an emotionally charged state. The reason I found this discussion and interpretation so difficult is, I suspect, connected to that very experiential intensity: verbalizing intense musical experiences is as difficult, and perhaps as futile, as verbalizing other moments of emotional intensity. And the reason I resisted—I could, after all, have said *something*—is perhaps that given the choice, allowing the moment to fade slowly is easier to bear than reducing it quickly to something known, controlled, and impotent. Another factor is revealed by my reaction to those website reviews—*Ah yes, it wasn't just me then*. In this way discourse can reassure us that intense personal reactions are to a degree shared within the community of listeners, which in turn acts as a kind of validation of that experience.

However reluctant I may be, Björk's performances and recordings are nonetheless surrounded by webs of discourse: some generated by the artist herself (in her book, in published interviews, in her lyrics); some by critics and reviewers; a great deal by fans. A sample of the latter can be observed in the form of fans' concert reviews, in which one can discern some common themes. A great deal of this informal public exchange concerns practicalities (what did she sing, what did she wear, what was the sound quality like, and so forth), while some is explicitly comparative ("Was this better than Union Chapel??" (SC); "one of the best [concerts] I have ever experienced in my life" [JD]).[2] But the issues that seem to emerge as most important are the emotional intensity of the performance, and the sense of relationship members of the audience feel with the singer. A few examples:

"Björk wanted to give us the full experience and succeeded beyond expectations" (SC).

"This evening's concert was extremely powerful and emotive, I felt Björk wanted us to experience something quite different . . ." (SC).

"I was very lucky to see Björk in concert on Sunday night. I'm having great difficulty finding words that can describe how brilliant the whole evening was" (JD).

"Last night was definitely a religious experience" (PP).

---

2. I am very grateful to the authors of these comments, Simon Cheung, John Dalgano, and Pierre du Plessis, for permission to quote them; also to Lina/lunargirl at bjork.com for her help in contacting these reviewers. Please see the website for these and other complete reviews.

Can this kind of discourse be compared to the theorizing about tala in Indian classical music? I suggest that it can: not that these discourses function in exactly the same way or have precisely the same effects, but that both exist in a dialectical relationship with particular musical repertories and performances. In both cases, familiarity with the discourse affects the way one experiences subsequent performances. In both cases, discourse begets discourse, metaphorically creating a field within which consensus may be reached over the meaning and importance of the musical experience.

An obvious difference between the two cases is that fans' reviews of Björk's concerts do not generally address musical theory per se. Such an approach is possible, and one imagines that it is realized in some contexts—perhaps by the musicians when rehearsing and recording the music, or by a minority of fans in other situations. But the dominant mode of discourse among fans is one in which the primacy of the occasion and the quality of the experience are affirmed and not transgressed. Experience and discourse cannot collapse into each other in this case.

In the case of music-theoretical discourse, such as I commented on and contributed to in *Time in Indian Music*, this collapse is all too likely. Since all music theory is discursive, it is always to some degree alienated from the experiences it describes. Much musicological writing tacitly assumes the existence of musical works, repertories, forms, styles, and systems: entities that can be described by a musicological discourse that nonetheless appears to remain outside those musical facts. Since I am arguing that these "facts" are all actually discursive artifacts, it follows that the work of musicology is not to describe musical facts but to be implicated in a wider discursive field. This implication has a purpose, and part of that purpose is the control or delimitation of musical practice and its interpretation. The illusion is that musical works and forms exist, but are only imperfectly described—in fact they exist only as imperfect descriptions, while the more immediate business of musical experience is denied serious attention.

In the one example then, fans' exchanges preserve the centrality of the experience, and refuse to collapse everything into discourse. This has the effect of strengthening the sense of community shared by listeners (and, perhaps, further estranges those who don't "get it"), but does little in terms of the production of academic knowledge: it tells us very little about why we felt as we did. In the second example, the theoretical discourse has vastly more to say about the music "itself." On the other hand (as Boretz suggests) the production of this discursive knowledge threatens to substitute itself for our musical experience, in such a way that we listen only for that which signifies the structures described by theory, and to deafen us to all other features of a given performance.

Comparative Musicology Compared

How, finally, do the issues I raised above relate to the legacy of "comparative musicology"? This discipline, now remembered as ethnomusicology's forerunner, was in fact listed by Adler as one of the subdivisions of his science (his field was divided into historical and systematic approaches; comparative musicology came under the latter). It is clear from Adler's work, however, that comparison—alongside ethnography—was reserved for "other" music, that it had little to do with the serious business of "tonal art." The succeeding generation, in the form of scholars such as Carl Stumpf (1911) and Erich Moritz von Hornbostel ([1905] 1975), confirmed the place of comparative musicology on the academic map, although the comparative method was mainly implicit in their development of general analytical principles (principles that were not, of course, applied to Western art music). Where Western art music and other repertories were considered together was in compendia such as Hubert Parry's *Evolution of the Art of Music* (1896). In such works it was abundantly clear that, while all musics might be part of the same evolutionary scheme, they by no means enjoyed equal status.

We must thank Hornbostel for setting out his vision of comparative musicology with great clarity. In an article of 1905 entitled "The Problems of Comparative Musicology," he explained his debt to anatomy and linguistics and their shared reliance on an evolutionary model.

> Systematization and theory depend on comparison. In this sense all learning is comparative, and comparison is a general and not a special method. Yet one generally speaks of *comparative anatomy, comparative linguistics,* etc. This surely infers the application of a particular approach. Medical anatomy is almost exclusively concerned with the structure of the human body; zoology . . . treats the anatomy of the individual animal species separately. . . . Now comparative anatomy presents cross-sections, so-to-speak, of the entire complex: it traces the individual organs through the entire realm of living beings and thus recognizes, for instance, vertebrae in the cephallic bones of man and a sort of eye in the outer epidermis of a leaf. The knowledge thus acquired yields new principles of classification and at the same time stimulates new and specialized investigations.

The development of linguistics followed a similar course. Initially, philology examined the individual languages separately, until comparative linguistics began to tie connecting threads. Here again the concept of evolution presented itself: it pointed to new paths and led to new groupings. (Hornbostel 1975 [1905], 250)

Whatever Hornbostel thought he was comparing in music, they were clearly *entities*, made up of *parts* that fitted together logically and according to common structural principles. The individual entities were, moreover, exemplars of species—the logic of his own comparison with other disciplines is that comparative musicology would look for deep similarities and differences among *types* (repertories, music cultures?), and would not be concerned with the detail of individual *instances* (performances?). Another implication of this approach is that the boundaries between musical repertories would be seen as relatively stable, and hybridization a slow and difficult process, while individual music cultures were related to each other more or less closely, like languages or animal species.

It is notable that early comparative musicology offered few attempts at large-scale comparison (Carl Stumpf's *Die Anfänge der Musik* being the most obvious exception). Grand surveys and sweeping generalizations were on the whole more the preserve of music historians such as Parry. If the hope was to rewrite such evolutionary history on a more scientific basis, the aim was hardly realized before the political traumas of the 1930s shattered the academic status quo. Comparative musicology reemerged in North America after the second world war with what proved to be a brief fluorescence. The most ambitious and commented-upon postwar comparative project was Alan Lomax's Cantometrics (Lomax 1968), a brave attempt to correlate features of singing styles with aspects of social organization. However, if anyone in this period can be regarded as Hornbostel's intellectual heir, it must surely be his student Mieczyslaw Kolinski, who developed a series of ingenious empirical (or quasi-empirical) methods of comparative analysis, described in a series of articles published from the 1950s to the 1970s (for a bibliography see Beckwith 1982). By this time, however, the intellectual climate was changing, and as a result Kolinski's work was largely ignored, and most of the potential his methods offered was wasted.

The comparative musicology project had effectively collapsed, and part of the reason for this was the place Adler and his followers had allotted it in the greater scheme of things. Evolutionism meant that however marginal comparative musicology may have been in Adler's scheme, it nonetheless formed an inseparable part of musicology as a whole. Back in the late nineteenth century musicology and comparative musicology had been united in their goal of describing a comprehensive history of world music. Once social evolutionism collapsed, Western music scholarship didn't feel the need for comparative musicology, and could retreat into the insular stance from which it is still slowly emerging, while comparative musicology's marginality intensified. On the other hand, if the ideology that had given comparison its urgency was now dead, why should comparative musicologists worry any more about comparison?

Comparative musicology was gradually superseded by ethnomusicology, with its anthropological methodologies and mistrust of grand comparative schemes. Where early comparative musicologists sought to compare different musical structures on a common basis, later ethnomusicologists tried to replace this with another view, structuralist in a different sense, in which the structural principles of music related to those found in other cultural domains. As I argued above, there were two major problems with this: (1) that comparison is inescapable, and a retreat from comparison results only in irrational implicit comparisons; and (2) that structure in music is itself contingent, and needs to be recognized as a discursive artifact. From the point of view of the epistemological basis of comparison in musicology, neither nineteenth-century comparative musicology nor late-twentieth-century ethnomusicology satisfies: it can hardly be denied that a new paradigm is needed.

I have argued that comparison is inevitable in musicology. I have also argued, however, that comparison is problematic as long as we confuse experience with discourse, and as long as we do not recognize the contingency of musical "structure." What we *might* look for is a kind of metatheory that is able to take into account the contingency of the very idea of the musical structure. The underlying intention of this metatheory would be to address the relationship among *sound*, as an integral aspect of human interaction; the *experience* of producing, perceiving, and responding to that sound; and the processes by which people imagine that sound to possess structure or to convey meaning.

I have discussed and illustrated comparison on a number of different levels, in order to demonstrate the point of its inescapability: to either retreat from or rush toward comparison would be equally futile. What can we learn from comparing Indian musical practice with Western music theory? One concert with others? The way fans talk about a Björk concert with the ways musicologists analyze a classical symphony? These examples are not far removed from the everyday business of musicology, although they perhaps make the basis of comparison more explicit than is normal, or take comparison into areas not previously explored. My point is not that we need more comparison, but that we could be more conscious of what we compare, and on what basis.

It would also be a long overdue step to acknowledge that Adler was wrong to restrict comparative musicology to the study of "others," and wrong to place comparative musicology as a subdivision of musicology rather than vice versa. Establishing a rational basis for comparison in academic musical discourse may one day prove to be the critical step in the still unconsummated rapprochement between subdisciplines, and the development of a post-Adlerian consensus on the organization of our field, if indeed such a hope is realistic in self-consciously postmodern times.

Further Reading

björk.com/unity. Website: www.bjork.com

Boretz, Benjamin. 1992. Experiences with no names. *Perspectives of New Music* 30: 272–83.

Cavicchi, Daniel 1998. *Tramps like us. Music and meaning among Springsteen fans.* New York: Oxford Univ. Press.

Clayton, Martin. 2000. *Time in Indian music. Rhythm, metre and form in North Indian rāg performance.* Oxford: Clarendon Press.

Falck, Robert, and Timothy Rice. 1982. *Cross-cultural perspectives on music. Essays in memory of Mieczyslaw Kolinski from his students, colleagues, and friends.* Toronto: Univ. of Toronto Press.

Hornbostel, Erich Moritz von. 1975. *Hornbostel opera omnia.* Edited by Klaus Wachsmann, Dieter Christensen, and Hans-Peter Reinecke. The Hague: Martinus Nijhoff.

Hornby, Nick. [1995] 2000. *High Fidelity.* London: Penguin Books.

Lakoff, George, and Mark Johnson. 1980. *Metaphors we live by.* Chicago: Univ. of Chicago Press.

Mugglestone, Erica. 1981. Guido Adler's "The scope, method and aim of musicology" (1885): An English translation with an historico-analytical commentary. *Yearbook for Traditional Music* 13: 1–21.

Nettl, Bruno. [1973] 1992. Comparison and comparative method in ethnomusicology. Pp. 148–61 in *Ethnomusicology: History, definitions, and scope: A core collection of scholarly articles.* Edited by Kay K. Shelemay. New York: Garland.

Nettl, Bruno, and Philip Bohlman. 1991. *Comparative musicology and anthropology of music. Essays on the history of ethnomusicology.* Chicago: Univ. of Chicago Press.

Smith, F. Joseph. 1979. *The experiencing of musical sound. Prelude to a phenomenology of music.* New York: Gordon and Breach.

CHAPTER 5

Music and Social Categories

JOHN SHEPHERD

The starting point of this chapter is the question, to what extent do musical structures and practices reflect, model, or resonate with the identities, experiences, or structural positions of social classes, and gendered and ethnic groups? This issue is a vast one, encompassing an impressive and imposing literature going back almost thirty years and begging some major questions in social and cultural theory. It is an issue to which I contributed during the 1970s and 1980s. My intent in this chapter is to explain why I think this issue and its exploration were important to the development of the cultural study of music during this time; why the work that resulted was superseded by other, more sophisticated work; and why the legacy of some of the thinking that occurred during the 1970s and 1980s might remain pertinent as an emergent paradigm for the cultural study of music is contemplated. This chapter is thus tinged with an element of intellectual autobiography.

It is also written largely, but not exclusively, from the point of view of popular music studies. This is because the issues discussed here found a striking focus during the 1970s and 1980s in work in this discipline, even though it can be argued that they are important to the cultural study of all music. Popular music studies were, however, influenced by wider developments, including some outside the study of music as a whole. Some of these developments are discussed in this chapter. Also, developments important to the issues discussed in this chapter occurred independently of popular music studies in disciplines such as ethnomusicology (e.g., Blacking 1973; C. Keil 1979). As the 1990s dawned, the importance of ethnomusicology to these issues increased considerably (e.g., Slobin 1993).

Music and Paradigms

When I studied music during the late 1960s and early 1970s, I did so in what was then a very conventional way. I studied the history of Western art music, and with only marginal reference to social and cultural forces. The emphasis was overwhelmingly on "the music itself," a music that was judged to be autonomous. The assumption was that, although Western art music was created at particular points in history, it was essentially beyond the influence of social and cultural forces. It was assumed to embody within itself universal, "otherworldly" values and truths immune to the impact of everyday life.

This same period witnessed considerable cultural and social turmoil. In the United States, this was evident in the Civil Rights movement and opposition to the war in Vietnam. Developments in the United Kingdom were less dramatic, but there was nonetheless considerable opposition to established social, cultural, and moral values, with an emphasis on a cultural rebirth emanating from younger generations. Common to all this "antiestablishment" activity was the role of popular culture, and particularly popular music. Much popular music of the time was for younger generations imbued with and expressive of a broadly based and broadly felt sense of cultural and political opposition and renewal. It had to do with the realities of everyday life, and was self-evidently and palpably "social."

For many studying music in institutions of higher education at the time, it was not difficult to perceive a disjunction between music as understood academically, and music as experienced as a part of everyday life. There existed few if any alternatives to the way that music was studied. By contrast, the role of popular music in the cultural politics of everyday life was unmistakable and compelling. To those of us naive enough to suggest that popular music and its politics were a legitimate object for study, the reply was swift and final. Popular music was inferior to "classical" music, and should not therefore be included in the curriculum. Its inferiority was marked and guaranteed by its clear social "content," which served to compromise its tonal values. "Classical" music was superior precisely because it was immune to such undesirable social forces. The cultural, musical, and, indeed, academic battle lines of the late 1960s and early 1970s were drawn very clearly.

This book on the cultural study of music is being written in very different times. While it would be misleading to say that the old "high cultural" attitudes are no longer evident in university music departments, there have undoubtedly been changes. This has been due to several factors: the contributions made to the study of music by a wide range of disciplines outside music, such as sociology, anthropology, and communication; the increasing and sustained influence of ethnomusicology, a discipline for which existing and interacting with the people whose music is being studied has been a central and defining methodology; and major changes within the historically more conservative disciplines of academic music.

The suggestion has been made that these disciplines have interacted with an intimacy that makes possible a new, emergent paradigm for the cultural study of music. This paradigm will certainly be in contrast to the one dominant during the quarter century following the end of the second world war. It is of significance that this earlier paradigm became susceptible to challenge in part because of the advent of the term and concept of *paradigm*. The concept's widespread currency derived from Thomas S. Kuhn's influential book *The Structure of Scientific Revolutions* (1962). Kuhn argued that scientific knowledge did not progress steadily toward "the truth," with erroneous knowledge being discarded and replaced by new, more accurate knowledge. He suggested that when one scientific paradigm, or body of premises, axioms, and theories, could no longer answer the questions it had generated, a crisis would occur in the scientific community supporting and advocating the paradigm. The crisis would be followed by a revolution in which the old paradigm would be replaced by a new one capable of answering the previously unanswerable questions. This new paradigm would be based on a different set of premises, axioms, and theories, and would, quite literally, see the world differently. A classic example of one such paradigm shift is that instigated by Einstein's theories of relativity early in the twentieth century. Scientists who accepted his theories at an early stage did so not because of any empirical "proof," which had to wait some years, but because of the elegance and effectiveness of their explanations. Kuhn concluded that scientists shifted paradigm allegiance not for scientific reasons, but for reasons that were primarily aesthetic.

While Kuhn did not say that scientific knowledge was a social construct, he opened the door for this controversial argument to be made in later years. The argument that *reality* is a social construct was, however, made in 1966 in Peter L. Berger and Thomas Luckmann's *The Social Construction of Reality*. According to Berger and Luckmann, reality was not something given that we receive and perceive neutrally, but something that is constructed by people acting together. These two books provided the intellectual basis for arguing that the way in which music was studied after the end of World War II was not something natural, given, self-evident, or unquestionable, but something that had been constructed socially for political and cultural reasons. What followed from this realization was that something that was made by people could be changed by people. The stage was set for a major paradigm shift in the academic study of music. Fundamental to this paradigm shift was the foundational premise that all music, including "classical" music, was a social construct, and thus something that had to be understood both socially and culturally.

Social categories played an important role in the early days of this paradigm shift. If music was a social construct, it followed that connections should exist between social groups and their music. This chapter traces the lines of this development, the problems to which such work gave rise, and the more sophisticated work that followed it. However, the chapter remains cognizant of something recognized by Kuhn: namely, that with paradigm shifts there are losses as well as gains. More specifically, Kuhn observed, with a paradigm shift questions that were previously important become much less important and sometimes get lost to view. A theme underlying this chapter is that if a new paradigm for the cultural study of music is on the horizon, then, in the spirit of the continual problematization of objects and methods of study, there should be a sensitivity to questions that appear to have receded from view.

Music and Social Categories

The idea that connections exist between social groups and the characteristics of their music began to emerge in the 1970s. In 1970, Andrew Chester drew a distinction between extensional and intensional forms of musical expression. Said Chester:

> [Western classical music] is the apodigm of the *extensional* form of musical construction. Theme and variations, counterpoint, tonality . . . are all devices that build diachronically and synchronically outward from basic musical atoms. The complex is created by combination of the simple,

which remains discrete and unchanged in the complex unity. Thus a basic premise of classical music is rigorous adherence to standard timbres. . . .

By contrast:

Rock . . . follows . . . the path of *intensional* development . . . the basic musical units (played/sung notes) are not combined through space and time as simple elements into complex structures. The simple entity is that constituted by the parameters of melody, harmony and beat, while the complex is built up by modulation of the basic notes, and by inflection of the basic beat. (Chester [1970] 1990, 315)

Chester saw important connections between musical characteristics and social groups. While "the internal coordinates of a musical form are not mechanically determined by its social base," he said, "to each social group correspond certain acceptable genres" (pp. 318–9).

This idea that the characteristics of a musical form could give life to the social reality of a culture gained increasing currency during the 1970s and 1980s. In 1977 I argued that the characteristics of functional tonality as the "language" of classical music embodied and gave expression to the temporal and spatial senses underlying and making possible industrial capitalism as a social form. In 1978 Paul Willis argued that early rock 'n' roll and progressive rock articulated the social realities of biker boy sub-culture and hippie counterculture, respectively. In 1982, I attempted to set out an encompassing model for the social analysis of classical music and many forms of African-American and African-American–influenced popular music important during the twentieth century. The idea behind this model was that of a "harmonic-rhythmic framework," comprised of three chords (the tonic, dominant, and subdominant) and simple duple and triple meters, which was common to both classical and popular musics. This basic framework, with its centralized and "controlling" keynote, was a code for, and articulation of, the encompassing social structures of industrial capitalism. Those with power and influence could manipulate this framework extensionally—hence the complex architectonic harmonic structures of classical music. Those with little power or influence tended to live within this social-musical environment—taking it for granted—and to develop musical complexity intensionally, through individualized sounds or timbres, and through the bending of pitches and rhythms in ways that would be unacceptable within classical music (hence

Chester's reference to "modulation"—actually an incorrect use of the term—and "inflection" in his description of intensional modes of musical development). The model thus incorporated the sociological categories of class, ethnicity, and, to a degree, age. In 1987, I extended this kind of analysis to gender, arguing that different voice types or timbres in popular music gave expression to different kinds of gender identities. It is symptomatic that all this work reflected the clearly drawn battle lines of the 1960s and 1970s.

Illuminating though this work seemed, it brought with it problems. Despite Chester's observation that "musical practice has a relative autonomy" ([1970] 1990, 319), the impression lingered that music was a secondary symptom of social and cultural forces. Music, in other words, seemed to be produced by the "social base." Second, this work operated *only* at the level of social groups. Little attention was paid to the social and cultural identities of individuals. Such identities could exist only because of group membership. Third, the fit between music and social and cultural realities was too tight and convenient. It was not difficult to demonstrate that the practice of music was more complex than theoretical models would allow. This problem was identified by Will Straw (1991) when he drew a distinction between musical communities and musical scenes. A musical community, observed Straw, "may be imagined as a particular population group whose composition is relatively stable . . . and whose involvement in music takes the form of an ongoing exploration of a particular musical idiom said to be rooted organically in that community." By contrast, a musical scene ("the most appropriate term for designating centres of musical activity today") is "that cultural space within which a range of musical practices co-exist, interacting with each other within a variety of processes of differentiation and according to widely varying trajectories of change and cross-fertilization." The break with the work of the 1970s and 1980s is clear in Straw's assertion that cultural theorists like himself encountering such studies for the first time "after an apprenticeship in the hermeneutics of suspicion may be struck by the prominence within them of notions of cultural totality or claims concerning an expressive unity of musical practices" (1991, 369–73).

At one level, Straw's observations signaled real changes in musical and cultural life as captured in concepts such as "globalization" and "postmodernism." The battle lines of the 1960s and 1970s had been replaced by an understanding that the musical world is more complicated than the work emanating from those politics and battles could reveal. Since then, cultural commodities including music had to a degree been drained of ideological or organically rooted meaning as a consequence of their increasing number and variety, and the speed and efficiency with which they were transmitted across the surface of the globe. One consequence was that musical practices no longer occurred just within the delimited geocultural spaces within which particular communities lived. Communities in part and musical communities in particular were created as a consequence of the transmission of music. The notion of place and its role in identity construction thus had to be reconceptualized, a process evidenced in the work of George Lipsitz (1994), Martin Stokes (1994), and Andrew Leyshon, David Matliss, and George Revill (1998). At another level, however, Straw's observations are more profound, signaling the distinct possibility that musical life has always been characterized by complex patterns of cross-fertilization and cultural hybridity, and that notions of organic rootedness and "authenticity" are largely mythical. It has only been the more modest rate of such changes during the course of history that has allowed for the *appearance* of tight fits between music and society.

It is perhaps not without coincidence that, in the same year that Straw was making his observations, Sara Cohen was also calling for a change in approaches to the cultural study of music. In an observation symptomatic of a move away from theory, she argued that "what is particularly lacking in the literature . . . is ethnographic data and micro-sociological detail" (1991, 6). Such detail has been provided not only by Cohen, but by Ruth Finnegan (1989), Deena Weinstein (1991), and Susan Crafts, Daniel Cavicchi, and Charles Keil (1993). It has also been provided by a generation of ethnomusicologists interested in world popular music (e.g., Manuel 1988; Waterman 1990; Stokes 1992; Guilbault et al. 1993; Slobin 1993; Erlmann 1996; Langlois 1996).

The 1990s seemed to evidence a watershed in the cultural study of music. A concern with particular social categories (class, gender, ethnicity, age, subculture, counterculture, and so on) had been replaced with a more embracing and pervasive concern with identity. This concern with identity has subsumed established social categories in markedly complex ways, and at the same time has required and been evidenced by an attention to the specific details of lived cultural–musical realities to a degree not on the whole characteristic of earlier work. The move to ethnography, together with a partial shift in focus from "traditional" to "popular" music in ethnomusicology, can be seen as a defining moment for the emergent new paradigm suggested for the cultural study of music. As Georgina Born and David Hesmondhalgh recently observed, "a common problematic across musicology, ethnomusicology and popular music studies in recent years has been the theorization of music and identity and, by implication, difference" (2000, 2).

Music and Meaning

In the early pages of *Studying Popular Music* (1990), Richard Middleton refers to Gramsci's distinction between "situations" and "conjunctures." In Middleton's words, "situation" refers to "the deepest, the organic structures of a social formation; movement there is fundamental and relatively permanent, the result of crisis"; "conjuncture" refers to "more immediate, ephemeral characteristics, linked to the organic structures but changing at once more rapidly and less significantly, as the forces in conflict within a situation struggle to work out their contradictions" (1990, 12). A question that might be asked of an emergent new paradigm for the cultural study of music is the extent to which the growing, necessary, and legitimate concern with the details of lived cultural–musical realities has nonetheless allowed the situational to recede in relative importance in musical analysis. It is symptomatic, perhaps, that, according to Born and Hesmondhalgh, "much recent work has attempted to move beyond the neo-Gramscian concepts of hegemony and resistance" (2000, 5). They also report that the postcolonial theory so central to recent developments in the cultural study of music "has been criticized" for treating issues of power "almost entirely in terms of textuality and epistemology" and sidelining "material conditions and the possibility of political practices oriented towards changing material conditions" in a manner that "has been the cause of some bitter Marxist polemics against the field" (p. 6).

A second and related question has to do with musical meaning. The paradigm shift that began in the 1970s had as much to do with the question of musical meaning as it did with the foundational premise of music's social and cultural constitution. Susan McClary (1991), in a book that played a seminal role in the development of critical thinking on questions of gender in music, identified the importance of this issue. "I was drawn to music," she said, "because it is the most compelling cultural form I know. I wanted evidence that the overwhelming responses I experience . . . are not just my own, but rather are shared." However, McClary soon discovered that "musicology fastidiously declares issues of musical signification off-limits to those engaged in legitimate scholarship" (1991, 4). In instigating the beginnings of a paradigm shift, the work of the 1970s and 1980s began to throw light on this question precisely by way of the premise that music was constituted socially and culturally. If music were constituted in this way, then it followed that its characteristics—its harmonies, melodies, rhythms, and sound qualities or timbres—embodied and gave expression to meanings that were pervasively social and cultural.

The work of the 1970s and 1980s spoke as much to the situational as it did to the conjunctural. If one question that might be asked of an emergent new paradigm is the extent to which the situational has receded in relative importance in musical analysis, an allied question might be that of the extent to which questions of signification in music have likewise been allowed to recede. A concentration on the details of lived cultural–musical realities has quite correctly involved a heavy reliance on the verbal accounts of those involved in musical practices. This concentration has nonetheless been consistent with the placing of considerable emphasis on the role of connotation in musical significance: the feelings and images capable of descriptive encapsulation that are customarily associated with such musical characteristics as, for example, the feelings of apprehension created by the use of high tremolo violins in film music, or in the images of the ocean—visual, rhythmic, sonic, and even, perhaps, olfactory— evoked by Debussy's *La Mer*. This is an emphasis that seems to have detracted from a concern with the way in which the structural elements of music—harmonic, melodic, rhythmic, and timbral—can speak directly to the structures of social, cultural and individual realities, and thus to the identities and structural positions of social classes and gendered and ethnic groups. This shift in emphasis is consistent with the Foucauldian "linguistic turn" that has been so influential in a wide range of disciplines in the humanities and social sciences. Although Foucault himself stressed the way in which discourses are embedded in the material practices and apparatuses of institutions (see for example, Foucault 1970, 1972, 1978, 1979), this turn nonetheless draws on a long line of French-language linguistic and cultural theory that has tended to eschew the material, whether the material bases of lived realities or those of various signifying practices such as music (in the case of music, its sounds). It is perhaps not without relevance that Born and Hesmondhalgh have recently quite baldly claimed that "connotation is undoubtedly the dominant mode of musical signification" (2000, 56).

If there is a new, emergent paradigm for the cultural study of music, then it may be important to ensure that the situational and the structural, in both life and music, do not get obscured from view. Any reassertion of the situational and structural will have to take on board the important insights resulting from more recent research on the ways in which music is involved and implicated in the construction of cultural identities. A hint as to how such analysis might work can be drawn from the opening pages of Middleton's book. One moment of situational change identified by Middleton "begins sometime after the Second World War—most strikingly with the advent of rock 'n' roll" (1990, 14). The role of Elvis Presley in this upheaval has been debated. As Greil Marcus observes, "it is often said that if Elvis had not come along to set off the changes in American music and American life that followed his triumph, someone very much like him would have done the job as well." However, concludes Marcus, "there is no reason to think this is true, either in strictly musical terms, or in any broader cultural sense" ([1976] 1982, 166). Because of his particular biography and musical talents, it can be argued that Presley was able to identify intuitively many of the cultural contradictions evident in the United States at the time—between black and white communities, rural and urban life, men and women, working and middle classes, young and old, the South and the North—and give them musical expression. This expression was not simply reflective, but also evidenced the relative autonomy of which Chester speaks. As Marcus notes, "Elvis inherited these tensions, but more than that, gave them his own shape" (p.166). Middleton echoes these sentiments in saying that "Elvis's importance . . . lies not so much in the mix of elements (blues/country/Tin Pan Alley) which he helped to bring into rock 'n' roll, but in what he did with it. He transformed them into particular patterns" (1990, 21). Presley gave a specifically musical shape to a situational moment in a manner that was structural as well as connotative, and powerfully corporeal. The question is whether this would have been possible through any other medium than music, and whether an understanding of this moment could be achieved without a heightened awareness of the social categories through which situational contradictions are generated and find expression.

Further Reading

Born, Georgina, and David Hesmondhalgh, eds. 2000. *Western music and its others*. Berkeley: Univ. of California Press.

Bradby, Barbara. 1990. Do-talk and don't talk: The division of the subject in girl-group music. Pp. 341–68 in *On record: Rock, pop and the written word.* Edited by Simon Frith and Andrew Goodwin. New York: Pantheon.

Frith, Simon, and Angela McRobbie. [1978] 1990. Rock and sexuality. Pp. 371–89 in *On record: Rock, pop and the written word.* Edited by Simon Frith and Andrew Goodwin. New York: Pantheon.

Koskoff, Ellen, ed. 1989. *Women and music in cross-cultural perspective.* Urbana: Univ. of Illinois Press.

Maróthy, János. 1974. *Music and the bourgeois, music and the proletarian.* Budapest: Akademiai Kiado.

McClary, Susan. 1991. *Feminine endings.* Minneapolis: Univ. of Minnesota Press.

Middleton, Richard. 1990. "Roll over Beethoven"? Sites and soundings on the music-historical map. Pp. 3–33 in *Studying popular music.* Milton Keynes, U.K.: Open Univ. Press.

Peña, Manuel. 1985. *The Texas-Mexican conjunto: History of a working-class music.* Austin: Univ. of Texas Press.

Radano, Ronald, and Philip Bohlman, eds. 2000. *Music and the racial imagination.* Chicago: Univ. of Chicago Press.

Shepherd, John. 1991. *Music as social text.* Cambridge, U.K.: Polity. 96–185.

Stokes, Martin, ed. 1994. *Ethnicity, identity and music: The musical construction of place.* Oxford: Berg.

Taylor, Jenny, and Dave Laing. 1979. Disco-pleasure-discourse: On "Rock and sexuality." *Screen Education* 31: 43–48.

CHAPTER 6

Music and Mediation
Toward a New Sociology of Music

ANTOINE HENNION

After a century of studies, there is no agreement on what it means to construct a sociology of music. From the beginning this "of" has been a place of tension, not of smooth coordination. If music has easily attracted social readings, there has been strong resistance to a systematic sociology of music whose aim would be to explain musical values or contents through reference to sociological factors. The most vehement prosecutor of such alleged reductionism was undoubtedly Adorno (e.g., 1976)—even though he himself became the worst reductionist when it came to popular culture (Adorno 1990); for him, only musics that are not really art deserve sociological treatment (it is difficult to know if this is more disrespectful of popular music or sociology!). By contrast, the opposite program—a positive explanation of the ways in which music is produced, diffused, and listened to—has been attacked on the grounds that, given its refusal to address "music itself," it cannot acknowledge music's specificity.

In this opposition between two programs, a part of the question is specific to the case of music, but another is common to the social interpretation of any art. To a large extent, the sociology of art has defined itself through opposition to aesthetics. The aim was both to criticize any claim of autonomy for works of art and aesthetic judgment, and to return the experience of aesthetic pleasure—often regarded as immediate and subjective—to its social and historical determinations. The two types of causality mobilized above have often been described in social studies of art in terms of a distinction between studying either "the art object sociologically" or "the art object as a social process" (Zolberg 1990, chapters 3 and 4). One approach displays the mediators of art, the other how art mediates society. The latter takes art as an empirical given reality, and provides explanations of its social conditions; it can be respectful vis-à-vis the "artistic nature of art": the task of sociology is to give an account of the social conditions of its production, diffusion, and reception. The former shows art as a social artifact, or construction, of a group—an "art world"; as such, it is more invasive (it looks for the social nature of art, as Blacking [1973] would put it, not for wider social factors), and sees the claim of art to be autonomous as problematic.

These two directions, one clearly empiricist and more devoted to specific case studies, the other more theoretical, are themselves divided into different trends. Across the board, though, sociology has set itself against a purely internal and hagiographic aesthetic commentary on artworks, "filling out" an art world formerly only including a very few *chefs-d'œuvre* and geniuses. Mainstream productions and copies, conventions and material constraints, professions and academies, performance venues and markets, and codes and rites of social consumption have been pushed to the front of the scene. These mediations range from systems or devices of the most physical and local nature, to institutional arrangements and collective frames of appreciation such as the discourse of critics, right up to the very existence of an independent domain called art. In so doing, scholars have produced a practical theory of mediation, conceived as the reciprocal, local, heterogeneous relations between art and public through precise devices, places, institutions, objects, and human abilities, constructing identities, bodies, and subjectivities.

A Sociology of Aesthetic Pleasure?

Nevertheless, the relationship of sociology and art remains problematic. For most of the classical forms of sociology, for critical theory (Bourdieu 1984), and for interactionist (Becker 1982) or constructivist (DeNora 1995) currents, the sociological analysis of art has always been less interested in creation, genius, or the works "in themselves" than in what makes these categories appear as such. For Bourdieu, who took the critical intention furthest, it means unmasking the magical role of "creation." In this view, culture is a façade disguising social mechanisms of differentiation, artistic objects being "only" means to naturalize the social nature of tastes; aesthetic judgments are but denegations of this work of natural-ization that can only be made if unknown as such. This critique of taste and of its social reproduction has led to many empirical surveys of musi-cal consumption (e.g., DiMaggio 1987; Lamont and Fournier 1992). A radical lack of concern for the works themselves characterizes most of these studies. Sociology refuses subjectivism, the cult of genius, and the self-glorifying discourse of artists, preferring to demonstrate the con-straints through which artists and amateurs are unknowingly determined, the conventions through which they recognize and create their world, and the formats used to mold the social construction of masterpieces.

In these conditions, any report on artistic experience in terms of beauty, sensation, emotion, or aesthetic feeling is thus automatically regarded as a manifestation of actors' illusions about their own beliefs (Bourdieu 1990), or the conventional products of a collective activity. The works do noth-ing, and the processes involved in their appreciation lose their specificity or specialness (Frith 1996); works and tastes—meaningless in and of themselves—are returned to the *arbitrariness* (a key word in any analysis in terms of belief) of a collective election based on a social, nonartistic principle. The argument is a powerful one, and should not be overlooked if we want to avoid the celebration of autonomous art simply being taken literally again. But one also has to measure the limits of such a view, par-ticularly in view of its dominant position now in the sociology of art. It is becoming essential to reconsider sociology's lack of interest in works of art and the aesthetic experience.

Understanding the work of art as a mediation, in keeping with the lesson of critical sociology, means reviewing the work in all the details of the gestures, bodies, habits, materials, spaces, languages, and institutions that it inhabits. Without accumulated mediations—styles, grammar, sys-tems of taste, programs, concert halls, schools, entrepreneurs, and so on— no beautiful work of art appears. At the same time, however—and against the usual agenda of critical sociology—we must recognize the moment of the work in its specific and irreversible dimension; this means seeing it as a transformation, a productive work, and allowing oneself to take into account the (highly diversified) ways in which actors describe and experi-ence aesthetic pleasure.

For various reasons, this has not been the case within social studies of music. The sterile opposition between theoretical and empirical programs has not yet been superseded. In the case of literature or the visual arts, the sociological approach was prepared by lengthy debate over the merits of internal and external explanations. Even if the terms of this debate proved to be unsatisfactory in the end, the debate has at least occured; in the case of music, the fight has not even taken place. Music has always puzzled the critical discourse of the social sciences: here there is an art obviously collective but technical and difficult to grasp, and with no visible object to contest. As music had a priori no explicit "content," the opposition between internal and external approaches was difficult to mobilize. To what could one refer an opposition between a formalist and a realist interpretation of musical works? The positivistic character of much traditional musicology, with little theoretical self-questioning, has often been criticized, while a purely grammatical analysis of musical language produced its own closed sphere. With little relationship to either, a history of music could then describe all the concrete forms through which music had been created, performed, and listened to. The social status of musicians, the technical and economic development of musical instruments, changes in concerts and musical life: studies of all these elements have accumulated, producing rich insights and results, but without any possibility of relating them to musical works, languages, or "contents" in other than very intuitive or metaphorical terms. Instead of giving birth to fruitful controversies and passionate polemics, music has allowed different disciplines to grow, and to ignore one another.

In the case of the visual arts, the materiality of the works, even and especially if challenged by the artists, has allowed a debate to take place about the social production and reception of art. Music is in the reverse situation: its object is elusive; social interpretations just take it as the expression of a social group (ethnic trance, rock concert), aesthetic studies as a nonverbal language of immediacy. Music has nothing but mediations to show: instruments, musicians, scores, stages, records. The works are not "already there," faced with differences in taste also "already there," overdetermined by the social. They always have to be played again.

The Lesson of Music

But what was a handicap for the older, formerly dominant critical approach can become an asset if the aim is to envisage a positive conception of mediation (Hennion 1993). Patrons, sponsors, markets, academies: from the first undertakings of the social history of art, mediations have always had a crucial role in social analyses (e.g., Baxandall 1972; Haskell 1976). Their critical dimension has been used against aestheticism to recall that works and tastes are constructed and socially determined. But music enables us to go beyond the description of technical and economic intermediaries as mere transformers of the musical relationship into commodities, and to do a positive analysis of all the human and material intermediaries of the "performance" and "consumption" of art, from gestures and bodies to stages and media. Mediations are neither mere carriers of the work, nor substitutes that dissolve its reality; they are the art itself, as is particularly obvious in the case of music: when the performer places a score on his music stand, he plays that music, to be sure, but music is just as much the very fact of playing; mediations in music have a pragmatic status—they are the art that they reveal, and cannot be distinguished from the appreciation they generate. Mediations can therefore serve as a base for a positive analysis of tastes, and not for the deconstruction of these tastes.

Recent trends have foregrounded the specificity of music's construction, either on the basis of ethnomethodologist or reflexivist claims to take into consideration the way people themselves construct a reality that they call music (Bergeron and Bohlman 1992), or to account for the fact that we find in music a very particular way of putting a social reality into a form and a practice, and need to cope with the enigma of this art, which is both very immediate, subjective, and emotive, and also highly symbolic, so powerfully able to mobilize groups and carry social identities. To make a sociological analysis of taste does not mean to acknowledge the existence of some general underlying social mechanisms responsible for the presumably stable and necessary relationship between self-enclosed works and preexisting tastes. Rather, taste, pleasure, and meaning are contingent, conjunctural, and hence transient; and they result from specific yet varying combinations of particular intermediaries, considered not as the neutral channels through which predetermined social relations operate, but as productive entities that have effectivities of their own.

One could expect that musical practices, publics, and amateurs would be privileged objects of study for sociologists of music. This is the case with changes in concert life and the development of new musical tastes (Weber 1975, 1992; Morrow 1989; Johnson 1995). The invention of a tradition and the social production of the past has been traced for several repertories, ranging from Beethoven (DeNora 1995) to country music (Peterson 1997). From a more political point of view, Fulcher (1987) has discussed French "Grand Opera" not as a mere petit-bourgeois form of divertissement, as usual, but as a vehicle for the risky political production of the newly restored monarchy's national-popular legitimacy. And after

Benjamin's much-debated essay (1973), modern media and the socioeconomic transformation of music and listening that they entail have been widely discussed; for example, in relation to the records of Callas (La Rochelle 1987), and rock and popular culture (Laing 1985; Hennion 1989; Frith and Goodwin 1990). More generally, popular music and rock have been sites for rich critical rethinking within cultural, gender, and ethnic studies (Willis 1978; Hebdige 1979; Wicke 1990): what appears to be a blasphemy for occidental music is inescapable for popular music, which is studied as a mixture of rites, of linguistic and social structures, of technical media and marketing strategies, of instruments and musical objects, and of politics and bodies. Often implicitly, social analysis refers to the power of music to establish and actualize the identity of a group, an ethnicity, and a generation, and points to the ambivalence of its political function: music both helps a social entity to access reality, and prevents it from expressing itself through more political means (Brake 1980; Frith 1981; Yonnet 1985; Middleton 1990). And after all, Max Weber ([1921] 1958) had done something similar in his much earlier essay—tentative and speculative but full of deep insights—establishing new relations among musical language, technique, and notation, and the social division of labor among audiences, musicians, and composers.

The theme of mediation as an empirical means for identifying the progressive appearance of a work and its reception is very rich; it is the means (for the sociologist) to reopen the work-taste duality, a duality that represents a closure of the analysis, with works on one side left to aestheticians and musicologists, who attribute the power of music to the music itself, and, facing them, a sociological denunciation, the reduction of music to a rite. In the next three sections I briefly exemplify such a "mediation perspective" from some of my own studies.

"Bach Today"

Bach was not a "modern composer," author of a "Complete Works," catalogued in the *Bach-Werke-Verzeichnis*, before musicology, the record industry, and the modern amateur. One can trace through the nineteenth century the long transformation of what was "music," and how it produced our taste for Bach as a musician, giving him the strange ability of being both the object and the means of our love for music (Fauquet and Hennion 2000). Bach is neither the solitary individual born in 1685 to whom history would ascribe an oeuvre, nor an artificial construct of our modern taste. We listen to him today by way of three hundred years of collective labor, and of the most modern mechanisms, mechanisms that we created to listen to him but also *because* we were listening to him. Those mechanisms keep on perfecting themselves in the desire for a "return to Bach" (thanks to musicology, organology, computerized recording, the progress made by performers, and the historicization of our appreciation). But in so doing, they invest themselves more and more in this active production of "Bach today," and the more and more modern they become!

How can one analyze Bach's grandeur? To answer such a question, one cannot just study "Bach's reception" musicologically. To speak of reception is already to admit that the oeuvre is constituted. Beauty is also in the eye of the beholder: the formation of a taste cultivated for classical music is not simply an independent development that enables the "reception" of the great composer always to be more worthy of him. But one cannot just sociologically critique the cult of Bach: there was, and continues to be, a simultaneous production of a taste for Bach, of an oeuvre corresponding to this taste and, more generally, of a new mechanism for musical appreciation. The hand is not dealt to two partners (Bach and us) but to three (Bach, us, and "the music"), none of which can be separated from the others: Bach's music continually changes in the process, and reciprocally, all through the nineteenth century, Bach helped a complete redefinition of the love for music to take place.

Bach "becomes music": not only a reference, an ancient Master, the statue of the Commendatore in the shadow of whom the music of the present time is written, but a contemporary composer. But the reverse is also true: music "becomes Bach," it is reorganized around his figure (and Beethoven's), resting on their production. Bach is not integrated into an already made musical universe: he produces it, in part, through the invention of a new taste for music. Throughout the century, we witness the formation both of a new way to love music, as a serious, demanding activity—a development that was primarily due to the influence of Beethoven and Bach—and of a new repertoire of masterpieces that respond to this appreciation. Bach's "early adopters" in France (Boëly, Fétis, Chopin, Alkan, Gounod, Franck, Liszt, Saint-Saëns) copied, paraphrased, transcribed—not because they were unfaithful, but because Bach was a means for making music, not a composer of the past. Through the way that each incorporated the insights that they discovered in Bach's work into their own compositions, these composers gradually developed our modern form of musical appreciation. Paradoxically, their interaction with Bach's oeuvre also led to the current stipulation that the past be respected, a stipulation that calls us to reject this nineteenth century that brought Bach to us, so as to return to a more original, more authentic Bach, a Bach who is "better" understood (Hennion and Fauquet 2001).

This account reveals the "musicalization" of our taste for the music: the formation of a specific competence, increasingly well defined and self-sufficient, that makes us appreciate the works according to a regime of connoisseurship—a format that we stop seeing as we come to belong to it most naturally and intimately. This is at the heart of the paradoxes surrounding the baroque revival (Hennion 1997): the appearance of a past to listen to in a particular fashion, by respecting its modes of production, is the incredibly elaborated—and very modern—fruit of a hypertrophy of musical taste, based on musicology and the progress in recording. It is the culmination of a transformation of musical taste, not a passive and anachronistic "return to sources." Nothing is more modern than an historical approach to an old repertoire.

Jazz, Rock, Rap, and Their Media

Comparing musics and genres on the basis of the media and modes of performance they use does not mean taking their self-descriptions at face value. It is too easy, for instance, to oppose the freedom of playing together and the pleasure of dancing bodies, identified in jazz or rock, to the way written music gives itself airs, while it is suspected by its opponents to be already dead. Against the supposed rigidity of a corseted classical music—prisoner of scores, orchestral hierarchies, harmonic "laws"—jazz, which is so fond of old records, assumes its sweetest voice to sing praises of improvisation. But, busy adorning the object of her love with these praises, the jazz lover forgets that this splendid transgression of centuries of written music did not come about by going back to the oral sources of a traditional music that cannot be written down on paper, but on the contrary by going forward with the use of new means to overfix music, through a medium that no former genre could lean on: jazz has been written by recordings. Testimonies from all the jazz greats converge: they have trained, they have practiced scales, with one ear stuck at the gramophone and radio. Parker learns how to "chorus" by listening hundreds of times to Hawkins's or Young's solos on an old record player, just as previous generations wore out their eyes on old scores, and he looks for the same thing they did: to read a music he could not hear at its source, but that these recordings allow him to work and rework, to analyze and copy, and to play, note by note, faster and faster.

As a result, far from obeying the millennial rhythm of traditional musics that (transmitted only through collective repetition) continuously change without changing, never stop moving while thinking themselves eternally the same, jazz covered in fifty years a history classical music took five hundred years to write. Between an old blues and a chorus by Coltrane, both officially improvised, lies a transition from orality to a music that on the contrary is overwritten, even more written than classical pieces. Records have written jazz's library. Its living history is the fruit of mechanical recording.

Another example: the sudden passage from rock to rap, quite similar to the revolution of rock itself in the fifties, also displays a conflict between different media—stage versus record. Through a face-to-face confrontation between the star and the public, rock constructed its power around a mythic stage in the quest for a lost hand-to-hand clinch between idols and people. This central place given to the stage was destroyed by rap from the very start, giving way to another definition of musical truth: where you live, where you hang out. The denunciation of rock's too-sophisticated techniques, already made by punks, and the bricolage with record decks and boom boxes, exposed rock's "archaic" conception of stage performance on the basis of an unexpected promotion of recording: not as a faithful reproduction medium, but a cheap means for local creation.

By explicitly refusing to refer to a place other than where one lives—the street, the pavement, shared and invaded places, where one talks, fights, discusses—rap at its origin interrupted the very gesture of the great stage performance. It commuted rivalries and fights into an improvisatory sparring match based on a given background music, played on equipment whose quality did not matter as long as the music was loud enough, to be listened to on the spot, by buddies, equals. The truth of music is not in music itself, not in any reconstituted collective, it is in the present performance you can give, here and now. The initial hostility of rappers toward the music business, money, and the mass media is less to be interpreted as political radicalism than as the technical means to stop the move of identities toward the big stage, always in the hands of intermediaries—and of the white man. So defined, rap is not so new: bebop in its time, punk more recently, or neobaroque musicians all began by escaping from the big stage and the media, before being seized back or dying. Rap has already suffered this common fate. But before it became just another musical genre and social style—racking up huge sales for the record industry—rap had produced, besides a blow to rock grandeur, a new and lasting instrumental use of "reproduction" technology.

Figures of Amateurs

When a sociologist questions somebody nowadays on what he likes, his subject apologizes. "My family is very bourgeois, my sister plays the violin. . . ." Far from revealing the hidden social reality of tastes thought of by amateurs as personal and subjective, irreducible and absolute, sociology has become one of the main registers in which to speak about them. Music lovers, fully aware that tastes are relative, historical, and the supports of various social rites, display them as arbitrary, socially determined signs. Strange paradox of a highly reflexive field: it is the sociologist who must henceforth "desociologize" the amateur if he wants her to speak back of her pleasure, of what holds her, of the astonishing techniques and tricks she develops in order to reach, sometimes, her joy.

Far from being the cultural dope at whose expense the sociology of culture built its critical fortune, the amateur (in the broad sense of art lover) is a virtuoso of experimentation, be it aesthetic, technical, social, mental, or corporeal. She is the model of an inventive and reflexive actor, tightly bound to a collective, continuously forced to put into question the determinants of what she likes. She is as self-aware about pieces and products as about the social determinants and mimetic biases of her preferences; about the training of her body and soul as about her ability to like music, the technical devices of appreciation and the necessary conditions of a good feeling, the support of a collective and the vocabulary progressively designed to perform and intensify her pleasure. Studying diverse amateurs, then, provides a better understanding of our attachments (Gomart and Hennion 1998; Hennion 2001).

Such a survey of classical music lovers, through all the means they can use to reach music (instruments, choirs, singing, but also records, concerts, media, and the Internet), displays the various and heteronomous moments, formats, and configurations in the careers of amateurs, their pattern depending less on past determinants than revealing the stages of a problematic relation to an evasive object. A systematic comparison between wine amateurs and music lovers puts under scrutiny the variable role of the heterogeneous mediations of taste: techniques of buying and tasting; belonging to clubs or organized groups; use of an idiomatic vocabulary somewhere between technical discourse and emotive self-expression; the role of critiques and guides; modes of evaluation, status games, and so forth. Bodies, spaces, durations, gestures, regular practice, technical devices, objects, guides, apprenticeship: both music as a performing art and wine because of its focus on a corporeal contact with the eye, the nose, and the palate allow us to understand taste not as a recording of fixed properties of an object, not as a stable attribute of a person, and not as a game played between existing identities, but as an accomplishment. It is not about liking music or being a wine taster, but about being touched by this piece or liking this bottle, here, now, with these people: a strange activity, the conditions of which are continuously discussed by amateurs themselves. It relies closely upon moments, places, opportunities: taste is not only an activity, it is an event, oversensitive to the problematic relationship between—as they nicely say—a combination of circumstances.

A Possible Return to the Work?

A last point, about the work "itself"—this silent other side of the coin for the sociology of art. A rewriting of music from the viewpoint of mediation makes artistic creation somewhat less distant, less difficult to think of for sociology. Creation does not need to be "taken away" from the great composers and given back to society or consumers: it is just more distributed. Creation is not only on the side of the creator; on the contrary, the more there is a collective work in defining and thus creating a domain such as music, the more we will end up attributing the origins of the works exclusively to certain creators—the paradox of the "author," which the theoreticians of literature have clearly pointed out (Foucault 1969). This mechanism is profoundly circular: it takes all the collectivity's love to be able to say that everything comes from Rembrandt or Mozart. This is why Elias (1993) is caught in a double bind when he speaks of Mozart as a "socially unrecognized" genius—a paradoxical pleonasm, considering how much this "unrecognition" is a central figure of the social production of "genius." Highlighting the work of mediation consists of descending a little from this slightly crazy position of attributing everything to a single creator, and realizing that creation is far more widely distributed, that it takes place in all the interstices between these successive mediations. It is not despite the fact that there is a creator, but so that there can be a creator, that all our collective creative work is required.

This collective redistribution of creation is a counterpoint to the single attribution—the "all to the author"—in the preceding period. There is an optimistic note here: This redistributed creation, always out of line, has no need to be compared to the original work as if to a sort of paralyzing challenge. Creation only uses the elements that it holds to make—with a slight discrepancy—something else: a new creation. It is less a question of understanding everything (a formula whose epistemological terrorism is readily apparent) than of grasping something at work, from which a constantly changing interpretation can be presented.

Further Reading

Bennett, H. Stith. 1980. *On becoming a rock musician.* Amherst, Mass.: Univ. of Massachusetts Press.

Bennett, Tony, Simon Frith, Larry Grossberg, John Shepherd, and Graeme Turner, eds. 1993. *Rock and popular music: Politics, policies, institutions.* London: Routledge.

Cutler, Chris. 1985. *File under popular. Theoretical and critical writings on music.* London: November Books.

DeNora, Tia. 1999. Music as a technology of the self. *Poetics* 26: 1–26.

Durant, Alan. 1984. *Conditions of music.* London: Macmillan.

Gumplowicz, Philippe. [1987] 2001. *Les travaux d'Orphée. Deux siècles de pratique musicale amateur en France; harmonies, chorales, fanfares.* Paris: Aubier.

Hennion, Antoine, Sophie Maisonneuve, and Emilie Gomart. 2000. *Figures de l'amateur. Forme, objets et pratiques de l'amour de la musique aujourd'hui.* Paris: La Documentation Française.

Laborde, Denis. 1997. *De Jean-Sébastien Bach à Glenn Gould. Magie des sons et spectacle de la passion.* Paris: L'Harmattan.

Leppert, Richard, and Susan McClary, eds. 1987. *Music and society: The politics of composition, performance and reception.* Cambridge, U.K.: Cambridge Univ. Press.

Peacock, Alan, and Ronald Weir. 1975. *The composer in the market place.* London: Faber.

White, Avron Levine, ed. 1987. *Lost in music: Culture, style and the musical event.* London: Routledge and Kegan Paul.

Willis, Ellen. 1992. *Beginning to see the light: Sex, hope, and rock-&-roll.* Hanover, N.H.: Univ. Press of New England.

CHAPTER 7

Music and Everyday Life

SIMON FRITH

In the British House of Commons on March 15, 2000, Robert Key, the Conservative MP for Salisbury, begged to move "That leave be given to bring in a Bill to prohibit the broadcasting of recorded music in certain public places" (Hansard [Parliamentary Debates]. Sixth Series, 1999–2000, vol. 346, p. 326–27)).

Key was speaking on behalf of Pipedown, the Campaign for Freedom from Piped Music, but suggested that there would be widespread public support for the measure. He cited a 1997 *Sunday Times* survey that found piped music to be number three in the list of things most hated about modern life. He noted that following a survey of its users, Gatwick Airport had stopped playing canned music. He drew on medical findings. "All uninvited noise raises the blood pressure and depresses the immune system." He added information from the Chartered Institute of Environmental Health. "The commonest type of offending noise is not pneumatic drills, cars or aircraft but music."

The bill was greeted enthusiastically in the media, perhaps because everyone knew it wouldn't get anywhere. But as a solution to the problem of public music, Key's bill was actually quite modest. He didn't seek to ban piped music from places where people choose to go (stores, hotels, sports clubs). His measure was meant to regulate involuntary listening. It covered hospitals and surgeries, local authority swimming pools, bus and railroad stations and journeys, and the streets. He didn't propose, as he might have, that in the future no one should listen to music except in premises licensed for that purpose.

It is not as if private places are free of musical pollution. How many people now travel by car in silence? Who now doesn't shave or bathe to music, cook or iron to music, read or write to music? Thanks to the radio and the record player and the tape recorder, music is now the soundtrack of everyday life, and no law is going to change that. And our ears are as likely to be assaulted these days by classical music as by pop. It's not just that music is everywhere but that all music is everywhere. Works composed for specific secular or religious occasions (marches, masses), in specific places (Thailand, Texas)—can turn up as if at random on TV commercials and restaurant tape loops. There's no longer any necessary connection between the occasion for making music and the occasion of listening to it. Hence the peculiarity of our present situation: If music was once that organization of sounds that could be distinguished from noise, it has become the epitome of noise itself, more offensive, if Robert Key is to be believed, than the sound of jackhammers.

One theme of twentieth-century composition was to make music out of noise, to reclaim the everyday for art, as it were, to write works *for* jack-hammers. Noise-as-music has as many instances as music-as-noise: Cage and Stockhausen wrote works including "live" radio (*Imaginary Landscape No 4* and *Kurzwellen [Short Waves]*). Avant-garde composers took up Pierre Schaeffer's and Pierre Henry's idea of *musique concrète* in a variety of genres. Eric Satie, following a different strategy, proposed *musique d'ameublement*, furniture music, which would be unnoticed in the every-day hubbub, an idea followed up much later by Brian Eno in his *Music for Airports*. And, of course, many rock musicians—in heavy metal bands and their offshoots, in the postpunk industrial and noise scenes—have made electronic amplification and the distorting effects of high volume and feedback a central part of their aesthetic.

But what concerns me here is another of John Cage's contributions, his question: What now is silence?

Two points are striking here. First, silence is so rare that it has become, in itself, increasingly valuable. We live now not just with the permanent sense of traffic roar, the routine interruption of sirens and car alarms and mobile phones, but also with the ongoing electric hum of the refrigerator, the central heating, the neon lights, the digital clock. Silence has become the indicator of an unusual intensity of feeling—emotional intensity in the Hollywood film; public solemnity in the two-minute silence on Veterans' Day; the one-minute silence before kickoff in which to honor someone's death. It was, presumably, this that prompted the Independent

Television Commission in Britain to censure Independent Television News (ITN) for broadcasting a "sick and tasteless" sequence of news in which "the collapse of the World Trade Center in New York was set to music." The music (from Charles Gounod's *Judex*) may have been, as ITN claimed, suitable, with "a sombre, funeral tone," but the very attempt to show these images in time to music "was inappropriate and breached the programme code." And silence, as something valuable, to be bought, means not complete silence, but the absence of human or electronic or artificial sounds. Nature—the country retreat, the unspoiled beach or bush or jungle, the mountain wilderness—is the most precious holiday resource.

Because we seem to value silence, to covet it, it is perhaps surprising that silence is also now something to be feared—on radio, in seminars, on the telephone. Here silence becomes something to be *filled*, and music becomes not that which isn't noise, but that which isn't no noise (i.e., silence). Popular music, something once used to drown out other sounds—on the streets, in the music hall and variety theater, in the pub and parlor singsong—is now used to ensure that there is never no sound at all. If the BBC were to reintroduce Lord Reith's rule that programs should be followed by silence, to allow listeners to reflect on what they had heard, I have no doubt that the switchboard would be jammed with complaints: Has something gone *wrong?*

In the House of Commons, Robert Key suggested that there is an important difference between choosing to listen to music in public places and having to listen to it, and given people's apparent need to fill their lives with music, the implication is that the problem is *what* we have to hear: other people's music, not our own. And certainly the routine use of the term *muzak* to dismiss a certain sort of light instrumental arrange-ment suggests that what's involved here is a matter of taste. But this may be misleading. People are equally upset by what seems to be the *inappro-priate* use of music they do like: Mozart as we wait for a plane to take off; Credence Clearwater or the Clash on a commercial; Miles Davis in a bank. I don't know of any systematic research into what most offends people about the use of music in public places but an unscientific survey of friends and newspaper columnists suggests that what is played matters less than its circumstances.

On the one hand, people seem less offended by live music: children singing on a playground, a brass band or choir in the park, an Andean troupe or reggae guitarist in the shopping mall. A busker singing "Wonder-

wall" or "Hey! Mr Tambourine Man" badly is less offensive than the original record. The issue here is not aesthetics but sociability. Live music
is music as a social event, an aspect of a social situation—play, display,
celebration, begging. It is an organic, a living aspect of public life (hence
the term *live music*), whatever its technical or aesthetic qualities. Canned
music, piped music (terms almost always used with negative connotations of the mechanical) has been removed from its social origins. Like
some alien force it moves relentlessly forward regardless of any human
responses to it.

On the other hand, anecdotal polling suggests that there are experiences of public music that are particularly offensive whatever the music
involved. Music while a telephone is on hold; Walkman leak on trains and
buses; the bass boom from a car at traffic lights; the endless loop of
Christmas songs in December; the sound of other people's parties. The
offense here is against one's sense of one's own space—it is being invaded;
but it reflects too, I think, resentment, resentment at being so obviously
excluded by other people. Music, that is to say, has become a defensive as
well as an offensive weapon (just as it has become a way of negotiating
shared space, as in the club or on the dance floor).

The question of how and why music got implicated in our sense of
personal space is fascinating and has been little explored. It is not just a
matter of music in public places; music is equally important in organizing
domestic space. From a sociological perspective, that is, we can better
understand the domestic relations of intimacy and distance, power and
affection, by mapping patterns of musical use than we can explain musical
tastes by reference to social variables. How is family space regulated musically? Family members (teenagers most notoriously) mark off their own
space with their music—volume as a barrier. But what happens in communal spaces—the kitchen, the car? Who decides what plays? What
music is ruled out *tout court* and why?

I doubt if there's anyone nowadays who couldn't map the history of
family relationships along musical lines. It's a moot point whether changes
in domestic ideology meant new markets for new kinds of domestic elec-
trical goods, or whether it was the new musical possibilities that changed
families, but I have no doubt that a sociology of contemporary courtship,
romance, sex, and friendship could start with the role of music in these
relationships: the exploration of each other's tastes, the shifting degrees of
tolerance and intolerance for other people's records, the importance of the
musical gift, the attempts to change other people's music habits, to resist

changing one's own. I'll come back to this. First I want to digress into some brief remarks about the role in all this of music radio.

I believe that radio was the most significant twentieth-century mass medium. It was radio that transformed the use of domestic space, blurring the boundary between the public and the private, idealizing the family hearth as the site of ease and entertainment, establishing the rhythm of everydayness: the BBC "Children's Hour," "Breakfast Time," "Friday Night Is Music Night!" It was radio that shaped the new voice of public intimacy, that created Britain as a mediated collectivity, that gave ordinary people a public platform (creating the concept of "ordinary people" in the first place). It was radio that made sport a national symbol, that created the very idea of "light entertainment." Where radio led, television simply followed. And it was radio (rather than film) that established the possibility of music as an ever-playing soundtrack to our lives.

If television in all its varieties were to be abolished, it would make little difference to a classical music world that is, though, almost entirely dependent on radio not just for broadcasts, but also for the support of orchestras and concerts, for commissions and record sales. And while the pop world would have to adapt its ways if television no longer played a part in star making, radio is still the most important source of popular musical discourse, defining genres and genre communities, shaping music history and nostalgia, determining what we mean by "popular" music in the first place.

It was radio that created the musical map that we now use to distinguish high and low music, youth and older people's music, the specialist musical interest, and the mainstream. Radio is important not least as a means of access to music otherwise inaccessible, whether in the BBC's systematic policy of musical education or in the furtive teenage use of Radio Luxembourg, the American Forces network, and pirate radio stations as windows on another world.

But here I want to use radio to address another issue: the question of musical choice. In the early days of the music industry, it was assumed that the phonograph and the radio were competing for domestic attention, and it is often suggested that the U.S. record industry only survived the Depression years of the 1930s because of the success of the jukebox (an interesting example of a technological device for imposing private musical choices on a public). It seemed a matter of common sense that if someone owned a record they could play at will, they wouldn't turn on the radio to hear it. Or, alternatively, if they knew the radio would be routinely playing the latest hits, why would they spend money on getting the records for themselves?

In practice, though, this is not how radio choice works. From the 1950s' rise of top 40 radio in the United States to the 1990s British success of Classic FM, it has become accepted industry wisdom that people are more likely to stay tuned to a radio station the more likely it is to play music that is familiar to them, records that they already own or have just bought. It is much harder to maintain listening figures for programs or stations that routinely play the odd or unfamiliar. And radio remains, of course, the essential tool for selling music of all sorts: The more a track is played, the more likely it is that listeners will buy it.

What seems to be involved in radio listening, then, is a constant movement between predictability and surprise. On "our" station we expect to hear our kind of music, without ever being quite sure what will come next. It's as if we're happy to let someone else have the burden of choice. And radio is also a way of suggesting a broader taste community. Our personal musical likes and dislikes are publicly confirmed, and deejays and presenters have a particularly important role in treating music as a form of social communication. The only kind of radio that acquires the condition of muzak is that deejayless ambient format in which no voice is heard (unless it is selling something).

Radio has also been important in developing the skill of switching attention, moving back and forth between hearing music and listening to it, treating it as background or foreground. It's a skill that is taken for granted by film scorers, and one that we exercise everyday without thought as we walk down the street or sit in the pub. Public music irritates, one could say, when what should be in the background forces itself on us as foreground, but the question that interests me and to which I will return, is why it is, when we are now so skilled at screening out music that doesn't much interest us, that some songs or voices or melodies or beats just reach out and grab our attention anyway.

For Adorno "all contemporary music life is dominated by the commodity character" and it is the resulting "fetish character in music" that explains "the regression in listening" (Adorno [1938] 1991). Or, as we would say these days, music is a matter of brand and lifestyle. Take this report from the music industry trade paper *Music Week*:

There was further good news for Classic FM last week when its TV-advertised Time to Relax entered the compilation chart at number nine. "Getting listeners to buy into the Classic brand is at the heart of what we do," says [Roger] Lewis [Classic FM program controller]. "As well as the albums we have the magazine, a credit card and even a dating agency. We are seeing a classical music phenomenon in the UK, as suddenly it's cool to be classical." (*Music Week*, November 3, 2001)

But underlying such brash commercialism are two broader transformations in how music now works in society, the transformations to which Adorno is in part referring when he uses the term *commodity character*. On the one hand, we primarily think of music in terms of its *use*; on the other hand, usefulness means *individual* use.

It is the use of music as a commercial tool to which we mostly object these days: its use to manipulate us in the market. There can be few people who are unaware of how music is used by advertisers and retailers. But it is equally important to note that people nowadays routinely use music to manipulate their moods and organize their activities *for themselves*.

The pioneering researchers of music and everyday life in Britain, sociologist Tia DeNora and psychologist John A. Sloboda, both emphasize the extent to which people now regard music as a personal tool, something to be used, in DeNora's terms, for "emotional self-regulation" (DeNora 2000). As a "technology of self," music has become crucial to the ways in which people organize memory, identity, their autonomy. Both writers suggest that the driving force of people's everyday use is the need to be in control, and that today this means integrating emotional and aesthetic control: creating the setting for the appropriate display of feeling (whether to oneself or to others). Sloboda's research also shows that people are more likely to use music to accompany chores than pleasures, tasks done as duties rather than enjoyed for their own sake (Sloboda and O'Neill 2001). Joggers routinely wear a Walkman; walkers do not. Once the dinner party conversation comes to life no one bothers to put on a new CD.

In many societies, as ethnomusicologists have told us, the functions of music could be described in almost exclusively social terms: Music was used in games and for dancing; to organize work and war; in ceremonies and rituals; to mark the moments of birth, marriage, and death; to celebrate harvest and coronation; and to articulate religious beliefs and traditional practices. People might have enjoyed music individually, but its purpose was not to make them feel good. Compare assumptions now about the use of music. In a survey of 210 works on "the power of music" (commissioned by The Performing Right Society), Susan Hallam notes how contemporary research is focused on the use of music for therapy and medical treatment, for enhancing children's learning abilities, and for influencing individual behavior. Among her "key points" are these:

Music can promote relaxation, alleviate anxiety and pain, promote appropriate behaviour in vulnerable groups and enhance the quality of life of
those who are beyond medical help.

People can use music in their lives to manipulate their moods, alleviate
the boredom of tedious tasks, and create environments appropriate for
particular social events.

The easy availability of music in everyday life is encouraging individuals to use music to optimise their sense of well being. (Hallam 2001, 1)

And she concludes her survey of research by suggesting that

[t]here is also need for more systematic investigation of the ways that
music can impact on groups of people in social settings. To date, research
has tended to focus on commercial and work environments. The way that
music may affect behaviour in public places has been neglected. Such
research, for instance, might explore whether particular types of music
might stimulate orderly exits from large public functions, reduce the inci-
dence of disorder in particular settings, increase tolerance when people
have to queue for relatively long periods of time or engender feelings of
well being and safety in public places. (Hallam 2001, 19)

There are, in fact, already reports of music being used for such social
engineering—classical music played in railroad stations to make them
unsuitable as youth hangouts, for example—and what I want to note
about this is less dismay that music should have become a technology of
discipline rather than delight, than that it marks a significant shift in our
understanding of *how* music is powerful. While the Taliban outlawed
music with the traditional anxiety that it is a source of collective disorder,
a challenge to religious authority, in modern societies discipline is internalized. What's at stake is not what people want to do but usually (until
released by music) don't, but what they don't want to do in the first place.
Music remains "a powerful medium of social order," but its power is exercised less through group psychology, the orchestration of crowds, than
through individual psychology, the articulation of self.

Tia DeNora concludes her book on *Music in Everyday Life* by suggesting that

[f]urther explorations of music as it is used and deployed in daily life in
relation to agency's configuration will only serve to highlight what

Adorno, and the Greek philosophers, regarded as a fundamental matter in relation to the polis, the citizen and the configuration of consciousness; namely, that music is much more than a decorative art; that it is a powerful medium of social order. Conceived in this way, and documented through empirical research, music's presence is clearly political, in every sense that the political can be conceived. (DeNora 2000, 163)

I want to conclude by reiterating DeNora's suggestion that music is much more than a decorative art. In *The Sociology of Rock*, published in 1978, I began with the observation that while recorded music was usually included in a list of the contemporary mass media in textbooks, it was rarely otherwise examined. Twenty and more years on and the situation hasn't really changed. The cinema, television, newspapers, magazines, and advertising are still regarded in the academy as more socially and politically significant than records. And so it needs stressing that what people listen to is more important for their sense of themselves than what they watch or read. Patterns of music use provide a better map of social life than viewing or reading habits. Music just *matters* more than any other medium, and this brings me back to my starting point and the ways in which music is now heard as offensive. It is because music is now used to mark private territory that it can also "invade" it; it is because music has become so deeply implicated in people's personas that it can be misused; and it is because music is now so widely employed as an emotional tool that its misuse is genuinely upsetting.

But there are two further points I want to make. First, DeNora and Sloboda tend to refer musical meaning to its emotional function for individuals, but music remains equally important as a means of communication and as a form of sociability. Most academic research on everyday music focuses, as I have focused here, on music listening. But what is equally remarkable is the sheer amount of *music making* in which people are engaged, and my point here is not just that people do, in large numbers, join choirs, form rock and pop groups, play around with record decks, and set up home studios, but also that these musical activities are central to their understanding of who they are. Music making provides, as Ruth Finnegan argues, critical pathways through life (Finnegan 1989). And music making is less about managing one's own emotional life than about enjoying being together in groups, real and imagined. Future research in music and the everyday needs to integrate the study of music making with the study of musical use. To my mind, ongoing investigation of people's tastes and the current research focus on issues of identity are much less interesting projects than an ethnography that would try to map in detail people's *timetable of engagement,* the reasons why particular music gets particular attention at particular moments, and how these moments are, in turn, imbricated in people's social networks.

Second, and to register finally my unease at treating music in simple functional terms, we need to balance accounts of how people use music to manage their emotions with accounts of how music still has the unexpected power to disrupt us emotionally. The ancient myths of musical power—the stories of the Sirens, Orpheus, the Pied Piper—have a continued force not primarily because of advertisers' ceaseless attempts to lead us astray but because of the much more mysterious power of music *in itself.* How is it that a voice suddenly reaches us, out of the background, whether we are paying attention or not? Whatever the strength of those commercial and technological forces that turn the transcendent into the trite, I don't think we have lost the sense that music, the musical experience, is *special,* that it is a way of one person reaching another without deceit. There's still no better way than through music to be surprised by life.

Further Reading

Bennett, Tony, M. Emmison, and John Frow. 1999. *Accounting for tastes. Australian everyday cultures.* Cambridge, U.K.: Cambridge Univ. Press.

Booth, Wayne. 1999. *For the love of it. Amateuring and its rivals.* Chicago: Univ. of Chicago Press.

Deleuze, Gilles, and Felix Guattari. 1988. *A thousand plateaus. Capitalism and schizophrenia.* Minneapolis: Univ. of Minnesota Press.

Hargreaves, D. J., and A. C. North, 1997. *The social psychology of music.* Oxford: Oxford Univ. Press.

Hennion, Antoine, Sophie Maisonneuve, and Emilie Gomart. 2000. *Figures de L'Amateur. Formes, objets, pratiques de l'amour de la musique aujourd'hui.* Paris: La Documentation Française.

Lanza, Joseph. 1994. *Elevator music: A surreal history of muzak, easy-listening and other moodsong.* London: Quartet.

Scannell, Paddy. 1996. *Radio, television and modern life.* Oxford: Blackwell.

CHAPTER 8

Music, Culture, and Creativity

JASON TOYNBEE

Although creativity might seem an obvious topic for the cultural study of music, little attention has been paid to it, certainly within the field of cultural studies. Perhaps the main factor has been a populist current that runs through this field as a whole (McGuigan 1992). Its logic can be set out as follows. Authorship and creativity are associated with high art; high art is elitist; therefore creativity is not an appropriate subject for cultural studies, concerned as it is with the culture of the people. Several intellectual tributaries have then strengthened this position. Structuralism, particularly important in the 1970s, focused on relations between elements in the text while ignoring the stage of production. Poststructuralism went even further. For example, in his highly influential essay "The Death of the Author," Roland Barthes (1977) lampooned the "author-god" and argued that the meaning of literature is realized at the moment of reception rather than creation. Finally, the ethnographic tradition in cultural studies, where culture equates to way of life, has focused almost entirely on the consumption of artifacts. Interestingly, the concept of creativity does persist here, but as "symbolic creativity," a phenomenon that animates everyday activities, like listening and dancing to music (Willis 1990). From this perspective, then, creativity is widely distributed through the cultural practices of ordinary people.

My response to all these tendencies in cultural studies that want to do away with creativity, or dissolve it into the everyday, is a banal plea for moderation: don't go so far. For in an obvious and quite literal sense, music (like any other symbolic system) is fashioned by those who design and perform it. Depending on the division of labor that exists in any particular case, composer, instrumentalist, and engineer all contribute directly to shaping the phenomenal form of the musical text. However, and this qualification is critical in any consideration of creativity, the making of meaning remains incomplete until the text is apprehended by an audience.

As Keith Negus and Michael Pickering (2000) suggest, to consider creativity must involve some form of evaluation. We need to establish which songs and symphonies are genuinely creative as opposed to merely competent. And that is where the issue of reception comes in. Quite simply, there is no satisfactory measure of value apart from the recognition of listeners. If we take as wide a range of musical creators as Chopin, Bix Beiderbecke, and the So Solid Crew, creativity is manifested precisely through post hoc evaluation, a process of diffusion and reception that is cultural in the widest possible sense. The issue cannot then be reduced to one of choosing either production or reception. Rather, *both* count in any analysis of creativity. To state this not only challenges the skepticism about creative work found in cultural studies, it also constitutes a reproach to Romanticism, the strongest account we have of creativity as a factor of production.

Romantic discourse asserts that music comes from within and is a direct product of the psyche of the creator. A passage from a letter by Tchaikovsky shows this quite nicely:

Generally speaking, the germ of a future composition comes suddenly and unexpectedly. If the soil is ready—that is to say, if the disposition for work is there—it takes root with extraordinary force and rapidity, shoots up through the earth, puts forth branches, leaves and, finally, blossoms. . . . It would be vain to try to put into words that immeasurable sense of bliss which comes over me directly [when] a new idea awakens in me and begins to assume a definite form. I forget everything and behave like a madman. Everything within me starts pulsing and quivering; hardly have I begun the sketch ere one thought follows another. (Tchaikovsky [1878] 1970, 57)

Three main points, utterly typical of Romantic discourse, can be pulled out of this passage, I think. First, the creative process is solipsistic. Both *germ* and *soil* are located within Tchaikovsky's own psyche and have no connection to other music making, past or present. Second, creation is involuntary, and involves possession by a creative demon that is not subject to conscious control. Third, composition takes place in stages, from inchoate "new idea" to "definite form." This is a transformational approach to creation whose origins, as George Steiner points out, can be traced to the Christian doctrine of transubstantiation (Steiner 2001, 46–48). Such an understanding of creativity has become hugely influential, and not just in the realm of art music. Both jazz and rock fans have adopted the heroic mode and, along with it, a tendency to lionize artist-creators (Frith 1996). It is clear too that the musicians themselves tend to understand their work in Romantic terms—as the outpouring of a tortured, solitary soul (e.g., Wenner 1972 for John Lennon; Mingus 1995). However, I want to argue that there are fundamental problems with such a conception.

Above all, it treats creation as a mystical process, and creators as a select band of individual geniuses. In doing so, Romanticism ignores the profoundly social nature of authorship in all forms of culture, including music. Several writers, none of whom is a music specialist, help to open this alternative approach to creativity. We might begin with the sociologist Howard Becker (1982), who makes the point that new art works only emerge through the interaction of artists, coworkers, and audiences. When interaction is intensely repeated, it may solidify in conventions that organize both the way the artist works and the audience responds. However, the artist is not necessarily aware of such conventions. Rather, in making a creative choice he or she works intuitively. Becker calls this the "editorial moment," that is, when the artist identifies creative options and then selects from them according to informal criteria that represent, in the case of music, an ideal listener's point of audition. For Becker, then, creation involves small amounts of individual agency and large amounts of regular, if complex, social interaction. Even the most intense and solitary moments of creative passion depend on careful monitoring of choices from a (virtual) position outside the creator's own subjectivity, and in the thick of the culture in which he or she works. As Becker puts it, "art worlds rather than artists make art" (pp. 198–99).

The Soviet literary critic Mikhail Bakhtin (1981), although he comes from an entirely different tradition, complements this approach. Like Becker, he is concerned with interaction, but more in relation to the ingredients of art—in his case speech as it feeds into the novel. The defining attribute of the novelistic form, Bakhtin suggests, is dialogue, and this consists not only of the idiomatic utterances of characters, but also of a huge range of "speech genres" quoted by characters or embedded in the discourse of the narrator. In an important sense, then, the novel is a fabric woven from voices that already exist, and that therefore have socially ascribed connotations and even structural significance. To use Bakhtin's terms, the dynamism of the novel derives from the "interanimation" of these voices, a process that "refracts" authorial intention rather than directly expressing it.

There is a problem with applying Bakhtin's theory of dialogism to music, however, namely its basis in a radically dissimilar system of communication—language. In everyday life in the industrialized world people do still produce music; for example, in amateur productions, karaoke, or casual whistling. But this is on a much smaller scale than the speaking they do. As a result, musical genres, whether classical or pop, are considerably less demotic than language genres. Furthermore, it is hard to find any musical equivalent of the utterance, a univocal syntagma with one dominating parameter in the shape of semantic content. Music, of course, is always multiparametric, generally polyphonic, and has little or no denotative meaning. A further significant divergence between language and music lies in the fact that dialogue is defined precisely by the diachronic segmentation of differently voiced utterances. Antiphony in music has a similar function, but its importance varies enormously by genre. Rarely is it of defining significance.

If these are necessary caveats, I still want to argue that the general principle of dialogism, particularly the notion that cultural production consists of the interanimation of social materials, is so cogent that it must lie at the center of any theory of creativity. How might it be applied to music then? Quite simply, music needs to be understood as an ensemble of coded voices. On the one hand, these may be sounds that come from a recognizable place and time: the sliding tones of the early Billie Holiday, say, or a baroque harpsichord in busy chime. In this respect coded voices are comparable to Bakhtin's utterances, being pieces of musical fabric with an identifiable source and therefore also a particular social milieu. On the other hand the emphasis may be more on what Umberto Eco calls, in his theory of semiotics, "system code," namely "elements oppositionally structured and governed by combinatorial rules that can generate both finite and infinite strings or chains of these elements" (1976, 38). Here it is relatively abstract rules and forms that are most at stake. Examples include the movement structure of the concerto or the metrical organization of that genre called drum and bass.

Now, as Eco stresses, while fabric and code may be distinguished for analytical purposes, in practice "[s]ignification encompasses the whole of cultural life" (p. 46). Or, in the terms used here, the coded voice can always be located on a continuum running between the formal and the phenomenal. Thus Billie Holiday's voice—the thing we hear—is also a generative, rule-governed system, while the structure of the baroque concerto can never be completely separated from the sound of a baroque concerto. Clearly, this approach runs counter to the strict separation of form and sounded work generally found in musical analysis. My point, though, is that it is much more productive to recognize that both aspects are copresent (albeit to varying degrees) in what I have been calling the *coded voice.* This certainly makes it a broad category. Yet that very breadth enables a powerful, large-scale theory of the process of musical creation to be constructed.

At a general level, the author's work can now be understood as the identification of coded voices and their arrangement in meaningful dialogue. Most of these arrangements will be already given. Whether we consider genres and movements in classical music (the sonata, the string quartet, impressionism, and so on) or in pop (rap, new country, sixteen bar verse-chorus structures, etc.), the collocation of coded voices is highly conventional. In effect, competence as a social author consists of being able to identify and deploy appropriate voices so as to meet a minimum threshold of stylistic accomplishment. However, this does not necessarily amount to creativity. Earlier on I emphasized the importance of listener recognition. We might say now that what is being recognized in the case of a "creative" work is a particular relation to the stylistic norm. This may involve transcendence of the norm, or even, in the case of avant-garde aesthetics, its transgression. But just as often, the work will strive to implement or express the norm completely. This is a centripetal tendency where what is at stake is crystallization of style.

Whatever form such relationships with stylistic norms may take, though, the question remains: how do they come into being? Or, to put this in a different way, why are some music makers particularly creative? We can usefully call on another sociologist of culture here. Pierre Bourdieu (1993b) argues that two structuring factors tend to shape the making of art. First there is the "field of production," marked by a system of positions. The contemporary musical field is clearly enormous. It is a great landscape of scenes and schools, each one made up of a cluster of music makers working with a particular set of stylistic norms. But the key point is that any particular position, with certain quantities and kinds of status attached to it, attracts particular music makers.

Second, from the other direction as it were, aspiring musical creators are disposed to aim for a particular position in the field according to "habitus," the way of going on in the world that every actor "carries" with her. It is largely acquired during the early years, and is determined by a complex of social factors such as class, education, and gender. Critically, the push of musician habitus and the pull of the field tend to converge, and it is through the highly charged *near* alignment of these forces that a "space of possibles" (Bourdieu 1993b, 176–77, 182–85) then opens up. What Bourdieu calls possibles are nothing less than creative choices in the terms I am using here. They are made much more frequently when the field starts to shift, or when new kinds of authors begin to push forward. In these circumstances the space of possibles expands, and creative possibilities further out along the "radius of creativity" become audible (Toynbee 2000, 35–42).

Let me try to depict this graphically. Imagine a circular space of possible creative choices delimited by a certain radius. At the center is what I call the "social author." A cluster of densely distributed dots around her represent those regularly selected choices required for the competent production of a text in a given genre. Moving out along the radius, an increasingly thin distribution of dots indicates not only the increasing difficulty of making choices beyond the datum of genre, but also a larger and larger space of possibilities. It is less predictable what will be done out here. Eventually, inscribed by the end of the radius is a fuzzy perimeter or virtual horizon of possibility beyond which the author cannot identify any coded voices at all.

Three points need to be made about the thinly dispersed choices toward the outside of the radius. First, they still represent the selection of *coded* voices. So, in the case of transgressive creative acts, which yield unlikely sounds and structures, there must be recognition of their meaningfulness on the part of the audience. To this end cues are offered or countercodes implied. Equally, where crystallization is at stake, detailed attention to the main strands of the style reveals subcodes that can then be explored and developed. In either case the new is produced through a process of linking back to that "body of conventions" (Becker 1982, 30) that governs the more obvious choices around the center. Such a process encapsulates a defining paradox about creativity: difference needs to be recognized. The second point is that the literally eccentric choices in the model depend on combination. Arthur Koestler (1975, 35–38) argues that "bisociation" is central to creativity. He means by this the putting together of previously unconnected components that then produce a surprising synthesis. Bi-sociation is very much what is at stake further out along the radius as choices become more and more thinly distributed. Third, highly creative choices are often made when a social author arrives at a position in the field that is *not* strongly indicated by habitus. In other words, the "wrong" kind of background and disposition can produce the conditions for a particu-larly creative combination of voices. Hector Berlioz with his less than fully adequate formal training in composition is a case in point. From another angle, so is John Cale—Welsh, working class, and overtrained for the emerging New York rock scene of the mid-1960s.

Up to now I have been making rather broad claims about creativity, and suggesting that they apply to all types of musical production. This is an important step in the argument. Too frequently Western art music and its Others are counterposed as radically distinct when in fact common problems of structure and meaning are encountered everywhere in musi-cal analysis (McClary and Walser 1990). Yet there *are* important differ-ences across the musical field and between popular and classical music in particular. In considering creativity we cannot avoid them.

To begin with there is the issue of distribution of creative roles. In Western classical music, composition and performance are generally sepa-rated. Composers may play or conduct their own works of course. Nonetheless, the apparatus of sheet music and concert hall reinforces the creative supremacy of the composer in her or his absence and the cor-responding subservience of performers (Small 1987). In contrast, pop's division of labor varies to a considerable degree. There is, however—partic-ularly since the 1960s—a strong tendency toward the sharing of creative functions. The small rock group with its own "writers" as in the Beatles (MacDonald 1995); the Motown "factory" system where responsibility for molding the sound of a recording is split among writers, arrangers, singers, players, and producers (George 1985): both examples involve a high degree of flat, art world interaction. This divergence between pop and classical music is then associated with another difference. Classical music consists of a canon of emphatically first-rate work composed by great *auteurs*. On the other hand, pop has a historically varying system of genres and stars, but also one-off hits and sublime oddities. Another way of putting this is to say that the field of classical music is relatively unified and stable, while the popular field is fragmented and volatile.

Finally, there are differences to do with form. Andrew Chester has argued that popular music may be defined by the "intensional develop-ment" of materials. He means by this inflection and variation within a basic form—the 12-bar blues, say. This is a method of creativity that involves "inward" movement toward complexity along many dimensions. And it depends too on articulation of parameters (intonation or the sound of the human voice, for example) that are assumed to be fixed in classical music. Conversely, classical music is characterized by extensional development. Here "[t]he complex is created by combination of the simple, which remains discrete and unchanged in the complex unity" (Chester [1970] 1990, 315). Nicholas Cook makes a similar point. Composers in the tonal tradition, he suggests, work by elaborating simple motifs so as to produce a progressively more complex structure (Cook 1990, 187–216).

It seems to me that the distinction between intension and extension is extremely illuminating for the study of creativity. What is more, it complements Franco Fabbri's semiotic approach to musical codes and generic change. Fabbri's musical code is very like the system code delineated by Eco—it is a set of combinatorial rules. Crucially, though, Fabbri sets up two historical types: "rich" and "poor" (1982, 61–62). Rich codes are associated with the durable rules of classical music. They are capable of generating complex musical texts. Clearly, rich codes also have the capacity to generate *long* texts where not only are motivic atoms recombined over the length of a piece, but large-scale harmonic development may also take place. By contrast, the poor codes of pop yield *short* texts (the mythical perfect pop record plays for 2 minutes 30 seconds), which deteriorate quickly as musical communities become "analytically competent," and find successive texts more and more predictable. It might be said, then, that the intensionality of the poor code consists of a movement down into the synchronic microcoding of texture and meter.

How does this way of conceiving the structure of classical music and pop impact on the analysis of creativity? In the first place we need to recognize that textual organization is fully social in both cases. Becker's point about conventions being highly regularized forms of interaction applies here. Code is simply repeated social action: a "doing it this way." But then, almost immediately, we encounter a significant difference between the two broad types. On the one hand the social authors of popular music tend to be code shapers. As we have seen, the poverty of pop codes means that sooner or later redundancy sets in, and this is quickly followed by bending or even breaking of rules. Moreover, because the field is relatively open there is no formal induction or exclusion through academic training. As a result the habitus of aspiring music makers varies strongly. Sometimes they may not achieve competence in a code before they enter the field. Sometimes it may not be clear exactly what competence consists of.

Thus, from a sociological perspective as much as a textual one, popular music is volatile and has a tendency to mutate. To put it another way, the most creative episodes in popular music making always involve code shaping and generic change.

In classical music, on the other hand, codes have been relatively stable. Edward Said describes functional tonality from Mozart to Mahler as "a police regime of the signifier." This was a language that suppressed radical transformation (1992, 56). It also involved a system of authorship whereby composers worked *through* a set of rules. Code might be adapted by the handful of great composers (in the conventional wisdom greatness consisted of "making one's own" the language of tonality), but it could never be fundamentally altered. Arguably, the advent of serialism did represent something more radical. Yet as Schoenberg himself proposed, serialism was actually "an organisation granting logic, coherence and unity." It would therefore enable one "to compose as before" (quoted in Griffiths 1978, 91). In the terms we have been using above, serialism represented a renewal of extensive composition through the application of a new rich code. Twentieth-century inflections of the tonal system (neoclassicism, for example) then constitute a less radical version of the same move. It is only with the various kinds of avant-gardism, minimalism, *musique concrète*, and electronica that code shaping itself becomes an important principle of the creative process. And even here the field demands academic credentials of a very particular and historically invariant kind from its novitiates. Composers must not only be competent in the use of consecrated codes, they must also be grammarians, able to state how breaking and making rules "works."

In this chapter I have been arguing that creativity in music needs to be reconceived as a cultural process rather than a heroic act. New music—in other words significantly different music—is made by social authors who work in networks, collaborating (and sometimes fighting) with coworkers, critics, industry, and audiences. Social authorship also implies a social semiotics in that creation is a matter of selecting from a pool of coded voices that are shared within a given musical community. If these are general characteristics, a relative openness of the field to authors from a variety of cultures, and hence with diverse forms of competence, has tended to differentiate pop from classical music. In addition pop's short texts and poor codes have demanded that its authors be code *shapers*, constantly making new combinations of voice.

Creativity is thus manifestly a cultural process. But how then to account for the persistence of a romantic myth of the individual creator in the post-Romantic age—from, say, Elliott Carter to Missy Elliott? It would perhaps be easiest to explain this in political-economic terms. The industry strives to reduce uncertainty of demand by marketing a few big stars (Miège 1989). And in popular music it has been convenient to graft stardom onto the authorship cult of small group or performer-writer that has predominated in the rock era. As for art music, the system of commissioning and state subsidy represents nothing but the bureaucratization of the individual creator in the modern age. Still, the romantic cult of creativity is not just imposed. Listeners actively embrace it, partly for reasons of efficiency. To admire a limited number of great artists makes learning and sharing knowledge about music more economic (M. Adler 1985). And music makers of course want romanticism too. Perhaps the key factor here is the endemic likelihood of failure. In such a situation, to imagine oneself a lone creator with a special gift provides both a pretext for autonomy—"I am instructed by my muse"—and an excuse for failure—"society cannot understand what I do." Finally, for a handful of stars the cult of individual genius justifies their copyright income.

In effect, then, romantic discourse about creativity ties together industry, artist, and audience. Or to put it another way, capitalist ideology built on insecurity and the profit motive suppresses the social nature of the creative process (Stratton 1982). Yet such ideological work can never be complete. For the myth of the heroic creator is always already premised on a utopian imperative: if music transcends everyday life (though arguably it *organizes* the quotidian too: see Frith, chapter 7, present volume), then so must its producers in their abundant creative capabilities and extraordinary personalities. Ultimately this represents a goal for everyone. We should all be creators together, and in this way transform the limited social practice of music making into something universal and collective. Looked at this way, the contradiction between romantic ideology and the reality of social authorship is simply one more symptom of the contradictions within the capitalist system as a whole.

Further Reading

Bourdieu, Pierre. 1996. *The rules of art: Genesis and structure of the literary field.* Cambridge, U.K.: Polity Press.

Csikszentmyhalyi, Mihaly. 1999. Implications of a systems perspective for the study of creativity. Pp. 313–35 in *Handbook of creativity.* Edited by Robert J. Sternberg. Cambridge, U.K.: Cambridge University Press.

Eshun, K. 2002. Sonotronic manifesto, *Fringecore* 7. (accessed April 2, at http://www.fringecore.com/magazine/m7-2.html)

Fernandez, James W. 2001. Creative arguments of images in culture, and the charnel house of conventionality. Pp. 17–30 in *Locating cultural creativity.* Edited by John Liep. London: Pluto Press.

Gardner, Howard. 1993. *Creating minds: An anatomy of creativity.* New York: Basic Books.

Keil, Charles. 1994. Participatory discrepancies and the power of music. Pp. 96–108 in *Music grooves: Essays and dialogues.* Edited by Charles Keil and Steven Feld. Chicago: Univ. of Chicago Press.

Moore, Allan. 1993. *Rock: The primary text. Developing a musicology of rock.* Buckingham, U.K.: Open University Press.

CHAPTER 9

Music and Psychology

ERIC F. CLARKE

> Music recognizes no natural law; therefore, all psychology of music
> is questionable.
> —Theodor Adorno

Always ready with his negatively dialectical hatchet, and never one to miss a polemical opportunity, Adorno provides an appropriately perverse starting point from which to argue a defense of the value of psychology to the cultural study of music. Adorno was a psychologist (as well as a composer, philosopher, and sociologist) who was strongly influenced by the work of Freud among others—not only in his specifically psychological writing, but also in his writing on music. However, the assumption that psychology must be concerned with natural laws that is implicit in Adorno's rejection of the psychology of music is unwarranted, and my aim in this chapter is to argue that psychological principles can help to shed important light on music from a variety of natural and cultural perspectives, and that the very idea of a sharp distinction between "nature" and "culture" is one that psychology itself (in at least some of its manifestations) rejects.

Since most people engage with music because they find it in some way meaningful, rewarding, or exciting—whether from an aural perspective or some broader behavioral or social point of view—psychology, variously defined as the "science of mental life" (James 1890) or the study of behavior (Watson 1919), should have quite a bit to offer to an understanding of music. But that abstract potential arguably remains frustratingly unfulfilled: while the psychology of music has seen dramatic growth since around 1980, its achievements have largely been concerned with establishing, or verifying, the processes by which people produce or make sense of what have been considered the "fundamentals" of music—pitches, duration sequences, the control of tempo and dynamics, basic tonal structures, the timbre of single sounds or small-scale complexes, and so on. While some work has made more concerted attempts to tackle issues on a larger scale and with more sense of how they might fit into a bigger picture, there is still a strongly reductionist impetus within the subject (reflecting the generally cognitive outlook that has been adopted), and little sense of an engagement with culture. In this chapter I argue that this need not be the case, and that a very fruitful interaction between music and psychology is possible that encapsulates a much more richly cultural view. It depends, however, on adopting a rather different view of perception and cognition from the one that has dominated until now—one that places the issue of musical meaning at the center of the whole endeavor.

Psychology is an extraordinarily hybrid subject. It is part philosophy, part biology, strongly influenced by ethology and sociology, and since the 1960s, by cybernetics, linguistics, and computer science. A crude institutional indicator of this disciplinary uncertainty is that psychology can be found across a whole range of university faculties including arts and humanities, social science, pure science, biological science, and cognitive and computing sciences, and that research in psychology in Britain is supported by the Arts and Humanities Research Board, the Economic and Social Research Council, the Engineering and Physical Sciences Research Council, and the Brain and Behavioural Sciences Research Council. A recent introduction to the subject (Butler and McManus 1998) concludes in the following terms:

> Today psychology is a far more diverse subject than it was even fifty years ago, as well as a more scientific one. Its complexity means that it may never develop as a science with a single paradigm, but will continue to provide an understanding of mental life from many different perspectives—cognitive and behavioural, psychophysiological, biological, and social. Like any other discipline, it is the site of conflicting theories as well as agreement . . . (130)

Note the tone of approval with which psychology's increasingly "scientific" character is mentioned, coupled with the admission of its sometimes uncomfortable heterogeneity. In considering its relationship with psychology, music (itself a diverse and heterogeneous subject) confronts a chameleon, and if there are shortcomings in achieving what could have been—and might still be—a "beautiful relationship" between the two, it is in part a result of the rather narrow range of encounters that have so far been contemplated.

One central feature of psychology that distinguishes it from musicology (and one of the hallmarks of a science) is that it is primarily concerned with the identification and investigation of general principles rather than particular manifestations. At the level of individual pieces of research this may not always be immediately apparent: A psychological paper may seem to be concerned specifically with the ability of a group of infants to recognize their carers' faces, for example, but the emphasis in such research is invariably on discovering *general principles* for face recognition, which can then be discussed in the context of still more general principles of perception or memory. It is seldom the particular perceptual or mnemonic attributes of one specific face that are the focus of interest. By contrast, a considerable amount of work in musicology (whether analytical, critical, or historical, "new" or "old") focuses on a detailed understanding of particular phenomena: a consideration of the role of music boxes and automata in Mozart's opera *The Magic Flute* may *relate* to more general issues of Enlightenment thought, but the emphasis is likely to be primarily on what's happening in the specific piece. This difference of perspective could and perhaps should represent a fruitful complementarity, an opportunity rather than a problem. But all too often the trade-off between broad explanatory power and local specificity leads research in the psychology of music to seem blandly obvious and lacking in bite to musicologists, while psychologists point to the apparently arbitrary particularity of musicological research, its speculative and discursive character, and raise the inevitable questions about empirical support and "evidence."

The contemporary phase of the psychology of music dates from around 1980, when within the space of about five years a number of important books were published, and new journals established. The sudden rise of the subject came on the back of what has often been called "the cognitive revolution" in psychology (which began some 20 years earlier) and which has continued to play a powerful role in shaping the psychology of music. The characteristic features of this approach are a combination of controlled experimental procedures, an emphasis on modeling of one kind or another (either in the form of "grammars" or computer programs), and a determined focus on individual human subjects stripped of their cultural context. Internal representations, mental models, and cognitive capacities are very much the order of the day, with human action, and in particular the cultural context of human action and interaction, held at bay so as to throw into relief fundamental psychological functions in their pristine state.

Deutsch's reference volume, entitled *The Psychology of Music,* originally published in 1982 and in a second edition in 1999, provides one opportunity to assess how the subject sees itself. The eighteen chapters of the second edition show a preoccupation with pitch perception (six chapters), with two chapters on rhythm, and single chapters on a variety of topics including timbre, performance, neurology, hierarchical structures, acoustics, and "comparative music perception and cognition." There are no chapters on emotion or meaning in music, the outlook is almost entirely concerned with the Western classical tradition, and any sense of the way in which music is culturally embedded is almost entirely absent. This looks like a bleakly unlikely prospect for any attempt to argue for the relevance of the psychology of music to its cultural study. But the cognitive tradition, for all its dominance in contemporary psychology, is not the only way to study mental life and human behavior, and a rather different prospect for the psychology of music comes into view if a different *psychological* starting point is adopted. I use the remainder of this chapter to focus on listening—the "central territory" of Deutsch's book, and thus home ground for the cognitive psychology of music—understood from a perspective that *does* make an important connection with the cultural study of music.

Consistent with the overall character of the modern psychology of music given above, listening has been tackled in a predominantly structuralist fashion: It has been widely assumed that the primary aim must be to investigate the kinds of abstract tonal, metric, grouping, melodic, and timbral structures that people accumulate as they listen (e.g., as reviewed in Krumhansl 1991), as well as the more dynamic processes to which these structures give rise. As a number of commentators have pointed out (e.g., Cook 1994; Serafine 1988), the assumption that the basic units of "standard music theory" are necessarily the salient features of listening is unjustified—and indeed as Cook argues, the very fact that the music-theoretic way of listening has to be learned through aural training programs rather suggests that these may not be important attributes of spontaneous listening. The kind of highly abstracted structural listening that characterizes both standard music theory and the cognitive tradition looks rather like an artifact or a fictional stereotype.

And yet there is a recognition within this cognitive tradition that listening is far more situated. In a spirited defense of empirical research and its relationship with music theory, Robert Gjerdingen (editor of the leading psychology of music journal *Music Perception*) observes that "A little reflection ... leads one to realise that a great deal of music perception is contingent, situational, and subject to biases of culture and experience" (Gjerdingen, 1999 168). Quite so—and in fact it would be hard to resist the assertion that *all* music perception involves "biases of culture and experience." How might a more situated and cultural approach to listening, but one that is still amenable to empirical inquiry, and based in psychological principles, tackle its subject? As Cook (2001) puts it:

> How can we understand the cultural production of music as prompted but not determined by acoustical or psychoacoustical phenomena, and correlatively how can we see musical meaning as prompted but not determined by verbal or other discourse? How in other words can we avoid the binary either/or that makes music *either* all nature *or* all culture, and that locates musical meaning *either* all in the music itself *or* all in its verbal or other interpretation? (180–81)

A number of authors have recently argued for the potential of an ecological approach to listening (Clarke 1999; DeNora 2000; Windsor 2000)—an approach in which the relationship between perceiver and environment (natural and cultural) is taken to be fundamental. Central to an ecological view is the idea that perceptual information specifies objects and events in the world, and that perception and action are indissolubly linked. If I hear glass breaking, for instance, I am likely to turn my head to hear and see where the breakage has occurred, and alter my behavior to avoid treading on the glass: the perceptual information (the sounds of impact followed by a cascade of irregular and dissipating tinkling sounds) specify an event (breaking glass), which I perceive by means of orienting actions (head turning), and which leads to further adaptive actions (changing my pattern of movements to avoid possible injury). The relationship between stimulus and object or event, and between perception and action, come together in an important concept for which the psychologist J. J. Gibson coined the term *affordance*. The affordances of an object are the uses, functions, or values of an object—the opportunities that it offers to a perceiver:

I have coined this word as a substitute for *values*, a term which carries an old burden of philosophical meaning. I mean simply what things furnish, for good or ill. What they *afford* the observer, after all, depends on their properties. . . . [T]he human observer learns to detect what have been called the values or meanings of things, perceiving their distinctive features, putting them into categories and subcategories, noticing their similarities and differences and even studying them for their own sakes, apart from learning what to do about them. (Gibson 1966, 285)

A lump of stone of an appropriate size, for instance, may afford being used as a missile or a paperweight, or being carved into a sculpture, but it does not afford being used as clothing or as a dwelling (for a human being). It simply doesn't have the right properties. The affordances of objects are, however, defined relative to the perceiving organism: "I mean by it [affordance] something that refers to both the environment and the animal in a way that no existing term does. It implies the complementarity of the animal and the environment" (Gibson [1979] 1986, 122). To a human being, a wooden chair affords sitting on, while to a termite it affords eating. Equally, the same chair affords use as a weapon to a human being who needs one (an illustration of the way in which an organism's changing *needs* affect affordances)—as in the archetypal barroom brawl. The relationship really is dialectical—neither simply a case of organisms imposing their needs on an indifferent environment, nor a fixed environment determining strictly delimited behavioral possibilities.

A concentration on everyday objects might lead to the erroneous conclusion that affordances are a simple matter of physical properties and perceptual capacities. But even the most cursory consideration of more "socially charged" objects demonstrates the importance of the social component. A wooden crucifix, for example, affords religious contemplation or prayer; it also affords use as fuel, but social factors ensure that this is a rather remote affordance—which might only be realized in extreme circumstances or by an individual who had no regard (or even a deliberate disdain) for the conventional religious context that regulates the affordances of the crucifix. Similarly, objects and events may afford clearly *social* actions (as when an outstretched hand or a smile affords friendly social engagement with another person), those actions being socially determined in infinitely variable and often highly particular ways—as a fist of solidarity, mistaken for a fist of aggression or disdain illustrates. The properties of objects are part of the material of a *social* fabric—but this makes them no less material.

As these examples demonstrate, there is a complex intertwining of attributes that are commonly ascribed to "nature" and "culture," and of supposedly "subjective" and "objective" properties. An ecological approach rejects these supposedly hard and fast distinctions, in the dialectical concept of affordance on the one hand, and in the following explicit statement on "nature and culture" on the other:

> In the study of anthropology and ecology, the "natural" environment is often distinguished from the "cultural" environment. As described here, there is no sharp division between them. Culture evolved out of natural opportunities. The cultural environment, however, is often divided into two parts, "material" culture and "non-material" culture. This is a seriously misleading distinction, for it seems to imply that language, tradition, art, music, law, and religion are immaterial, insubstantial, or intangible, whereas tools, shelters, clothing, vehicles, and books are not. Symbols are taken to be profoundly different from things. But let us be clear about this. There have to be modes of stimulation, or ways of conveying information, for any individual to perceive anything, however abstract.... No symbol exists except as it is realized in sound, projected light, mechanical contact, or the like. All knowledge rests on sensitivity. (Gibson 1966, 26)

It is in these respects that an ecological approach has something important to offer to the cultural study of music. By considering music in terms of its affordances, discussions of musical meaning (which have often been excessively abstract, or diverted into a consideration of emotional responses to music, or caught up in discussions of music's relationship with language) can combine with a consideration of its social uses and functions in a manner that recognizes the plurality of music's social functions without being swept away by total relativism.

To make this approach clearer, I offer three specific examples. The first comes from DeNora's book on *Music in Everyday Life* (DeNora 2000), in which she looks at the way in which music is used in step aerobics classes. An aerobics class typically uses a carefully planned sequence of musical materials that takes the participants through a specific pattern of physical activities: warm-up, pre-core, core, cool down, and floor exercises. Considerable care is taken in assembling these tapes, since getting the music right can have a dramatic effect on the success of an aerobics class. In this case the music affords different kinds of physical movement with varying degrees of physical exertion, pace, and stamina. To the women in these classes, the primary affordance of the music is a pattern of physical engagement, arising out of a socially defined context (an exercise class), the properties of the music (tempo, texture, dynamic shape), and the women's particular focus (an exercise motivator and regulator).

A second and contrasting example of music's affordances comes from Windsor's (2000) discussion of acousmatic music. Windsor points out the paradoxical character of acousmatic sounds: they often specify objects and events of the everyday world with considerable power and explicitness, while at the same time concealing their sources through the very fact of their acousmatic presentation—sound in the absence of any visible source. Furthermore, acousmatic presentation allows sound to play with a listener's sense of the relationship between everyday reality and the "virtual" reality of the objects and events specified by the sounds of the piece. Impossible objects, or impossible relationships between objects, can be specified in acousmatic sound, and one of the consequences of this, Windsor argues, is that listeners are driven to try to find an interpretation of what they hear, somewhere on a continuum between the lawfulness of everyday reality and the special context—the virtual reality—that the piece itself creates. Acousmatic music therefore affords (even demands) interpretation. This move to a more generalized notion of affordance allows for a wider-ranging application of the idea to music: music can afford emotional catharsis, persuasion, structural listening, the accumulation of cultural capital, synchronized working, group solidarity, seduction, and dancing. The question is whether, and how, the specific attributes of both the musical materials and the perceiver's capacities and circumstances, which give rise to any particular affordance, can be determined, and it is here that the psychology of perception could make a real contribution to the cultural study of music.

My third example takes up this last point more directly, and also relates to DeNora's study of music in aerobics. As I discuss in more detail elsewhere (Clarke, 2001), a powerful component in the impact and meaning of much music is the sense of motion and agency that listeners hear. A great deal of contemporary dance music makes use of this—not only to afford the dancing for which it is designed, but also to explore various kinds of virtual spaces and virtual motions with which the real spaces and movements of actual dancing interact. There are established techniques that dance music producers use to achieve these effects (filtering techniques, withholding and introducing/substituting beats and silences, etc.) that not only exploit basic perceptual processes (the sense of occlusion/ distance and directness/proximity that variable low-pass filtering specifies, or of "looseness" versus "tightness" specified by different amounts and styles of synchronization), but also engage with the vast repertory of other dance music. Producers and DJs manipulate this complex environment, using the transformation of clubbers' perceptual experiences to elicit both virtual actions in the virtual spaces that the sounds specify, and the real actions of dance. This interaction of the virtual and the real is often powerfully evident at the start of dance tracks, where the texture and meter of the music is often deliberately poorly defined, specifying rather loose and "spacey" environments and making dancing difficult, but becomes gradually more clearly articulated. Often this process of gradual clarification accelerates until a suddenly climactic point is reached as the energizing and anchoring beats of the music are laid down, galvanizing clubbers into coordinated dance and transforming or supplanting the preceding "spacey" virtual environment in their heads. The interdependence of perception and action, a cornerstone of the ecological approach, could hardly be more directly manifested.

This chapter has tackled the relationship between music's social meaning and its material, and has argued that the relationship can be understood as much more perceptual than has hitherto been understood. The resistance to doing so has come on the one hand from a suspicion on the part of musicologists and critical theorists that a perceptual approach implies determinacy, and a failure to recognize the social and historical nature of both human subjects and musical materials; and on the other hand from psychologists, who have regarded accounts of music's social meaning as too speculative, and discourse-based, to be amenable to psychological inquiry or explanation. Both of these resistances are unwarranted: perception is not determinate, as its variability in even quite simple and everyday circumstances illustrates—and in aesthetic contexts it is particularly and deliberately so. If this indeterminacy leads to diverse and sometimes unanticipated perceptions of "what is going on" and what it means, this is no reason for us to reject them, or to regard them as somehow rarified or fantastic. Perception is all about being tuned to the opportunities that the environment offers, and aesthetic objects offer exceptionally multivalent opportunities. We shouldn't shy away from recognizing that this leads to diverse perceptions, that some of these will reflect the particular preoccupations and perceptual tuning of an individual, and indeed that stimulus information can only be properly described relative to the perceptual capacities, sensitivities, and "interests" of a perceiver. If people (critics, commentators, teachers, friends) use their perceptions to guide the attention such that they perceive in that way too, this is not evidence for the nonperceptual character of the resulting experience, but rather an illustration of the much more general and pervasive principle of perceptual learning.

The contribution of ecological theory is thus to ground the elusive relationship between musical material and social meaning by insisting upon the manner in which the stimulus information in musical sounds specifies a whole range of invariants—from the instruments on which it is played, through the musical structures of which it is composed, to the social conditions from which it arises (cf. Dibben 2001). The problem is not in bringing these elements together, but is rather to trace explicitly *how* any particular invariant is specified in the stimulus, and to consider music's affordances in a properly "perceiver-specific" fashion—as the concept of affordance requires. The perceptual framework sketched in this chapter is one particular way to understand the relationship between musical materials and social meaning—not through the language of codification and representation, but through the perceptual principles of specification and affordance. An advantage of this approach is that the arbitrariness and abstraction of codification are replaced by the realism and directness of perception, restoring the connection between the aesthetic consciousness of musical listening and the practical consciousness of "everyday" listening.

It also exposes, however, a deep-seated uncertainty within both music theory and the psychology of music about the significance of musical structure: There have been times when both music theory and the psychology of music have claimed that structure is really all there is—or perhaps all there is that's worth talking about—followed by reactions to such a totalizing stance (for instance by Cook 1994; Levinson 1997) that have questioned how much structure, and of what kind, listeners can pick up. The point on which I finish, then, is this: The idea that the social meaning of local, small-scale musical materials can be picked up by listeners is not too controversial. What is more problematic is the question of whether and how these "immediate" perceptual meanings relate to larger musical form, and in particular whether this relationship should be understood as some kind of abstract and discursive mediation, or as another aspect of a thoroughly perceptual state of affairs. I have pushed for a perceptual view both because it emphasizes the continuity between different types of listening, and because it encourages a close consideration of the properties of musical materials as specified in relation to different listeners. But in the end it may also boil down to a proper investigation of some of the empirical questions that are raised by such an outlook, and that have so far received little or no attention.

Further Reading

Clarke, Eric F. 1999. Subject-position and the specification of invariants in music by Frank Zappa and P. J. Harvey. *Music Analysis* 18: 347–74.

Cook, Nicholas. 1990. *Music, imagination and culture.* Oxford: Oxford Univ. Press.

DeNora, Tia. 2000. *Music in everyday life.* Cambridge, U.K.: Cambridge Univ. Press.

Gaver, William W. 1993. How do we hear in the world? Explorations in ecological acoustics. *Ecological Psychology* 5: 285–313.

———. 1993. What in the world do we hear? An ecological approach to auditory event perception. *Ecological Psychology* 5: 1–30.

Musicae Scientiae (2001). Special issue on *Perspectives on musical meaning.* 5(2).

Serafine, Mary Louise. 1988. *Music as cognition. The development of thought in sound.* New York: Columbia Univ. Press.

Windsor, W. Luke. 2000. Through and around the acousmatic: the interpretation of electroacoustic sounds. Pp. 7–35 in *Music, electronic media and culture.* Edited by Simon Emmerson. Aldershot, U.K.: Ashgate Press.

CHAPTER 10

Subjectivity Rampant!
Music, Hermeneutics, and History

LAWRENCE KRAMER

> The hardest of all the arts to speak of is music, because music has
> no meaning to speak of.
> —Ned Rorem, *Music from Inside Out*

> But I've gotta use words when I talk to you.
> —T. S. Eliot, *Sweeney Agonistes*

The two epigraphs tell my story in miniature. No one doubts the formidable power of music to communicate on its "own" terms, but to communicate about it you have to use words. When words are added, though, they are commonly felt to say the wrong thing, no matter what they say. In one sense they say too little. Many would agree with Nietzsche ([1901] 1969, 428) that "compared with music all communication by words is shameless; words dilute and brutalize; words depersonalize; words make the uncommon common." Music that fails to cultivate its difference from language betrays "the law of its being" (441). In another sense words say too much. They are specific where music is suggestive. Words carry more meaning than music, which "has no meaning to speak of," can bear.

The purpose of this chapter is to say the contrary: to suggest, in so many words, that music does important cultural work by being spoken of, and would not be what we call "music" otherwise. Words situate music in a multiplicity of cultural contexts, both those to which the music "belongs" in an immediate sense and those to which it stands adjacent in ways that often become apparent only once the words are in play. In the process, words invest music with the very capacity to "speak" of its contexts that it is usually thought to lack, and is often prized for lacking. Neither the speech nor the contexts—this can't be stressed too much—are "extrinsic" to the music involved; the three terms are inseparable in both theory and practice.

But how, really, can we *say* what music means? Surely the music doesn't say, and a good part of our response to music is intuitive and physical—unspeaking, and all the better for it. In other words, our responses are deeply subjective. Even if our statements about musical meaning are guarded, generalized, and resigned to being inadequate—as most have generally been—this is a hurdle too high. Even these limited efforts are vulnerable to the charge that inevitably greets attempts to address music with the rich conceptual and verbal resourcefulness routinely applied to texts and images: given music's semantic poverty, any attempt to say what it means is not just subjective but hopelessly so. It makes no difference whether the subjective utterance is merely depreciated or valued as "personal" or "poetic." Either way, musical meaning forfeits in advance any possible claim to represent musical knowledge.

The result is a familiar paradox. Although both the everyday conduct and ceremonial forms of culture are filled with music, regarded in its own right music is cut off from its cultural relationships, and indeed used as a means of escaping or denying them. Aside from familiar talk about the expression of feeling—as if feeling, too, were not socially and culturally conditioned—there is nothing more to be said. But it is one thing to enjoy not filling in music's semantic blanks, and quite another to prohibit filling them: to turn a custom into a law. The prohibition is pointless in any case. Semantic energies are irrepressible; the voices of culture refuse to be stilled. But until quite recently there has been a consensus that enforces a certain silence about music by requiring that any meanings ascribed to it be both vague and modest, as befits their origin in mere subjectivity.

Only since around 1990 has there been a concerted effort to ascribe complex, broadly intelligible meanings to music without restriction to feelings and without constraint by music's lack of representational-semantic richness. Usually called "the new musicology"—I prefer to speak of "cultural musicology"—this trend resists easy summary. It represents a habit of thought more than a program or consensus. Nonetheless, it seems fair to say that there has been widespread interest in the interaction of music with social and cultural forms. Attention has gone particularly to the way music helps shape historically specific modes of subjectivity on grounds that are, taking the term in its broadest sense, ideological. Beethoven's "Tempest" Sonata might be found to uphold the links drawn by Enlightenment anthropology between sympathy and social evolution (Kramer 1998), or Schubert's "Unfinished" Symphony to model a hedonistic alternative to bourgeois masculinity (McClary 1994), or Ravel's *Daphnis and Chloe* to link colonial fantasies with the pleasures of mass consumption (Kramer 1995, 210–26). This choice of examples from "classical" music reflects my own interests, but most cultural musicology destabilizes firm distinctions between cultivated and vernacular forms, and in principle takes all music as its province.

For those persuaded by it, cultural musicology solves a number of important problems about musical meaning. It answers the charge of the interpreter's subjectivity by taking that very subjectivity as the object of inquiry, understanding it as a socially constructed position made available by the music and occupied to a greater or lesser degree by the listener. Subjectivity so understood is not an obstacle to credible understanding but its vehicle. The semantic problem is solved by seeking, not to decode music as a virtual utterance, but to describe the interplay of musical technique with the general stream of communicative actions. Musical hermeneutics is asked, not to decrypt a hidden message, and far less to fix the form of anyone's musical experience, but to suggest how music transcribes some of the contextual forces by which the process of listening to it may be or may once have been conditioned. Having detailed these positions elsewhere (Kramer 1995, 2001), I will provisionally take them for granted here to focus on a new aspect of the general problem.

Cultural musicology can claim to show that music has cultural meaning despite its lack of the referential density found in words or images. But musical meaning can be made explicit only by language, and the process of "translation" therefore presupposes some sort of vital relationship between music and text. Yet the nature of that relationship is just as problematical, if not more so, in cultural musicology as elsewhere. Interpretations like those sketched above inevitably involve a gap between what is said about the music and what can be said to be "in" it. Music per se is not only nonsemantic, but "unsemanticizable"; even the simplest interpretations of it rapidly exceed anything that might be conceivably encoded in its stylistic and structural gestures. Where interpretation is practiced the most, the pragmatic arenas in which meanings are negotiated and shared as music is talked about, taught, visualized, and rehearsed, there is rarely a demand for reference to such codes. People are literally taken at their word.

The gap between music and meaning does not have to be glaring; in statements that seem sensible, obvious, or otherwise unobjectionable, it may often go unnoticed, or at worst be written off as an accidental effect of metaphor. Consider, for example, what seems—indeed, is—a fairly innocuous remark by Robert Schumann about the first movement of Chopin's piano sonata in B♭ minor (1837–39, published 1840). Reviewing the newly published score, Schumann says that the "stormy, passionate" character of the movement is relieved by a "beautiful cantilena" that "leans toward Italy via Germany," but that "when the song is over, the Sarmatian flashes from the tones in his defiant originality" (Schumann [1840] 1946, 141). The impassioned storminess is easy enough to ground in the music's tempo, mode, and texture, and the contrast of national characters is conventional for both composer and critic in 1840; but the image of "flashing out" as a sign of defiant (why defiant?) originality has no unambiguous musical correlative, and nothing in the music mandates the use of the term *Sarmatian*, which refers to a legendary race of mounted hunter-warriors who supposedly ruled primeval Poland. In the nineteenth century, with Poland politically dismembered, the image of the Sarmatian band of brothers, natural aristocrats on horseback "equal before each other and invincible to foreigners" (Schama 1995, 38), was an important source of nationalist nostalgia and revolutionary fantasy. Schumann's language thus constructs a metaphor of creative originality as a combination of feral energy and primitive nobility, a force from beyond the social and geopolitical boundaries of modern western Europe. The metaphor is one that the music might well be able to convey, but could hardly be said to signify.

Gaps like this are endemic in musical hermeneutics, and their presence is usually used to discredit the whole idea of musical meaning, which, it is argued, is an arbitrary construction of the interpreter that at best addresses the strictly musical qualities of a work in superficial terms. Plausible as it may seem, this view is untenable. Not only are these hermeneutic gaps not a sign of arbitrariness, they are the enabling condition of musical meaning, and the site where the interplay of music and culture is most fully realized. To make sense of this argument, it will prove helpful to consult a neighboring process of interpretation. That process is descriptive, and the most suggestive account of it I know of is a philosophical poem, Wallace Stevens's "Description Without Place" ([1945] 1954, 339–46). The poem is an attempt to define precisely what kind of statement calls meaning forth across hermeneutic gaps, whether "on the youngest poet's page,/ Or in the dark musician, listening/ To hear more brightly the contriving chords" (stanza 3).

Stevens is interested in getting beyond the classic empiricist distinction between fact and value. To that end, he takes up a special type of vivid description that does more than simply convey information, if it conveys any at all. Description in this sense has the peculiar quality of "sticking" both to its object and in the mind. It enhances the object in our cognizance by infusing the object with meaning, but it does not disappear in the process; on the contrary, in enhancing the object it also enhances itself. For Stevens, this sort of description is "a sight indifferent to the eye" (stanza 5); it has sensory acuity without sensory limitation. It combines real or virtual sight with "the difference that we make in what we see" and again with our "memorials of that difference" (5). In other words, the description is less a representation than an invention, not a description at all in the ordinary sense of the term but a construction from which meaning is extended to the object addressed.

Far from being merely fabricated, however, constructive description is a form of truth: "Description is revelation. It is not / The thing described, or false facsimile.// It is an artificial thing that exists,/ In its own seeming" (6). The effect of this seeming, a seeming that is revelation, is not simply to repeat or reaffirm something about the object described, but to reconstitute the object in the act of describing it. In a sense, all description can be said to do this, but constructive description does it so forcefully as to produce a qualitative shift, a quantum leap. Constructive description, "description without place" (i.e., without a literal referent) endows its object with meanings that return to it from the object in a new form: it is "the column in the desert, / On which the dove alights" (5), "a sense / To which we refer experience" (5). It is even a specifically musical sense, "a point in the fire of music/ Where dazzle yields to a clarity and . . . we are content" (3).

Verbal attributions of meaning to music have the force of constructive descriptions: they do not decode the music or reproduce a meaning already there in it but attach themselves to the music as an independent form or layer of appearance, "its own seeming." The language does not have to be eloquent to do this; the constructive dimension is a function, not a trait. Something in the music—music played, heard, or remembered—or someone involved in the musical experience prompts the description, which may pass through several versions or be negotiated with others before it "sticks" with a typical sharp fusion of knowledge and pleasure.

But sticks for how long? Any constructive description that outlives the circumstances of its utterance becomes a historical artifact. As time passes, particular descriptions may seem to retain their freshness, or to become dated, or comfortably familiar, or disturbingly unfamiliar, or legendary, or strange. This is not to say, however, that past descriptions are necessarily "finished," that they are hermeneutically inert, either because they are regarded as obsolete or, on the contrary, regarded as speaking with the voice of history itself. The very vicissitudes of constructive descriptions form new sources of meaning. Worn or faded descriptions can be revitalized by sympathetic acts of interpretation and contextualization; still vivid descriptions, and new ones as well, rely on the same process to animate and transform the meanings they provide. So constructive description is more than a historical artifact; it is a historical agency, a cultural practice that installs the past in the present, and installs its objects in history even in the absence of overtly historical language. I discuss that installation and its consequences next.

To broach the topic, we have to look more closely at constructive description as a type of statement. It is virtually axiomatic in modern hermeneutics that all acts of understanding depend on frameworks of prior supposition and disposition: what Hans-Georg Gadamer calls "prejudgment" (*Vorurteil*, the common German word for "prejudice"). In contrast to the classical assumption that the responsible interpreter must set prejudgment aside, Gadamer argues that no understanding is possible without it. Prejudgment does not—or should not—determine or exhaust understanding; it is a catalyst, and as such indispensable, but it is not a cause. The proper way to use prejudgments is to put them at risk. Maybe so, says Jürgen Habermas (1977), but Gadamer tends to immunize prejudgment from risk by grounding it in a tradition that is not open to criticism (1975). My use of Gadamer here risks believing that it's possible to adopt his analysis of prejudgment without giving it a preemptive or coercive foundation.

In practice, of course, helpful disposition and blind predisposition are not always easy to tell apart. Prejudgment commonly operates tacitly, without reflective awareness. That it does so is what gives the classical view a continuing kernel of truth: no one wants to be *merely* prejudiced. In practice, too, therefore, viable acts of understanding seek (at least ideally) a variety of middle grounds between blind prejudgment and full-fledged philosophical reflection. One such ground is occupied by constructive descriptions, which can be characterized as statements that are simultaneously recognized as expressions of prejudgment and accepted as expressions of good understanding. In constructive description, the structure of prejudgment assumes a manifest, palpable, even dramatic form.

In this context, music emerges as perhaps the paradigmatic object of constructive description. Because it is semantically underdetermined, music renders the inevitable gap between meaning and the object of meaning much more palpable than texts or even images do. In music, therefore, the structure of prejudgment becomes lived experience more plainly, palpably, and dramatically than virtually anywhere else. But prejudgment is not an abstract or unconditional form; it is a contingent cultural–historical formation. When music brings prejudgment to life, it brings culture and history to life, too, and in exactly the same open space between semantic lack and constructive description.

It follows from the recognition of this process that music is saturated with meanings attributed to it by the subjects it addresses, which are always already a part of any music we actually hear or play. Musical meaning is produced less by the signs of a musical semiotics than by signs about music, signs whose grounding in historically specific forms of subjectivity is the source of their legitimation, not of their—literal—insignificance. The historical presence of these signifiers cannot be excluded from the constitution of whatever we understand as music itself.

More broadly, it follows that the question of musical meaning and its relation to subjectivity is far more political than epistemological. The disengagement of music from worldly contexts and constructive descriptions offers a certain pleasure in return for observing a rule that prohibits certain kinds of speech and devalues others. If speech is understood as the primary medium through which subjectivity is negotiated, then this same pleasure is the reward for surrendering a certain portion of one's rights or privileges as a subject. The politics of disengaged listening is based on the systematic misrecognition of this surrender as either a transcendence of subjectivity or, contrariwise, a fundamental enhancement or expression of it. These alternatives are only apparently in opposition, because both enact the same compliant relationship to music regarded as an agency of socialization. In the language of Michel Foucault (1979, 195–230), disengaged listening is a disciplinary practice in which the subjective power of music is policed by the very subjects who enjoy it, subjects who experience their discipline as a form of freedom. In some circumstances they may even be right; disengaged listening can offer real pleasure, and certain forms of engaged listening—for instance with attention mandated to national or racial character—can be as coercive as their opposites. Be that as it may, music is never more engaged with subjectivity than when it is disengaged from the worldly grounds of subjectivity, and when, accordingly, "subjective" verbal responses to it are written off as inessential or merely personal.

Once these relationships are recognized, the familiar objections to the idea of musical meaning collapse, and the notion that music, or some inviolate part of music, floats somewhere beyond cultural contingencies collapses with them.

Take the core argument that because music is nonsemantic, claims about its meaning are necessarily subjective and arbitrary. This would hold good only if subjectivity were extrinsic to meaning, whereas the exact opposite is the case. The structure of prejudgment grounds subjectivity in a specific sociocultural situation, and thereby allows sense to be made of experience; subjectivity and meaning are historical correlatives. Interpretation is contingent on particular structures of prejudgment but never completely determined by them. With music, as we have just seen, this process is at its most explicit, but the musical case involves nothing not also present in the interpretation of texts or images.

To illustrate, consider once more Schumann's simple statement about the first movement of Chopin's B♭ minor sonata. One of the presuppositions of this statement is the concept of a true or original self (Chopin the Sarmatian) that may be deceived by its own false or borrowed appearances (a Chopin who leans toward Italy via Germany). However beautiful, the secondary character is inauthentic; Schumann stresses that the end of the movement leaves it behind. The true self is identified with defiance and difference, and assigned a character both primitive and exotic with respect to western European norms. (In the process, certain stereotypes, including Chopin's sensuous effeminacy and the opposition of German and Italian styles, are pointedly ignored.) Strictly speaking, this characterization would apply only to someone like Chopin, an eastern-European "other" by birth. The evident value that Schumann places on

Chopin the Sarmatian, however, points to a more general resonance. Underlying the contrasts of east and west, primary and secondary self, there lies a characteristic bourgeois separation between private or interior identity and public demeanor, the former of which escapes or transcends the social determinations that the latter obeys. For Schumann, Chopin's Sarmatian character serves as a paradigm for what he takes to be the socially resistant quality of authentic identity.

For Schumann, too, Chopin carries the expression of authenticity to its limit in the sonata's last movement, which defies all available resources of prejudgment: "[In] this joyless, unmelodious movement breathes . . . an original and terrifying spirit that holds down with mailed fist everything that seeks to resist [it], so that we listen fascinated and uncomplaining to the end—though not to praise: for this is not music." The movement's only intelligible element is the aggressive power, the mailed fist, of the Sarmatian self, which Schumann associates with an eastern identity even older and more remote: "the sonata closes as it began . . . like a Sphinx with an ironic smile" (Schumann [1840] 1949, 142). Some three-quarters of a century later, the influential American music critic James Huneker would more fully assimilate this last movement to Schumann's model for the first. With the imperial adventures of the later nineteenth century behind him, Huneker links the movement's "sub-human growling . . . expressive of something that defies definition" with a definite "Asiatic coloring . . . like the wavering outline of light-tipped hills seen sharply in silhouette, behind which rises and falls a faint, infernal glow" (Huneker [1909] 1927, 299).

Nothing in either Schumann's statement or Huneker's is unwarrantably "subjective" in the sense—a problematical sense, but let that go—of being idiosyncratic or ungrounded. On the contrary, their remarks are informed by a structure of prejudgment with a serious track record, something both durable and flexible. When interpretive statements do seem "subjective" in the pejorative sense, the reason is not their necessary origin in a historical subject and cultural subject-position. When the great pianist and conductor Hans von Bülow writes (after Schumann, before Huneker) that Chopin's Prelude no. 9 in E Major portrays the composer bludgeoning himself in the head with a hammer (cited by Schönberg 1963, 128), the statement is—famously—absurd. What makes it so, however, is not (or not only) Bülow's personal perversity, but the lack of any plausible connection to a structure of prejudgment. The remark might make sense as satire, but it is not meant satirically; it might make sense in psychopathological terms, but it is not meant that way, either. Like the sonata finale, but without its artistic license, Bülow's remark alienates itself from the available resources of sense making.

Two other objections can be considered more briefly. It is sometimes argued that musical meaning cannot readily be heard in musical sounds; to do so the listener would have to quickly piece together an improbably long and specific chain of signifiers. This argument mistakenly prescribes that meaning must arise immediately in the act of listening rather than in anticipation, retrospection, or some combination of the three. Even more importantly, the argument fails to acknowledge the power of constructive description to live up to its name. The description is what constitutes the music as a particular kind of object, and allows that object to be experienced as meaningful in concrete ways. Without at least a rudimentary discursive or descriptive background, listening could not take place. But there is no need to stay rudimentary. Schumann's and Huneker's descriptions of the finale of Chopin's sonata allow them, and anyone so inclined, to "hear" an extreme esotericism in the music that challenges (even though it does not escape) both the social and conceptual norms of Western rationality.

Finally, music is sometimes acknowledged to have meaning in a general sense, but musical detail, the musical nitty-gritty, because (once more) it lacks semantic value, is said to have only musical meaning, which is the real object of musical understanding. This argument is a holding action that tries to redraw the boundary breached by its own admission of a general though inferior kind of musical meaning. Music has no means to reserve some specific layer or pocket for meaning. Once it has been brought into sustainable connection with a structure of prejudgment, music simply becomes meaningful. There is no guarantee that any particular detail will become hermeneutically active, but no detail is exempt from the possibility. In light of Schumann's description, the end of the first movement of Chopin's B♭ minor sonata—a booming proclamation of the major mode—might well be heard as a "defiant" affirmation of the original Sarmatian self.

The affirmation extends to details of the movement's sonata form, which, most unusually, begins its recapitulation with the second theme, that is, with the cantilena in which Schumann heard a borrowed identity. The cantilena resolves the harmonic drama of the movement in the tonic major, but the resolution, though structurally correct, is rhetorically unstable. At the end of the recapitulation the minor and major modes clash dramatically, leaving the coda to begin with the major in shambles, beset by dissonance and presented in the weakest, most ambiguous of chord positions (the second inversion). When the closing measures finally right the balance, their "Sarmatian" vehemence may thus appear as the true resolution—or else as a rhetorical excess that, perhaps self-consciously, deconstructs the idea that a resolution is ever simply true.

All of these hermeneutic arguments lead straight to culture and history, and all of them counteract the familiar social practice of using music to erase its own social specificity. Musical meaning, like meaning generally, carries its contingent, socially constructed character as part of its content. The moment that part is recognized, culture, history, and society come flooding in. This is a moment that twentieth-century musical aesthetics sought to defer indefinitely, but that in some sense has always already arrived. Constructive description is a fact of musical life, and more, one of its foundations. Particular descriptions may be either informal or scholarly, improvisatory or deliberative. They may also, of course, be good or bad, perceptive or silly. Even failed descriptions, however, reflect the condition that successful ones depend on: a full, open engagement with music as lived experience, experience rendered vivid and vivified by a host of overlapping cultural associations. Why bother with anything less?

Further Reading

Cook, Nicholas. 1998. *Analyzing musical multimedia.* Oxford: Oxford Univ. Press.

Cook, Nicholas, and Mark Everist, eds. 1999. *Rethinking music.* Oxford: Oxford Univ. Press.

Kerman, Joseph. 1985. *Contemplating music.* Cambridge, Mass.: Harvard Univ. Press.

Kramer, Lawrence. 1990. *Music as cultural practice, 1800–1900.* Berkeley: Univ. of California Press.

———. 1998. *Franz Schubert: Sexuality, subjectivity, song.* Cambridge, U.K.: Cambridge Univ. Press.

Leppert, Richard. 1993. *The sight of sound: Music, representation, and the history of the body.* Berkeley: Univ. of California Press.

Leppert, Richard, and Susan McClary, eds. 1987. *Music and society.* Cambridge, U.K.: Cambridge Univ. Press.

McClary, Susan. 1991. *Feminine endings: Music, gender, and sexuality.* Minneapolis: Univ. of Minnesota Press.

———. 2000. *Conventional wisdom: The content of musical form.* Berkeley: Univ. of California Press.

Scott, Derek, ed. 2000. *Music, culture, and society: A reader.* Oxford: Oxford Univ. Press.

Subotnik, Rose R. 1991. *Developing variations: Style and ideology in Western music.* Minneapolis: Univ. of Minnesota Press.

Williams, Alastair. 2001. *Constructing musicology.* London: Ashgate.

CHAPTER 11

Historical Musicology: Is It Still Possible?

ROB C. WEGMAN

In recent years, historical musicology has come close to critiquing itself out of business. Scholars have argued ever more vigorously that the pursuit of music history is driven—and its results contaminated—by the values, creative impulses, dreams, illusions, and neuroses of our time. Historical inquiry, they concur, is fundamentally *creative*, expressive of who we are. Nor could it be otherwise. Without the firm interpretive hand of the music historian, the massive flood of unsorted, undigested, unprocessed material that we euphemistically call "historical evidence" would remain devoid of any apparent sense or meaning. That material is the clay, the raw material, that we are irresistibly driven to cut, shape, and mold in our image. We pick and choose, select and combine, whatever evidence we need to fill out the patterns we wish to perceive. That is why history is so rewarding. It is the creative act of imposing order on chaos.

Of course we do need the illusion that the shape, the pattern, and the order are more than just the products of our imagination—that they have a basis in historical reality. This illusion has traditionally been provided by the ideals of objectivity and authenticity. Yet these ideals have been questioned as well, and with good reason. A historical fact, by itself, may be objective and incontrovertible. But the choice to single it out, from among innumerable other facts, is unavoidably arbitrary, revealing of our interests. Still, it is that choice, and the interpretation that guides it, that endows a fact with its historical significance. Without interpretation, we are not engaged in history, but in collecting and storing raw data. Positivists might insist that it is possible for interpretations to be objectively valid if they are inductively derived from empirical evidence, somewhat like natural laws or universal principles. Yet the endeavor to prove that induction can yield objective and incontrovertible knowledge defeated epistemologists long ago.

More problematically, perhaps, what is the touchstone of objectivity and authenticity? "Objective" or "authentic" in terms of what? "Historical reality," one might be tempted to answer. Yet historical reality cannot by definition be objective, or at least not objectively knowable. It is a metaphysical entity. It cannot be empirically known by us (otherwise it would not be historical), only postulated—that is, once again, created. This is not to deny that people in the past must have had a sense of their reality. Yet that sense would have been *subjective* even then: it might well have varied enormously depending on whom you asked. If there is such a singular, objective, and transcendent thing as "historical reality," then surely it can be knowable only to God.

Even after the modernist ideals of objectivity and authenticity are abandoned, however, there typically remains a powerful yearning for a past that has a reality of its own, an autonomous existence, transcending the distorting fictions inherent in our modern perspective. This yearning has recently given rise to a new proposal: the idea of a dialogue with the past. Starting, once again, from the premise that history ought to be more than the product of our creative imagination, advocates of this approach insist that the past can be—and indeed should be—an equal partner in a cross-historical dialogue. This so-called ethnographic approach, advocated especially by "new musicologists," has come under criticism as well (Taruskin 1997, xx–xxx). The chief objection is that it succeeds merely in replacing one illusion with another. We can disown the products of our imagination by attempting to show that they correspond to historical truth, and we can disown them by postulating "others" whose "authentic" voice we then hope to hear somehow within our own ventriloquizing. But what's the difference? If the Other is not the product of our historical imagination, then what can it be, except yet another metaphysical postulate?

Whither historical musicology? Is it still possible? That is the critical question. It concerns every historical musicologist, and it affects all our work. In the following essay I outline an introduction to the debate, clarifying its terms, and, in a polemic conclusion, offering some of my own thoughts.

The problem outlined above is of course anything but new. What we are reliving in the current debate over historical musicology, arguably, is the same "crisis of historicism" that erupted in German scholarship in the 1920s. That crisis affected musicology no less than it did other disciplines. Its impact can be witnessed, for example, in Heinrich Besseler's well-known textbook on the history of early music *Die Musik des Mittelalters und der Renaissance*, published in 1931. Besseler opened his book with a separate chapter devoted to the "core problem" of historicism, a problem whose causes he explained as follows (Besseler 1931, 3; my translation):

> In the nineteenth century, early music, as a living tradition, retained an active presence only in isolated vestiges. As a phenomenon in its totality it had to be rediscovered, yet this discovery was guided by the needs and longings of the present. What modernity failed to offer was sought and found in history. It was inevitable that its image [of the past] would conform to its own wishful dreams, that selection and interpretation, evaluation and cognizance, were determined by the ideas of an age which yearned for the past in order to use it for its own fulfilment. No consideration of history may pass over the task of elucidating the motives behind such discoveries, and of raising awareness of the manifold reinterpretations which the legacy of earlier eras undergoes as it passes from one generation to another.

These words were written more than seventy years ago, yet they seem to have lost none of their relevance today. What is perhaps most noteworthy about them, given musicology's traditional aspirations to scientific status, is their emphasis on the *psychological* nature of the problem. The issue was not merely one of methodology. According to Besseler, the rediscovery of early music had been driven by unconscious needs and longings, wishful dreams, and a yearning for fulfillment. At the root of all this, he suggested, was a sense of disillusion with modernity, which had failed to offer what the encounter with history was hoped to provide.

If this was indeed the core problem, then it should not surprise us that its recognition provoked a crisis. The ideals that had captivated nineteenth-century scholars turned out to be contaminated by the very problems from which the past had seemed to offer an escape. The needs, longings, dreams, and yearnings had finally been exposed for what they were: symptoms of modernity. Even the encounter with history, in short, had ended in disillusion. If musicologists were to draw any lessons from this, Besseler concluded, they should continue to expose those symptoms in all historical inquiry, by engaging in rigorous self-scrutiny and self-criticism.

This injunction is of course still being repeated in current debates over historical musicology. Gary Tomlinson, for instance, has argued that "in broad terms, a postmodern musicology will be characterized most distinctively by its insistent questioning of its own methods and practices" (Tomlinson 1993, 21). If we are to implement genuine renewal in the discipline, he suggested, "we might begin to interrogate our love for the music we study" (p. 24). As these words indicate, the terms of the debate may not have changed all that much since the early twentieth century. Our passion for the music of the past may be as ardent as were the needs, longings, dreams, and yearnings of nineteenth-century musicology. Yet for Tomlinson, no less than for Besseler, they may also be self-serving and self-centered. That is why they need to be interrogated.

It can never hurt to repeat that injunction, perhaps not even after seventy years. At the same time, one wonders if persistent self-interrogation is likely to tell us much that we didn't already know. In essence, after all, the problem we are confronting here is that of the *subjectivity* of human knowledge, the fact that it always bears the imprint of the feelings, thoughts, and concerns of those who produce it. This problem is of course paradigmatic of the Western intellectual tradition, and surely there is no need to remind ourselves of it at every turn. We are fallible human beings, and everything we do will always have its problems: so what else is new? On the other hand, the particular psychological mechanism that Besseler identified—history as the projected fulfillment of modern longings—does seem to invite closer analysis. This mechanism has been studied by a number of writers, and it is commonly understood as exhibiting *narcissistic* impulses (Davies 1989). I suspect that this was Besseler's understanding as well, even if he didn't say it in so many words. For the archetypal myth of Narcissus matches his analysis very closely, and in fact matches the current debate over historical musicology equally well.

Like Narcissus, or so critics remind us, we have gazed into a fountain, and have become enamored of the image reflected in its surface. The fountain, one might say, is the totality of the available historical evidence, and the image it returns is the product of our historical vision. We have wanted that image to be real, objective, autonomous, authentic, other. Like Narcissus, however, we have been frustrated in our attempts to capture the image—that is, to demonstrate its objective reality. Sooner or later we were bound to make a painful discovery. "Oh, I am he!" Narcissus cried, "now I know for sure the image is my own; it's for myself I burn with love; I fan the flames I feel" (Ovid 1986, 64–65). That was the moment of truth. Historical evidence, by itself, may be as real and tangible as the water in the fountain. Yet the past, as we read it into that evidence, has no objective reality, no independent existence, no autonomy, no otherness. Rather, it is always and necessarily the reflection of the viewing subject, the product of our historical imagination. That is why the Narcissus myth is of enduring relevance: it epitomizes the Western discovery of subjectivity (Kristeva 1987).

Let us pause briefly to review the key issues in this analogy. First of all, what have we lost with the discovery? What we have lost is "the past," as a realm that has an autonomous existence independent from our historical vision—just as Narcissus lost the object of his love when he discovered it to be his own reflection. Second, what do we think we have gained? Like Narcissus, we may have gained self-knowledge. The past "as it really was" may be a delusion, yet at least we can try to understand how we have fashioned it in our image. That, as noted before, is what Besseler urged historians to do, and that is what we are still being urged to do today. Finally, why was the discovery a painful one? Because historical musicology, like Narcissus, had invested its deepest needs, longings, dreams, and yearnings in the image it perceived. Its love for the past was staked precisely on the objective reality of that image. Yet this love affair ended in the 1920s, and the aspirations of historical musicology have remained unfulfilled ever since.

The syndrome is a recognizable one: what causes the pain is, in effect, a narcissistic injury. We have loved the past, in all its apparent authenticity and objectivity, but we have been duped. We have made fools of ourselves. There is no past that could have asked us to love it, and like Narcissus, we feel shame and embarrassment at having imagined one. For Narcissus, the initial response was one of despair. Grieving over the lost image that had fueled his love, he cried out: "What now? Woo or be wooed? Why woo at all?" (Ovid 1986, 466). The response in our time is not dissimilar. What now, we wonder? Why pursue historical musicology at all? Is it still possible? Why aspire to authenticity in performance, to objectivity in historical knowledge? Why converse with imagined others, as if they actually had the power to speak to us? It has all been exposed as a fruitless pathological delusion.

Another response, however, is indignation. The past that we knew and loved has let us down, and so it must be repudiated as the delusion it was. Such repudiation has become a popular pastime in present-day scholarship. When scholars dismiss every image that was ever constructed of the past, preferably by previous generations of musicologists, they are not merely expressing a difference of historical interpretation. There is more at stake. We cannot forgive traditional musicology for having indulged and gratified its infatuation with the past, for this is a pleasure that we must deny ourselves. We are only too aware of, after all, how deeply satisfying it can be to identify with the past, to imagine it to be real, to love it with a passion. As we all know, there is an irresistible attraction to exercising the historical imagination: its very subjectivity confirms how much it is a part of who we are.

To indict and interrogate that subjectivity may be conscientious, but it does involve us in inner conflict. We settle that conflict at a high price. When an archival scholar is thrilled about the discovery of a new document, and when a critic dismisses such work as positivistic fact-gathering, it is the latter who is the poorer, not the former. For the archival scholar is capable of perceiving historical meaning and significance in the document, whereas the critic cannot acknowledge it as more than a "mere" fact. The latter may be right, of course. The fountain is just a body of still water. And where we perceived an image of a living past, there is in fact just a mountain of inert evidence. It will always be tempting to be carried away by the historical imagination, yet we must remind ourselves that this faculty is, in the end, subjective. For that very reason, however, it is painful, exceedingly painful, not to be able to allow it free rein, to deny ourselves the sheer exhilaration of exercising it without inhibition.

The chief reward for this self-restraint, this self-abnegation, is the knowledge that we are at least more conscientious than others have been. That knowledge may do little to ease our pain, yet it does bring a further reward. For we have also earned ourselves the right to cast judgment on those who have been less conscientious than we. It is here that we can give free rein at least to our indignation, and allow ourselves the *ersatz* exhilaration of exercising it without inhibition. Targets are easy to find. For there are many things for which we cannot forgive traditional musicology— Western hegemony, positivism, objectivism, modernism, metaphysics, essentialism, reification, whatnot. It is not that those paradigms are merely unsatisfactory or inadequate. That, after all, would be true of every paradigm we might adopt in their place. The problem is that they have offered us a past that we must forsake. The more we have loved that past, or envy others for their love of it, the more we resent the paradigms for having accommodated that love.

Yet our anger is directed at musicology as well, and this anger is of a particularly bitter and unforgiving kind. To the extent that we have only ourselves to blame, the narcissistic injury calls for punishment. "Then in his grief he tore his robe," as Ovid wrote of Narcissus (Ovid 1986, 3: 480–81), "and beat his pale cold fists upon his naked breast." We, too, must engage in merciless self-criticism, perpetually reminding ourselves of our failings, and finding even a perverse pleasure in exposing them. "The narcissistic self," as historian Martin L. Davies noted, "evinces a depressive, destructive aggressivity, repudiating the unworthy Other [that is, our image of the past] with an intensity matched only by its own internal self-castigation [that is, our self-criticism]" (Davies 1989, 266).

These, needless to say, are not the signs of healthy critical debate. They are symptoms, rather, of a profound and despairing sense of melancholia. In recent years, historical musicology has developed a moral conscience, a superego, of unprecedented righteousness and severity. Under the guise of critical reflection, it keeps reminding the discipline of its unworthiness. Everything you do, it says, everything you have ever done, has been self-serving, self-centered, and self-indulgent. Or, to put it in more familiar terms, everything has been hegemonic, positivist, objectivist, modernist, essentialist, totalizing. We indulge and placate that superego not just by accepting its accusations, but also by seeking to satisfy its demands. We cannot simply throw ourselves into an encounter with the past, or so the reasoning goes, for we have no idea how base our hidden motives may be, and how badly we may need to expiate them. That is why, over the last decade or so, musicologists have become engaged in a desperate search for legitimation—a predicament summed up by the question, is it still possible? This search has typically led away from historical inquiry as such into the realm of critical theory. By now, we are close to reaching the stage where we cannot make any step, no matter how small, without theorizing it first. Without such legitimation, we feel, historical musicology may not be possible at all.

This search for legitimation is doomed to failure, however. As I said before, the problem comes down, at bottom, to the subjectivity of human knowledge. If this problem is paradigmatic of the Western intellectual tradition, then of course we cannot theorize ourselves out of it, no matter how hard we might try. Why then do we persist? Chiefly, I suspect, because we feel *incriminated* by our subjectivity. And we cannot see any legitimation for the pursuit of history if everything we do is bound to incriminate us further. We are fallible human beings, true, but we ought not to be. That is why we have lost the confidence to look into the fountain. Every image we see reminds us of our subjectivity, and confirms our unworthiness to engage in historical inquiry. If only we could prove ourselves worthy again, if only we could discover some legitimation for what we do, that confidence might be restored.

And yet: worthy of whom, worthy of what? Surely our subjectivity cannot make us unworthy of ourselves. For to be subjective is to indulge oneself—and self-indulgence typically fosters a sense of self-worth. That is why the pursuit of history is so rewarding, and yet so problematic. We distrust our subjectivity precisely because it has made us too self-indulgent, too pleased with ourselves. If this makes us unworthy, then surely we must be unworthy of the Other—that is, the past, which we readily confess to having stifled under our mastery pose, our "hegemonizing" gestures. That is what our moral conscience tells us. Go theorize, it says, and then look again: you will see that there really is an objective past where you used to see your own image, that there really are others where you used to hear your own voice. Your work so far has been unworthy of that past, unworthy of those others. But you can redeem yourself, and renew the discipline, if you can manage to see them now, in all their reality, through the corrective lens of critical theory.

This, needless to add, is merely another lapse into narcissism. And yet, it is this perpetual relapse, alternated by the perpetual rediscovery of our subjectivity, that keeps the debate going round in circles. For every image that is exposed as subjective, a new one is theorized as real. If we are to follow Gary Tomlinson, for example, "the primary stimulus for musicology, instead of our love for this or that music, might more luminously be our love of, concern for, belief in, alienating distance from—choose your words—the others who have made this or that music in the process of making their world" (Tomlinson 1993, 24). That is to say, if narcissistic identification with music is self-serving, narcissistic identification with others might be selfless. One would like to believe Tomlinson, but the premise does strain credulity. No amount of theorizing can endow historical others with an objective existence. They are dead and gone, and can only be revived in the historical imagination. Surely one cannot blame that imagination for being unworthy of the others it calls into being. Yet for Tomlinson, its inherent subjectivity is detrimental to the *real* others who (he imagines) exist beyond its ken. If only we could prove worthy of those others, by escaping from the prison of our subjectivity, historical musicology might be redeemed at last. This aspiration does indeed seem to motivate his call for disciplinary renewal. Several critics have drawn attention to the "aversion to old-fashioned subjectivity," "distrust of subjectivity," indeed "antisubjectivity" that appears to underwrite his harsh indictments of traditional musicology, and his desire to break away from it (Kramer 1993, 32, 33; Taruskin 1997, xxv). As Charles Rosen concluded, "he ends up by asking, in short, for a value-free history, although he knows that this ideal of objectivity is impossible" (Rosen 1994b, 62).

Can we break away from this vicious circle? If we want to, I suspect, we probably can. As far as narcissism is concerned, the solution seems deceptively simple. Throughout Western history, at least until the modern period, it has been taken as self-evident that the past has no objective reality or existence (Ligota 1982, 3–6; cf. also Schott 1968, 192–93). "When a true narrative of the past is related," as St. Augustine observed in his *Confessions* (XI. xviii. 23), "the memory produces not the actual events, which have passed away, but words conceived from images of them" (St. Augustine 1991, 233–43). For St. Augustine this was not a painful discovery at all; on the contrary, it was a matter of common sense. After all, "who can measure the past which does not now exist, or the future which does not yet exist, unless perhaps someone dares to assert that he can measure what has no existence?" (XI. xvi. 21). To the extent that the past has any reality, it dwells only in the memory of those who narrate history. There is no Other to fall in love with, only a self that may choose to dwell in "the fields and vast palaces of memory" (X. viii. 12).

Still, I doubt that narcissism is necessarily the problem here. Nor, for that matter, are Western hegemony, positivism, objectivism, modernism, metaphysics, essentialism, reification, and all the rest. The real issue probably lies elsewhere. Let me put it quite bluntly: if we cannot accept that we are fallible human beings, that everything we do will always have its problems, then historical musicology will indeed be possible no longer. To put it even more bluntly: There is a certain arrogance in depreciating a worthwhile endeavor, in this case historical musicology, merely because we cannot attain perfection in it. Narcissism may be a human weakness, but instead of excoriating it for that reason, we might learn to live with it. True, narcissistic history may potentially trap us in delusion. Yet the fiction of a "real" past has undeniable heuristic value, and may well bring out the best in us—our historical imagination, for instance, or our subjectivity, or excitement, or yes, our love.

What, exactly, have we become afraid of? We know that there is no real past, that there are no real others of whom we could be unworthy. The only world that is real is the one we live in today. History adds a rich dimension to that world. If we are in danger of being unworthy of anything or anyone, it is probably our readers—*real* others, whom we may perplex with our scholarly angst, annoy with our narcissistic self-torment, and exasperate with our defensive theorizing. It is only the paralyzing fear to take human risks that might render historical musicology impossible. Or rather, perhaps, it is the fear that we may not be forgiven for our failings. Yet we cannot ask anyone's forgiveness if we are unable to forgive ourselves, and the scholars who worked before us. That, I suspect, may be the hardest thing of all: to find it in our hearts to understand and accept those failings—before we blame them on the discipline, and critique it out of business altogether.

Further Reading

Besseler, Heinrich. 1931. *Die Musik des Mittelalters und der Renaissance.* Potsdam: Akademische Verlagsgesellschaft Athenaion.

Davies, Martin L. 1989. History as narcissism. *Journal of European Studies* 19: 265–91.

Kramer, Lawrence. 1993. Music criticism and the postmodern turn: In contrary motion with Gary Tomlinson. *Current Musicology* 53: 25–35.

Kristeva, Julia. 1987. Narcissus: The new insanity. Pp. 103–21 in *Tales of Love.* Translated by Leon S. Roudiez. New York: Columbia Univ. Press.

Ligota, Chistopher R. 1982. "This story is not true": Fact and fiction in antiquity. *Journal of the Warburg and Courtauld Institutes* 45: 1–13.

Ovid. 1986. *Metamorphoses.* Translated by A. D. Melville. Oxford: Oxford Univ. Press.

Rosen, Charles. 1994. Music à la Mode. *New York Review of Books,* June 23, 55–62.

Schott, Rüdiger. 1968. Das Geschichtsbewusstsein schriftloser Völker. *Archiv für Begriffsgeschichte* 12: 166–205.

St. Augustine. 1991. *Confessions.* Translated by Henry Chadwick. Oxford: Oxford Univ. Press.

Taruskin, Richard. 1997. *Defining Russia musically: Historical and hermeneutical essays.* Princeton, N.J.: Princeton Univ. Press.

Tomlinson, Gary. 1993. Musical pasts and postmodern musicologies: A response to Lawrence Kramer. *Current Musicology* 53: 18–24.

CHAPTER 12

Social History and Music History

TREVOR HERBERT

"The past is dead and gone. History is what historians make of it." This aphorism neatly summarizes the key issue. Unlike historians, some musicians and sectors of the listening public believe that the past can be reclaimed. They expect its musical artifacts—its past repertoires and practices—to be regularly enacted. In fact, the word *past* in this context can be something of a misnomer. The repertoires of our own time are the repertoires of all time, to the extent that we know of them and choose to call on them. This is a condition that music shares with other creative disciplines. But to music historians it has a special edge because of the concerns of both the academy and the box office.

There are other disjunctions between history and music history. Historians, particularly those for whom social and cultural history have been subsidiary to political and constitutional history, have typically used music as the fodder of footnotes, merely illustrating social and cultural patterns. But can social history—particularly in its newer cultural forms, and employing wider discourses than are offered simply by economic and demographic parameters—offer anything new to music history? The critical reflection within both disciplines in the closing decades of the twentieth century, forced as it has been by wider theoretical debates, makes such questions especially compelling.

My purpose here is to give an overview of some traditions of history and music history, and—in the light of newer, more radical approaches to historical discourse—to examine convergences and divergences between the two disciplines. The main question I want to pose is whether there are new avenues for genuine social histories of Western art music.

History and Social History

There are long-standing debates about how historians do what they claim to do. They center on the philosophical, methodological, and even ethical assumptions that underpin the business of being an historian. The polemic most often utilized in Britain for illustrating this is the one that emerged in the 1960s between E. H. Carr and other English historians, especially Sir Geoffrey Elton. Carr's contention was that histories are as much about the time of their making as they are about the past. He held that the barrier that stands between historians and their subjects is made from their own cultural and ideological baggage. He counseled skepticism about the historian's "fetishism for facts." Like Croce, he held that all history is "contemporary history" (Carr 1961, 21) because it inevitably interprets the past in light of prevailing conditions. This does not mean he believed that history could not be written. He answered his own question, "What is history?" with the retort that it is "a continuous process of interaction between the historian and his facts, an unending dialogue between the present and the past."

Elton (1967), on the other hand, held faith with the notion that the accumulation of authentic facts and the application of skilled synthesis through sophisticated historical method provided a perfectly reliable basis for the assemblage of an objective history. In effect, he believed that it was possible, through the careful scrutiny and objective synthesis of primary sources, to write histories that—if they were done properly—could be definitive. Elton, like many of his generation and persuasion, saw grand narratives of political and constitutional history as both the basis upon which, and the framework within which, any history should be constructed. It is easy to see why the Carr/Elton dichotomy became the primary exercise most commonly encountered in British universities by brand-new history students who had left home harboring the innocent and optimistic assumption that the past was there before them, just waiting to be discovered.

Social history developed uneasily and relatively recently as a subdiscipline of history. On April 7, 1966 the *Times Literary Supplement* famously devoted most of its pages to an evaluation of history, the British history profession, and historical writings. Several of Britain's leading figures set out their stalls. Prominent on the front page was a piece by Geoffrey Thomas in which he reported that the long-established *English Historical Review* had already been eclipsed by the social history–oriented *Past and Present*, whose subscribers held conferences at which such sociological topics as "work and leisure," "social mobility," and "popular religion" were featured.

The impact of social history on the discipline of history represented a sea change for those steeped in the Great Men tradition. The French *Annales* school was an important force for change. Its participants sought to understand society as "a total, integrated organism." Strong advocacy for social history as a distinct species of history also came from those who developed a broadly Marxist focus. Many embraced a wider range of evidence than political historians would have countenanced. They identified culture as "the driving force of historical change" and denied "simple correlations between economic forces and cultural constructs" (Desan 1989, 50–51). They also espoused methodologies that would routinely pay equal, or more than equal, regard to society as a whole, as opposed to just its dominant figures. The most important presence in this respect was probably E. P. Thompson, whose massive and influential *The Making of the English Working Class* (1963) offered both a new type of narrative and a working illustration of his "history from below" thesis—a systematic reversal of the practice of tracing the past by following the downward flow from the highest point of hegemony. His mission, as he famously put it, was to "rescue" the people "from the enormous condescension of posterity."

It became tempting to associate social history with themes that are primarily positioned to the political left, but this is misleading. Equally misleading was the claim by its detractors that it is a "soft history" or that it merely functions as an indicator of political change. When the *Journal of Social History* was launched in 1976, its editors self-confidently announced that "Social history must be iconoclastic, corrosive of received explanations; creative in producing new concepts and deriving new methods; and aggressive, encouraging incursions into all fields of historical analysis." Those editors may not have anticipated how soon their words would be put to the test. The theoretical upheavals that emerged in light of debates centered on structuralism and more especially postmodernism stimulated waves of self-examination that questioned the fundamentals of the historian's craft.

Music History

Music history has been conditioned by concerns that have been prevalent in musicology since the nineteenth century. Central has been the perceived need to identify, verify, classify, and catalog the sources for works that make up the body of Western art music. Additionally, and especially since the late 1960s, music historians have sought to gain an understanding of historic performance practices. These lines of inquiry (and their attendant ideologies) gained focus and emphasis through key forums in the musical establishment, especially learned societies, which were oriented around quite particular discourses, and the musical academy, which developed similarly focused curricula.

The preoccupation with the assemblage of data about a canonical repertoire and how it was performed implied an essentially linear approach to music history, in which the main points of reference—periodizations, canonical composers, the emergence of genres, styles, and so on—appeared obvious and unquestionable. Inherent too was the implication that the past (as reflected in its histories) was a progression, in which each historical "moment" developed out of, or in reaction to, that which preceded it. A further nuance that might be drawn from this (if certain historical models were followed) was that such narratives told of a continuous path of positive progression from which societies and their cultures benefited incrementally. The task of the music historian was to add more detail to the musical "grand narrative," to fill in some gaps, or to tell the story with a different accent and different points of emphasis—but the basic story was almost always, more or less, the same.

The other underlying assumption of many music histories up to the closing decades of the twentieth century is that music is essentially autonomous: that social and other cultural factors have a contextual, rather than a more intimate or even causal, relationship with musical creativity or practice. Richard Leppert and Susan McClary recognized this when surveying the musicological map in 1987:

> Briefly stated, the disciplines of music theory and musicology are grounded on the assumption of musical autonomy. They cautiously keep separate considerations of biography, patronage, place and dates from those of musical syntax and structure. Both disciplines likewise claim objectivity, the illusion of which is possible only when questions considered valid can, in fact, be answered without qualification. (Leppert and McClary 1987, viii)

The parallels between trends in the disciplines of history and music history are easy to spot. By the late 1960s both had become susceptible to central positivist narratives in which a certain type of knowledge and inquiry was privileged; both sought to garner historical "facts" and use them as the basis for "objective" histories; and both became infatuated with orthodox methodologies. Eventually both also came to be challenged from within and without.

Music History, Social History, Postmodernist History

Henry Raynor's substantial *Social History of Music* (1972) opens with the declaration that it attempts "to fill some part of the gap between the normal and necessary history of music which deals with the development of musical styles and the general history of the world in which composers carried out their function" (vii). Whatever are the merits of Raynor's book, there are no prizes for guessing what "the normal and necessary history of music" means, who the "composers" are, or that to him the term *general history of the world* is a largely unproblematic concept. But others were pioneering alternative ways of interrogating musical processes from social, economic and cultural perspectives. Among the more obviously important publications are those of Cyril Ehrlich (1985, 1990), John Rosselli (1984, 1991), Lawrence Levine (1988), and William Weber (1992). Each of the aforementioned (none of whom is primarily a musicologist) has demonstrated that musical practices are usually dependent on social, economic, and cultural interactions traversing a wider terrain than is immediately occupied by the music makers. This paradigm will hardly surprise ethnomusicologists and anthropologists, but music historians have always questioned the legitimacy of discursive approaches that are not demonstrably focused on musical texts.

A further albatross that music historians have shared with historians is born of the preoccupation with historical "facts" and the spooky notion that, in the right hands, their original meaning is resistant to the layers of interpretive, cultural, and ideological mediations to which they are submitted. In the positivist tradition, it often seems, legitimate histories are those that are not merely objective but *neutral*: devoid of imaginative engagement with their subjects. This is hard to countenance, given that all histories are exercises in conjecture based on the chance survival (sometimes following careless disposal) of documents and artifacts. The patchwork of musical topics that has received close scrutiny is also partly random: a consequence of fashion, taste, ideology, and accident. Then there is the mode of historical rhetoric, the figures of speech and tones of which are utterly of the present. A denial of imaginative engagement between the music historian and historical material implies a denial of what is already embryonic in much musicological writing.

It would, of course, be grotesquely inaccurate to ascribe to all music histories written since the middle of the twentieth century the characterization that I have given here. Such perspectives have long been questioned by historians and musicologists (e.g., R. G. Collingwood, Hayden White, Arthur Mendel, Richard Taruskin, Joseph Kerman). To these names can be added many more who have focused on popular music. But the prevailing orthodoxy of Western art music history remains primarily positivist and elitist. There is certainly little that genuinely addresses the social history of music. That topics relating to the canonical repertoire are central to most research is hardly reprehensible; more questionable are the self-limiting methods that are employed, and the neglect of the "lost peoples" of music history who are left to languish in a historical void—constituencies whose obscurity is made more certain by the effects of globalization. For example, little is known about the lives and culture of rank-and-file musicians, of the attitudes of popular audiences, or of the interaction between amateurs and professionals.

Many historians regard postmodernism with skepticism, and not without some justification, because at its most extreme, postmodernism relativizes knowledge to the point where it is hardly possible to conceive of any knowable history at all. But in its more moderate manifestations, postmodernism offers ways of building upon the methods and concerns of social historians in dealing with those whom music history has often overlooked. Social histories of music must as a matter of course expose the interactions between the widest spheres of society and musical practices. One can identify a range of revitalizing elements that postmodernism has introduced into the discipline of history that could invite a closer engagement between music history and social history. Postmodernism emphasizes a range of social determinants (such as gender and ethnicity) that challenge the Marxist focus on class, and accommodates incidents, events, and characters that fall outside the modernist emphasis on reason and progress. Above all, it resists prioritization of one aspect of history over another, rather than accepting a central privileged narrative as the point of reference for events and movements that fall outside it.

The postmodernist emphasis on themes and practices that fall outside the more traditional parameters of historical methodology is especially evident in microhistory, an approach that emerged in Italian historical thinking in the early 1980s (e.g., Ginzburg 1980; Muir and Ruggiero 1991). Microhistories take the opposite tack to the large-scale, "grand narrative" approach that deals with major themes running over several centuries: "they build on the obscure and unknown rather than on the great and the famous. . . . [They] take very small incidents in everyday life and retell them as stories, analysing them as metaphorical and symbolic clues to larger things" (Evans 1997, 245). Thus they often disclose something of the relationship between the popular and the elite so as to inform a wider historical picture.

Can and should such approaches inform music history? The obvious difference between music history and history in its most general sense is the one that I indicated at the start of this chapter: Music histories always carry some responsibility to cast light on repertoires and their creation, performance, and reception. Can music be autonomous and yet need a social history to enliven our understanding of it? Does Western art music history suffer from a lack of narrative depth—especially in terms of the social strata that its investigations touch upon—even in the parameters that it has defined for itself?

An Illustration: The Case of the Valve—Music History or Social History?

In 1814, Heinrich Stölzel, an otherwise obscure horn player working in the orchestra of the Prince von Pless in Prussia, invented what is believed to be the first widely adopted valve brass instrument. Soon, other makers adopted this or similar inventions and applied them to treble instruments such as trumpets. These instruments provided the raw prototype for the valve trumpets that are used today. Before Stölzel's invention, and leaving aside some of the transitional models (such as the *Klappentrompete*) that were contemporary with it, "natural trumpets" with crooks were essentially identical to those that had probably been in use since at least the sixteenth century. The implications of this invention were important: Valve instruments are much easier to play than "natural" instruments, the players of which had rare skills that were taught privately, mainly within family dynasties.

Any good music history book will tell you that valves were invented in the second decade of the nineteenth century. Few mention that hardly anyone used them for the best part of the next quarter century. There were two related reasons for this. First, few people needed them: there was little standard repertoire that actually required them, and players of instruments of older designs saw no need to desert their sophisticated techniques in order to learn the use of a new contraption. Second, the market for these instruments was entirely among professional players—a small group of men, probably no more than a handful in each of the larger European and American towns that supported professional musicians. These men lived distant from, and were probably unknown to, each other. Indeed, even though Stölzel's invention was listed in the *Allgemeine musikalische Zeitung* in 1815, one wonders how widely valve instruments were known and understood by players across Europe, let alone across the Atlantic.

At this point, social and economic factors combined to initiate one of the most momentous changes to the idiom of a family of instruments in the history of Western music. The earlier designs were given considerable refinement by (among others) the Belgian inventor Adolphe Sax, who moved to Paris in the 1840s. There, in 1844, he had a chance encounter with an itinerant group of British brass-playing entertainers called the Distins—an encounter that turned out to be cataclysmic. Following the meeting the Distins adopted the British sales agency for Sax's valve instruments. British makers, following the Distins' lead, recognized that a new market existed in the sprawling industrial conurbations of Victorian Britain. They seized on the possibility that groups of working men could be encouraged to form bands. Realizing that the main barrier to their ambition lay in the economic circumstances of their potential clients, they opportunistically seized on issues of social cohesion that worried the dominant classes. They extolled communal music making to community leaders (such as factory owners) as a "rational recreation": a recreation that would be morally—even spiritually—constructive, and would promote civic responsibility. They then put into potential purchasers' heads the idea that if the said community leader's name could be used to guarantee a loan, the instruments could be delivered promptly and paid for on a deferred payment basis.

The strategy worked like a charm. Thousands of bands were formed, and industrialists across the country happily underwrote the debts. Railroad companies also saw a chance to make a profit by sponsoring band contests for which trains were needed to carry bandsmen and their hundreds of supporters. Such congregations of brass players had never previously assembled. They provided unprecedented opportunities for the standardization of a new brass-playing idiom. The repertoire they played was drawn from third-hand arrangements of Italian operatic overtures and the like. Some of it survives, and it reveals that many of these players were consummate virtuosos.

But how did they play? What were the sonic values that they had in mind when they were learning? Who did they imitate other than each other? They had no relationship with the continuum of the art-music brass-playing tradition. It is virtually certain that what we have here is an *ab initio* encounter of a vernacular population with the sophisticated tools of art music.

Miscellaneous fragments of documentary evidence, together with the handwritten (sometimes crudely annotated) music, give important insights into these questions. The repertoires can be reconstructed. Exchanges about how contest adjudicators evaluated performances, personal exchanges between players, and similar documents allow us to get close to establishing a series of snapshots of the lives and musical preoccupations of these bandsmen. This type of investigation informs a wider music history. The brass band phenomenon occurred throughout the world in one guise or another. The American manifestation is especially interesting, because a version of it is so germane to embryonic forms of jazz.

Should this narrative be read as music history or as social history? Perhaps it is both, but it deals with a topic with which the traditional positivist music history, by default, has never sullied its hands. Undoubtedly part of the reason for this is that few brass players have found their way into the academy (compared, say, to keyboard players). The reason that some might offer for regarding this example as merely contextual is that it does not touch on any repertoire that can stand up to the value judgments or assumptions that are normally present in music histories. But does that matter?

Of course such approaches bring their own set of problems. Some have cast doubt on cultural history "defined only in terms of topics of inquiry" (Hunt 1989, 9). But histories in which evidence about small units of the past are investigated to analyze the relationships between musical and socioeconomic processes, and to inform wider structures of music history, offer potential. Such histories might focus on the experience of individuals and groups in order to understand the larger social mass. One group ripe for such treatment is the professional rank and file of instrumental players, a sector of Western music history that has generally been left in obscurity.

By necessity, this type of endeavor requires the sustenance of traditional empirical historical methods to provide reliable data about people, societies, institutions, and their economic and cultural condition. History that is based merely on ideas and that is contemptuous of the need for a relentless pursuit and sensitive scrutiny of sources is not really history at all—it is historical fiction. Microhistorians demonstrate meticulous concern about questions of selectivity and significance, and also "respect the strictest positivist standards" of source evaluation (Muir and Ruggiero, 1991, xii), but they use the information in new and highly imaginative ways. However, such approaches to the social history of music should also imply a setting aside of the goal of cool objectivity in favor of open advocacy—a refreshing tendency often found in gender and gay studies in music. Empiricist data are not self-revealing. They require and demand clear mediation and forthright advocacy. What is needed now are social histories of music that are both intimate and red in tooth and claw. E. P. Thompson always wore his subjectivity on his sleeve. His work engaged with the type of grand narrative that I now suggest is inappropriate for social histories of music, but his style and manner are difficult to quarrel with. In 1966 he commented on a passage in the preface to Volume 6 of the *Cambridge Economic History of Europe*, in which the editors signaled that a distant future volume would "perhaps … deal with the social changes involved with the modern world." "In that 'perhaps'," Thompson observed, "we have the poor bloody infantry of the industrial revolution, without whose labour and skill it would have remained an untested hypothesis." It is a pity that Thompson wrote nothing about music.

Further Reading

Arnold, John H. 2000. *History: A very short introduction.* Oxford: Oxford Univ. Press.

Carr, Edward H. 1961. *What is history?* New York: St Martin's Press.

Ehrlich, Cyril. 1985. *The music profession in Britain since the eighteenth century.* Oxford: Clarendon Press.

Elton, Geoffrey R. 1967. *The practice of history.* London: Methuen.

Evans, Richard J. 1997. *In defence of history.* London: Granta Books.

Hunt, Lynn A., ed. 1989. *The new cultural history.* Berkeley: Univ. of California Press.

Jenkins, Keith. 1995. *On "What is history?": From Carr and Elton to Rorty and White.* New York: Routledge.

Leppert, Richard, and Susan McClary. 1987. *Music and society: The politics of composition, performance and reception.* Cambridge, U.K.: Cambridge Univ. Press.

Levine, Lawrence W. 1988. *Highbrow/lowbrow: The emergence of cultural hierarchy in America.* Cambridge, Mass.: Harvard Univ. Press.

Muir, Edward, and Guido Ruggiero, eds. 1991. *Microhistory and the lost peoples of Europe.* Translated by E. Branch. Baltimore: Johns Hopkins Univ. Press.

Rosselli, John. 1991. *Music and musicians in nineteenth-century Italy.* Portland, Ore.: Amadeus Press.

PART II

Issues and Debates

CHAPTER 13

Musical Autonomy Revisited

DAVID CLARKE

> Attempts to annul what is contradictory in the development of art,
> by playing off a "moralizing" against an "autonomous" art, miss the
> point because they overlook what is liberating in autonomous and
> what is regressive in moralizing art.
>
> —Peter Bürger

Exposition

The concept of musical autonomy has been having a hard time of it lately.
Be it from quarters sociological, new-historicist, or feminist (the list goes
on, but this gives the gist), the word is out that to construe music purely
as an art for its own sake is to perpetuate a discredited ideology. Charges
against the autonomy concept are several. It is bourgeois and hegemonic:
it wants to present its socially and historically specific paradigm as universal and as the measure against which all other musics are evaluated (so distorting our reception of popular, vernacular, and non-Western musics). It
is reifying and atrophying: its promotion of music as meaningful purely in
its own terms, allegedly floating free from historical and social contingencies, underwrites a canon of putatively timeless masterworks—the fos-
silized museum culture of classical music. It is patriarchal and sexist: until
recently this canon has deflected both feminist critique and female participation because, on the one hand, its music, putatively formed only out of
its own stuff, denies the influence of anything so worldly as gender

159

(McClary 1991, 55), while, on the other hand, in the record of actual social practice, the principal genres of autonomous music—symphony, sonata, string quartet—and their associated aesthetic of greatness have been the prerogative of male composers (Scott 1994). Carrying the burden of so many sins, then, it is only to be expected that the autonomous music has found it necessary to commit suicide (Chua 2000, 221–23, 266–75), only to find itself "as dead as Elvis," surviving like the inert cinders of a formerly living practice (Kramer 1995).

Look around you, though, and these critical generalities get muddied in the complex particulars of empirical life. Consider, for example, how for a season in parts of Britain free instrumental lessons in schools and a flourishing culture of local youth orchestras held out the possibility of breaking the middle-class monopoly on access to the practice of classical music (and its associated autonomist aesthetic). Consider too the game of cultural negotiation required of a schoolkid learning, say, the violin under this initiative, who has to juxtapose a classical musical practice—with its connotations of effeminacy—alongside a youth culture infused by conspicuous mass musical consumption. From this perspective, what is hegemonic and what is emancipatory, what is atrophied and what is vital, may look a little different. Readers will have probably suspected an autobiographical element at work here; but the intention is not to be anecdotal. Rather I want to suggest that the social and cultural mediations acquired by autonomous classical music in the grand sweep of history may be open to redefinition and revaluation, and that this possibility may be prompted by, among other things, personal and local histories that don't entirely square with the characterizations of autonomy in recent critical accounts.

In advancing the possibility of other critical positions, however, I don't wish to institutionalize a simplistic for-or-against model of argument or allegiance. It seems to me to be as futile to deny that autonomous musical practices are ideologically problematic as it is to claim that they no longer have valuable cultural work to do. I am more inclined to argue for bringing these contradictions to a fuller consciousness and considering how they can be worked through within our contemporary cultural situation. This is a position broadly analogous with Frederic Jameson's refusal to come down squarely on one side or the other of the modernism–postmodernism debate, citing instead the idea of a "historical and dialectic analysis" which "cannot afford the impoverished luxury of . . . absolute moralizing judgements: the dialectic is 'beyond good and evil' in the sense of some easy taking of sides" (1988, 381). Part of that dialectical consciousness certainly involves heeding Lydia Goehr's call for a revaluation of the autonomous artwork's alleged "universal and absolute validity" (1992, 273)—in other words putting the autonomy aesthetic in its place, as one musical species among many. But I want to argue for a more dynamic, frictional view of musical autonomy within this pluralist situation: as a modern concept that may still have important critical currency within a postmodern cultural landscape. In this sense, then, Jameson's framework is indeed relevant (and I mention it again below), as is his call for a historically informed understanding of the situation.

Development

The historiography of autonomous music—music emancipated from ritual or ceremonial function; music whose meaning is not dependent on an accompanying text or imagery—is itself a site of polemic, not least regarding dating (cf. Strohm 2000; Goehr 2000). These differences notwithstanding, I pursue below one of the dominant narratives of autonomous music, which locates its emergence around 1800. This situates aesthetic autonomy within the wider conditions of *modernity* in which—following the Enlightenment's cultivation of Reason—rationality, morality, and sensuality separate into radically independent modalities of knowledge (Bernstein 1992, 5–6). There is space here only to sketch some of the key points of this history, but more detailed accounts may be found in writings referenced in the process.

What also needs stressing—something implicit in this account so far—is the potential for slippage between the idea of autonomy and other concepts that while not synonymous nevertheless overlap semantically. Start talking about such autonomous forms as the symphony and sonata, for example, and the concept of a musical *work* (as opposed to the n-dozenth piece exemplifying a genre) lurks not far behind; and this notion in turn is something peculiar to, though not a sole defining criterion of, *Western classical music* (Horn 2000). On a broader canvas still, the idea of autonomy is difficult to unhitch from the idea of the aesthetic as such—that strong concept of art (Art with a capital A) that differentiates it from merely socially functional practices. And then there is the concept of *absolute music* (and its associated notion of *formalism*), often treated as interchangeable with the idea of autonomous instrumental music, but in fact, like all the other terms mentioned, arising within its own historically and culturally specific discourse. In one way or another all these terms contribute to a constellation around the musical autonomy idea. Indeed it is arguably their convergence in the period following the Enlightenment that defines what I term the *strong* autonomy concept. (And I later consider whether new configurations of the idea could be related to a dispersal and redistribution of these elements.)

The roots of the concept lie in changing constructions of the musical meaning, specifically the meaning of *instrumental music*, at the turn of the eighteenth and nineteenth centuries. Already among the Enlightenment *philosophes* we can detect a move away from previous understandings of instrumental music as *mimetic*—as emulating sounds in nature, or imitative of the human voice itself, or an analogue for rhetorical oratory—toward a view that such music may be its own justification. For example, the encyclopaedist Marmontel writes: "If through a veil of sound [instrumental] music allows the listener to see and feel what he pleases depending on his individual state of mind at the concert then it has served its purpose" (quoted in Ford 1991, 42.) For Kant such a "play of sensations" ([1790] 1952, 184) put music at the top of the merely *agreeable* arts but at the bottom of the more highly rated *fine* arts (p. 195). However, other theorists writing around the turn of the nineteenth century developed a concept of fine art that, more than just accommodating instrumental music under its banner, would eventually make it its definitive paradigm.

This predominantly Germanophone line of thought belongs to the moment of early romanticism or idealism—related but not identical philosophical–aesthetic movements (cf. Goehr 1992, 148–75; Bonds 1997, 389ff.). Key writers include Wackenroder, Tieck, Novalis, Schelling, and E. T. A. Hoffmann. But there were numerous others, among them, Christian Gottfried Körner, who in an essay published in 1795 posited a new level to which a composer might elevate music: "he should *idealize* his material. . . . he should . . . present the infinite as an intuition [*Anschauung*], which outside of art is permitted merely as thought [*zu denken*]" (quoted in Bonds 1997, 402 n. 46; my translation). Similar sentiments are found in Hoffmann's famous 1810 review of Beethoven's Fifth Symphony: "Music reveals to man an unknown realm, a world quite separate from the outer sensual world surrounding him, a world in which he leaves behind all feelings circumscribed by intellect in order to embrace the inexpressible" (Hoffmann [1810] 1989, 236).

Taken together, Körner's and Hoffmann's statements suggest a contract between composer and listener—and their mutual empowerment. The lofty responsibilities ascribed to the former by Körner (entirely consistent with romantic notions of genius) are reciprocated in the equally committed attentiveness assumed of the latter in Hoffmann's comments. What Rose Subotnik has identified (and critiqued) as the "structural listening" (Subotnik 1991, 277–83) assumed of art music today is already evident in idealized notions of listening promoted by the early romantics—for example, by Wackenroder in 1792 as "the most attentive observations of the notes and their progression" (cited in Bonds 1997, 394). But, given Bonds's claim that "it was not a change in the contemporary repertory that was transporting listeners to a higher realm, but rather a change in the perceived nature of aesthetic cognition," it seems unlikely that listeners were propelled toward the absolute merely by their own perceptual projections: something was also happening to the work of music itself.

Indeed it was becoming just that—a work: not merely a transient event in sound, but some *thing* with the potential to endure, a textlike object for "reverent contemplation" [*Andacht*] (Herder's phrase of 1800: see Bonds 1997, 410). This is evident in the changing appearance and status of the symphony—the most exemplary and public genre of "independent music" at this time (Dahlhaus, 1989a, 10–14). From its beginnings in Enlightenment concert life as a rococo genre amounting to little more than a curtain-raiser—literally an overture—the symphony had become, by the end of the eighteenth century, something composed on a larger, more complex scale (see Zaslaw 1989, 517–25). The last symphonies of Mozart composed in 1788 would provide as good an illustration as any of what Friedrich Schlegel may have had in mind when a decade later he rhetorically posed the question: "Must not pure instrumental music itself create a text of its own? And does not its theme get developed, confirmed, varied, and contrasted like the object of meditation in a philosophical sequence of ideas?" (quoted in Dahlhaus 1989a, 107). Music can attain the status of a philosophical discourse, Schlegel implies, through an affinity with philosophy's own discursive medium, language. A striking paradox: music becomes most essentially itself ("pure ... music") through its mimesis of something other than itself;[1] it extends toward the infinite by intending into itself.

A further paradox ensues: Music's very self-referentiality, its articulation of the linguistically unsignifiable, elicits a whole new style of highly

---

1. In Clarke (1996a) I explore in greater detail how music might acquire an autonomous dimension when its own structural processes achieve certain homologies with linguistic structures.

poeticized writing about music from critics of the time. As Bonds points out, this paradox need not be perplexing if the tendency to rhapsodize poetically is seen as a free subjective response to the experience of musical immanence, and not as an attempt to translate into language what a piece "really" means (Bonds 1997, 413ff.). It was only later in the century with Eduard Hanslick's polemical conception of *absolute music* (a term used pejoratively by his adversary Wagner, but which Hanslick adopted and sought to transvalue in his own riposte) that the suppression of such subjective poetic responses began to be institutionalized. Hanslick's rigorously objective, formalist conception of music—of which "it is impossible to form any but a musical conception, [and which] can be comprehended and enjoyed only for and in itself" ([1885] 1974 , 70)—could be seen to be close to that assumed in many music-analytical methodologies of the nineteenth and twentieth centuries. Yet while Hanslick's understanding of absolute music had paradoxically stamped out any reference to the absolute, this was only achieved by cutting certain poetic, extramusical references from the first (1854) edition of his treatise *The Beautiful in Music* (Dahlhaus 1989a, 28–29; Bonds 1997, 414–17) so that subsequent editions established a greater critical distance from exponents of program music such as Liszt, and from Wagner's total artwork, which sought a synthesis of musical and literary content.

Retransition

From the time that Kant ascribed to it the character of "purposiveness without a purpose," the independent realm of the aesthetic can be seen as possessing an implicit political dimension. Music's very longing for an "other" world transcending the here and now in fact bears critical witness to the historical and cultural conditions it disdains to acknowledge. Stephen Rumph (1995) interprets Hoffmann's music criticism in just such a light: while Hoffmann claims that for musicians "our kingdom is not of this world," the poetic imagery he deploys in his review of Beethoven's Fifth and other writings alludes to the very real political conditions of a Prussia under Napoleonic occupation (see also Chua 1999, 8–11). Similarly, Goehr explores the notion of a "double-sided autonomy" in which the formalist properties of music were attractive to romantic composers of various persuasions precisely because, having "no meaning to speak of," music could be used to envision an alternative cultural and political order—while escaping the scrutiny of the censor (Goehr 1993, 186–88). And for bourgeois consumers in a modernizing society, characterized by increasing scientific rationalization, growing industrialization, and an associated market economy, autonomous art offered a world of imaginative experience that was Other to the means– end orientation and commodity production of the empirical social world (Paddison 1996, 38). Moreover, as romantic hopes for social transformation faded after the failed revolutions of 1848, the realm of the aesthetic increasingly came to represent a retreat from life (arguably still a kind of political gesture). This moment coincided with Hanslick's formalist agenda, and was followed by the Wagnerphile French symbolists' search for a hermetic poetry that would emulate music's apparent disconnection from the everyday world of things.

We now approach the moment of aesthetic modernism at the turn of the twentieth century, when, decades before the critiques of scholars, the domain of the aesthetic acquired a critical self-consciousness of its own ideology while asserting its continuing social necessity. The result was a situation in which, as Adorno puts it, "art revolts against its essential concepts while at the same time being inconceivable without them" (1984, 465). The prismatic distortion of form in Stravinsky and the distension of tonal connections beyond the breaking point in Schoenberg's quest for emancipated dissonance are both manifestations of the immanent critique of the very devices musical art used to construct an autonomous domain for itself. Repudiating historically established codes of communication, autonomous music now denies its bourgeois consumers illusory solace from reality. Further, in the multiple serial works of the 1950s, such as Pierre Boulez's *Structures 1a*, autonomous music reaches an absolute of objective musical formalism in which total structural integrity is achieved at the price of maximum indifference to sensuous appearance and subjective enjoyment. This extreme is iconic of high modernism's resistance to the world of commodities: contemporaneously with the rise of rock 'n' roll, such music now radically asserts, "under the guise of a self-referential, formal autonomy, . . . its absolute difference from popular musics" (Born 2000, 16). On the one hand, then, there is a high modernist practice that retains its purity as an autonomous art by moving to an aesthetic vanishing point where only a minority care to venture; on the other hand, there is a mass cultural practice assimilated to its role as part of a market economy and embracing its mundaneness, its worldliness. This polarized cultural condition—what Andreas Huyssen (1986) has termed *The Great Divide*—forms the context against which any revaluation of the autonomy concept must be considered.

Recapitulation/Development II

We are too knowing these days not to recognize the paradox of "independent music" as a historically situated cultural category. What is necessary, I argue, is fully to embrace the dialectics of the situation. I don't think we need regard the sentiment behind Scott Burnham's statement that "[o]ne might . . . claim that we *need* to understand music as music, as an autonomous language, if we want to grant it the power to speak of other things" (2001, 215; emphasis in original) as conciliatory liberalism. Rather, this might support the dialectical notion of an autonomous *moment* of musical signification within the larger interplay of social and cultural codes that bring that signification to its full articulation. Goehr's depiction of musical autonomy as *double-edged* (as an inwardly oriented resistance to outer political circumstances) might be worked up to its full tension; indeed something cognate is implicit in Lucy Green's dialectic of inherent and delineated musical meaning. For Green music is inherently meaningful on one level by dint of its temporal organization of sounds. Nevertheless those sounds do not point "only to themselves": on another level they also "point outwards from music and towards its role as a social product"; they delineate their situation within "a web of meanings in the social world" (1988, 27–8). What's also interesting in this formulation is that its application is not specific to any particular kind of music; classical and popular styles could equally be considered to operate both facets of this dialectic. Likewise, Adam Krims, in arguing forcibly for rap music's consideration as a cultural formation (and indeed for music theory as a subdivision of cultural studies), also argues for its identity-constituting processes as being played out in the sonic particularity of the songs themselves: "One must, at some point, work through [rap's] musical poetics . . . , not to aestheticize it or abstract it away from social life, but *precisely to factor in that the people one is studying are taking the music seriously, as music*—and that their cultural engagement is mediated by that 'musical' level" (2000, 40).

Hand-in-hand with the autonomy concept's double-edgedness, then, comes the possibility of its *dispersal.* If we are open to thinking of autonomy as dialectically enmeshed in music's social and cultural formations, so, conversely, we might also speculate whether elements of its constellation might also be recognizable within other genres of music, including those usually documented more explicitly for their sociocultural significance. This could be figured as a loosening or unbonding of various elements of the strong autonomy concept (the cognate features outlined earlier—work concept, high-art aesthetic, and so on). For example, under this dispersed paradigm we might endorse the possibility of an autonomous moment in Indian classical music—which demands an attentive listenership, and reflects a strong focus on its own musical processes, but which, crucially, carries no concept of a musical work;[2] or in rock music—which places emphasis on composition (though not in isolation from performer and performance), and whose aesthetic values include "seriousness," subjective authenticity, and autonomy, but which clearly (except for progressive rock) does not seek "high art" status as such (Keightley 2001, 127–39). Another case might be certain subgenres of present-day dance music concerned largely with "purely musical" sounds, such as Detroit techno or garage. Most obviously a celebration of collective hedonism, a resource for identification as, variably, black, white, young, or gay (or some combination, mediation, or blurring of these categories), this musical genre also contains ample possibility for celebrating creativity through its formations and transformations of sounds in time, its play of sounds across actual and virtual spaces (perhaps a quite literal example of "sounding forms in motion"—as Hanslick aphoristically characterized absolute music).

Lest this last seem an anachronistic (or, worse, imperialistic) projection of a nineteenth-century concept onto present-day practices, possible links between these two conjunctures are suggested by historical accounts of the cultural mediation of music technology. David Toop (1994) refers to the "labyrinthine entwinements of culture" that connect present-day electronic evocations of "possible worlds" to scores such as Satie's *Parade* of 1917, with its evocation of machine noises, and to the player piano technology and other "musical automata" of the earlier twentieth century. Such connections would find corroboration in research by Anna Sofie Christiansen (2001) into the aesthetic discourses that mediated the reception of mechanical music in Weimar Germany.[3] Christiansen describes how, in writings of the 1920s, mechanical instruments such as

---

2. Martin Clayton's equivocation as to whether "cultural ideology, patterns and norms may be reflected in [in this case Indian] music" is not unconnected with this argument (Clayton 2000, 5–7, 10–11).

3. I am grateful to Matthew Sansom for drawing my attention to Toop's sleevenote and the Warp album that it accompanies; and to Anna Sofie Christiansen for kindly making her unpublished paper available to me.

player pianos were seen to hold the potential to attain a more absolute, objectivized relationship between composition and performance by cutting out the expressive mediation of the performer to attain a kind of transcendent piano playing "in itself" (the Kantian *an sich*) or an idealized form of expression, an absolute immediacy between the geometric patterns of the piano roll and "the sounding forms in motion" that resulted (an allusion to Hanslick in a review by Alfred Einstein of a mechanical concert). This unexpected convergence of twentieth-century technology and nineteenth-century idealism offers a suggestive gloss on Toop's speculations regarding the potential of present-day electronica to recover some remnant of spirituality within a world of "mechanisation and commerce."

Of course such a recontextualization of the idea of absolute music does not make it any less ideological. Simon Reynolds for one is entertainingly disparaging of the kind of dance subgenres found on the Warp label for which Toop writes. Such "'electronic listening music' or 'new complexity techno': the particularly use-less, uselessly peculiar sonic *objets d'art* constructed by the likes of Autechre and Christian Vogel" is pilloried as nothing more than "small boys playing with tekno toys, lost in their own little world of chromatics and texture and contour" (Reynolds 1998, 90–91). Reynolds's spleen is vented at the complicity of dance genres in promoting a contradictory aesthetics in which radical political potential is simultaneously melded with and undermined by a depoliticized escapism: this is "music of resistance and acquiescence, utopian idealism and nihilistic hedonism" (p. 92). While clearly a different figuration of an idealist escape from the empirical world than that described by the likes of Hoffmann (with underpinnings now perhaps more pharmacological than philosophical), the situation is not dissimilar—and prompts similar critique, albeit now from the standpoint of a postmodern rather than post-Enlightenment culture. What is more important however, is to see this debate now being played out on the other side of "the great divide" between classical and popular culture.

Reynolds's comments seem to tell of a frustration at the blunting of the double-edged potential of dance music. On a broader canvas this might be symptomatic of a postmodern condition, in which individuals' engagement with culture involves a degree of acquiescence toward its basis in a market-driven economy dominated by the commodity—an acquiescence that in its most radical postmodern guise might take the form of outright celebration (emblematically, learning from Las Vegas, [Venturi et al. 1977]). If, as Frederic Jameson suggests, "we are *within* the culture of postmodernism to the point where its facile repudiation is as impossible as an equally facile celebration of it is complacent and corrupt" (1988, 381), this is nevertheless not to preclude fostering a consciousness of resistance from within. And it is here that cultural forms of all kinds have a role to play—a role to which the epithet "modernist" might still be appropriate, and a role in which a critically aware autonomist practice might still have something to contribute. On the one hand this might mean the ongoing "classical" modernism of a Harrison Birtwistle or Brian Ferneyhough—a modernism that, while getting long in the tooth, retains a necessary critical bite. On the other hand, and pursuing the notion of an autonomy dispersed across "the great divide," we might also look for resistance within popular musical genres (Bloomfield 1993) in which a reflexive, creative use of sonic materials cuts into our normative social consciousness, and provides a phenomenal space in which we might for a moment experience the world differently, without simply becoming amnesiac about its problematics.

The music of postdance composer David Kosten, produced under the alias Faultline, offers a glimpse of such a possibility (and a constructive response to Reynolds's critique). Belonging less to the genre of crossover music, the Faultline album *Closer Colder* (1999) is compelling more for the way it invites oppositional categories and then deconstructs them—dualisms such as classical/popular, modernist/postmodernist, physical/mental, and autonomous/referential. The groove of the CD's opening track, "Awake," is made from spluttering, distorted splinters of sounds that invoke a harsh, desolate postindustrial landscape, over which is mixed the periodic entries of effulgent singing cellos—the humane embrace of the maternal and personal. In similarly non- (or only partially) synthetic fashion, the urges to dance, to listen, and to reflect are copresent but not coterminous. We are simultaneously drawn inward, to the artifice of the music's own poetic strategies, and oriented outwards to the social world referenced by its samples (including, on the final track, "Partyline Honey," a telephone sex chatline); intrinsic and extrinsic musical meanings are rendered utterly permeable to each other.

Coda

My intention with these few pointers is emphatically not to argue for so-called "intelligent dance music" as a monolithic paradigm for some would-be idea of "new autonomy." But there are alternatives between making a fetish of the autonomy idea and wanting to bury it; it is imaginable that (borrowing Peter Bürger's phraseology) what is truthful about autonomous art, its "apartness ... from the praxis of life," need not lead to untruth, "the hypostatization of the fact," the occlusion of the social and historical determination of that apartness (Bürger 1984, 46). Hence I invoke dance and postdance genres here as possible examples on the way to envisioning a more mutable, pliable construction of autonomy, adapted to our relativized, postmodern frame, oblivious neither to other determinants of musical experience—words, dancing, images, bodies, technology, and so on—nor to the social medium in which it operates. In societies whose history has rendered them less than fully congenial places for all their members, the autonomous moment available to music—embodying the notion of something valuable in and for itself—might still offer a moment of subjective resistance against social domination or means–end oriented rationality. It may still serve as a reminder that, to paraphrase Adorno (Jarvis 1998, 216), "that which is" need not be "*all* that there is."

Further Reading

Biddle, Ian D. 1995. Autonomy, ontology and the ideal: Music theory and philosophical aesthetics in early nineteenth-century German thought. Ph.D. thesis, University of Newcastle upon Tyne.

Dahlhaus, Carl. 1982. *Esthetics of music.* Translated by William W. Austin. Cambridge, U.K.: Cambridge Univ. Press.

———. 1989b. The metaphysic of instrumental music. Pp. 88–96 in *Nineteenth-century music.* Translated by J. Bradford Robinson. Berkeley: Univ. of California Press.

Kivy, Peter. 1990. *Music alone: Philosophical reflections on the purely musical experience.* Ithaca, N.Y.: Cornell Univ. Press.

Neubauer, John. 1988. *The emancipation of music from language.* New Haven, Conn.: Yale Univ. Press.

Scruton, Roger. 2001. Absolute music. Pp. 36–37 in *The new Grove dictionary of music and musicians.* 2d ed. Edited by Stanley Sadie. London: Grove's Dictionary.

Stravinsky, Igor. 1942. *Poetics of music: In the form of six lessons.* Cambridge, Mass.: Harvard Univ. Press.

Treitler, Leo. 1989. Mozart and the idea of absolute music. Pp. 176–214 in *Music and the historical imagination.* Cambridge, Mass.; London: Harvard Univ. Press.

Wolff, Janet. 1987. The ideology of autonomous art. Pp. 1–12 in *Music and society: The politics of composition, performance and reception.* Edited by Richard Leppert and Susan McClary. Cambridge, U.K.: Cambridge Univ. Press.

CHAPTER 14

Textual Analysis or Thick Description?

JEFF TODD TITON

Comparative musicology, a forerunner of ethnomusicology, was the first academic discipline to undertake a systematic cultural study of music. The founders asked grand questions: How did music originate, and how did it grow and spread among the world's peoples? How could musical affinities among varied human groups reveal the paths of migrations and diffusions? What did the variety of musical instruments found throughout the world signify, and how could they be classified and compared? The comparative musicologists of the early twentieth century borrowed scientific methods from linguistics and evolutionary biology but failed to achieve the success of their colleagues in those disciplines, and in the 1960s and 1970s their project exhausted itself in Alan Lomax's cantometrics (Lomax 1968; Lomax and Berkowitz 1972; Lomax et al. 1978). Today, the cultural study of music asks different questions, ones that bear on the relation of music to region, race, class, gender, politics, ethnicity, belief, identity, money, power, and the production of knowledge. Our questions concern music as lived experience, as commodity, as social practice, and as cultural symbol. No scholar has had more impact on ethnomusicological representations of people making music during the last quarter century than the anthropologist Clifford Geertz, whose methodology involving "thick description" of cultural "texts" moved the discipline away from scientific method and toward the interpretive practices of the humanities. By incorporating textual analysis into thick descriptions, and by representing   *171* people making music using hypertext and multimedia, ethnomusicologists have gone beyond Geertz's methodology to the point where readers of ethnomusicological works can now experience what it is like to be an ethnomusicologist involved in the cultural production of knowledge about music.

Ethnomusicologists are not, of course, the only academics producing knowledge about music. The same can be said of musicologists and of scholars in the discipline of cultural studies. As an ethnomusicologist, however, I write as a representative of my discipline on the ways in which we have come to view the cultural study of music. Whereas traditional musicologists regard "culture" in the Arnoldian sense of "getting to know . . . the best which has been thought and said," we regard culture in the anthropological sense as the learned inheritance that makes one people's way of thinking and doing different from another's. Traditional musicology understands "serious" music as not only good for a person's intellectual development and emotional maturity, but also as locked in combat with other, lesser musics motivated by the cheap rewards offered by industrial and postindustrial society. For the traditional musicologist, the cultivation of classical music and the other fine arts offers a defense against the commodified popular music carried by mass media; it offers a means of refinement and civilization amidst the hellish modern industrial state. Ethnomusicologists do not make such value judgments; indeed, by focusing on everything but Western art music (and, lately, even that) we invoke a cultural relativism in which all musics have a legitimate claim to be understood: first in the terms that their own culture understands them, and then in terms of their contribution to our understanding of music as a worldwide phenomenon.

Challenges to traditional musicology's values have also arisen from within. A generation of musicologists influenced by cultural studies and practicing the "new musicology" is enlarging the predominantly male canon to include women composers and composers who are people of color; is broadening the scope of musicology's subject to include jazz, Broadway show tunes, and other formerly déclassé musics; and is challenging traditional musicology's historical and theoretical procedures on grounds of race, class, and gender discrimination. Much music research in cultural studies takes place in popular music, where youth are viewed not simply as passive victims of corporate musical manipulation, but also as cultures of active participants in listener–fan communities that, paradoxically, resist and to a degree co-opt the values of mass culture and corporate capitalism while consuming their products. Themes of cultural studies involve not only class and the nature of the popular, but also gender, race, systems of power and behavior in the face of it, centers and margins, commodification, and a host of related issues (e.g., Shepherd 1991). Cultural studies and the new musicology pose challenges to ethnomusicologists also. While modern ethnomusicologists have largely abandoned claims of scientific objectivity, most have not abandoned ethnographic fieldwork, even in the face of challenges from scholars in cultural studies and anthropology who critique its colonialist heritage and challenge the very concept of "the field" and "the other." Rather, we have attempted to reform the cultural study of music based upon changing ideas of subject/object, self/other, inside/outside, field/fieldwork, author/authority, and the application of ethnomusicology in the public interest (Barz and Cooley 1997; *Ethnomusicology* 36:3 [1992]). Here Geertz's work in the representation and interpretation of culture has been very influential and yet, at the same time, very necessary to move beyond.

Geertz's intellectual project is to reconfigure cultural anthropology through redefining its key concept, culture, as an assemblage of texts: not texts as words on a page, but texts in a larger sense, as any objects of interpretation (Titon 1995b). "Thick Description: Toward an Interpretive Theory of Culture" (Geertz 1973), "Deep Play: Notes on the Balinese Cockfight" (Geertz [1972] 1973), "From the Native's Point of View: On the Nature of Anthropological Understanding" (Geertz [1974] 1977), and "Blurred Genres" (Geertz [1980] 1983) have proven to be the key essays. In them Geertz states, refines, and illustrates the idea that culture is not like an organism whose structures and functions are to be analyzed; nor like a game with tacitly understood rules governing behavior; nor like a drama, with stages, actors, and performances; but, rather, culture is a system of symbols embedded in social action. Now, drawing on the French philosopher Paul Ricoeur's idea that "meaningful action" could be understood as a "text"—that is, "read" and interpreted as if it were a text—Geertz declares that this symbol system, residing in social action, is in fact a great text; that "the culture of a people is an ensemble of texts, themselves ensembles, which the anthropologist strains to *read* over the shoulders of those to whom they properly belong" ([1972] 1973, 452; my italics). Geertz asserts, further, that cultural anthropologists are not only readers but also, fundamentally, writers; that is, they "inscribe social discourse" and turn a passing event into an "account which exists in its inscriptions and can be reconsulted" (1973, 19). Reading, interpreting, and writing as a model may not seem remarkable at first, but it was a cry for a humanities-based approach to the work of cultural anthropology, and was very much opposed to the then-dominant model based on the natural sciences (hypothesis, observations, measurements, conclusions).

Geertz's theory of "thick description" follows from these assertions. *Thick description* is best understood as a method by which to apprehend and interpret cultural texts. Borrowing this term from the English philosopher Gilbert Ryle, Geertz explains how often a subtle and complex understanding is required to grasp the meaning of even the simplest act: in Ryle's thought experiment, the act is the blink of an eye (Geertz 1973, 6). Is this an involuntary twitch, asks Ryle, or is it a wink? And if a wink, is it a conspiratory signal, or is it perhaps a faked wink meant to deceive a third party? Ryle thus distinguishes between "thin description" (the blink described as a contraction of an eyelid) and "thick description" (the wink understood as "practicing a burlesque of a friend faking a wink to deceive an innocent into thinking a conspiracy is in motion"). To put this into Geertz's terminology, thick description renders a more satisfactory "reading" (interpretation) of the "text" (the wink).

For Geertz, then, thick description is what anthropologists ought to do: unpack the meanings of the symbols that reside in texts and comprise a culture. This involves understanding the layers, the "multiplicity of complex conceptual structures" that the anthropologist "must contrive somehow first to grasp and then to render" in writing (1973, 6–7, 10). No easy task, even in one's own society, let alone among complete strangers. Although Geertz has published a number of ethnographic works, his essay on the Balinese cockfight, which appeared at about the same time as his groundbreaking theoretical articles, is usually taken as his case in point, his best exercise in thick description. The essay is a tour de force, a dazzlingly persuasive, densely detailed, dandily written account of how cockfights in Bali symbolize much in Balinese culture and character. The essay contains elaborate descriptions of the cocks, the fighting, the wagering, how wagering symbolizes social relations, and the way Balinese beliefs and character can be read in the varieties of behavior exhibited around the cockfight; it is impossible to summarize. I only restate my admiration for it below and comment on a few aspects of it as I begin to tug at the loose ends of Geertz's enterprise—not in an attempt to unravel it all, although I do unravel it some; but rather to show how it might be redone in a more persuasive way.

One of the striking early things in Geertz's cockfight essay is his story of how he and his wife gained community acceptance by "getting caught, or almost caught, in a vice raid." Geertz and his wife were observing a cock-fight; the police raided it; everyone ran away; Geertz and wife (alas, she is never named; she always appears as "my wife") joined a fleeing Balinese man and wound up in his courtyard. The Balinese man's "wife, who had apparently been through this sort of thing before," set a table, the two couples sat down and composed themselves, and they presented a united front when the police arrived. The next day "the village was a completely different world for us," Geertz wrote, and they were "suddenly the center of all attention, the object of a great outpouring of warmth, interest, and most especially, amusement.... In Bali, to be teased is to be accepted. It was the turning point as far as our relationship to the community was concerned, and we were quite literally 'in.'" The incident made it possible for Geertz to achieve "that mysterious necessity of anthropological fieldwork, rapport.... It led to a sudden and unusually complete acceptance into a society extremely difficult for outsiders to penetrate. It gave me the kind of immediate, inside-view grasp of an aspect of 'peasant mentality' that anthropologists not fortunate enough to flee headlong with their subjects from armed authorities normally do not get" ([1972] 1973, 416).

This charming and clever narrative functions to establish Geertz's ethnographic authority as someone who is "in," who is "accepted," who has established "rapport" with, and therefore has good access to, the people and culture under study. Yet, a little later, in his essay "From the Native's Point of View," Geertz dissociated himself from those social scientists who, following George Herbert Mead, advocated rapport as a means toward empathetic understanding. For Geertz, "Understanding the form and pressure of ... natives' inner lives is more like grasping a proverb, catching an allusion, seeing a joke—or, as I have suggested, reading a poem—than it is like achieving communion" ([1974] 1977, 492). From that point in his essay, he is enmeshed in thick description of the cockfight. By the end of the piece we learn that the cockfight is a "paradigmatic human event" in which "the Balinese forms and discovers his temperament and his society's temper at the same time" (1973, 450–51). He is so thorough, so smart, so graceful, and so reassuring that the reader is lulled, and does not worry that Geertz's is the only authoritative voice speaking from within the inscribed account. Geertz very seldom quotes his Balinese informants, and when he does it usually appears in a footnote, well below the level of the discourse inscribed as thick description. That is, although we are given to understand that Geertz has conversed with the Balinese about cockfights, the kind of meaning he is after is presumably not something that most Balinese would be able to articulate.

Upon reflection, one wonders what the Balinese think of Geertz's take on the cockfight. We never know, and he implies that it does not matter.

For many ethnomusicologists in the twenty-first century, it does matter. Suppose that a Balinese wrote an account of North American culture based on the "paradigmatic human event" of the professional football game. As a ritual, Sunday afternoon football in the United States surely rivals the Balinese cockfight in rich cultural symbolism. Ritual violence and mock war drama; hierarchy and racism (the Balinese might remark on the preponderance of black athletes at every position except quarterback and head coach); gambling and organized crime; spectating and various kinds of vicarious behavior and misbehavior in the stands; sports talk shows—all this and more would be grist for the symbol mill, as football becomes a quasi-religious ritual akin to the Balinese cockfight in which, to paraphrase Geertz, "the American forms and discovers his temperament and his society's temper at the same time."

Well, some Americans. Males, principally, and presumably (though not entirely) of a certain social, educational, and economic class. Surely not university professors. But note that this interpretation is not something that a Balinese has supplied; as a participant in the culture, my culture, I have articulated it on the basis of a few seconds' thought. A Balinese ethnographer would come up with something different. Of interest, then, would be to show the Balinese and his or her American informants in dialogue over the interpretation of football. Interpretive accounts and inscriptions thus become multivoiced, and meaning in them often turns out to be incomplete as well as contested. This is the direction in which ethnomusicological ethnography has moved "thick description" in the past quarter century.

In reconfiguring thick description to include dialogue and to show the process of interpretation proceeding through fieldwork into reflection and inscription, a more engaged relationship is obtained between the ethnomusicological ethnographer and those people whose music is under study. Words like *rapport* and *informant* and *interview* do not always suffice to describe it; they give way to words like *friend* and *conversation*. Indeed, researchers enter into friendships that require reciprocal obligations. In his ethnographic book on music in Bulgaria, Timothy Rice writes of his long-time friendship with Kostadin, a bagpiper and his principal "informant," who became, among other things, Rice's bagpipe teacher. The relationship made Rice understand that just as he expected certain things of Kostadin, so Kostadin had invested a good deal of expectation in Rice's study of the bagpipe (Rice 1994). In becoming bimusical (i.e., in becoming competent in a second music) Rice understood that Kostadin was his teacher in more ways than one (Titon 1995a). In his ethnographic work on "sound and sentiment" among the Kaluli in Papua New Guinea, Steven Feld discusses the reception of his book among the people he wrote about. Just as the Balinese cockfight is paradigmatic for Geertz, among the Kaluli the myth of the boy who turns into a muni bird is paradigmatic for Feld. Yet Feld reports that his Kaluli friend asked why he had chosen that particular myth and not another that in his view had an equal, if not better, claim (Feld 1990). It would be as if an American had questioned the Balinese ethnographer's choice of football, suggesting that something different, but equally important, could be learned about American culture by examining the behavior of couples on a "date," the activities surrounding a rock concert or the purchase of a house, or a day in the life of a fast food restaurant; and then as if the resulting discussion were included in the ethnography, further thickening the description to the point of contestation.

Empathy in ethnomusicology's "new fieldwork" (Barz and Cooley 1997) not only thickens the description through dialogue, it also introduces the subjectivities of emotion and reflexivity. European intellectuals, in my experience, are skeptical of empathy as a scholarly method; but as developed in American ethnomusicology, or in the practice of medicine for that matter, empathy does not mean standing in the other person's shoes (feeling his pain) as much as it means engagement. Better than the distanced procedure of symbolic analysis, empathy, or the experience of those moments of "subject shift" when one is thrown outside of oneself (Titon 1995a), offers insight into what Geertz described as "the structure of feelings" in a society. Empathy has led, also, to a resurgence of applied ethnomusicology; that is, to ethnomusicology in the public interest: ethnomusicologists advocating on behalf of musical communities as well as, or instead of, extracting musical life from them and then producing ethnomusicological knowledge primarily for the academic world (*Ethnomusicology* 36:3 [1992]).

In these new ethnomusicological writings the thickening description not only names the people and shows them in dialogue, thus becoming multivocal (Levin 1996 is a fine illustration); it also restores texts in the more narrow sense of words (and music) on the page (Kisliuk 1998). Interpretation of meaningful action as a text requires that the ethnographer inscribe the observed action into a narrative description-interpretation. So, for example, Geertz evokes, describes, and narrates the cockfight; the result is a highly processed account from the ethnographer's viewpoint. Missing, as I have said, from Geertz's text are the voices of the handlers, the wagerers, the spectators, and what it is, exactly, that they say—that is, the texts, in the conventional sense, generated in the performance of the cockfight. These, if given in Geertz's ethnography, would be on display, as it were, as grist for the mill of everyone's interpretive efforts, whether Geertz's or the reader's.

Geertz has been criticized for being too much a literary critic, reading culture; but the problem in the cockfight essay is that he is not enough of one. That is, a literary critic always places the text of the poem, play, or novel in front of the reader so that the process of interpretation can be followed with the exact words of the original text in mind. Geertz's text is both highly processed and predigested; the original text has long since disappeared. Geertz would surely respond that, in observing human activity, there is no such thing as apprehending an original text; that every text is always already an interpretation. This, however, is one of the difficulties with treating meaningful action as a text. The fact is that certain meaningful actions do generate texts (words) in the conventional sense, and the endless conversations in the field generate them as well. As a writer Geertz operates more as a Jamesian novelist than a literary critic, a comparison that I think would please him.

Geertz has pointed out that even when the ethnographer includes many voices in a written account, the ethnographer retains control over those voices, writing as a kind of ethnographic ventriloquist. To be sure, just as an ethnographic filmmaker selects those scenes, filmed from "real life," to be ordered into the final sense-making film cut, so, unless we have multiple authorship (Guilbault et al. 1993; also Titon, Cornett, and Wallhausser 1997), the ethnographic writer selects, from among the many statements by the many voices, what will be included in the ethnographic account. But when the multiply voiced texts are on display, they offer the reader far more interpretive possibilities than are present when the interpretation comes through the inflection of a single voice. To illustrate this procedure I do something below that Geertz often does, that is, discuss one's own research and writing; in this case, the Preface to *Powerhouse for God* (1988), and a computer-based, multimedia hypertext about a musician's world and music (1991).

The Preface to *Powerhouse* is an exercise in multivoiced, thick description, a narrative of a luncheon conversation in which my friend John Sherfey, the principal figure in this ethnographic monograph on music, language, and life in a Baptist church in rural Virginia, presents himself to a visitor from the Library of Congress, by telling a story from his own experience to illustrate, indirectly, the kind of person he is. I evoked the scene, describing it as best as I remembered it; I printed the text of the dialogue between Sherfey and the man from Washington; I interpreted the dialogue in light of my particular concerns once it was finished. Is this "ethnographic ventriloquism?" (Geertz 1988, 145). It cannot be, for the text of the dialogue is given complete (although my description of people's gestures had to be reconstructed from memory) and verbatim, because I had tape-recorded it. (I was, at that time, in that fieldwork stage of documenting everything.) My understanding of the dialogue in its context and in the context of my research is meant to introduce the reader both to John Sherfey and to the subject of the book; but the reader is free to interpret it otherwise, for the reader always has the text of the conversation at hand, not a highly processed or predigested description of the conversation. Including conventional (what Geertz would call "raw") texts for analysis not only thickens the description but allows for the possibility of multiple interpretations.

The Clyde Davenport HyperCard Stack (see Further Reading for details) was my attempt to write multiple interpretations into a multi-media computer presentation of the virtual reality of a musician's world. Davenport is an old-time fiddler from Kentucky whose music and ideas about music are represented within a web of sounds, images, musical transcriptions, and words. In some parts of the program he is shown narrating incidents from his life; in other parts he is shown in dialogue with me. At one point the reader is led to hear two fiddle tunes Clyde performs: "Davy Dugger" and "Shoot That Turkey Buzzard." From that listening experience, one linked path leads through musical transcription and analysis toward an understanding that the tunes are very similar in structure. But another series of links leads to a dialogue among Clyde, Steve Green, and me in which Clyde states that what matters to him is that the two tunes are different; and then he proceeds to play the fiddle and demonstrate the difference. The person sitting at the computer is left having to decide whether, and how, the two apparently opposing interpretations may be reconciled. In the HyperCard version (but unimplementable in the Web version) the computer user interacts by leaving comments for future users to read, thereby becoming an author and altering the representation.

The computer information revolution has already occurred. Most research already takes place in front of the computer screen. Linked, hypertextual multimedia representations of music not only further thicken the descriptive stew but also, at their best, they offer the computer user the opportunity to enter the virtual world of the ethnographer puzzling his or her way toward "reading" the "texts" that contain the symbols of social action with which Geertz, advocating "thick description," reconfigured the project of cultural anthropology. That is, multimedia hypertext represents the partial, the contested, the ambiguous, the complex structures and symbols of cultural life; and for the cultural study of music it requires one to become far more active as a participant-observer. It encourages the student of music to be not simply a spectator looking over an ethnographic shoulder but also an ethnomusicologist drawing interpretive conclusions.

Further Reading

Barz, Gregory F., and Timothy J. Cooley. 1997. *Shadows in the field: New perspectives for fieldwork in ethnomusicology.* New York: Oxford Univ. Press.

Feld, Steven. 1990. *Sound and sentiment. Birds, weeping, poetics, and song in Kaluli expression.* 2d ed. Philadelphia: Univ. of Pennsylvania Press.

Geertz, Clifford. [1972] 1973. *The interpretation of cultures.* New York: Basic Books.

———. [1974] 1977. "From the native's point of view": On the nature of anthropological understanding. Pp. 480–92 in *Symbolic anthropology: A reader.* Edited by Janet L. Dolgin et al. New York: Columbia Univ. Press.

———. 1983. Pp. 19-35 in *Local knowledge: Further essays in interpretive anthropology.* New York: Basic Books.

———. 1988. *Works and lives.* Stanford, Calif.: Stanford Univ. Press.

Rice, Timothy. 1994. *May it fill your soul: Experiencing Bulgarian music.* Chicago: Univ. of Chicago Press.

Titon, Jeff Todd. 1988. *Powerhouse for God.* Austin: Univ. of Texas Press.

———. 1991. *The Clyde Davenport HyperCard Stack.* Providence, R.I.: the author. A noninteractive World Wide Web version may be found at http://www.stg.brown.edu/projects/davenport/CLYDE_DAVENPORT.html

———. 1995a. Bi-musicality as Metaphor. *Journal of American Folklore* 108: 287–97.

———. 1995b. Text. *Journal of American Folklore* 108: 432–48.

CHAPTER 15

Music, Experience, and the Anthropology of Emotion

RUTH FINNEGAN

Attempts to capture the variegated experiential dimensions of music are now attracting increasing interest. Replete with problem and controversy as they are, and scarcely a central concern of traditional musicology, such attempts, I suggest, deserve our serious attention.

Emotion, Mind, and Body

The background partly lies in current debates around that powerful theme-with-variations running through Western thought—the value-laden oppositions between mind and body, intellect and emotion. Romanticist accounts used these polarities to celebrate the emotional side. More commonly reason was set on top, its role to control our lower "animal" nature and lead upward into the scientific, emotion-free enlightenment of human language and writing. It was these cognitive elements, furthermore, that were regularly (if not quite invariably) taken as the fit focus for scholarly analysis.

These ideas have long influenced our models of culture and, with it, of music. Western classical music—the assumed norm—has often been implicitly assigned to the "rational" side of the equation, connected with written formulations, and the intellectual elements of cultivated human society. Scholars privileged music's cognitive and nonbodily features, high-lighting composition, written scores, and the rationality of classic music theory: *these* aspects, not the primeval emotions, were the appropriate subject for scholarly analysis. Emotions are not irrelevant in traditional musicology (my opening comment was oversimple); but as something bodily and opposed to the intellect they must be controlled and refined by reason. In a common twentieth-century view, music (i.e., Western classical music) is: "a language of the emotions, through which we directly experience the fundamental urges that move mankind. . . . A dangerous art. . . . But under the guidance of the intellect and the enlightened moral sense, it is surely as safe as anything human can be—as safe . . . as religion or science (Cooke 1959, 272).

The musicological task was not to dwell on the fundamental urges but to provide the intellectual guidance for regulating them (feasible for "true" music, unlike unwritten forms like jazz, rock, or African drumming, seen as irredeemably "physical," the "mindless" outflow of primal emotion). Prolific twentieth-century "listeners' guides" offered intellectual expositions of the expressiveness in the musical work (not in the listeners), focusing on the musical text and teaching listeners "how musical elements fit together" (Ratner 1977, 1). Similarly Leonard Meyer's *Emotion and Meaning in Music* did not present ordinary people's experiences but the "syntax" of musical works and the judgments of "composers, performers, theoreticians and competent critics" (1956, 197).

This cluster of assumptions is now in question. We are nowadays ready to challenge limiting ethnocentric models, among them traditional musicology, and in so doing to go beyond prescription, intellectual theory, and written products into people's (varied) practices. Added to this are new approaches to experience and emotion as objects for serious study in people's everyday actions rather than as matters of speculation, disapproval, or buried mystery.

This is where the anthropology of the emotions comes in. Anthropologists had long noted links between ritual and sentiment, and in the later twentieth century were explicitly tackling the subject of emotion. The anthropologist John Blacking pointed to experiential processes like falling in love, ecstasy, or joy in dancing (1977, 5), and his analyses of music (1973, 1987) brought together body and thought, feeling and practice. Meantime Vic Turner was developing the "anthropology of experience" (Turner and Bruner 1986), and from the 1980s anthropological work on emotion was increasingly taking off (Crapanzano 1994; Heelas 1996; Lutz and White 1986; Lutz and Abu-Lughod 1990; Schwartz et al. 1992).

As one would expect from anthropologists, the emphasis was on cultural relativity. Contrary to what had often been assumed, emotions turned out not to be universal facts of nature but to be differently formulated in different times and places. We *learn* how to feel, and how to deploy particular emotions in ways and contexts appropriate to our situation. People also learn the discourses through which their emotions are more, or less, verbalized, for conceptualizations differ too, ranging from the "hydraulic metaphor" underlying many Western views to the Sudanic Dinka concept of forces acting from outside (Lutz and White 1986, 419; Heelas 1996, 182). The study of experience has to be cognizant of such cultural specificities.

Anthropological work has now increasingly diversified, interacting both with recent surges of interest in emotion across other disciplines and with transdisciplinary feminist, poststructuralist, and postmodernist trends (Bendelow and Williams 1998; Lupton 1998; Lutz and Abu-Lughod 1990, Introduction; Williams 2001). Emotions are also "managed," it emerges. Emotional experience can be arranged and manipulated, as with flight attendants trained to shape their feelings to the job (Hochschild 1983). The medieval Christian church organized sights and sounds to encourage reverence and exaltation just as religious and political movements today deliberately deploy identity-bringing musical performances. As Gordon comments (1990, 168), elites everywhere endeavor to control the material and symbolic resources for emotion production. But behind the diversity of approaches, the emphasis on cultural rather than biological construction remains. In Helga Kotthoff's succinct summary, "feelings are no longer regarded as something innate and inward, but rather as a culturally interwoven and shaped mode of experience" (2001, 169).

The boundaries between mind and body, cognition and emotion, inner and outer are correspondingly dissolving. Experience is increasingly envisaged not as mysterious inner state or unthinking primeval impulse but as embodied and lived, intertwined with culturally diverse epistemologies. The Enlightenment ideology of language, and the scholars' preoccupation with cognition and verbalized texts are undermined and enlarged by a growing appreciation of human life as everywhere intershot with imagination, with value, with connotation. In Michelle Rosaldo's memorable formulation, "feeling is forever given shape through thought . . . and thought is laden with emotional meaning" (Rosaldo 1984, 137).

The debates continue (I return to some later). But what is important about these recent perspectives is that they help analysts of music to bypass the tendentious mind–body polarity and the prescriptive model of music associated with it, to bring up questions about the *diverse* ways people actually experience music in practice.

Studying Musical Experiences

Some brief examples can give a flavor of the studies now being undertaken. Differ as they do, they share a preparedness to attempt in-depth ethnographic study, culture-sensitive and nonjudgmental, in pursuit not of universals but of the embodied experiences of participants in music in specific situations. And for *all* participants. In Ola Stockfelt's provocative overstatement, "the listener, and only the listener, is the composer of the music" (1994, 19). Musical experience in other words belongs not just to musical work, composer, or accredited "expert" but also, crucially, to the variegated audiences.

Take the anthropologist Steven Feld's pioneering *Sound and Sentiment* (1990), based on long participant observation among the New Guinean Kaluli. He explores their music not as text but as interwoven into all the associations that Kaluli learn to feel between "birds, weeping, poetics, and song." Feld uncovers the complex sonic world in and through which Kaluli live, the ways they describe and experience it, and the interaction among the sorrowful songs of their night-long ceremonies, the tears these stir in their hearers, the rage with which these deeply moved participants retaliate—and are expected to retaliate—against their mythically informed experiences, and the acoustic epistemology that resonates through their lives. The songs, thoughtfully composed and deliberately rehearsed, are oriented to making the listeners sad and nostalgic, eventually moving them to tears. They are performed by a dancer

> whose downcast demeanor and paced solitude, moving up and back the center aisle of the house, creates an image of loneliness and isolation. The act of moving the audience to tears is marked most socially by the instant retribution of burning the back of the dancer, a mark he wears for life. . . . The way the songs persuaded the audience to tears is what dominates both the aftermath and the remembrances of [the event]. (Feld 1990, 215, 7)

Kaluli organize feelings of sadness and rage. Other traditions differ. The anthropologist Simon Ottenberg describes the free-lance Limba

musician Sayo in northern Sierra Leone, his vocal-instrumental performances marked by their sense of sadness and misfortune, of a lack of ability
to control life or destiny. But the listeners to these sorrowful songs do not
show sadness. As members of the chorus—participant listeners—they
seem concerned not with the words but with the enjoyment of responding, clapping, and dancing (Ottenberg 1996, 92–93). Their reactions,
culturally specific, stand in stark contrast to those of the Kaluli—but are
no less a real dimension of their musical experiences.

Different again is the musical lamenting in (Caucasian) Georgia, where
the women "carry out emotion work" for the community (Kotthoff
2001, 25). Their laments are not the outcome of spontaneous irrational
forces, but worked-on artistic performances. The singers' management of
their feelings structures the emotional occasion and enables the audience
to grieve.

> For the lamenters aesthetical grieving means to keep control over their feel-
> ings. They cannot let themselves go. For some of the listeners the process is
> the other way round. They are inflicted with their pain. . . . [The occasion]
> involves the audience in grieving . . . coming to terms with the loss.
> (Kotthoff 2001, 192, 25)

Or take Daniel Cavicchi's work on music and meaning among
Bruce Springsteen fans (it is not just among "other cultures" that musical
experience can be studied). Cavicchi uncovers the complex ways fans experience the music: their shared enthusiasms, experiential conventions in "becoming-a-fan" narratives, sense of personal connection with
Springsteen. The performances are not to watch passively, but to join.
"I'm tired after seeing a Bruce show," says one fan, "I've been on my feet,
I've been applauding and I've been yelling and screaming" (Cavicchi
1998, 93). Another describes "the feeling that one has just been to a religious revival. . . . Faith and Hope and Joy!," while for yet another:

> It gets you into it physically, because you're dancing, you're moving around,
> you're waving your arms, you're clapping your hands. You get into it men-
> tally because you know the lyrics or you're listening to them again, maybe
> you're getting another meaning out of them, a new meaning or an old
> meaning, whatever. It's just such an energizing experience, and it's a spiri-
> tual experience. So, it gets you, mind, body, and soul. (Cavicchi 1998, 95)

It is not just "fun" but personal critical appreciation. Rejecting generalizations about illusion or hegemony, rooted, he posits, in armchair

theorizing rather than study of participants, Cavicchi explains how fans' experiences interact with their individual lives. "During the commute, at work, at school, . . . most fans are still 'listening' . . . making associations between perceived musical structures, potential messages, and the contexts of their experiences" (p. 126).

Experiential expectations are molded through specific groups, genres, and contexts. In the English town of Milton Keynes, people's experiences in the contrasting "worlds" of jazz, folk, or classical music are interwoven with differing practices and conceptualizations of performance, composition, and learning (Finnegan 1989; see also Hennion 1997). Expectations differ over time as well. Someone who heard Chopin playing the piano, for example, formulated the experience through the otherworldly metaphors that were then current: "I could think of nothing but elves and fairy dances . . . [The music] seems to descend from heaven—so pure, and clear, and spiritual" (Kallberg 1994, 52). Specific genres too come to have particular associations at given times or places: some with overtones of nostalgia and loss; others excitement, dance, or rowdy laughter; others again gaiety, solemnity, exuberance, reverence, humor, trance. Some are conventionally heard with full attention or intense feeling; in others these sonic experiences are mingled with other sounds or materials, or ebb and flow over time.

Rituals are often intershot with music, managing fraught occasions in human lives and presenting organized occasions for emotional deployment where, again, it makes no sense to draw an opposition between thought and feeling. Musical performances have been seen as occasions for exploiting the encompassing capacity of sound to marshal a sense of *communitas*, of trance, or of transformation from one state to another where, as Van Leeuwen suggests (1999, 197), "listening is connection, communion." Experience is dynamically cocreated too as people smile at or dance with each other, beat time, move together, construct and reexperience their recollections later—realizations of human sociality that recall Schutz's "mutual tuning-in relationship" (1951, 92). We should not overromanticize. As Gerd Baumann insists,

> Every experience of collective "communion" . . . forging an experiential "us" . . . can [also] be abused. Whether it is engendered by [raindances in the Nuba mountains], or associated with the rousing rendition of a Nazi hymn . . . it can be exploited, and perhaps even induced, in the interests of powerful elites, sectional interests, or seductive hegemonic ideas. (Baumann in Baily 1995, 38)

But this potential for group-aggregating experience, harmonious and/or divisive, is nevertheless a feature of music now on the research agenda. The experiential dimension also comes through in accounts pointing to the transcendent power of music. The Georgian lamenters created "a non-ordinary experiential and imaginative involvement and a space where the living are seemingly in contact with the dead" (Kotthoff 2001, 173), while among Liverpool rock performers music "creates its own space and time where all kinds of dreams, emotions, and thoughts are possible" (Cohen 1991, 191). Limba musical performances altered everyday time and thought, overshadowing the here and now (which in Sierra Leone could be grim indeed). Instrumentalists and chorus were "happy in a sort of pleasant, timeless musical world" as troubles and conflicts were publicly expressed, "giving people as groups a chance to deal with the reality of their feelings under the appearance of happiness" (Ottenberg 1996, 192–93). Further,

> The repetitiveness of the instrumental music and song, the steady rhythm, sometimes the repetitive movements of dancers in a circle, and the minimizing of everyday time allowed not only for a sense of momentary social solidarity but also for a special sort of inner individualism ... swinging back and forth between full consciousness and daydreaming. (193)

The varying experiences of time and imagination in differing contexts, elusive as these are, are now becoming topics for in-depth research exploring the complex and subtle intertwining of cultural expectation, specific setting, and individually embodied practice.

Commentary

Studies like those sketched above need to be brought into the mainstream study of music, to be supplemented, assessed, and debated. But if that is my central point, let me also briefly comment on a handful of the many controversies that arise.

First, just what is meant by musical "experience" here? A tricky issue: Theoretical discussions of emotion say surprisingly little about music specifically. Krumhansl notes "the marginal position of music in the emotions literature" (2000, 88), and most accounts of musical experiencing are little concerned with verbal definition. The examples above are also in fact quite heterogeneous. But I argue that this open-ended heterogeneity, for all its problems, is actually at this stage quite healthy. Cultural relativity has rightly made us cautious about essentializing definitions but, more than that, a preoccupation with precise boundaries can fetter us back into exactly the kinds of contrasts—intellect–emotion, mind–body— that have proved constraining in the past. Work in the anthropology of the emotions and elsewhere suggests that we can productively focus not on trying to penetrate and pin down hidden internal states but rather on the *manner*, variably practiced and conceptualized in different contexts, in which people are personally involved in their musical engagements. This may be varied and complex—but it *is* something that can be observed and discussed. When Ottenberg, Feld, or Cavicchi describe people's musical activities in such terms, we do not dismiss what they say as unintelligible (though we may want to debate their interpretations). In other words I am not advocating a bounded definition but rather indicating a broad and variegated facet of human life to which words like *emotion, affect, mood, imagination, expressiveness, passion,* and *overtone* can direct our attention. Such aspects have in the past been downplayed by scholars but by now we can surely find something recognizable in detailed studies like those discussed above, the more so because these accounts are tied into overt and specific practices.

It is not always a matter of elaborated sonic epistemologies or highly charged "inner feelings," far less flattening terms like *sexuality, pleasure,* or *desire* to which they are all sometimes reduced, but also of quieter resonances. Consider the overtones of Wagner's music for some listeners; or the multilayered clusters of associations, partly personal, partly shared, of a childhood carol, a particular recording, the opening of Beethoven's 5th symphony. Amusement, happiness, intellectual satisfaction, excitement, disapproval—in specific contexts these too are part of people's musical practice. It is not so much self-conscious internalized "feelings"—though in some cultural settings that is indeed one element—as the contextualized manner of people's musical engagements: joyfully, fearfully, inattentively, reflectively, proudly; in a spirit of exaltation or energy or irritation; in sorrowful, celebratory, or nostalgic mood; with boredom (that too!), with dance, with tranquility. Whether in deeply intense fashion or more light-touch action, music provides a human resource through which people can enact their lives with inextricably entwined feeling, thought and imagination.

Second, many analysts currently focus on "practices" rather than "musical works." I would go further, however, and urge that for exploring musical experience we would do well to abandon the fashionable concept of "text" as well. "Text" turns us away from people's diverse experiences back into that limiting approach of locating emotion in the work and its exposition by experts (the "semiotic decodings," for example, so effectively criticized in DeNora 2000, 21ff). But people participate in music in multifarious ways in the different roles they take, the occasion, or their own personal histories—experiences of "the same" text are not necessarily uniform. In the Balkans, Serbian epic-singing is heard with pride by Serbs but terror by their Croat neighbors (Petrovic in Baily 1995, 69), while in Ireland listeners of different backgrounds experience the sounds of Orange flutes and drums in contrasting ways, bound into long historical-mythic associations. Different participants organize their experiences differently, and in musical rituals people may move in and out of the "appropriate" emotions. Textual analysis cannot replace time-consuming ethnographic investigation of the actual experiences of variegated participants in all their dynamics and multiplicities.

Further, even in the expanded senses in which the term is now sometimes used, the connotations of "text" inevitably privilege linguistic and cognitive matters: easier for scholars to capture, admittedly, and in keeping with the academic tradition of studying ideas, but for musical experience definitely not the whole story. Thus the *words* of songs—the verbalized texts—often get the prime attention. For some genres, some individuals, and some occasions these words are indeed significant. But this is not always so, nor are their meanings necessarily agreed on (musical analysts have been slow to echo the "reader-response" and meaning-as-emergence perspectives that have elsewhere moved analysis from authors/producers to readers/users). Simon Frith (1996) insightfully criticizes overemphasis on lyrics, stressing instead performance and listeners' multiple interpretations. Cavicchi similarly shows how the words of Springsteen's songs, though resonant for many individuals, did not carry one single message, and seemed less central than the shared expectations of energizing religious experience and personal interpretation (Cavicchi 1998). "Text" is unilluminating, even misleading, here, inclining us away from experience and multiplicity.

Third, the concept of "cultural construction" needs revisiting. It was helpful indeed for challenging universalized concepts of emotions as primeval internal impulses; but the pendulum can swing too far, substituting cultural for biological determinism. We may all nowadays agree in criticizing the traditional model of "culture" as homogeneous external entity, and instead stress differentiation and multiplicity. But at a lower level it is easy to slip back into a species of sociologism through a preoccupation with the constraining power of social and institutional arrangements. Insights from social interactionist and processual traditions help to restore the balance, illuminating the creative roles of individuals as they interact with, and themselves mold, cultural expectations.

This is not to deny that people's experiences are indeed interwoven with conceptualizations and conventions that are shared (more or less) with others—and not always equitably so. But these are at the same time *resources* that human agents draw on and fashion to their own occasions. The processes are too multisided to be reduced to one-dimensional cultural constraints. The Nigerian Yoruba explicitly use band performances to generate happiness, relaxation, and enjoyment, where the music "rushes over the listener in a continuous stream . . . or blows flutteringly, like a flag in a strong wind"; pragmatics, sensuality, and aesthetics are inextricably intertwined as "social power, musical sound, poetic rhetoric, and sentiment are woven via performance into whole experiential cloth" (Waterman 1990, 187–88). Tia DeNora's *Music in Everyday Life* presents music as "a material that actors use to elaborate, to fill out and fill in, to themselves and to others, modes of aesthetic agency and, with it, subjective stances and identities . . . a resource for producing and recalling emotional states" (DeNora 2000, 74, 107). The imagery of Chopin listeners, Kaluli myth, classical music ideologies, Yoruba musical metaphors, biographical particularities—all in their different ways are resources through which people actively construct their experiences.

Thus Ottenberg traces how the individual lives of three blind musicians interpenetrated their musical performances (1996), just as Cavicchi (1998) describes individual Springsteen fans intertwining their personal histories with how they experience his music and build it into the fabric of their lives. DeNora explores how "Lucy" uses Schubert's *Impromptus* to "retreat into" and "soothe" herself, actively putting together memories, musical recordings, furniture, current emotional state, timing, and biographical associations (DeNora 2000, 42–43):

> There is nothing untowardly mysterious about this process . . . [where] the sum is greater than its parts: music, plus the ways that [Lucy] attends to it, plus the memories and associations that are brought to it, plus the local circumstances of consumption. Through this alchemical process of pulling together a range of heterogeneous materials, Lucy herself is . . . a contributor to the constitution of the music's power over her, its ability to move her from one emotional location to another. (43)

We must leave space for such individual creativities and the active coconstructing of experience.

Finally let me highlight the bodily dimension of music. This is now increasingly appreciated, from Barthes's characterization of music as in part manual and muscular, "as if the body was listening, not the 'soul'" (1986, 261), to Simon Frith's felicitous comment that "*all* music-making is about the mind-in-the-body" (1996, 128). We do not have to accept the old body–mind dichotomies to recognize that sound resonates in the body, and that the experience of music includes its patterned corporeal engagements. But this embodied musical experiencing is the more compelling, I would add, because it is so often multisensory. Musical performances are "multimedia events," Blacking remarks, their sound patterns only one of several communication channels (1987, 123), and as Leppert's *The Sight of Sound* illustrates, the "visual-performative" aspects are as significant for music as for dance or theater (1993, xxi). All this brings yet further resonances to music's experiential potential—images of place, artifacts (instruments, dress, programs), visual associations, tactile impressions, bodily rhythms, somatic remembrances, intertextualities across a range of senses. These complex multimodalities deserve a central rather than marginal place in our experience-ful analyses of music.

We should welcome this multiplicity of musical experiencings, interfused overlappingly with thought, embodied affect, and personal creativity. Their study is not easy, for they can only emerge through sensitive critical attention to ethnographic specificities with all their complications of multiple groups, roles, outlooks, senses, artifacts, and individuals— and, without doubt, their controversial interpretations too. But widening the analysis of music to include such issues lays the foundation for both a more realistic appreciation of music and a richer model of human beings and human culture.

Further Reading

Cavicchi, Daniel. 1998. *Tramps like us: Music and meaning among Springsteen fans.* New York: Oxford Univ. Press.

DeNora, Tia. 2000. *Music in everyday life.* Cambridge, U.K.: Cambridge Univ. Press.

Feld, Steven. 1990. *Sound and sentiment. Birds, weeping, poetics, and song in Kaluli expression.* 2d ed. Philadelphia: Univ. of Pennsylvania Press.

Frith, Simon. 1996. *Performing rites. Evaluating popular music.* Oxford: Oxford Univ. Press.

Heelas, Paul. 1996. Emotion talk across cultures. Pp. 17–99 in *The emotions. Social, cultural and biological dimensions.* Edited by Rom Harré and W. Gerrod Parrott. London: Sage.

Lupton, Deborah. 1998. *The emotional self.* London: Sage.

Lutz, Catherine, and Geoffrey M. White. 1986. The anthropology of emotions. *Annual Review of Anthropology* 15: 405–36.

Ottenberg, Simon. 1996. *Seeing with music: The lives of three blind African musicians.* Seattle: Univ. of Washington Press.

Schwartz, T., Geoffrey M. White, and Catherine A. Lutz, eds. 1992. *New directions in psychological anthropology.* Cambridge, U.K.: Cambridge Univ. Press.

Turner, Victor, and Edward Bruner, eds. 1986. *The anthropology of experience.* Urbana: Univ. of Illinois Press.

Williams, Simon. 2001. *Emotion and social theory. Corporeal reflections on the (ir)rational.* London: Sage.

CHAPTER 16

Musical Materials, Perception, and Listening

NICOLA DIBBEN

Based on the history of research into music perception and cognition one could be forgiven for assuming that the cultural character of music has little to do with the perceptual capabilities of individuals. Research into the perception and cognition of music has largely focused on the perception of auditory events such as pitch, grouping, and tonal and rhythmic structures. One of the most influential accounts of music cognition in the last twenty years has been the idea that listeners hear relationships between abstract underlying structures in music, as well as surface relationships, and that a hierarchy of tonal structures is fundamental to the listening experience (e.g., Lerdahl and Jackendoff 1983). The titles of work in this domain, such as Steven Handel's *Listening*, belie an almost exclusive focus on musical sound conceived in terms of "raw" parameters.

Much of this research converges with a particular branch of music theory and analysis: Many theoretical concepts such as pitches, chords, harmonies, scales, keys, voice-leading, and rhythmic structures have received empirical verification. However, while some of these theoretical constructs do seem to be heard, others seem to bear little relationship to listeners' experiences. For example, despite much research into the cognitive reality of large-scale structure there is little evidence that the large-scale hierarchical structures posited by cognitive theories play an important role in listeners' aesthetic appreciation of music. Furthermore, while attempting to describe the perceptions of experienced listeners, these models tend   *193* to result in a "view from nowhere": the listening subject is deleted in favor of an apparently objective reading of musical structure (Cross 1998).

The conception of material implicit in these approaches is in direct contrast with the historically or socially informed approaches within music theory and criticism. For example, semiotic theories conceive of music not in terms of raw parameters and structures but in terms of "topics" or "archetypes"—musical materials that come with a history of use (e.g., Agawu 1991). And in the last two decades, "new musicology" has presented interpretations of works in which musical structures are read in terms of social meanings. Thus, there appears to be a sharp divide between conceptions of musical material implicit in studies of music perception, and those implied by some branches of music theory and history.

One interpretation of the absence of empirical research into the perception of musical "material" is that listeners don't really "hear" the structures and meanings identified in music theory and criticism, and that therefore there is no need, or indeed point, to carrying out perceptual studies to show the cognitive reality of these materials. Indeed, the way in which the relationship between music perception and music theory has generally been conceived is that whereas music perception and cognition studies what listeners hear, music theory persuades the listener of what they might or could hear. Taken at face value, this is a problematic distinction. On the one hand, it seems to suggest that the cultural and social meanings identified by theory and criticism are not related in any way to historically situated musical materials heard by an individual, and that, on the other hand, there is a level of musical experience that is unmediated and to which a sociologically informed hermeneutics is subsequently applied. In this chapter I review some empirical evidence that listeners hear musical "material," not just "sound," and consider implications of the cultural construction of listening for understanding the perception of music. I start by presenting an account of musical structure that brings together a more veridical account of listening with a culturally informed conception of musical material.

Associative Structure

An alternative to hierarchical models of musical structure is the idea of "associative" structure. Little empirical or theoretical research has been conducted into associative structure. Leonard Meyer (1973) provides a discussion of the associative structure of melody, and more recently Jerrold

Levinson (1997) has argued that music is heard on a "moment-to-moment" basis (what he terms *concatenationism*), rather than in terms of large-scale structural relationships between events separated in time. According to Levinson, knowing that large-scale relationships exist may have some effect on the listening experience, but knowing that is not necessary to the aesthetic experience of music. In effect, his theory rehabilitates the untrained listener, and attempts a more veridical account of the listening experience. Despite criticism of the idea of concatenationism by some music theorists (critics have argued that large-scale structural relationships do play a part in the listening experience for them), Levinson's approach is important because it is a systematic attempt to clarify what a nonhierarchical experience of musical structure might be like.

The approach that I propose differs from both Meyer's and Levinson's in that it encompasses associative links in two axes, which are somewhat similar to the syntagmatic and paradigmatic axes of Saussurean linguistics. Meyer primarily discusses the syntagmatic axis, analyzing and categorizing the associative links between elements occurring within the same piece of music but displaced in time. It is in this domain that subsequent empirical research has been conducted. The paradigmatic axis (Saussure himself originally called this the "associative axis") is concerned with the relationship between any instance of an element and the other elements belonging to the same category with which it could be substituted. This axis captures the manner in which musical materials refer beyond themselves to other instances (archetypes, prototypes) that may not be present here and now but that give a basis for evaluating those that are. The difference between this theory of associative structure and hierarchical theories of music perception mentioned earlier is that it treats the substance of musical sound as "material" rather than as raw parameters. This alternative conception of musical material can be thought of as operating in two dimensions: first, intraopus, forging relationships within a particular piece, and giving rise to a sense of coherence; and, second, extraopus, by virtue of reference to other specific, or generic, works and styles.

There are a number of clues to the existence of musical "material." One such clue lies within hierarchical perceptual theories themselves. Although *A Generative Theory of Tonal Music* (Lerdahl and Jackendoff 1983) specifies a set of rules that remove successively higher levels of structure, it is not able to do this with the two-membered cadence. The authors argue that "we must regard cadences as signs, or conventional formulas" (1983, 134), and in doing so they render the theory open to historical style analysis. This treatment of the cadence is an example of a more widespread phenomenon identified by music theory and analysis: the idea that musical material does not consist only of the "raw" parameters of pitch, rhythm, contour, and so on, but is socially and historically constituted. Influenced by semiotics, music theory refers to this material as "topics," "schemata," and "archetypes," and proposes that, due to the compositional and social use of particular materials, their meanings or functions have become stabilized over time. Drawing on the writings of Theodor Adorno, a number of scholars have elaborated on this idea (Green 1988; Paddison 1996). In very broad terms it suggests that musical materials are heard in terms of their historical usage, such that if they have been associated with particular social (or musical) contexts or functions those meanings remain when they are used outside of those contexts or functions. The discourse surrounding music (program notes, narratives, lyrics, visual accompaniment, and so on) provides an interpretative context that reinforces those meanings. This idea underlies Philip Tagg's analytical method (1982). An often-cited example used to illustrate Tagg's method is the television theme song to the American detective series *Kojak*, in which, among other motifs and associated meanings, the use of brass signifies predatory behavior (due to the history of the use of brass instruments in hunting calls) and is associated with masculinity (due to the hunting reference, but also to other musical and film contexts in which this figure accompanies the appearance of the male hero).

In sum, I argue that listeners make associative links between musical elements that are present in any given piece, and at the same time make associations with similar or functionally equivalent elements or gestures in the wider repertoire of music with which they are familiar. This approach is based on the premise that musical materials are heard in terms of their historical usage, whether that be their compositional use with regard to fulfilling particular structural functions, or their association with particular social contexts. The advantage of this approach to music is that it does away with a crude distinction between intramusical and extramusical attributes: Sounds always have a compositional function, and are part of a social situation. This is, in essence, an argument for paying more attention to the historical nature of musical material, rather than simply treating it as raw materials in the here and now. And in doing so, one finds that these associative links lead beyond what is commonly regarded as the domain of music into a more general system of cultural reference.

Hearing "Material"

The idea that people hear music in terms of material rather than sound is central to applications of ecological psychology to music (see chapter 9 by Eric Clarke in this volume). Drawing on ecological psychology, William Gaver (1993) distinguishes between two listening modes, which he equates with two types of sound: "musical listening," in which the listener attends to the acoustic characteristics of sound, and "everyday" listening, in which the listener attends to the sources specified by sounds (such as the way in which a sound specifies the size and material of the object that produces it, and the manner in which it has been produced). Subsequent applications of ecological psychology to music differ from Gaver's approach in two important respects. First, the distinctions between "everyday" and "musical" listening are theorized not as two different types of sound, but as two different listening modes. The question then becomes one of when and why listeners hear sounds in one way rather than another. This is addressed through the notion of "affordance" (the way in which the meanings of things are a function of the mutuality of organism and environment) and captures the way in which the meanings specified by sounds are always meanings for someone rather than being properties of an object. The second important difference is the extension of source specification to include not only physical sources of sounds, but also the cultural and historical meanings of material, and their compositional functions (cf. the work of Eric Clarke and of Luke Windsor).

Relatively few empirical studies have investigated the perception of music in terms of this notion of musical "material." Robert Francès's book *The Perception of Music* (1988) includes an account of listening studies that show that listeners are sensitive to the cultural and historical meanings of musical material. Carol Krumhansl (1998) has investigated perception of "topics" in classical music, although this is in terms of their occurrence rather than their specific content. And a number of studies, Francès' among them, have shown that listeners are sensitive to the structural functions in music (for example, the way in which diverse musical material may have a closural function in a piece of music). One study that contextualizes its findings in relation to listening as a cultural practice is John Baily's study of Herati Afghans' perceptions of a range of musical and everyday sounds. Baily asked his listeners to describe a selection of musical and everyday sounds, and found that his informants tended to describe sounds in terms of their meanings and values. Baily concluded that "Afghans do not generally perceive sounds as abstract entities, as pure sounds, in the way that Europeans may do" (1996, 173).

Following from this research, I carried out a listening study that investigated the range of meanings sound material has for Western listeners (Dibben 2001). In one task (similar to that used by Baily), participants were presented with forty-eight short sound examples of musical and nonmusical sounds, and asked to describe the thing they were hearing. The range of responses included reference to acoustic attributes, physical source, genre, compositional function, physical space, proximity of the sound to the listener, performance skill, emotional character, and social context. Overall, listeners described sounds in terms of their physical and cultural sources more frequently than in terms of their acoustic characteristics. This indicates that, for these listeners, listening to music involves more than listening to its acoustic attributes; it involves hearing meanings specified by sounds. This finding serves to highlight the narrowness with which perception is traditionally conceptualized within music perception research. It also shows that listeners are sensitive to the physical and cultural sources and associations of sounds, contrary to constructions of Western music, and of the Western listening aesthetic as one in which listeners pay attention to "pure" sounds.

In itself, the finding of this listening study is no great revelation; intuitively it seems obvious that listeners hear sounds in terms of their meanings and contexts. What are more important are the questions it raises regarding subjectivity, and the apparent tension between subjectivity and the idea of sedimented meaning. Although there was a great deal of agreement between listeners' descriptions of sounds (as might be expected given a shared cultural context and listening conditions), there were nonetheless differences between the descriptions of sounds given by different participants. Why is it that some listeners described sounds in terms of one kind of attribute rather than another? These differences seem to be due to a number of factors. First, listeners may simply be mistaken about some aspect of the sound, as for example in the case of a six-second recording of vinyl hiss that listeners described variously as the sound of vinyl, the sound of burning, and the sound of bees. In this case, differences between listeners arise from the paucity of the information presented, leading to confusion over the sound source. Second, listeners may simply not be aware of a culturally significant attribute: some listeners described the sound of a stringed instrument accurately as a koto, whereas others, less familiar with this genre, described the sound in terms of its acoustic attributes. Third, listeners privilege certain meanings over others according to their needs and preoccupations and the information available to them. For example, responses to an excerpt from Beethoven's violin concerto in D Major, op. 61, included descriptions of the sound source ("violin concerto— Beethoven"), genre ("Classical"), structural function ("development part"), physical space and social context ("church"), reflecting differences of background and training among other factors. And for one informant—a seventeen-year-old student from a relatively disadvantaged background with little if any training in classical music, and participating in my study as a visitor on an outreach program run by the university—the salient aspect of an extract from Beethoven's Violin Concerto in D Major, op.61, was its class allegiances ("posh"). On the face of it these differences seem to argue against the idea of sedimented meaning and serve to highlight the question of whose meanings these are. The notion of sedimented meaning, is problematic to the extent that it is an analytical convenience—an averaging out of interpretations of material arising from an assumed common cultural context. Yet it is still commensurate with a dialectical notion of the relationship between listener and material: In other words, the perceptual characteristics of the stimulus are dependent on the needs of the individual, and the properties of the object (cf. Eric Clarke, chapter 9 this volume)—although stating it in this way already suggests a misleading polarization.

The descriptions of the extracts given above highlight one way in which this dialectical relationship of listener and material works to produce meanings. Just as the Beethoven example mobilized particular meanings to do with social class for the participant in my listening study, so too DeNora has argued that music focuses particular meanings for musicologists and critics:

> Telling what the meaning is, and deftly deflecting dispreferred meanings and readings, is part and parcel of the semiotic skills of daily life. We need to learn to see professional semioticians in a similar vein—as mobilizing particular features of utterances in order to produce meanings. (DeNora 2000, 38)

Musicological interpretation and criticism have come to be seen as *formative* of the meanings and significance of music rather than as simply "reflecting" truth. The most notorious example of this type of writing, and one that invited most response along these lines, was Susan McClary's feminist analysis of Beethoven's 9th Symphony in which she interprets the first movement recapitulation as a rapist's murderous fantasy. Detractors of McClary's approach argued that such interpretations were fabrication, arbitrarily related to the musical trace, and justified by nothing more than the need to make them. One reason for the heated debate that surrounded this critical reading was its failure to articulate the basis for its interpretative claims, which led to a mistaken assumption as to how and what music means: McClary's analysis provides a way of perceiving the musical work, and in light of this we may also perceive what she perceives, and mistakenly assume that it was there all along (cf. DeNora 2000; Cook 1990). Seen in this way, musicological writings have a specifically instructional role, often for political ends—whether that be to point up constructions of gender and sexuality in the music of Beethoven in a way relevant to a late-twentieth-century reaction against formalism, and concern with sexual equality, in the case of McClary, or, in the case of some of her detractors, a means of protecting the notion of autonomous music. The important point is that music analysis and criticism are concerned with persuasion rather than proof, with providing ways of experiencing music—the ramifications of which are only slowly becoming apparent for psychological approaches to music listening. As others have argued, one function of theoretical accounts is to provide new ways of hearing (or imagining) music—in effect, to produce music.

Listening Practices and Musical Culture

The approach to music listening that I have presented here understands musical materials as having a history of use due to their sociohistorical associations, and is in direct contrast to the view espoused in hierarchical models of perception and cognition. I have argued that hierarchical models of the perception of music are premised upon the idea that listeners' perceptions can be described adequately without taking into account the historical character of musical material, and that in these models the musical work is viewed as a concrete, self-contained unit specified by the notes of the score. By contrast, the theory of associative structure makes possible the interpenetration of immanent analysis with the sociohistorical and extramusical context. The history of research in music perception and cognition reflects a prevailing reception ideology of Western art music in which listening has been conceptualized as attentive but passive listening to musical structures. However, to paraphrase

Nicholas Cook on the aesthetics of Western art music: To interpret music in terms of an interest in sound and its perceptual experience does not transcend cultural values, it expresses them (1990, 7).

Knowing how to listen, and what to hear, are parts of what constitutes musical culture. Nicholas Cook has argued that "a musical culture is essentially a cognitive entity . . . to define a musical culture means defining the things a people must know in order to understand, perform and create acceptable music in their culture . . . ear training forms the basic means by which the identity of a musical culture is maintained" (Cook 1990, 222).

From this perspective "contemplative" listening, the act of listening afforded to audience members by Western classical concert music, is just one of a number of ways of listening. An ecological perspective argues that whether one pays attention to the acoustic character of sounds, or to their social and physical specifications, is determined by the needs and preoccupations of the moment. However, it is also determined by a set of listening practices into which listeners are enculturated.

As I have argued, the passive and laboratory-based listening context required by most research in music perception is modeled on a prevailing ideology of Western art music as "works" that are subject to attentive, passive listening. However, as any historical or cross-cultural survey shows, there is a coevolution of beliefs about music and listening practices. James Johnson has traced the way in which changing listening practices coincided with new ways of thinking about music's materials and forms in nineteenth-century France (Johnson 1995). And in terms of more recent developments, the impact of recording technology on listening is the most obvious focus of research into changing listening practices: in particular, the experience of music removed from its original social and cultural context (Benjamin 1970–73; Chanan 1995); and the invention of a new kind of listener produced by a historicized musical repertoire (Hennion and Fauquet 2001). However, this should not be taken solely as an argument for the "impact of recording": In a remarkable reversal of the one-way conception of the relationship between listening and recording (an influence running from recording to listening), Jonathan Sterne has shown how ideas about listening, and about music, have shaped the development and use of sound reproduction technology, as evidenced by that most macabre of hearing devices, the "ear phonautograph" (Sterne 2001).

One way in which research in music perception can contribute to an understanding of music listening is to offer psychological explanations of why we hear what we hear, and of what effect particular listening practices might have in determining this. For example, there is empirical evidence from ecological psychology that under circumstances where people are unable to explore a particular perceptual event they tend to describe it in terms of its perceptual qualities rather than in terms of its properties and identity. James Gibson (1966, [1979] 1986) found that when presented with a haptic (i.e., tactile or kinesthetic) stimulus participants described it in terms of sensations on the hand, whereas a participant allowed to explore it actively tended to report object properties and identity. In the domain of sound, William Gaver found that listeners tended to describe sounds in terms of their acoustic characteristics when the source of the sound was ambiguous (1993). And in a similarity task in which listeners were asked to pair two out of three sounds related either by acoustic similarity or source similarity, participants tended to group sounds on the basis of acoustic similarity (Dibben 2001). Luke Windsor has argued that music and other aesthetic objects afford interpretation because of the very ability of music to deny the possibility of exploration with the other perceptual senses one would normally employ to make sense of the world (2000). Where the immediate information from the perceptual source (e.g., sound) is insufficient, the listener searches for additional information from the social and cultural environment: by observing the behavior of others, by discussions with others, and by exploring the music through the discourse and other information that surrounds it.

What are the implications of this for a more culturally informed approach to research in music perception? First, it suggests that sound should be conceptualized not only in terms of "raw" parameters, but also in terms of musical "materials" heard in terms of their history of use. Second, it suggests that research needs to investigate the relationship between music theory and music perception—not to show if and how the two match up, but to investigate how musical discourse impinges on experience. Third, and perhaps most importantly, it suggests an alternative way to theorize about listening as social action (cf. Small 1998). At the crux of this argument is a critique of the Western ideology that the material of music history lies in the creation of forms rather than social action. Once this conceptual shift is made, it allows studies of perception to take into account the social and physical mediation of listening. If we are able to do this then we may really be capable of a culturally informed theory of music perception.

Further Reading

Clarke, Eric F. 1999. Subject-position and the specification of invariants in music by Frank Zappa and P. J. Harvey. *Music Analysis* 18: 347–74.

Cook, Nicholas. 1990. *Music, imagination and culture.* Oxford: Clarendon Press.

Cross, Ian. 1998. Music analysis and music perception, *Music Analysis* 17(1): 3–20.

DeNora, Tia. 2000. *Music in everyday life.* Cambridge, U.K.: Cambridge Univ. Press.

Du Gay, Paul, Stuart Hall, Linda Janes, Hugh Mackay, and Keith Negus, eds. 1997. *Doing cultural studies: The story of the Sony Walkman.* London: Sage.

Johnson, James H. 1995. *Listening in Paris: A cultural history.* Berkeley: Univ. of California Press.

Small, Christopher. 1998. *Musicking: The meanings of performing and listening.* Hanover, N.H.: University Press of New England.

Sterne, Jonathan. 2001. A machine to hear for them: On the very possibility of sound's reproduction. *Cultural Studies* 15(2): 259–94.

Windsor, W. Luke. 2000. Through and around the acousmatic: the interpretation of electroacoustic sounds. Pp. 7–35 in *Music, electronic media and culture.* Edited by Simon Emmerson. Aldershot, U.K.: Ashgate.

CHAPTER 17

Music as Performance

NICHOLAS COOK

The case for the prosecution is easily made. You can blame it on Stravinsky, who claimed that music should be executed and not interpreted, or on Schoenberg, who wrote that the performer was "totally unnecessary except as his interpretations make the music understandable to an audience unfortunate enough not to be able to read it in print" (Newlin 1980, 164). Or you can blame it on the recording industry, which has created a performance style designed for infinite iterability, resulting over the course of the twentieth century in a "general change of emphasis . . . from the characterization of musical events to the reproduction of a text" (Philip 1992, 230), or on musicology's origins as a nineteenth-century discipline modeled on philology, and therefore treating music as a written text. Any way you choose, the charge is the same: Because they think of performance as in essence the reproduction of a text, musicologists don't understand music as a performing art. In fact this orientation is built into our very language for music: You can "just play," but it's odd to speak of "just performing," because the basic grammar of performance is that you perform *something*, you give a performance "of" something. In other words, language—and especially musicological language—leads us to construct the process of performance as supplementary to the product that occasions it, and it is this that leads us to talk quite naturally about music "and" its performance, just as
film theorists speak of the film "and" the music, as if performance were

not as much part of music as music is of film. (As it happens, this chapter was originally commissioned under the title "Music and Performance.")

The 1990s saw a sustained critique of the idea of the reified musical work, triggered largely by Lydia Goehr's *The Imaginary Museum of Musical Works* (1992). This critique is the necessary starting point for developing a concept of performance that is not just performance "of," or—as I have expressed it in my title—thinking of music *as* (not *and*) performance. Richard Taruskin (1995) and Christopher Small (1998), to name just two, have suggested some ways in which this might proceed, but in this chapter I want to draw on aspects of interdisciplinary performance studies and ethnomusicology that I see as particularly relevant to an understanding of music as performance. The shift from a text-based to a performance-based understanding of music is closely comparable to the breaking away of theater studies from literary studies that took place during the last generation, the flavor of which is conveyed by the dance and theater theorist Nick Kaye's characterization of performance as "a primary postmodern mode": as he sees it, the performance-oriented practices of artists like Foreman, Cunningham, or Cage subvert the "discrete or bounded 'work of art'" definitive of modernism, or dissolve it into "the contingencies and instabilities of the 'event' . . . penetrated by unstable and unpredictable exchanges and processes" (Kaye 1994, 22, 32, 117). Given the extent to which the reified musical work is built into the very language of musicology, the same kind of tension is probably inherent in any attempt to write about music as performance. But then nobody without a taste for the impossible should become a musicologist.

Keir Elam (quoted in Aston and Savona 1991, 104) has written, with reference to theatrical performance, of the "relationship of mutual and shifting constraints between two kinds of text, neither of which is prior and neither of which is precisely 'immanent' within the other, since each text is radically transformed by its relations with the other." Though his characterization of performance as "text" reflects an earlier phase of theatrical semiotics (the quotation dates from 1977), Elam's formulation vividly captures the interaction that is constitutive of music as performance. The contemporary performance studies paradigm stresses the extent to which signification is constructed through the act of performance, and generally through acts of negotiation either between performers, or between them and the audience. In other words, performative meaning is understood as subsisting in process, and hence by definition is irreducible to product; as Charles Bernstein (1998, 21) expresses it with reference to poetry reading, "Sound . . . can never be completely recuperated as ideas, as content, as narrative, as extralexical meaning."

To understand music as performance, then, means to see it as an irreducibly social phenomenon, even when only a single individual is involved. (There is a comparison with religious ritual, which involves the enaction of socially agreed-on forms of expression even when conducted in private.) According to Ingrid Monson (1996, 186), "the formal features of musical texts are just one aspect—a subset, so to speak—of a broader sense of the musical, which also includes the contextual and the cultural. Rather than being conceived as foundational or separable from context, structure is taken to have as one of its central functions the construction of social context." Seen this way, however, the term *text*, with its connotations of New Critical autonomy and structuralism, is perhaps less helpful than the more distinctively theatrical term *script*. Whereas to think of a Mozart quartet as a "text" is to construe it as a half-sonic, half-ideal object reproduced in performance, to think of it as a "script" is to see it as choreographing a series of real-time, social interactions between players: a series of mutual acts of listening and communal gestures that enact a particular vision of human society, the communication of which to the audience is one of the special characteristics of chamber music.

Thinking of music as "script" rather than "text" implies a reorientation of the relationship between notation and performance. The traditional model of musical transmission, borrowed from philology, is the stemma: a kind of family tree in which successive interpretations move vertically away from the composer's original vision. The text, then, is the embodiment of this vision, and the traditional aim of source criticism is to ensure as close an alignment as possible between the two, just as the traditional aim of historically informed performance is to translate the vision into sound. But the performance studies paradigm in effect turns this model by 180 degrees: as Richard Schechner (1998, 28) expresses it, it emphasizes "explorations of horizontal relationships among related forms rather than a searching vertically for unprovable origins." In other words, it seeks to understand performances primarily in relation to other performances (Schechner's "related forms") rather than to the notated text; a given performance of Beethoven's 9th Symphony, for example, will acquire its meaning from its relationship to the horizon of expectations established by other performances.

The reorientation does not stop there. Busoni famously refused to admit any ontological distinction among scores, performances, and arrangements, because he saw all of them as equally transcriptions of an abstract, platonic idea. Current performance theory reaches the same conclusion from the opposite premise: there is no ontological distinction among the different modes of a work's existence, its different instantiations, because there is no original. Charles Bernstein (1998, 10) invokes Alfred Lord's study of the Homerian epic in order to oppose the reduction of poem to text: "I believe," wrote Lord, "that once we know the facts of oral composition we must cease to find an original of any traditional song. From an oral point of view each performance is original." And Stan Godlovitch (1998, 96) sees the related practice of storytelling as the best model for musical performance, not only because it emphasizes presentation, skill, and communication, but also because "this view of the relationship between works and performances puts the former in their proper musical place primarily as vehicles and opportunities for the latter in the larger business of making music." Instead of a single work located "vertically" in relation to its performances, then, we have an unlimited number of instantiations, all on the same "horizontal" plane.

Or have we moved too fast and too far? Is it really credible to claim that we have no "original" in the case of, say, the 9th Symphony when we have Beethoven's text? I have two answers to this. The first is that Beethoven's text exists only as an interpretive construct; there is a variety of largely contradictory sources (the autograph, copyists' scores, early printed editions, and so on), and it might be argued that the urtext editions of Beethoven's symphonies, which are at last beginning to appear, do not so much replace earlier texts as add new ones. (To put it another way, new editorial work constantly constructs new "originals.") The second answer is that while these historically privileged texts have a particular significance and authority within the field encompassed by the 9th Symphony, they do not exhaust the work's identity: in a passage that I have quoted so often that I might as well quote it once more, Lawrence Rosenwald (1993, 62) characterizes the identity of the 9th Symphony as "something existing in the relation between its notation and the field of its performances." This precisely captures what I am trying to convey: that Beethoven's text (whatever that means) has an obviously privileged role and yet relates horizontally, as Schechner would put it, to the symphony's other instantiations, resulting in just the kind of intertextual field to which Elam referred. In other words, the work does not exist "above" the field of its instantiations, but rather encompasses it—which, of course, is why the 9th Symphony is still evolving. There is a sense, then, in which to refer (like Godlovitch) to work "and" performance is just as wrongheaded as speaking of music "and" performance.

But somehow there is a remainder. It is only when you have started thinking of music as performance that the peculiarly time-resisting properties of works in the Western "art" tradition come fully into relief. The real-time process of performance routinely leaves not a few, fragmentary memories (like a holiday, say) but rather the sense that we have experienced a *piece* of music, an imaginary object that somehow continues to exist long after the sounds have died away. "The belief that quartets and symphonies of Mozart and Beethoven rise above history can never be completely erased," Charles Rosen (1994a, 89) affirms, because "the autonomy was written into them." Rosen's confident tone belies the fragility of this snatching of eternity, so to speak, from the jaws of evanescence: the extraordinary illusion—for that is what it is—that there is such a thing as music, rather than simply acts of making and receiving it, might well be considered the basic premise of the Western "art" tradition.

But what kind of musicological practice might this translate into? The most obvious way of studying music as performance is to study those traces or representations of past performances that make up the recorded heritage, thereby unlocking a century-long archive of acoustical texts comparable in extent and significance to the notated texts around which musicology originally came into being. Some musicologists, such as José Bowen, have used computers to make comparisons of performance timing across large numbers of recordings of "the same work"; this approach directly reflects the idea of music as a horizontal field of instantiations, and allows for a range of stylistic measures and the extrapolation of statistical trends, but does not easily provide the kind of insight into the specific qualities of specific interpretations that score-based analysis characteristically offers. (It suffers, in short, from the traditional problems of style analysis.) The alternative, as illustrated by the work of Joel Lester, is to seek to relate performance interpretation to the available analytical readings of a particular composition, in effect working from analysis to recording; here the danger is of replicating what the theater theorist Susan Melrose (1994, 215) terms the "page to stage" approach, and so reinforcing the very presupposition (that music is in essence a text reproduced in performance) that studying music as performance was supposed to interrogate.

Another route to understanding music as performance might be to focus on the functioning of the performing body, both in itself and in relation to other dimensions of the performance event (see Clarke and

Davidson 1998). But again the conceptual framework is crucial. Melrose (1994, 210) observes that structuralist approaches to theatrical perform- ance attributed significance to the body only to the extent that they con- structed it as "text" (and the same might be said of the performance timing approaches I have just described). The contemporary perform- ance studies paradigm, by contrast, seeks to understand the body in the same way as it understands sound, as a site of resistance to text, for as Charles Bernstein (1998, 21) puts it, "Sound is language's flesh, its opac- ity, as meaning marks its material embeddedness in the world of things." And in both cases performance is understood to be in "fundamental opposition to the desire for depth," as Kaye (1994, 69) puts it. His choice of words is particularly suggestive in a musical context, given the extent to which analytical discussions of performance represent it as a more or less transparent revelation of underlying structure (the obvious example is the Schenkerian concept of performing from the middle- ground). Set that aside, and a variety of terms might come into play to articulate the opacity of the relationship: quotation, commentary, cri- tique, parody, irony, or travesty, for example.

But a further conceptual ingredient is crucial. Melrose (1994, 225) quotes Ariane Mnouchkine's observation that "the goal of text analysis is to attempt to explain everything. Whereas the role of the actor . . . is not at all to explicate the text." It is just this distinction that theoretical approaches to musical performance generally seek to deny. After all, you cannot perform from the middle ground unless you have an authoritative knowledge of the text, and William Rothstein reveals the assumption that this is the foundation of articulate performance when he says (by way of the exception that proves the rule) that it is sometimes better to conceal than to project structure: on such occasions, he says, "the performer adopts *temporarily* the viewpoint of one or two characters in the drama, so to speak, rather than assuming omniscience at every moment" (Rothstein 1995, 238; my italics). By comparison a postmodern approach, as advo- cated by Kevin Korsyn (1999, 65), would question the possibility of what he calls "a central point of intelligibility, a privileged position for the spec- tator"—or, in this case, the performer. As might be expected, Korsyn invokes Bakhtin's concept of dialogic in order to make his point, drawing a comparison between music and Bakhtin's concept of novelistic discourse as "an artistically organized system for bringing different languages in con- tact with one another, a system having as its goal the illumination of one language by means of another" (p. 61). This image of different languages being brought into contact with one another—an image strikingly reminiscent of the Elam quotation—provides a fertile framework for the analysis of musical performance, and indeed it is hard to think of an area in which the Bakhtinian concepts of heteroglossia and double-voiced discourse might be applied in a more literal manner.

This is not an original observation. Richard Middleton (2000) has appropriated Bakhtin's concepts for the analysis of popular music, linking them to Henry Louis Gates Jr.'s (1988) concept of "Signifyin(g)"; Monson (1996, 98–106) has made the same linkage in connection with the tissue of intertextual reference that is jazz improvisation, also adding W. E. B. Du Bois's concept of African-American "double-consciousness" into the mix. Such approaches not only add depth to such concepts as parody, irony, and the rest, but also throw the emphasis firmly on the quality of creativity, of performative difference, which Gates invokes when he defines Signifyin(g) as "[r]epetition with a signal difference" (discussed in Monson 1996, 103); this semiotically charged figuring of iteration as commentary, ventriloquism, or even impersonation lies at the core of, for instance, Hendrix's Monterey covers of *Like a Rolling Stone* or *Sgt. Pepper's Lonely Hearts Club Band*. That approaches such as these, developed for the articulation of characteristic features of African-American culture, should be well adapted for the analysis of jazz and popular music is not surprising. I would go further, however, and suggest that just as the spread of African-American musical practices has gone far toward establishing a global lingua franca, so the concepts of Signifyin(g) and double-consciousness can help to articulate the creativity that has always been present in the performance culture of Western "art" music, but has long been repressed by the text-dominated discourses of musicology. Or to put it another way, thinking of "art" performances as reproductions may be less useful than thinking of them as monolithic, culturally privileged instances of intertextual reference.

The issue of omniscience, of the availability or otherwise of a central point of intelligibility, also has a direct effect upon the relationship between the performance analyst and the phenomena under investigation, and it is the component of the contemporary performance studies synthesis that I have not yet directly discussed that makes this clearest: ethnomusicology. Through its functionalist orientation (i.e., its insistence on understanding any practice within the totality of its cultural context), ethnomusicology from the start distanced itself from the model of detached observation and synthesis that characterized its predecessor discipline, comparative musicology. Instead, it emphasized the necessity of fieldwork, understood as prolonged residence within the target culture, during which musical practices would be observed in context and an understanding of native conceptualization acquired. Nevertheless the aim remained one of, if not omniscience, then at least an authoritative and objective understanding of cultural practice.

More recent approaches to fieldwork, however, question the availability of such a central point of intelligibility in just the same way that Korsyn does; it is for this reason that Michelle Kisliuk (1997, 33) describes the claim of ethnomusicological and other ethnography "to interpret reality for its 'informants'" as a "pretense." The result is that, in Jeff Todd Titon's words (1997, 87), "Fieldwork is no longer viewed principally as observing and collecting (although it surely involves that) but as experiencing and understanding music," and he continues: "The new fieldwork leads us to ask what it is like for a person (ourselves included) to make and to know music as lived experience." In a word, it stresses personal participation in the performative generation of meaning that is music, and as most conspicuously represented by such books as Kisliuk's *Seize the Dance!* (1998), it gives rise to a literary practice that is as close to travel writing or even autobiography as to the traditional literature of ethnomusicology, and which is also acutely conscious of its performative nature as writing. As Titon (1997, 96) puts it, citing Geertz, the performative approach "forces us to face the fact that we are primarily authors, not reporters."

Applied to more traditional musicological contexts, an ethnographic approach questions conventional constructions of relevance. For the drama theorist Baz Kershaw (1992, 22), it is "a fundamental tenet of performance theory . . . that no item in the environment of performance can be discounted as irrelevant to its impact," and Bernstein (1998, 14) provides an all-too-graphic illustration of what this might mean when he characterizes "gasps, stutters, hiccups, burps, coughs, slurs, microrepetitions, oscillations in volume, 'incorrect' pronunciations, and so on" as "semantic features of the performed poem . . . and not as extraneous interruption." The point Bernstein is making is that "one of the primary techniques of poetry performance is the disruption of rationalizable patterns of sound through the intervallic irruption of acoustic elements not recuperable by monological analysis" (p. 13), and one might say that in music the performance "of" paradigm—the equivalent of Bernstein's "monological analysis"—filters out such dimensions of performance as are not directly referable to the work being performed. An ethnographic approach, by contrast, seeks to understand the performance of a particular piece in the context of the total performance event, encompassing issues of program planning, stage presentation, dress, articulation with written texts, and so forth. To date, this approach is more familiar in the context of popular music than of the "art" tradition, and the work of Les Back offers a representative example that parallels both Kisliuk's self-consciously performative writing and, in its invocation of Deleuze and Guattari's cultural "rhizomes," Schechner's concept of the horizontal: Back shows by such means how the performances of the Birmingham (U.K.)-based musician Apache Indian function as an arena for complex negotiations of cultural identity reflecting, as he puts it, "a diasporic triple consciousness that is simultaneously the child of Africa, Asia, and Europe" (1996, 75).

For the musicologist such work may be simultaneously stimulating, because of the virtuosity with which cultural meaning is read in the multifarious dimensions of the performance event, and frustrating, because of its lack of engagement with the specifics of music. How might we put the music back into performance analysis? One model is provided by Monson's analyses of jazz improvisation, in which extended transcriptions are aligned with prose commentary, and counterpointed by quotations from and discussions of performers' discourse. Again, the kind of communicative interaction between performers that Chris Smith (1998) has analyzed in relation to Miles Davis is equally evident within the dynamics of—to repeat my previous example—a string quartet playing Mozart: Here there is an opportunity to combine ethnographic and traditional music-theoretical approaches, as well as the computer-based measurement of timing to which I have already referred, in an analysis of the relationship between notated "script" and social interaction. And if this kind of work is harder with the Western "art" repertory than with jazz improvisation, because of the danger of relapsing into the performance "of" paradigm, then a useful halfway house is offered by analysis of the longitudinal process by which "art" music interpretations come into being, that is, of rehearsal; this is a topic beginning to attract interest from music theorists, psychologists, and sociologists (see, e.g., Goodman 2000).

But analyzing music as performance does not necessarily mean analyzing specific performances or recordings at all. John Potter (1998, 182) offers an analysis of a passage from Antoine Brumel's *Missa Victimae Paschali* that focuses on the intimate negotiations and conjunctions between the performers, and the manner in which these inflect the performance: "Throughout, the voices are setting up patterns of tension and relaxation, acutely conscious of each other, both seeking to accommodate each others' desires and to satisfy themselves." At the end of the first bar, a particular dissonance "is only a passing moment but it creates a moment of acute pleasure that they may wish to prolong," thereby subverting the tempo (p. 180); the third voice (with successive eighth notes on the first beat of the following bar) has to reestablish the tempo, but by the suspension at the end of the bar it is the superius who controls the negotiations of tempo between the performers. "I have not chosen an actual performance," Potter writes, "since the potential degree of realization of the points I wish to make will vary from performance to performance" (p. 178). But the points themselves are scripted in Brumel's music; that is, they can be recovered from the score provided the analyst has the requisite knowledge of performance practice (Potter is a professional singer whose experience ranges from medieval music to *Tommy*)—and provided that the dissonances in question are understood not just as textual features, as attributes of the musical object, but as prompts to the enaction of social relationships in the real time of performance.

And the analysis of social interaction between performers offered by writers like Potter and Monson prompts a final thought on the potential of performance analysis for a culturally oriented musicology. The underlying objective of such a musicology, to understand music as both reflection and generator of social meaning, is most ambitiously expressed in Adorno's claim that music "presents social problems through its own material and according to its own formal laws—problems which music contains within itself in the innermost cells of its technique" (Adorno 1978, quoted and discussed in Martin 1995, 100). Music, in other words, becomes a resource for understanding society. Adorno's own analyses of music have proved a constant source of frustration, however, while even his apologist Rose Subotnik (1976, 271) has described his concept of the interface between music and society as "indirect, complex, unconscious, undocumented, and mysterious." But the problem disappears if instead of seeing musical works as texts within which social structures are encoded, we see them as scripts in response to which social relationships are enacted: The object of analysis is now present and self-evident in the interactions between performers, and in the acoustic trace that they leave. To call music a performing art, then, is not just to say that we perform it; it is to say that through it we perform social meaning.

Further Reading

Bowen, José A. 1999. Finding the music in musicology: Performance history and musical works. Pp. 424–51 in *Rethinking music*. Edited by Nicholas Cook and Mark Everist. Oxford: Oxford Univ. Press.

Davies, Stephen. 2001. *Musical works and performances: A philosophical exploration*. Oxford: Clarendon Press.

Day, Tim. 2000. *A century of recorded music: Listening to musical history*. New Haven, Conn.: Yale Univ. Press.

Godlovitch, Stan. 1998. *Musical performance: A philosophical study*. London: Routledge.

Goehr, Lydia. 1992. *The imaginary museum of musical works: An essay in the philosophy of music*. Oxford: Clarendon Press.

Kivy, Peter. 1995. *Authenticities: Philosophical reflections on musical performance*. Ithaca, N.Y.: Cornell Univ. Press.

Lester, Joel. 1995. Performance and analysis: Interaction and interpretation. Pp. 197–216 in *The practice of performance: Studies in musical interpretation*. Edited by John Rink. Cambridge, U.K.: Cambridge Univ. Press.

Monson, Ingrid. 1996. *Saying something: Jazz improvisation and interaction*. Chicago: Univ. of Chicago Press.

Philip, Robert. 1992. *Early recordings and musical style: Changing tastes in instrumental performance, 1900–1950*. Cambridge, U.K.: Cambridge Univ. Press.

Potter, John. 1998. *Vocal authority: Singing style and ideology*. Cambridge, U.K.: Cambridge Univ. Press.

Talbot, Michael, ed. 2000. *The musical work: Reality or invention?* Liverpool: Liverpool Univ. Press.

Taruskin, Richard. 1995. *Text and act: Essays on music and performance*. New York: Oxford Univ. Press.

CHAPTER 18

Of Mice and Dogs
Music, Gender, and Sexuality at the Long Fin de Siècle

IAN BIDDLE

This chapter is an attempt to locate a particularly crucial moment in the history of European music when we began to think about gender and sexuality in ways that we would recognize as "modern." When, for example, did we begin to think of gender as something that is "performed"? When, furthermore, did we begin to conceive of sexuality as an "unceasing flow," to use Freud's imagery, never fully satisfied by its "objects" of desire? It is my contention that a striking reorientation of attitudes to gender, sexuality, and the body can be located at what might be termed the "long" fin de siècle, and that this reorientation has striking consequences for European musical practice. It is "long" for two reasons: (1) because the "moment" of which I speak (circa 1870–1930) is far too long to be characterized simply as a calendar-induced moment of transition (its classically modernist articulation); and (2) because, in several very powerful ways, the intellectual "revolutions" that marked the long fin de siècle are still very much with us. I concentrate my attention in this chapter on two late short stories by the German-Jewish homosexual writer Franz Kafka that deal explicitly with music and its relationship with gender and/or sexuality as a topic: "Josephine the Singer or the Mouse Folk" and "Investigations of a Dog" (completed in 1919 and 1920, respectively, and both published in 1922). By a close reading of how that relationship is dealt with in the two Kafka stories I hope to place the ways we think about the interconnectedness of European music, gender, and sexuality under intense scrutiny.

Three qualitative revolutions impact upon the discursive appropriation of music in this period: the advent of recording technology (1877, with Edison's phonograph) and the subsequent acceleration of the "objectification" and commoditization of music; Freud's (and Breuer's) work on hysteria and sexuality, in which "desire" is posited as a kind of aimless "flow" without any fixed object to which to attach itself or in which to satiate itself; and crucially, the collapse of what Friedrich Kittler has termed *universal translatability* (1990)—for Kittler, the advent of the new technologies of recording, mechanical typing, and film constitute a radical breakdown in the assumption that the "message" of an artwork is somehow easily separated from the medium in which that message is presented (its "mediality") and readily "translatable" into another medium.

We begin, in perverse counterchronological logic, with Lacan, specifically his discussion of a striking passage from Sartre's *Being and Nothingness*: "you will see that, far from speaking of the emergence of this gaze as of something that concerns the organ of light, [Sartre] refers to the sound of rustling leaves, suddenly heard while out hunting, to a footstep heard in a corridor" (Lacan [1964] 1979, 84).

The gothic frisson of this passage from *The Four Fundamental Concepts of Psycho-Analysis* is remarkable for its faithfulness to the long fin de siècle. The uncanny reciprocity of looking and listening that so fascinates Lacan in this passage is a curious articulation of the fatal tendency, in discourses about the self since Freud, for the one looking or listening to readily turn into the one looked at or listened to: "And when are those sounds heard? At the moment when he has presented himself in the action of looking through a keyhole. A gaze surprises him in the function of a voyeur, disturbs him, overwhelms him and reduces him to a feeling of shame" (Lacan [1964] 1979, 84).

Sartre's choice of sound, the "rustling of leaves" or a "footstep in a corridor," to mark the uncanny anxiety of "being beside oneself," draws on the rather ancient conceit that sound is somehow beyond the limits of what we can rationally know. In this sense, sound (and music in particular) has been made to take on many of the functions of discourse that language fails to enunciate. This is by no means a recent trope. Indeed, it is a commonplace, and has been for a long time, to conceive of sound/ music, as a boundary. And, like so many overdetermined boundaries, music often takes on the characteristics of a zone of danger, of anxiety, of promise: it is perilously porous, and thus intensively policed. But boundaries are also the sites of discourse formation and/or dissolution, the place where the shape and scope of discourse can be tested and reformulated ad infinitum. In this perilous play at the edge of discourse, boundaries are intensely and frequently contested: as many scholars have shown, in this contested zone—a "dangerous crossroads" as George Lipsitz recently termed it—discourse is anxious (Sedgwick 1985, 1990; Butler 1990; Haraway 1991).

When threatened by possible collapse, discourse—especially the discourse of the self we identified above—shores itself up by appealing to a range of resources that seem to offer it security. As feminist commentators have demonstrated over and over, these resources—epistemological, metaphorical, and ideological—are *densely gendered* (Irigaray 1985; Cixous 1980, 1990). This insight is grounded in the observation, made most explicitly by Jacques Derrida in his critique of Lacan's seminar on Poe (Derrida [1979] 1987; Lacan 1972), that Western epistemology is characterized by a ubiquitous *phallogocentrism*. A conflation of *phallo-* and *logo*-centrism, this term designates the "old and enormous root" that characterizes our use of language: "the 'description' is a 'participation' when it induces a practice, an ethics, an institution, and therefore a politics that ensure the truth of the tradition" (Derrida [1975] 1987, 481n). For Derrida, language arrives to us *always already* marked by the deployment of a misogynistic discourse, and we can only counter this linguistic phallogocentrism by constant vigilance. It is not surprising that the figuration of music as a boundary has facilitated its appropriation as a way of doing important cultural work, not least at the points where gender and sexuality are constructed.

Kafka's Mice, or, Music and Gender

When music is characterized as a boundary, it is so characterized in order to place it under pressure to do the cultural work that discourse cannot undertake for itself. When it comes to the cultural work of gender and sexuality—both discursive formulations and yet both impish in their refusal of the constraints rational discourse seeks to place on them—music can operate as a way of effecting a particular discursive outcome: she sings like an angel; he marches with conviction; she dances like a woman possessed; he really hammers that piano. In each case, the "description" is densely gendered, sounding out the production of what Derrida would call an "ethico-institutional discourse" in its appeal to deeply embedded assumptions about femininity and masculinity.

The phallogocentrism of the Western rational epistemology marks music as a particularly volatile yet profoundly effective (and affective) cultural resource in the imagining, policing, and managing of discourses on gender. This is clear in a striking passage from the first of our Kafka short stories, "Josephine the Singer or the Mouse Folk." This story tells of a "great singer" who "whistles" for the mouse folk, an "unmusical people," as Kafka terms them. Many have suggested that the mice represent the Jews and, according to this reading, the tale is an ironic recasting of the commonly held fin de siècle view that Jews were incapable of original creativity, mere nomads who drifted through "rooted" European culture and mimicked the outer forms of that culture. But there are also other things to say about this story: at one point in the narrative, the narrator characterizes Josephine's bodily vibration when she sings in the following manner:

> So there she stands, the delicate creature, shaken by vibrations especially below the breastbone, so that one feels anxious for her, it is as if she has concentrated all her strength on her song, as if from everything in her that does not directly subserve her singing all strength has been withdrawn, almost all power of life, as if she were laid bare, abandoned, committed merely to the care of good angels, as if while she is so wholly withdrawn and living only in her song a cold breath blowing upon her might kill her. (Kafka [1922] 1993b, 236–37)

A multitude of discursive effects is activated here: the alignment of physical delicacy with femininity; song as a site for the construction and performance of female gender; the body as the primary site for the construction of the feminine; the proximity of the feminine to sickness and so on. And it is to a sort of degraded "song" (the "whistling" [*Pfeifen*] that we mentioned above) that Kafka looks for a site in which to lay out in ironic form the complexities of fin de siècle gender designations. For our purposes here, it is this aspect of the story that requires our attention. In Josephine's singing, as Boa (1996) has shown, Kafka is able to articulate the material conditions that sustain the "profession" of the female singer, her closeness to images of prostitution, her manner of *representing* a particular (misogynistic) imagination of the feminine as itself a marker of the alienation of feminine labor, its aestheticization (Boa 1996, 179).

Nonetheless, as a "singer" who merely "whistles," one who is so precariously endangered by this act of whistling and so comprehensively deeroticized, Josephine also serves to subvert the hysterical misogyny that attends the construction and consumption of the diva in the long fin de siècle. The cultural work that Kafka asks musical performance to undertake here is activated in no small measure by the use of music to mark a contested boundary between erotic play and the law. It is music that denies the appropriation of the feminine form as an object of desire, and generates a discursive play in the confrontation of the narrator's masculinity—itself ironically performative of a certain masculine "assuredness," "rationality" etc. (the narrator states at one point that "she cannot very well go on limping forever . . .")—with Josephine's femininity. This play is furthermore reliant on music's performative qualities: the "arbitrary" distinction the mouse folk draws between Josephine's whistling and the everyday whistling of other mice is reflected in her spatial deployment on a stage, away from the others. What separates her whistling from the others' equally mundane whistling is an agreement among the members of the mouse community that her whistling is different. In appealing to a model of musical meaning that relies first and foremost on the active construction of meaning by a community of the music's users, Kafka thereby also draws our attention to the performative dimension of *gender*. If music's meanings are made, and performed, so, by implication, are the meanings of gender: We learn to subvert the "given" nature or "law" of meaning by witnessing the ironic juxtaposition of music and gender. The proximity here helps undo the phallogocentric work of language.

This structural trope, the proximity of music and gender performativity, is grounded in the working through of a relationship between the various "stuffs" of discourse—between media—that Friedrich Kittler (1985) has described as "to a degree arbitrary, a manipulation." In this view, the passing of "messages" [*Botschaften*] from music into literature or literature into music, for example, comes to be viewed, somewhere around 1900, as a process that has to be constantly remade, refashioned at every delicate site of exchange. This moment is characterized by a sudden cohering of historical processes around this single principle of the impossibility of translating cultural materials from one medium to another. This is termed by Kittler a "discourse network" [*Aufschreibesystem*]: a historical "knot" governed by a single structuring principle. It is crucial here to distinguish this "delicate exchange," as I am calling it (Kittler terms it "transposition"), from "translation" which, as we have seen, refers to an older premodernist view of the message as somehow independent from its medium (this would be the structuring principle of the 1800 discourse network associated with romanticism in particular). This is how Kittler defines the later network:

Given Medium A, organized as a denumerable collection of discrete elements $E^a_1 \ldots E^a_n$, its transposition into Medium B will consist in reproducing the internal (syntagmatic and paradigmatic) relations between its elements in the collection $E^b_1 \ldots E^b_m$. Because the number of elements *n* and *m* and the rules of association are hardly ever identical, every transposition is to a degree arbitrary, a manipulation. It can appeal to nothing universal and must, therefore, leave gaps. (Kittler 1990, 265)

If music is often deliberately implicated in debates about gender, then it is inevitably thereby implicated in debates about how discourse transposition (from "gender" in law, biology, or popular psychology to "gender in music") is possible. It is crucial to recognize in Kittler's theory of media a profoundly historicist articulation of the exchange: the nature and scope of discourse exchange is reliant upon the local technologies and cultural resources that are available to the wielders of discourse. The extent of the implication of discourses on gender in literary or operatic forms, for example, is intimately connected to the ways in which the various data of those discourses came to be stored: "color and sound, light and the voice have become recordable, become part of the general acceleration, 'in the sense of the technical maximization of all velocities, in whose time-space modern technology and apparatus can alone be what they are' [Heidegger]. Henceforth, command will conflict with command, medium with medium" (267).

In this conflicted economy of exchange, the relationship between gender and music at the long fin de siècle must be explored, therefore, in the context of developments of new technologies, especially the technology of recording. If, for example, the singing or spoken voice can be *recorded*, it can also be constituted as a *fixed* object of scrutiny; sounds can be transported, moved from one location to another, and yet remain sounds, retain their "mediality" as sonic material. There is no longer a need for discourse translation in order to achieve a circulation of the "stuff" of sound in culture. As a result, the sounds of the voice can become stable carriers of human character, and of sexual and gender pathologies that hitherto resided only in the internal invisible world of the psyche. Hence, these externalized sounds become mobile, powerfully characterized markers *both* of healthy communicative norms *and* pathological deviance: voice now comes under the scrutiny of the rationalizing medical impulse. The operatic voice (especially the "pathological" feminine voice) can be seen as an elaboration of this new knowledge: Lulu/*Lulu*, for example, is unthinkable before the phonograph.

Kafka's Dogs, or, Music and Sexuality

Eve Sedgwick (1985, 1990) has famously shown how the phallogocentric tendency is invariably accompanied by its complement, homophobia. The conceptual pairing hetero/homo, which Sedgwick locates in fin de siècle medical discourses, is possible only after the term (and type) *homosexual* has entered medical discourse. This is also the point at which the need to "police" sexuality becomes particularly acute since to "medicalize" homosexuality is not only to "recognize" it (thereby constituting it for the first time as a sexual *identity* and thus bringing with it the need to conceive of *rights* and *laws* for that identity), but also to bring it into existence as a sexual *pathology*. This effects a new form of homophobia, the rise of which is dependent upon new conceptions of a medicalized "perverse" or nonnormative sexuality incubated in the already well-formed fin de siècle fascination with criminology, pathology, and raciology. One need only look to the densely sexualized reception of, for example, Gustav Mahler in order to see how sexual "perversion," gender "deviance" and racial "difference" overlap in the musicocritical discourses at the end of the nineteenth century (Franklin 1991).

If, as Foucault (1987) would have us believe, sexuality operates in the manner of a deployment rather than as a kind of state of being, then it is in the very *act* of its deployment, in a kind of discursive gear shift or *discourse transposition*, that sexuality can be said to exist at all: In this sense, sexuality, like gender, is the "invention" of the 1900 discourse network, reliant on a location of desire within a logic of exchange that is framed by the immutability of media. This observation is crucial to our understanding of sexuality at the fin de siècle. Just as Freud liquidates the "material" phenomenon of the dream in his *The Interpretation of Dreams* (1900) by seeking to differentiate fundamentally the "stuff" of the dream from the "language" we use to interpret it, so media transpositions "liquidate the Medium from which they proceed" (Kittler 1990, 275). Sex is obliterated in the act of writing; writing is obliterated in the production of sound. Only desire, the emptied-out, brilliant, fluid, overwhelming structurality of sex, seems to remain. It operates as a ghostly polymorphous carrier of shifting object relations from one medium to another, never completely entering the medium, never quite being taken up, always somehow *outside*.

Hence, the "deployment" that sexuality might be said to constitute will necessarily be activated at those same contested regions we have identified as music's operational territory at the fin de siècle, the boundary. How, then, does this boundary zone operate for discourses of sexuality? And how can music intervene in this operation? In the medicalization of the interior life of the psyche at the fin de siècle, music continued to help shape or articulate debates about *gender* through its appropriation by the wielders of discourse as a territory in which these debates could be rehearsed (a "zone" or site). Its encounter with *sexuality* was, as we might expect, similar but by no means the same. Whereas music was often appropriated as a secondary "site" or proxy for debates about gender, in its encounter with fin de siècle sexuality, music was often called upon to undertake highly explicit, indeed contested work: it would often have to conjure up, even as it announced its cultivated artifice, the very "stuff" of desire as an aestheticized material "flow." This powerful yet ultimately banal transposition allows the polymorphous nature of desire to find a crude analogue in the "flux" of sound. In our second Kafka short story, "Investigations of a Dog," an old dog recounts his encounter, many years earlier, with a group of "strange creatures" whom he takes also to be dogs. At the moment of this encounter, our dog narrator is overwhelmed, and music is here given extraordinary cultural work to do:

> [T]he music gradually got the upper hand, literally knocked the breath out of me and swept me far away from those actual little dogs, and quite against my will, while I howled as if some pain were being inflicted upon me, my mind could attend to nothing but this blast of music which seemed to come from all sides, from the heights, from the depths, from everywhere, surrounding the listener, overwhelming him, crushing him, and over his swooning body still blowing fanfares so near that they seemed far away and almost inaudible. (Kafka [1922] 1993a, 424)

The omnidirectionality, the overwhelming plurality of this music, its ego-debilitating effects, the source of an unbearable pain: all these figurations of music point to an extraordinarily terrifying bodily encounter with the underside of paternal law. Indeed, as the narrator observes, "those dogs were violating the law" and, like all idealized others, they fail to answer the Lacanian *che vuoi?* ("what do you (the Other) want?") in the young narrator's entreaty: "But they—incredible! incredible!—they never replied, behaved as if I were not there. Dogs who make no reply to the greeting of other dogs are guilty of an offence against good manners which the humblest dog would never pardon any more than the greatest" (425).

The law is invoked here in a dialectical formulation: the one side of the law generates its opposite, transgressive Other. What is particularly striking in this passage is the disturbing incursion of the unfettered gaze into the narrative:

Could I not see the last and youngest dog, to whom most of those cries were addressed, often stealing a glance at me as if he would have dearly wished to reply, but refrained because it was not allowed? But why should it not be allowed, why should the very thing which our laws unconditionally command not be allowed in this one case? (425)

Sound—the cries of the other dogs and the debilitating music—both *disturbs* the youngest "dog's" surreptitious gaze at the dog-narrator and *frames* its transgressive frisson: sound is both the marker of (warning against) transgression and a carrier (instigator) of desire; it is both a *signpost* to moral deviation and its *enabler*. The same-sex intimacy that might have ensued between the lawful and the lawless young dogs is transposed (foreclosed) by the music: whenever the dog-narrator reenters his legalistic phallogocentric discourse, the world falls silent; whenever sound intervenes (and especially music, which is here juxtaposed with occult knowledge or "magic") the narrator misses the transgression, lets it slip past unnoticed.

Great magicians [*Zauberer*] they might be, but the law was valid for them too ... and having recognized that, I now noticed something else. They had good grounds for remaining silent, that is, assuming they remained silent from a sense of shame [*Schuldgefühl*]. For how were they conducting themselves? Because of all the music I had not noticed it before, but they had flung away all shame, the wretched creatures were doing the very thing which is both most ridiculous and indecent in our eyes; they were walking on their hind legs. Fie on them! They were uncovering their nakedness, blatantly making a show of their nakedness ... as if Nature were in error. (426)

The display of the genitals, which Freud had already by 1905 linked to the interplay of exhibitionism and what he termed scopophilia, a highly eroticized mode of "looking" charged with the eroticism of touching (Freud [1905] 1977, 67), takes on the role here of an ironic, hyperbolic over-Freudian imagery. This ironic play on the Freudian orthodoxy also returns us to the extraordinary uncanny reciprocity of looking and listening that Lacan recognized in Sartre: Since music causes the narrator to miss the "shame" (Freud uses *Scham*) of exhibitionism, it functions here as a way of exploring taboos in a highly charged but safely "transposed" manner. Kittler's view of the 1900 discourse network as locked into media specificity is thus particularly apposite here: Lacan and Sartre's reciprocity of looking and listening, Kafka's dialectic of law and transgression, Freud's interplay of exhibitionism and scopophilia, all these fragile attempts at conjuring forms of equivalence across media are responses to the devastating fixity of media at the long fin de siècle.

The Homologizing Ideology

The devastation of this fixity is implicated in every anxious, overwrought "homological" coupling that stalks recent musicological attempts to implicate music in gender performance and to mark it as a substitution for the deployment of sexuality. I begin this final section by contending that homology, as an interpretative device whereby the structural proclivities of one cultural form are made to find a structural equivalent in another medium, uncritically reproduces the kinds of cultural patternings that characterize the phallogocentric impulse. Such patternings in musicology characterize a practice that is still grounded, as we shall see, in what might be termed an *Oedipal logic* (by which I mean the tendency, in even the most "radical" critiques of misogynistic practices and assumptions at work in musicology, to appeal ultimately to the Law of the Father and to surreptitiously reinstate the patriarch), and which fundamentally avoids explicit examination of *how* the connectedness of music to gender and sexuality is brought about. We might map a typical example of this practice in the following manner:

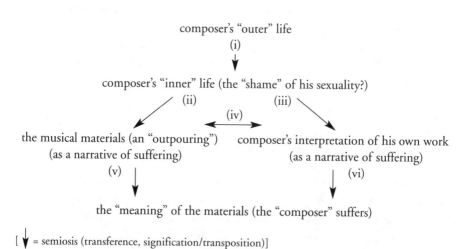

[↓ = semiosis (transference, signification/transposition)]

Figure 18.1. A typical relay of homological couplings in the oedipal economy of deviant creativity.

In this schema, a male homosexual composer, living and working in Europe some time after the explicit pathologization of homosexuality, is implicated in a deviant (or subversive, but always *spectacular*) compositional practice because of his sexuality. The composer's outer public life (his succumbing to an external law) is taken (via [i]) into his inner world (what Freud has termed the *superego*, the internalized Law of the Father). The suffering (shame) that the composer thereby feels is transformed (along [ii]) by a cathartic creative act into the aestheticization of that suffering, into "suffering," but safely doubly coded (via [iii]) by the composer's public counterpronouncements on the work's meanings. The task of the musicologist in this schema is to unpick the codification of the so-called "real" meaning in the subtle smoke-screening of the composer's public self-interpretation by considering the evidence of contemporaneous legal and popular discourses on sexuality, thereby constructing a template of how the composer will suffer *for us* along paths (v) and (vi). And it is for "us" that the composer suffers: this homological series is grounded in a view of that "suffering" (i.e., the suffering of the composer as "figured" in the musical work) as a *spectacle*.

1. The composer's "suffering" is paraded as a titillating spectacle for the liberal heterosexual critic fascinated by (desirous of) the homosexual Other.
2. The status of the "suffering" as spectacle is reliant upon the authority granted to that "suffering" by the same epistemological mechanisms that generate the suffering in the first place (since, to figure homosexuality as synonymous with suffering is to reproduce the idea that it is pathological and will inevitably *cause* suffering).
3. The work's signifying energies are largely focused on displaying that "suffering."

The heterosexist assumptions of this view aside, the Oedipal logic of the homological chain inevitably leads to the assumption that, like women, homosexual men "inevitably emerge in the only way the Oedipal story will let them be seen: as sources of problems" (Kearns 1997, 23). Hence, the assuredness of the homological chain mistakes the epistemological *content* of the Freudian revolution for its radical *consequences*. While there is much in Freud that allows us to make these kind of biographical observations, Freud's work is nonetheless structurally at odds with Oedipal biography. It is in the *mediality* of Freud's revolution—in his unwillingness to accept the homological coupling of dream content to dream interpretation, for example—that the revolution recognized by Kittler is grounded. In Kafka's ironic over-Freudian narrator-dog, in Lacan's fractured discourse of the self, in Freud's psychoanalytic recasting of narratives of the self, we encounter the crucial characteristics of the 1900 discourse network: the *technological operation* of the new media dispensation. In this new dispensation, music's connectedness to gender formation and the deployment of sexuality is extraordinarily fragile, and much more contested than musical scholarship has so far been willing to acknowledge.

Further Reading

Brett, Philip, Gary Thomas, and Elizabeth Wood, eds. 1994. *Queering the pitch: The new gay and lesbian musicology.* New York: Routledge.

Butler, Judith. 1990. *Gender trouble: Feminism and the subversion of identity.* New York: Routledge.

Citron, Marcia. 1993. *Gender and the musical canon.* Cambridge, U.K.: Cambridge Univ. Press.

Cook, Susan, Judy S. Tsou, and Susan McClary. 1994. *Cecilia reclaimed: Feminist perspectives on gender and music.* Urbana: Univ. of Illinois Press.

Ericson, Margaret. 1996. *Women and music: A selected annotated bibliography on women and gender issues in music, 1987–1992.* New York: G. K. Hall.

Green, Lucy. 1997. *Music, gender, education.* Cambridge, U.K.: Cambridge Univ. Press.

Groos, Arthur, and Roger Parker, eds. 1988. *Reading opera.* Princeton, N.J.: Princeton Univ. Press.

McClary, Susan. 1991. *Feminine endings: Music, gender and sexuality.* Minneapolis: Univ. of Minnesota Press.

Nattiez, Jean-Jacques. 1993. *Wagner androgyne.* Princeton, N.J.: Princeton Univ. Press.

Sedgwick, Eve Kosofsky. 1994. *Tendencies.* London: Routledge.

Solie, Ruth, ed. 1993. *Musicology and difference: Gender and sexuality in music scholarship.* Berkeley: Univ. of California Press.

Vice, Susan. 1996. *Psychoanalytic criticism: A reader.* Cambridge, U.K.: Polity Press.

CHAPTER 19

Contesting Difference
A Critique of Africanist Ethnomusicology

KOFI AGAWU

Difference may well be *the* sign of our times. In the United States, for example, feminist theories seeking to negotiate the problematic of gender, come to terms with various forms of essentialism, or to counter real world discrimination, have placed difference firmly on the critical agenda. Gay and lesbian studies, too, are centrally concerned with alternative episte-mologies, and with resisting coarse constructions of difference that may prove to be sociopolitically disadvantageous to their communities. And perhaps most notably, race as a category permeates a good deal of humanistic discourse, providing innumerable opportunities for a wide range of reflection upon difference. There are, as is to be expected, many points of divergence, but if we had to isolate one overriding concern, it may well be the attempt, in Gayatri Spivak's words, to undermine "the story of the straight, white, Judeo-Christian, heterosexual man of prop-erty as the ethical universal" (Spivak with Rooney 1989, 146).

Discussion of difference among music scholars is already under way, inspired in part by a number of interdisciplinary conversations, and in part by a widely shared feeling that only a few of music's many contexts have been given adequate scholarly attention (e.g., Solie 1993; Brett, Wood and Thomas 1994; Born and Hesmondhalgh 2000; Radano and Bohlman 2000). It is perhaps a little surprising that such discussion is not more prominent in Africanist ethnomusicology, a field that regularly traf-fics in difference. Although Martin Stokes characterizes the 1990s as a period in which the larger discipline of ethnomusicology "was absorbed by the question of difference, particularly in relation to matters of ethnicity, nation, race, gender and sexuality" (Stokes 2001, 388), signs of this absorption and subsequent reflection are not prominent in the subfield of Africanist ethnomusicology. Indeed, Christopher Waterman proffered an opposing view in 1991, claiming that "the portrayal of similarity and difference" is a subject "infrequently discussed" in Africanist ethnomusicology (Waterman 1991, 179). Waterman was well aware that ethnomusicology had always drawn *implicitly* on notions of difference, distance, and alterity. Explicit, open, and critical discussion of such notions was, however, strangely muted.

The purpose of this chapter is to develop a critique of notions of difference manifest in writings on African music. I proceed in three stages. First, I quote and comment upon a handful of thematizations of difference in Africanist ethnomusicology. Then I ask whether difference is "real." Finally, I take an explicitly political stance in urging a resistance to difference.

Thematizing Difference

Difference is regularly invoked by ethnomusicologists. Erich von Hornbostel, for example, opened his seminal 1928 article on "African Negro Music" with the question, "What is African music like as compared to our own?" His brief answer was, "African and (modern) European music are constructed on *entirely different principles*" (my emphasis). Why Hornbostel chose to emphasize differences over similarities, instead of granting similarities alongside differences, probably had less to do with the comparative method as such than with an inherited tradition of European representations of others. Perhaps Hegel's ghost was hovering over Hornbostel's pages, reminding the comparative musicologist of words written a century earlier: "[The African character] is difficult to comprehend, because it is so totally different from our own culture, and so remote and alien in relation to our own mode of consciousness" (Hegel [1822-8] [1975], cited in Eze 1997, 126; see Eze 1997 for other Enlightenment texts on race and Taiwo n.d. for a discussion of Hegel's view of Africa).

Interesting is the way in which Hornbostel, in the course of the article, concedes many points of similarity between the two musics. In fact, his phrase "entirely different principles" could easily be replaced by "similar principles" or, more daringly, by "the same general principles" without altering the (in)coherence of his argument. There is a danger of undercomplicating the challenge of comparison, however, for in the absence of explicit criteria for distinguishing between similarities and differences, a rigorous analysis cannot be undertaken. My interest here is not in proving the truth or falsity of Hornbostel's remark but in observing that his initially declared "difference" is a summary of his knowledge, not some fictional, unenlightened starting point to be proven untenable by a process of discovery. As such, it contradicts the other summary of his knowledge, the analytically achieved sameness that emerges from the article per se. This contradiction is fascinating: by constructing phenomena, objects, or people as "different," one stakes a claim to power over them.

A. M. Jones, too, opens his *Studies in African Music* of 1959 with a loud bang on the difference cymbal:

Anyone who goes to Africa is bound to hear the music of the country and is equally certain to notice that it is not the same as our Western music. True, the people sing, in solo or chorus, as we do, and their instruments though lacking the precision of Western technology, will still recognizably belong to the familiar families of wind, string, or percussion. Yet the music produced is obviously not the same sort of music as that to which we in the West are accustomed. . . . The plain fact is that African music is a strange and novel object when encountered by a Western musician. (Jones 1959, 1)

Jones acknowledged similarities and differences but, like Hornbostel, *chose* to give the edge to "strange[ness] and novel[ty]." Difference for him constituted premise as well as conclusion. As premise, difference served to enliven the process of discovery insofar as it allowed the Englishman to read African musical procedures as originating from an unfamiliar conceptual base. As conclusion, difference facilitated a symbolic affirmation of a prior, indeed naturalized view of African music as phenomenologically distinct from that of the West. Such acts of framing are not inevitable; they represent choices made within a broader economy of representational practices and impulses.

Hugh Tracey was equally forthright when, as Honorary Secretary of the African Music Society, he addressed the International Folk Music Council on July 14, 1953, on "The State of Folk Music in Bantu Africa":

We Europeans are at a great disadvantage in talking about African music. Unlike most other members of this conference we do not represent or discuss our own music but that of *a people radically unlike ourselves* among whom we live. It is only because we have found that the African is pathetically incapable of defending his own culture and indeed is largely indifferent to its fate that we, who subscribe wholeheartedly to the ideals of our International Council, are attempting to tide over the period during which irreparable damage can be done and until Africans themselves will be capable of appearing at our conferences as well-informed representatives of their own peoples. (Tracey 1954, 8; my emphasis)

The ringing characterization of Africans as "a people radically unlike ourselves" speaks to a persistent strategy of "differencing" that reaches back to the European Enlightenment. It is a habit that remains as alive today as it was in the 1950s, though it may take less blatant forms. Although Tracey understood that one consequence of the rise of global capital was the subjugation of African voices, although he construed the European's role in Africa as historically temporary, and although he felt confident that Africans would eventually possess the wherewithal to represent themselves, his own project and that of other Africanist ethnomusicologists did not pursue the task of transferring power to "Africans themselves" with any urgency. Nor was such a strategy finally implementable, for maintaining an imbalance of power is logically necessary for ethnomusicological practice. Balancing the distribution of power would remove one of ethnomusicology's crucial enabling mechanisms.

Hornbostel, Jones, and Tracey belong to an earlier generation, and so it may be thought that such acts of "differencing" are now a matter of the past. Yet, in more recent writing, Hegelian ideas of difference continue to be promulgated, sometimes in a direct and aggressively essentialist mode. Peter Cooke, for example, in a 1999 article subtitled "Listening to Instrumental Music in Africa South of the Sahara," sets out to prove that Africans "may well listen in a different way from the way Europeans do" (Cooke 1999, 73). Similarly, John Chernoff finds a peculiar link between the senses of hearing and smelling in Ghana: " 'Hearing' music, like 'hearing' a language or 'hearing' the truth or 'hearing' the scent of a soup, refers to perception as a form of recognition" (Chernoff 1997, 23).

The impulse to cast African realities into a priori categories of difference is so strong that both authors are led to make generalizations and inferences on the basis of questionable evidence. Thus Cooke makes much of the words attributed to an illiterate but highly skilled musician (Kakraba-Lobi), while Chernoff invests in a literal translation of the verb "to hear" by an individual with limited fluency in English. Both authors in effect strategically undercomplicate European practice in order to demonstrate Africa's ostensible uniqueness. Doing so, however, deprives Africa of full participation in our global critical conversation. While Africans deserve full recognition for whatever is unique about their critical and cultural practices, they do not need fake or facile attributions.

Is Difference Real?

At first sight, difference is a real, commonsensical phenomenon. Faced with a range of objects, I may distinguish them by number, size, color, texture, or function. The system of language enables me to invoke basic, meaning-producing oppositions. Thus, notes played on an instrument may be high or low, short or long, soft or loud, dark or bright. Chords may be consonant or dissonant, mellow or harsh, open- or close-spaced. These and thousands of such distinctions are employed routinely in (musicians') daily discourses. They are for the most part self-evident at a first level of articulation.

Meaning is difference. This fundamental insight has been worked over many times, with discussions extending into semiotic, linguistic, psycho-analytical, and other areas. Without difference, the ethnomusicologists would say after Saussure, there can be no meaning. So while a specific construction of meaning can accentuate one or another political or ideo-logical motivation, the will to communicate and the practical need to build from difference are shared by all producers of texts about music. The enterprise of ethnomusicology is, in this sense, not different from any other branch of learning.

A little reflection on the complex processes of meaning formation, however, undermines our confidence that differences are self-evident or natural. They are, in fact, propped up by other textual constructions and motivated in ways that are not (necessarily) immediately apparent. What, for example, does the term *black* mean when applied to a group of people in the United States? To some, it is a perfectly adequate descriptive cate-gory for one's racial makeup. "Race" in this understanding is distributed into two essential categories, "white" and "black" ("yellow" is underused since it does not carry the force of the two polar opposites, while various hybrids are generally consigned to the categories "black" or "nonwhite," never "white"). But since very few people are literally "black" or "white"— "brown" and "pink" might be more accurate substitutes for the meta-phorically challenged, those enamored of iconic signs—we need to translate signs from one realm of experience into another. But what about "black" as a social construction? Here, and depending on context, one might consciously (or, more often, subconsciously, and hence dangerously) tap into a series of historical or social texts that construe blackness in terms of slavery, sports, entertainment, preferential policies, urban violence, and so on. So, while at one level the terms *black* and *white* seem self-evident as descriptive categories, they are, in fact burdened with meaning (Gates 1986 provides an excellent introduction to issues of race and interpretation).

Differences, then, are not simply there for the perceiving subject. We do not perceive in a vacuum. Categories of perception are made, not given. Every act of perception carries implicit baggage from a history of habits of constructing the world. It should not seem strange at all—to choose a final set of examples—that not all of us notice hair types as markers of distinction among people. Similarly, in societies where intergenerational intercourse is marked, aging does not carry a stigma, and reference to an ethnographer as "an old man" is not an insult. Nor should one be upset at being described as "fatso" in communities in which plumpness is a sign of well-being. (Those who are thin are those who have not had enough to eat.)

To return to music: there is nothing self-evident about the categories used to distinguish African musics from Western music: functional as opposed to contemplative; communal rather than individualistic; spontaneous rather than calculated; rhythmically complex rather than simple; melodically unsophisticated rather than ornate; improvised rather than precomposed; and based in oral rather than written practices. These binarisms range from the possible to the irrational. Each subtends an asymmetrical relation in which one term is marked, the other unmarked. As ideology, these enduring characterizations speak to meaning as difference constructed by particular individuals for particular purposes.

Resisting Difference

There are two possible responses to the conditions described in the first part of this chapter: deny that there is anything problematic about the acts of differencing; or, accept the problem and abandon the Africanist ethnomusicological project altogether. The former recommends continuing with business as usual, while the latter advocates the end of all transactions. Might there be a less radical solution? In what alternative terms might we cast a principled pursuit of difference?

In a discussion of multiculturalism, Charles Taylor sought ways of interpreting degrees of difference and distance between cultures (Taylor 1994). Here is his Gadamer-inspired recommendation, one that has the added benefit for us of a musical analogy:

> [F]or a sufficiently different culture, the very understanding of what it is to be of worth will be strange and unfamiliar to us. To approach, say, a raga with the presumptions of value implicit in the well-tempered clavier would be forever to miss the point. What has to happen is what Gadamer has called a "fusion of horizons". We learn to move in a broader horizon, within which what we have formerly taken for granted as the background to valuation can be situated as one possibility alongside the different background of formerly unfamiliar culture. The "fusion of horizons" operates through our developing new vocabularies of comparison, by means of which we can articulate these contrasts. (Taylor 1994, 67)

A very reasonable proposition, this, indeed one that, far from being new, has been endorsed by social anthropologists committed to participant observation. It is also well known to ethnomusicologists whose ethnographies consciously incorporate "the native's point of view." Taylor's strategy for cross-cultural understanding promises to overcome certain ethical dilemmas raised by our dealing with Others. It provides a way of acknowledging, contextualizing, and eventually containing difference.

But isn't Taylor's program (and the numerous others that resonate with it) essentially a "Western" or "European" program? How does one decide, to start with, that a given culture is "sufficiently different"? If differences are constructed, then doesn't the judgment that one culture is "sufficiently different" from another presuppose a prior set of analytical acts? Isn't there a danger of monopolizing the ability to name something as different, a danger of granting that ability to those in the metropolis and denying it to those in the South? And whose are the resulting "broader horizons"—ours or theirs? Are they not essentially an expansion of Western horizons? Is it possible to achieve a genuine fusion of horizons between cultures located in radically different economic spheres? Is cross-cultural understanding ultimately possible?

These questions prompt us to consider an alternative strategy. Taylor notwithstanding, we might approach a raga with "the presumptions of value" implicit in Bach's *Well-Tempered Clavier* in order to pursue to the limits our initial impression—for it is no more than that—that the two musics are "sufficiently different." If we probe the contexts of both musics with equal commitment and sensitivity, and if we accept the theory that the impulses that lie behind certain expressive gestures are translatable (Henrotte 1985), we may well find that operating at different levels of perception are differences as well as residual similarities. We should be able to bring the "presumptions of value" implicit in a raga to bear upon an investigation of the *Well-Tempered Clavier*, thus allowing flow in both directions. For although Taylor, writing from "our" point of view, naturally assumes that we have the first option of checking out the other's horizon, it ought to be possible to imagine a reversal of this scheme. In short, it ought to be possible for others to "other" us if they so desire.

Taylor's efforts here suggest an attempt to relativize and ultimately decenter the West in order to draw other world cultures into a discussion space arranged along more egalitarian lines. ("Arranged by whom?" we should remember to ask, in order not to forget that the construction of egalitarianism itself represents an exercise of power.) Such a reorientation may produce a convergence at the background level of ostensibly different cultural systems. Backgrounds or deep structures bear uncanny resemblances to one another, so what Taylor calls our "background of valuation" may turn out to be a version of the Asian's, Australian's, or African's. But as we approach this "fusion of horizons" from the discrete polarity separating "our horizon" from "their horizon," we need to ask where this third space is located, and (since space is usually owned) to whom it belongs. Taylor implies that the new space is ultimately an extension of the West's; it is *our* "vocabularies of comparison" that will be enriched in the process. So while bringing more of the Other into view, Taylor's program does not—indeed cannot—eliminate the foundational terms of *Self* or Other, terms locked in a violent hierarchy in which Self as subject reproduces and completes itself as object or other. So, once again, a version of "Eurocentric cross-culturalism" is what is likely to emerge from an attempt to fuse horizons (Spivak with Rooney 1989, 133; see also Bhabha 1994, 85–92).

Embracing Sameness?

If differencing has produced such distorted, ideologically one-sided, and politically disadvantageous representation, and if a reasonable proposition to fuse horizons fails to overcome its core difficulty, why not eliminate it altogether and substitute a carefully defined sameness? The proposition that we dispense with difference might sound reactionary at first, scandalous perhaps, or merely silly. To attempt to eliminate that which is not ultimately eliminable is to attempt a critique in the spirit of a deconstruction (Spivak with Rooney 1989). It is to gnaw at limits and to resist the naturalized oppositions upon which knowledge of African music has been based without escaping the regime of oppositions. It is to insist on the provisional nature of our musical ethnographies, to persist in reordering concepts positioned at center or in the margin. Only through such a persistent critique can we hope to refine theories born of a will to difference; only through critique can we stem the tide that reduces the hugely complex edifice of African musical practices to a series of "characteristics."

There is no method for attending to sameness, only a presence of mind, an attitude, a way of seeing the world. For fieldworkers who presume sameness rather than difference, the challenge of constructing an ethnographic report would be construed as the challenge of developing a theory of translation that aims to show how the materiality of culture constrains musical practice in specific ways. The idea would be to unearth the impulses that motivate acts of performance, and to seek to interpret them in terms of broader, perhaps even generic, cultural impulses. Such a project would ultimately look beyond the immediate material level, not by denying that Africans blow on elephant horns, cover drums with animal skin, or make flutes out of bamboo, but by emphasizing the contingency of their material and conceptual investments. Objects function as means to an end, and it is the complex of actions elicited by such objects that betrays the translatable impulses behind performance. Focusing on such impulses promotes a cross-cultural vision without denying the accidental specifics of local (African) practices.

Contesting difference through an embrace of sameness might also prompt a fresh critique of essentialism. Such a critique should facilitate a better understanding of the peculiar juxtapositions of cultural practices that define modern Africa. It would explain how a Sierra Leonean, Nigerian, or Ghanaian can be equally moved by a hymn, a traditional dance, a local proverb, a quotation from Shakespeare, a piece of reggae, the Wedding March, and the latest Highlife music. Eliminating the will to difference facilitates a better appreciation of the precarious grounds on which contemporary African reality stands, grounds shaped by religious, political, and ethical impositions that are sedimented at various levels of depth. Sameness prepares an understanding of (modern) African culture as a form of improvised theater, a makeshift culture whose actors respond to social pressures on an ad hoc, ongoing basis. It is not a culture of frozen artifacts imbued with spiritual essences.

A premise of sameness might also reorient our studies of theoretical (including aesthetic) discourses by causing us to regard with suspicion some of what is reported to have been said by informants in their own languages. Languages evolve according to need, and needs are defined across a spectrum of human activities. Accidents occur just as frequently as intended actions. So the condition of any African language today is best considered in light of its genealogy and refracted histories, including real and hypothetical occurrences. The fact, for example, that there are no terms corresponding directly with *music* or *rhythm* in many African languages—a fact, incidentally, that has caused difference-seeking ethnotheorists to rejoice—is significant only in a restricted sense. Its significance is retrospective, not prospective. For what matters is not what is known but *what is knowable.* This future-oriented appraisal paves the way for empowerment by placing the accent not on what an objectifying Western discourse deems significant but on the potential of African languages to support a self-sufficient and sophisticated practice of critical reflection.

The transformative, contingent, if-only, frankly political approach advocated here has certain practical consequences. One of them concerns the production of ethnography. Awareness of the precarious nature of material investments should lead to an abandonment of ethnography and an embrace of fiction. It should lead to a rejection of all first-level, ostensibly objective descriptions, and a substitution of second- or third-level suppositions, some of them openly speculative, none of them realist. If realism is capable of producing only partial, misleading, or distorted truths, then why not follow an approach that rejects realism's pretensions without denying its own imperfections? Why not tap the imaginative realm for possibilities?

The idea of sameness makes some people nervous. We surely do not want to all look alike, play the same instruments, listen to the same music, deploy the same critical language. Sameness carries the threat of hegemonic homogenization analogous to the cultural effects of the movement of global capital. What I am arguing for, however, is not sameness but the hypostatized presumption of sameness, which in turn precedes action and representation. We no longer worry about the exact traces left by our acts of representation because the ethical bases of our motivations are beyond question. Restoring a notional sameness to the work of ethnomusicology will go a long way toward achieving something that has hitherto remained only a theoretical possibility, namely, an ethical study of African music.

Further Reading

Agawu, Kofi. 1995. The invention of "African rhythm." *Journal of the American Musicological Society* 48(3): 380–95.

Appiah, Kwame Anthony. 1992. *In my father's house: Africa in the philosophy of culture.* New York: Oxford Univ. Press.

Ekpo, Dennis. 1995. Towards a post-Africanism: Contemporary African thought and postmodernism. *Textual Practice* 9(1): 121–35.

Minow, Martha. 1990. *Making all the difference: Inclusion, exclusion, and American law.* Ithaca, N.Y.: Cornell Univ. Press.

Mudimbe, V. Y. 1988. *The invention of Africa: Gnosis, philosophy, and the order of knowledge.* Bloomington: Indiana Univ. Press.

Nzewi, Meki. 1997. *African music: Theoretical content and creative continuum: The culture exponent's definitions.* Olderhausen, Germany: Institut für Didaktik populärer Musik.

Radano, Ronald, and Philip Bohlman, eds. 2001. *Music and the racial imagination.* Chicago: Univ. of Chicago Press.

Scherzinger, Martin. 2001. Negotiating the music-theory/African-music nexus: A political critique of ethnomusicological anti-formalism and a strategic analysis of the harmonic patterning of the Shona Mbira song *Nyamaropa. Perspectives of New Music* 39(1): 5-118.

Solie, Ruth. 1993. Introduction: On difference. Pp. 1–20 in *Musicology and difference: Gender and sexuality in music scholarship.* Berkeley: Univ. of California Press.

Spivak, Gayatri. 1999. *A critique of postcolonial reason: Toward a history of the vanishing present.* Cambridge, Mass.: Harvard University Press.

CHAPTER 20

What a Difference a Name Makes
Two Instances of African-American Popular Music

DAVID BRACKETT

In 1959, after a ten-year reign as the "Queen of the Harlem Blues" or "Queen of the Juke Boxes" (depending on which source one reads), Dinah Washington, an African-American rhythm and blues star known for her gospel-tinged, blues–jazz vocal style, recorded "What a Diff'rence a Day Made." This recording, which became Washington's biggest pop hit, bathed her voice in the amniotic fluid of sumptuous strings and ooh-ing choruses redolent of that part of "mainstream" (read: white) popular music that had not yet succumbed to rock 'n' roll—but even this treat-ment could not quench her unrivaled ability to make even the most cosmopolitan ballad funky. It was not until 1993, however, by which time her 1959 hit had little in common with contemporary R&B, that Washington achieved the ultimate in crossover recognition when the U.S. Postmaster General issued a postage stamp bearing her visage.

What a difference thirty-four years had made: The name of African-American popular music now gestured toward a different bundle of musi-cal styles and cultural discourses, while the arrangement of popular music categories continued to produce a vision of difference in which that name remained marginal to the mainstream. Complete, nonmarginalized accep-

Work for this project was supported by a grant from the National Endowment for the Humanities.

tance could only occur, or so it would seem, according to a time frame resembling that of the acceptance of subjects for postage stamps: the rule for this time frame states that all such subjects must have died at least ten years prior to acquiring an exchange value of twenty-nine cents (the value of a first-class stamp in 1993; Dinah Washington died in 1963).

In the preceding paragraphs, I used the terms *rhythm and blues, mainstream popular music*, and *crossover*: conventional signs used by those who make, consume, and profit from popular music in the United States. The very conventionality of such terms may obscure their demographic associations, the functions they have served, and the images of society they both model and produce. When the demographic associations of one of these terms, *rhythm and blues*, become explicit and are then folded into the more general category of "African-American music," questions occasionally arise as to the connections between musical style, biology, and historical origins. Debates circle around either the assertion of an essential connection between race and style based on the phantasmatic power of such ideas in subjects' everyday lives, or the refutation of such connections due to the difficulty of producing a scientifically delimited list of traits, leading in some cases to a concomitant assertion that African-American music is constructed through discourses about race, power, and identity.

I attempt to chart an alternate path between these positions, a path not dissimilar to Paul Gilroy's "anti-anti-essentialism" (Gilroy 1993, 99–103; see also hooks 1992; Brackett 1995, 108–19). I do this by examining one particular practice that both constructs and emerges from the concept of African-American music: the process of categorizing styles sustained in the relationship among musicians, audiences, and the mass media/music industry apparatus. This process is part of the "phantasmatic power" of identification (Ivy 1995) alluded to in the preceding paragraph. The term *phantasmatic* does not indicate that identities are fictions, but rather refers to the role of temporal deferral or displacement that characterizes the process of identification in relation to a sense of racial, gender, national (etc.) origins.

To examine how this sense of difference emerges as "real," I look at two moments in recent U.S. history: the years around 1947, and those around 1996. Examining how styles are categorized illuminates how a sense of "black music" emanates from its relationship to other categories of music coexisting within a given period, and thus demonstrates how structures of difference permeate the circulation of both musical sounds and verbal dis-

1939–1949	1949–1969	1969–1982	1982–1990	1990–1997	Contemporary Radio Format	Video Channel/ Show
Popular	Popular/ Hot 100	Hot 100	Hot 100	Hot 100	Top 40/ Contemporary Hit Radio	MTV Top 20 Video Countdown
Harlem Hit Parade (1942–44)/ American Folk (1945)/ Race (1946)	Rhythm and Blues	Soul	Black	Rhythm and Blues	Urban Contemporary (UC)/ Quiet Storm/ R&B/Rap	MTV Jams/ BET
Hillbilly (1939)/ American Folk (1945–49)	Country and Western/ Country (1960)	Country	Country	Country	Country	CMT
Other categories					Adult Contemporary	VH-1
					AOR (Album Oriented Rock)	

Figure 20.1. Popularity chart and radio format nomenclature, 1939–97 (as found in *Billboard* magazine).

course about music (Middleton 1990, 241). While the experience of popular music as connoting particular demographic groups may be widespread and gain tacit acceptance in a particular place at a particular historical moment, it need not derive from a belief solely in either transhistorical essences or in arbitrary rhetorical effects. Somewhat paradoxically, the linkage between musical style and demographics, while experienced and acted upon as "real," may also be revealed as arbitrary when similar categories of popular music are compared from contrasting historical periods.

The context for the particular connotations of musical categories under discussion in this chapter centers around social and historical relations in the United States: My remarks may be suggestive for other geopolitical contexts to the extent that the particular connotations studied here have been successfully exported. Associations among musical categories, style elements, and audiences have existed in the United States since the 1920s, when the recording industry organized the popular music field around the divisions of "popular," "race," and "hillbilly" musics, each supposedly referring to a distinct musical style with its own audience. These categories developed in tandem with popularity charts that reflect the intersection of three forces: the public's fascination with the measurement of its preferences, its tacit acceptance of categories, and the music industry's use of these categories. While various charts had tracked the success of "mainstream" popular music since 1890, the economic importance of race and hillbilly music had grown by the 1940s to the point that popularity in those fields began to be represented in separate charts (see Figure 20.1). While historically the content of the term *mainstream* is malleable and stylistically heterogeneous, its durability lies in its continuing ability to provide a "center" for other, "alternative" or "marginal" genres (Toynbee 2002; Brackett 2002). At this point in the 1940s the assumed mainstream pop audience was Northern, urban, middle or upper class, and white. The charts for the "marginal" musics also assumed an audience—African-American for "race"; rural, Southern white for "hillbilly." Note particularly the instability (displayed in Figure 20.1) of the nomenclature used to describe "black music" relative to country or pop. Although rhythm and blues or R&B is the default name for popular music associated with African Americans, neither of the other categories is so explicitly tied to race.

To understand how a distinct black popular music circulates in relation to the mainstream, one must look closely at the *specific* interconnections among institutional policies, discourses of categorization, and elements of musical style within a narrow period of time. The years around 1947 prove instructive: while the music industry was in the process of slowly recognizing the importance of black popular music, it effectively excluded the representation of black music from the mainstream. Or, perhaps I should say that the mainstream at that moment included only one form of black music, and one of its more curious manifestations at that. A stand-out among these curiosities was Count Basie's smash hit from 1947, "Open the Door, Richard": Hitting number one on the Honor Roll of Hits on March 1, 1947, "Open the Door" stakes its claim as Basie's most successful recording, and one of relatively few recordings by African-American artists to appear on the (mainstream) pop charts during the period in question. Basie's success is particularly marked in that the Honor Roll of Hits ranked the top ten songs by synthesizing the radio play, record sales, and jukebox play charts from the "popular" category; reaching the top of this chart thus represented a greater achievement than topping any of the individual charts.

However, if we are to avoid charges of essentialism, the name of an African American on the label of "Open the Door, Richard" is not enough to qualify it as an example of black popular music. In fact, the presence of Basie's recording on the Honor Roll might militate against understanding "Open the Door" as "race music" due to its very appearance on a mainstream chart. It takes but a glance across the page of the March 1, 1947, issue of *Billboard* to reassure us that "Open the Door, Richard" is indeed well represented in the race charts, with different versions of the song (including Basie's) occupying five of the seven slots. As some five versions of the song appear on the mainstream top 30 "jukebox" chart, "Open the Door" would seem to be an archetypal example of a crossover song: a song that appears on more than one chart, thus by implication appealing to more than one segment of the *Billboard*-partitioned audience.

Determining what difference, if any, existed between songs represented on the race charts and those on the mainstream charts requires closer scrutiny of the constitution of the categories at this time. *Billboard's* definition, that "Records listed are race-type disks most played in the nation's juke boxes, according to the Billboard's weekly survey among juke box operators" is of little help, for the identity of those "race-type disks" remains a mystery. Analyzing the race chart tells us that at the crudest level there does appear to be a simple relationship of racial identity, as almost all the recordings on the chart are secular recordings made by African Americans. The majority of crossovers from the race chart to the mainstream chart during this period, however, do tend to be novelty tunes such as "Open the Door, Richard."

The sound of "Open the Door," along with the fact that it was Count Basie's most successful foray into the mainstream charts, may come as a bit of a surprise to those who know Count Basie as the innovative pianist and leader of one of the most successful black swing bands. In terms of musical style, the song certainly departs from what jazz fans would associate with Basie: his trademark tinkling piano is present but subordinated to novelty effects such as the repeated snare drum "knocks," the vamp that marks time during the narrative, the chorus sung in unison, and the spoken narrative itself, which describes the misfortunes of one of Basie's band members (Harry "Sweets" Edison) when he is locked out of his apartment by his roommate, a fellow band member by the name of Richard. The lyrics and performance style reveal that this novelty number presents a type of vaudeville humor with a long history in minstrelsy. The associations with novelty and minstrelsy also occur in many of the most successful recordings of the man widely regarded as the first crossover artist, Louis Jordan. Jordan's jukebox hits such as "Choo Choo Ch'Boogie" and "Ain't Nobody Here But Us Chickens," however much they might have been signifyin' trickster tales, double-coded to provide empowering messages to African Americans, at least partly invoked minstrelsy codes to white audiences (Lott 1993).

Jordan is often cited as the first crossover artist, but closely examining music industry publications during this time, though not literally contradicting this commonplace, reveals a layer of complication. While the race charts recorded only jukebox activity, there were many separate charts for mainstream popular music representing record sales and radio play in addition to jukebox revenue. A handful of recordings by African-American artists did register on the mainstream record sales and jukebox charts, but they almost never showed up on charts representing radio play, and they never appeared on the chart surveying network radio play (network radio shows were nationally syndicated and had the broadest audiences). It is open to question, therefore, how widely Jordan's recordings were actually played on the radio, the medium least bound by physical or geographical limitations.

A cautionary word is in order here: the preceding discussion does not endorse the idea of *Billboard*'s charts as transparent windows through which the popularity of recordings may be viewed in an absolute sense; rather, the charts are particular representations of popularity that circulated and thereby affected public notions of what was popular. However, to dismiss the information contained in popularity charts is to believe in the possibility of an unmediated means of conveying popularity. If we can relinquish the vision of a perfect re-creation of a historical moment, then a space is opened where analyzing the charts as a symbolic mediation of that period becomes plausible. The charts at this time may then be understood as *representing* the idea that crossover artists such as Louis Jordan were selling records and being played on jukeboxes but not being heard widely on the radio, unlike the vast majority of mainstream popular hits. This scenario suggests that these recordings became popular without the aid of network radio, and were not likely to have been heard by white audiences who did not happen to purchase the record or find themselves in a venue where a jukebox was playing "Choo Choo Ch'Boogie."

The most telling deviation from the mainstream that one finds among the race records chart—as well as, one assumes on the jukeboxes and the few radio shows devoted to black popular music at the time—is a *variety* of styles that did not cross over to the mainstream (in addition to the novelty songs that did). If the categories of race music and mainstream popular music are depicted as two overlapping circles (see Figure 20.2), then the crossover novelty songs exist within the portion of the circles that overlaps, while the noncrossover songs reside in the nonoverlapping part of the circle. Here, in the part of the race music circle that does not overlap, resides the critical difference that separates black popular music from mainstream popular music at this time.

Hence, listening to the most popular race recordings of the time that did not crossover—songs such as Cecil Gant's "I Wonder," Wynonie Harris's "Good Rockin' Tonight," or Amos Milburn's "Chicken-Shack Boogie"—may indicate the musical practices that differentiated race music from the mainstream. These noncrossover songs feature up-tempo boogie-woogie rhythms, slow blues grooves, guitars and saxophones with distorted or "dirty" timbres, strongly emphasized back beats, and extensive improvisation; they include lyrics filled with current African-American slang and playful double-entendres that extol the virtues of partying, enunciated with diction that may not have been easily intelligible to white listeners of the time. In the style that was coming to be called rhythm and blues or "jump blues," listeners could hear echoes of the small-band jazz that had emanated from Count Basie's Kansas City Six or Kansas City

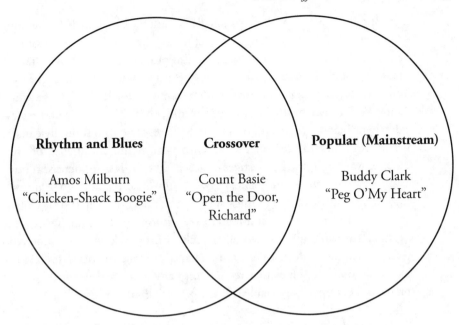

Figure 20.2. The circular logic of race and mainstream popularity charts, ca. 1946–47.

Seven groups, recordings that Basie made around ten years earlier when his songs were not heard on popular radio stations, back when there was little thought of asking for a door to be opened. In 1946–47, on jukeboxes in black neighborhoods, and on the few isolated radio shows scattered throughout the country that played race music for an hour or two, listeners could hear new permutations of the country blues, the classic blues, or piano-based boogie-woogie, now filled out with ensembles of bass, drums, guitar, saxophones, and trumpets, and fronted by blues shouters, gospel wailers, and jazz insinuators—musical elements, personas, and styles that were rare or nonexistent in the mainstream popular music of the time.

During the same years, a new phenomenon began to gather momentum. The possibility arose that, under certain amorphous circumstances, an African-American performer could sing mainstream pop ballads in a style that differed little from the crooning that had come to dominate popular music following World War II. Most closely associated with Bing Crosby in the years before 1946, after the war this relaxed singing style had spread to ascending male stars such as Perry Como, Dick Haymes, and Buddy Clark, as well as to female balladeers like Dinah Shore and Margaret Whiting. Nat "King" Cole, still recording under the aegis of the "King Cole Trio" at this point, was the exception that proved the rule. In recordings such as "You Call It Madness (But I Call It Love)" and "(I Love You) For Sentimental Reasons," Cole crooned effortlessly with flawless "standard" American diction in front of his subdued, yet jazzy and taste-ful, trio of piano, guitar, and bass to spatially separate (but sonically equal) lovers, regardless of their race. Benefiting from the confluence of the crooner wave with the last vestiges of acceptance for jazz-influenced music associated with the swing bands, a year later Cole parlayed this success into orchestra-backed recordings such as "Nature Boy" (in 1948). Cole's success flew in the face of music industry wisdom of the time; he, as well as other African-American vocalists such as Billy Eckstine, encountered resistance in their efforts to record pop ballads, frequently being limited to recording only the blues that record company personnel deemed appro-priate and commercially viable (DeVeaux 1997, 340–63).

To look at the concept of "African-American music" in action fifty years later is to observe both the persistent meaningfulness of the term and its radical instability. Two examples from 1996 illustrate how the concept continued to mark difference, thereby participating in the process of producing meaning in the popular music field while at the same time continuing to float free from essential connections to biology or from historically invariant style traits. By the mid-1990s the relationship between style and marketing category had become simultaneously sim-plified and more complex. Many of the same factors involved in cross-over still existed, but were adapted to the new medium of music television, with different channels targeting specific demographic groups, or with different programs on a single channel employing niche market-ing. Beginning in the early 1980s, music television channels and music video shows interacted with a greatly expanded number of style cate-gories for popular music, some of which had strong correlations with radio formats, others of which responded to the vibrations of dance clubs (see Figure 20.1). The properties of the new medium heightened aware-ness of the social connotations of pop music categories, granting crossover a visual immediacy that it had previously lacked in its deference to the aural. Music television reveals the physical characteristics of recording artists and putative cultural contexts in a way that radio cannot (unless we include that material signifier of the body conveyed through sound waves alone: *Le grain de la voix,* residue of the real), and these, together with the types of advertisements played during shows, supplement informal ethnography in analyzing the relationship of audience demographics to particular shows.

Music videos also provide a graphic reminder of who we, the audience, are to imagine ourselves to be, as videos represent a diegetic audience corresponding to the demographic of the target audience. For example, many rap videos are staged to show the participants partying and having a good time in what appears to be the artist's community, surrounded by his or her "posse" or group of friends (see Rose 1994, 8–15). In the video for the Southern dance-rap hit from the summer of 1996, "C'mon n' Ride It (the Train)," we find a group of African Americans located somewhere between outer space and a frenzied bumping and grinding dance party, while the performers, the Quad City DJs, are represented as shamanic personages summoning the image of African-American hypersexuality from the mass-cultural unconscious. This video followed a classic crossover pattern, appearing first on MTV's video "ghetto," the MTV Jams Countdown (a show paralleling the R&B chart—see Figure 20.1) in June, and eventually making it to the cynically innocent, multiracial, all-beautiful teen family of the MTV Top 20 Video Countdown (a show paralleling the mainstream, Hot 100 chart) in August. "C'mon n' Ride It" never did show up on the VH-1 countdown, which caters to a bourgeois, twenty-five to fifty-four, largely white audience, and parallels the Adult Contemporary chart, which arose with a new radio format in the 1980s (Barnes 1988). The song has tight links to other contemporary R&B hits with its incessantly repeated short riff; its largely synthesized, electronic, instrumental sound; and its alternation of sung chorus with rapped verse.

Another almost exactly contemporaneous video unsettles any potentially essential linkages. "Give Me One Reason" is recorded/performed by Tracy Chapman, who, although she is African American, has, since her emergence in 1987, been associated with the modern singer-songwriter pop genre, a genre with connotations of a predominantly white audience. Her song quickly hit number 1 in June of 1996 on the VH-1 countdown, slowly climbed up MTV's Top 20 countdown, making it as high as number 8, and never appeared in the MTV Jams countdown. The representation of the audience in "Give Me One Reason" differs markedly from that in "C'mon n' Ride It," with images of racially mixed couples dancing to an integrated, sexually androgynous band. Musically, the differences are quite profound as well; Chapman's song is a blues, which

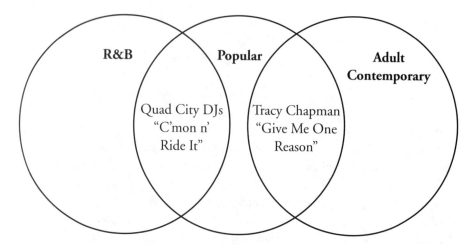

Figure 20.3. The circular logic of the R&B, popular, and adult contemporary charts, ca. 1996.

is, of course, a form associated historically with African Americans, but one that has been more often used by white musicians over the last thirty or so years. The instrumentation is that of the urban blues bands from an earlier time, and the song features a guitar solo, another performance gesture enacted most often in public since 1965 by white males, and one enacted in the video, in yet another act of musico–semiological reversal, by an androgynous woman.

In fact, this "earlier time" of the urban blues band is the period fifty years ago discussed previously in this chapter, and in many ways, "Give Me One Reason" has more in common with "race music" of the forties than with contemporary R&B. Is Tracy Chapman the Nat King Cole of the 1990s? Well, no: as the Quad City DJs demonstrated, a recording that is strongly coded as "black" could cross over in the midnineties to MTV's mainstream countdown if not to VH-1's. Conversely, while Cole had a large, African-American audience, it is most likely that Chapman's core audience lies in the (mostly white) Adult Contemporary category, if the formats in which her recordings are heard have any correlation with who actually listens to them (Figure 20.3 provides a graphic representation of the different crossover trajectories of "Give Me One Reason" and "C'mon n' Ride It").

Regardless of how many rap recordings show up on the mainstream Hot 100 chart or how many white rappers or black singer-songwriters receive mass exposure, the concept of crossover remains viable because popular music categories continue to create meaningful distinctions between demographically marked styles or genres of music (in a tempting homology, we could observe that regardless of how "integrated" U.S. society may be at any given moment, census workers must still check off a racial designation on their forms). And to think of crossover is always to think of the inseparability of marketing and style in U.S. popular music despite the dreams of those who envision a popular music in which separate styles existed autonomously before that fateful day when musical style was supplemented by marketing.

While I have stressed here the radical discontinuity of several examples of black popular music separated by fifty years, my approach need not exclude historical continuities or gradual transformations. For example, Samuel A. Floyd, Jr. (1991, 1995) has described the musical elements that developed within the ring shout, elements that have subsequently constituted a group of musical "tropes" that black music repeatedly draws from. In both the periods described in this chapter, at least part of the sense of difference between black popular music and mainstream popular music derives from the way in which these elements are employed. Perhaps Amos Milburn's "Chicken-Shack Boogie" is linked to "C'mon n' Ride It" by Floyd's call-response trope; or by other theories, such as Olly Wilson's (1974) "conceptual approach," Amiri Baraka's (1967) "changing same," or Ralph Ellison's (1964: 131) "concord of sensibilities," all of which seek to explain the practical expression of that sense of constantly reinforced racialized subjectivity that goes by the name of African-American difference. This sense of difference, reiterated in synchronic reformulations of the popular music field, marks a phantasmatic zone in the generalized (un)consciousness of the U.S. consumer who uses it to decode (in the words of Tower of Power) "What Is Hip" and to find CDs in the local megastore.

"Race Music," "The Harlem Hit Parade," "Rhythm and Blues," "Soul Music," "Black Music," "R&B," "Urban Contemporary": to repeat a point made earlier, of all the categories used by the popular music industry, the category associated with African Americans has been the most explicitly tied to race and the most unstable. One can speculate that this instability of naming is tied to changing mainstream notions in the United States about what might constitute acceptable modes of representation for African Americans. This speculative analysis could be pressed further still, to the idea that the naming of categories in popular music mediates (and simultaneously participates in producing) U.S. society's vision of itself and the position of African Americans in that society. This catharsis for sociohistorical cognitive dissonance influences the range of the possible: that is, who can hear what at any given time and who will reap the economic rewards. The process of crossover indicates that the category of African-American popular music exists as a colony for the mainstream, producing goods that may then circulate as part of a tarnished golden triangle (the same is true of country music). Recordings by black artists are thus held to a different standard by having to "prove themselves first" with success on the black chart, unless they already have a track record of crossover success (see Brackett 1994).

The arrangement of categories in the popular music field continues to make a difference: to imagine the field without difference is to imagine popular music without meaning. And to imagine the erasure of race from the play of this difference is to imagine a stage of society in the United States that has not yet come into existence.

Further Reading

Baraka, Amiri. 1967. *Black music.* New York: William Morrow.

Brackett, David. 1994. The practice and politics of crossover in American popular music, 1963–65. *Musical Quarterly* 78(4): 774–97.

———. 2002. (In search of) musical meaning: Genres, categories, and crossover. Pp. 65–83 in *Popular music studies.* Edited by David Hesmondhalgh and Keith Negus. London: Arnold.

DeVeaux, Scott. 1997. *The birth of bebop: A social and musical history.* Berkeley: Univ. of California Press.

Floyd, Samuel A., Jr. 1991. Ring shout! Literary studies, historical studies, and black music inquiry. *Black Music Research Journal* 11(2): 265–88.

———. 1995. *The power of black music: Interpreting its history from Africa to the United States.* New York: Oxford Univ. Press.

Gilroy, Paul. 1993. *The black Atlantic: Modernity and double consciousness.* Cambridge, Mass.: Harvard Univ. Press.

hooks, bell. 1992. *Black looks: Race and representation.* Boston, Mass.: South End Press.

Ivy, Marilyn. 1995. *Discourses of the vanishing: Modernity, phantasm, Japan.* Chicago: Univ. of Chicago Press.

Rose, Tricia. 1994. *Black noise: Rap music and black culture in contemporary America.* Hanover, N.H.: Univ. Press of New England.

Toynbee, Jason. 2002. Mainstreaming: Hegemony, market and the aesthetics of the centre in popular music. Pp. 149–63 in *Popular music studies.* Edited by David Hesmondhalgh and Keith Negus. London: Arnold.

CHAPTER 21

Locating the People
Music and the Popular

RICHARD MIDDLETON

Who are "the people"? The Founding Fathers of the United States of America had no doubt about the answer to this question: "We the people ... ," they declared in the new Constitution (1787), with the confidence proper to a new epoch. A few years later, Thomas Paine, defending the French Revolution with equal assurance, insisted that "the Authority of the People [is] the only authority on which Government has a right to exist in any country" (Paine [1791–92] 1969, 131). Such confidence was inspiring but oversimple. The Revolutionary Terror set a horrifying precedent for a host of subsequent attempts to establish popular authority by violence. The founding "we" of the United States was not universal but limited to men of property, excluding not only less-affluent white males but also Native Americans, all women, and (naturally) all slaves. The political moment was in any case part of a broader shift, in which, as Raymond Williams (1983) has shown, the rise of commodity culture led to an emergent and soon predominant usage of the term *popular* to mean "well-liked by many people." By the time that Alexis de Tocqueville was dissecting American society—the 1830s, a period when "Jacksonian democracy" was refocusing U.S. politics on the interests of the "common man"—he was as amazed that "The people reign in the American political world as the Deity does in the universe; everything comes from them, and everything is absorbed in them" (Tocqueville [1835] 1956, 58) as he was depressed by the prospect of leveling down that he saw resulting from the "tyranny of the majority."

From an early-twenty-first-century vantage point, the tiredness of the people idea seems self-evident. The grotesqueness of the concept of the Nazi *Volk* (from which Jews, gypsies, and homosexuals were excluded: no *Volkswagen* for them) was matched, for cynicism, by that of the "People's Democracies" of the Soviet bloc; Brecht's ironic advice to his masters, on the occasion of the failed East Berlin uprising of 1953, that they should perhaps dissolve the people and elect another, was the definitive riposte to "totalitarian populism" (Esslin 1959, 165). Popular Fronts for the Liberation of X (and, usually, the oppression of Y) have lost their allure (as marked by the comic demolition job on the phenomenon in the Monty Python movie *The Life of Brian*). Those of us living in Blairite Britain, with the reality of the "people's lottery" and "the people's Millennium Dome," not to mention the memory of the "people's princess" and of Margaret Thatcher's invocation of "the people" in the service of a multitude of reactionary causes, inhabit that farcical stage that, in familiar historical style, follows tragedy. Everywhere, distinctions between "the popular" and its others struggle to survive, it would seem, amid the assumptions of a vulgar relativism.

But the complexities were endemic from the start. The German Romantic W. G. Herder (1968, 323) carefully distinguished the folk-singing people (*das Volk*) from the "shrieking mob" (*der Poebel*), a distinction maintained in Arendt's *Origins of Totalitarianism* (1966); the "mob" was a key character in eighteenth- and nineteenth-century political and cultural discourses, and maintained its hold in the twentieth: the idea, explored by such diverse writers as George Orwell and T. W. Adorno, that capitalism's best hope for defending class injustice would lie in a program of cultural debasement of the masses is worth taking seriously at the same time that we note the element of condescension implicit in a perspective that fed a history of "moral panics" over "mobs" of ragtimers, jazzers, rock 'n' rollers, punks, and hip-hoppers. The nineteenth century saw a host of new communities imagined into being (Anderson 1991), in Europe and elsewhere, almost always with an appeal to a "national soul" embodied in their folk culture heritage. Small wonder that such a company of Celts, Magyars, Poles, Bohemians, generic Slavs (etc.—not to mention, further toward the margins, gypsies, Jews, "niggers" and orientals) dances and sings its way through the popular musical repertories of the period. Yet it jostles for space both with political and revolutionary songs fixed to class projects (from "La Marseillaise" through songs of the British Chartists, for whom, to quote one of their banners from 1848, "The voice of the People is the voice of God," to socialist anthems like "The Red Flag" and the "Internationale"), and with a huge expansion in market-oriented production, which by 1900 demanded that, in the words of Tin Pan Alley's Charles Harris, "A new song must be sung, played, hummed and drummed into the ears of the public, not in one city alone, but in every city, town and village, before it ever becomes popular" (Hamm 1979, 288). The character of the "people," despite its radical origins and potential, journeys through a landscape which, to use Althusser's phrase, is "structured in dominance," both in general and in the specific forms generated by the historical unfolding of capitalism; and in the maintenance of these hierarchized formations, cultural distinctions play an important role, as Pierre Bourdieu (1984) has taught us. Today, the historical trajectories, in exhausted anticlimax, precipitate inversion, detritus, and perversion, as in (to choose examples almost at random) the "turbo-folk" used as an instrument of ethnic cleansing in the Yugoslav wars of the 1990s; in the "Red Flag" simulacra passing for performances at Labour Party Conferences; and in the frankly celebratory sadocynicism of *Popstar* and *Pop Idol* (British TV talent discovery shows broadcast in 2001).

The people/popular concept, then, is irrevocably "dirty," and in two ways at least. First, it covers a discursive space whose content is mutable and open to struggle; just as, according to Bourdieu (1993a), there is no such thing as an objective "public" but only a shifting social character defined by varying survey methodologies, so, in the words of Stuart Hall (1981, 239), "there is no fixed content to the category of 'popular culture' ... [and] there is no fixed subject to attach to it—'the people.'" Second (and connected), the politics of the concept are "always already" corrupted (always already, because they are produced in a discourse with no clear origin), and, today, their rescue for progressive uses would require considerable cultural work—not least by intellectuals, so often popular culture voyeurs, but also would-be fellow travelers and even guides, for whom Fanon's injunction (1967, 187) to "work and fight with the same rhythm as the people" represents both a necessity and an impossibility.

The discourse we are uncovering is one specific to modernity. "The people" names a character seen as inhabiting an imagined social space (which is not to say that there is not a real social space in a relation with this). The configuration of this space varies historically and in accordance with ideological assumptions, and hence the character of "the people" is variably delineated too—as a social body, a political actor, a cultural voice—with implications for interpretation of its musical manifestations.

(We might suppose that many of the disagreements over definition—for example, of "the popular" seen as social-commercial success, as political representation either of tradition or of struggle, or as transformative figuring of an Imaginary—arise through confusing these registers. At the same time, we might also suppose that politically there is a point to trying to bring these into alignment: this would happen optimally when a music finds a way to speak with a fully politicized consciousness to and for a social bloc.)

The stage on which "the people" moves is commonly structured in alteritous fashion, and a variety of psychic mechanisms comes into play: projection, overcompensation, objectification, abjection. In general, "the people" is figured as a subordinate other—a periphery validating by difference both a central elite and a centered self. (In a happy coincidence, elite music acquired its first histories, became conscious of itself, in works published by Charles Burney and Sir John Hawkins in 1776, the same year as the American Declaration of Independence gave dramatic voice to the idea of popular sovereignty.) This figure is both gendered (the people inhabits a "motherland," and mass culture is "effeminate": passive, intuitive, affective, hysterical [Modleski 1986, Huyssen 1986] and racialized [the popular is imagined as "barbaric" and/or "exotic"—mapped, most commonly, onto "black"]). But peripheral elements can be appropriated by "the center," as they have been, arguably, in much of today's hegemonic popular music culture in the advanced societies. Alternatively they can answer back, as spectacularly evidenced in the long-lived, intricate workings of the "Black Atlantic" (Gilroy 1993); when, for instance, according to Lhamon (1998), an early-nineteenth-century New York cross-racial working-class fraction used the blackface mask to construct a subversive alternative to elite culture—a "Plebeian Atlantic"—at the very moment when the Founding Fathers were construing "we the people" as men of property and education. The working out of these tensions takes hugely varied forms. In Britain, the early beginnings of the late-modern phase constituted an important bourgeois fraction in the eighteenth century as a "polite and commercial people," with "popularity" defined by consumption patterns, within a by-now well-legitimated state; consequently the folk-national trope took the form not so much of a politically potent radicalism as an archaizing nostalgia or an instrument of English imperialism (Scots and Irish songs sounded endearingly quaint in London). In the United States, the agenda was fundamentally twisted by race (of course) and by the demotic triumphalism associated with a "Fordist" political economy. It was also mediated by the trope of migrancy, so the pioneer/hobo/beat/ ethnic outsider became a core popular type (prefiguring the postmodern cult of the border-crossing nomad).

The subject/object people is, then, necessarily fragmented, variable, and unstable: in the language of Freud and Lacan, *split*. As such, its very appearance is dependent on an apparatus—the regime of *representation*— specific to post-Renaissance (Cartesian) modernity (Foucault 1970), and given a new twist by Hegel's dialectics of subject and object, self and other. Earlier, the commoners were simply what was left over, but with the Cartesian revolution they became bound into a system whereby the out-there is a constituent of the problematic of the self: the representation of "reality" reflects, refracts, distorts, and guarantees the subject's presence, and the dynamics of popular and nonpopular interaction become an aspect of the processes of subjectivity. (Gary Tomlinson [1999] has explored this problematic for the realm of opera—but strangely the "people," whose nameless, numinous, but gross materiality, felt "from the near side" of discourse, acts as a guarantee of transcendent signification, is absent from his exposition, along with—more predictably—any hint, from the "far side," of their *speech*.) For Enlightenment thinkers, the evident contradiction between alterity (the inescapability of difference) and a politics of inclusivity could in theory be squared through the principle of universalism: all of humankind could potentially perfect itself in Reason. Mozart's *The Magic Flute* (1791) represents a neo-Kantian essay along these lines: Reason triumphs, with the "lower" characters located, musically and socially, firmly in the place appropriate to their cultural stage of development, yet at the same time narratively shadowing the revelatory trajectory followed by their "betters." By 1824, Beethoven's cry in the 9th Symphony, "O ye millions, I embrace you," has moved on to a neo-Hegelian reach for the Absolute. The shift from Kant's programmatic universalism of taste to Bourdieu's critique of distinction and its socioeconomic basis exemplifies a later skepticism. It remains true, however, that it was only with the advent of "modern" thought that this type of discourse became available at all. In the early eighteenth century, Giambattista Vico offered the innovatory means to think of all of a society, and even all of humanity, together, through a world historical image of human development. Tracing the journey from the Enlightenment to twentieth-century modernism reveals metaphors of cultural ladders (progress; upward mobility) joined by, perhaps giving way to, more synchronically structured models (highbrow-middlebrow-lowbrow; the interrelations of modernism, mass, folk, and primitive). At this point the figure of the *cultural field* (variably mapped to "corresponding" social and politicoeconomic fields) achieved a dominance eventually theorized by Bourdieu (1993b) among others, and in such concepts of Gramsci (1971) as "historical bloc," "hegemony," and the "national-popular."

Although the European Union's adoption of Beethoven's 9th Symphony "freedom tune" as its anthem might suggest that the Enlightenment project is still under way, it also marks its trivialization. Living (arguably) *after* the heyday of the modernity system, we often, it seems, find it problematic, embarrassing, or even ludicrous merely to name "the people." This grand subject appears to have turned into a simulacrum of subjectivity constituted in the reification of desire in advertising—"one market under God," as Thomas Frank's ironic rewriting of an earlier national-democratic ambition puts it (2002). At best, the people are elsewhere—in unnoticed Third World catastrophes, asylum camps, sweatshops; at worst, the popular is figured in terms of the mystifying flatness of self-improvement (the Blairite "people's meritocracy," with its boy and girl bands reflecting the self's narcissistic self-sufficiency). Digging within the musical repertories of this moment, can we find ways of reading the people back in?

Without proposing priority for any of the "fields" mentioned above—social, politicoeconomic, cultural—we concentrate here on the *discursive* sphere (using the term in the broadest, translinguistic sense). Whatever determinations and mediations are in play, the popular in music comes to us through the effects of sounds, words, and words about sounds: in short, through the work of the *signifier*.

Think of John Lennon's "Working Class Hero" (*John Lennon/Plastic Ono Band*, Apple PCS 7124, 1970). This is, evidently, a song about the people conceived in terms of class—or more exactly, about the disjunction of this relationship, that is to say, the culture forced on working-class people as a result of their lack of political consciousness; implicitly, it is also a song about leadership, or perhaps its lack or failure: "a working-class hero is something to be," as Lennon bitterly if ambivalently puts it. The style is terse, stern, and didactic, with lyrics foregrounded, melody plain, and accompaniment limited to simple acoustic guitar, summoning up memories of the equally spartan approach of the early Bob Dylan, down to the relentless ("deathly") guitar riff keeping the singer right on the straight and narrow message, forbidding all semiotic play. But an element of doubt about the references of pronoun shifters ("I," "we," "you," "they") clouds the issue: the flow of identifications is disrupted. Similarly, behind the stern paternal voice we hear a shadow—a would-be lyrical, "feminine" reach beyond the meaningful surface, audible in occasional tremulous cracks in timbre, anxious stretching for high notes, and little inflections and melismas around the main melody notes; and perhaps also in the disruption of the otherwise insistent minor tonic chord, once toward the end of every verse, by a single appearance of the "yielding" major chord on the subdominant (conventionally coded "feminine" in the Western tonal system, in relation to the "masculine" dominant). Will Lennon *cry*, we ask?

Historically, the song is richly contextualized. On a biographical level, it comes between, on the one hand, the traumatic Beatles breakup and Lennon's primal scream therapy earlier in 1970 with Californian psychotherapist Arthur Janov, when he spent much of his time crying and screaming, and on the other hand, the "silence" of the period 1975–79, when Lennon gave up musical production to be a ("feminized") househusband. In terms of cultural history, it punctuates the transition from "John Beatle" to "John Lennon," taking this to stand for the shift from the fetishizing, macho heroics of the 1960s star system (false hero worship, in Lennon's eyes) to the more skeptical, ironic, often gender-bending discourses around star presence characteristic of the 1970s. On the level of political economy, it engages the contemporaneous restructuring of class associated with the move away from social democracy toward the Thatcherism to come. "Working Class Hero" is both suspiciously insistent and revealingly fractured, signaling what Lawrence Kramer (1990) calls a hermeneutic window organized around scream/cry on the one hand and silence/death on the other. Lennon's figure of the people here is inscribed in the complex relationships set up at the intersection of shifting meanings attached to the tropes of "star" and "class," as these generate a tantalizing image of the popular other, desired but errant, and always receding from grasp.

For my argument in this chapter, the manifest content of "Working Class Hero," although obviously relevant, is less important than the exemplary interpretive lessons we can derive from its latent dynamics. Its voice, doubled and fractured, points clearly to the conclusion that, if popular songs can be related to underlying social formations, such relationships take culturally specific forms that, moreover, are never stable, always multivalent.

The Spice Girls' "Wannabe" (*Spice*, Virgin CDV2812, 1996), noisily surrounded by proclamations of "girl power," focused on gender rather than class. The singers issue instructions, give us their demands, tell us "what they really really want"; and the verses, where they do this, are delivered in a sort of rap style, borrowing and inverting the machismo of male hip-hop. No female group, however, can avoid summoning references to sixties girl groups, especially those of Motown, with their approach oriented around more traditional themes of "romance"; and sure enough, the choruses turn to a poppier style, complete with vocal harmonies, a melodic hook, and a stress on togetherness. The bridging of individual empowerment (verses) and collective feeling (choruses) is meant to target and construct girl power's own community (eliding the issue of class, of course). But verse and chorus are also contrasted: rapped call-and-response backed by rock-style minor-pentatonic bass riff in the first, major-key vocal harmonies in the second; it is as if the inclusivity strategy couples popular music's two main ideological categories and their gender associations, "feminine" pop fantasy being grounded by "masculine" rock realism—and further, calls up historical memories of dance-couplets (pavane and galliard, minuet and trio, etc.) reaching right back to the European Renaissance. The claim of contrast is deceptive, however. Verse and chorus flow seamlessly into each other, the rhythm track is continuous, and bits of vocal style from the verse increasingly find their way into the choruses; moreover, the bass/harmonic patterns of the two sections perform closely related gestures. Similarly, the dialogues within the verses are superficial: calls and responses from the different girls are much the same, and come from much the same place on the stereo spectrum. The song is a closed binary—nothing is left over—and the hint of teleology (tonally, the relationship of the two bass patterns—minor pentatonic and major, respectively—recalls that between *passamezzo antico* and *passamezzo moderno* that marked the dawn of "modernity" in the sixteenth and seventeenth centuries) leads nowhere.

Just as girl power offered a fake individual and collective empowerment at the extreme end of Thatcherism (there is no such thing as society, she told us), so "Wannabe" rehearses a simulacrum of difference, a wannabe teleology, a fantasy in which nobody fails and nothing is left out: rock and pop, romance and raunch, black (rap) and white (singalong), past and future are seamlessly stitched together. But the stitching (the suturing, as Lacan would call it) is overdone: it could not last—as became evident, on the level of biography, with the Spice Girls' disintegration, and, on the level of society, with the passage from Thatcherite postfeminism to the pseudomeritocratic populism that followed, accompanied as this was by a wave of emollient girl and boy bands on the one hand, and an underground subchorus of unorthodox gender poses on the other.

White rappers became commonplace in the 1990s. Most notoriously, the success of working-class white trash Eminem demonstrated the continuing potency of the blackface stance, his records exploiting (by implication) the blackface mask to proclaim white disempowerment. Produced by black rapper Dr Dre but most conspicuously successful (as with most rap by this date) with a middle-class white market, Eminem's extravagantly brutal, misogynistic, and homophobic narratives work against the background of a cross-race, class-based economic split in the United States (bourgeois affluence booming, workers impoverished, neglected, or imprisoned), but also draw the traditional *frisson* from the image of violence long associated with black ghetto society: rap's "posses" and "gangstas" reinscribe the discourse of mob and moral panic. Eminem's "My Name Is" (*The Slim Shady LP*, Interscope 490 287-2, 1999) adds further dimensions to the masking operation. The insistent repetitions in the choruses of the statement "My name is . . ." summon memories of the long African-American tradition of naming games and rituals (the street game, the dozens, for instance); they also echo boxer Muhammed Ali's equally insistent question, "What's my name?" to his opponent Sonny Liston, soon after the name change accompanying his conversion to Islam, and Black Muslim refusals of slavery surnames (by Malcolm X, for example). Small wonder that the persona Eminem adopts here, named for us, significantly, by a distant, other, and highly technologized voice, way back in the mix, is "Shady."

In a sense, the narrative of the song, telling of Shady/Eminem's brutal, oppressive early life and schooling, and bringing together issues of identity, charisma, and class, works similar territory to "Working Class Hero." But the fragmentation of voice is much more overt here. Shady's apparent identity and location shift constantly, and are embedded in complex dialogues with other voices. The play of name, identity, and voice is a work of what black theorists such as Gates (1988) have termed Signifyin(g), a key practice in African-American culture that operates through manipulation of a "changing same" by constant variation of given material, disrupting the signifying chain in the interests of semiotic play. Another element in this intra- and intertextual work is the instrumental backing, shaped—typically for rap—from a sample, here a four-chord riff taken from Labi

Siffre's "I Got The," which repeats in varied forms throughout. Again, technology (digital sampling in this case) mediates a shift in the parameters of the popular music community. The process of Signifyin(g) makes fun (play; play as fun; funny, incongruous, or uncanny connections) of sense, of the signification process itself, its orientation around doing rather than meaning pointing toward the sphere of the body. Although "My Name Is" adheres to the typical rap duality of "rhymes" and "beats" (word and act, logos and body), the lyrics are noticeably "musicalized" through the operations of the vocal polyphonies, and the underlying riff, reduced to the basic drum/bass groove, is what fades out the song, inviting but always retreating from bodily response.

These three songs are offered as symptomatic rather than representative examples. Their intricate maneuvers around the registers of race, gender, and class remind us of Hall's point that there is no *essence* of the popular—"the people" can only be defined dialogically. Their points of address from "below," no less (and no more) than their positionings in the power textures of capitalist society, confirm that the discourse of "the popular" is closely tied to the project of modernity. This, as we have seen, guaranteed the subjectivity of the emergent Western self through an apparatus of representations of his others, "masters" and "slaves" warring on, but also maintaining, each other (to draw on Hegel's celebrated dialectical image, produced [1807] in the same moment that the "people," conceived as potential subject, made such a dramatic historical step forward).

This does not of course imply that hierarchies of musical categories do not exist elsewhere. Indeed, probably "elite" and other categories (however labeled) have been found in all stratified societies. But the historically specific figure of "the people" as an agent in such dramas has been widely exported from "the West," as part of the globalization of the modernity discourse, and this has tended to restructure old hierarchies. Indeed, this process, although speeding up enormously in recent years, arguably began with colonialism as part of the birth of the modern itself. This hint of a universalism is alluring but tricky; on the level of the world picture, "modernization" has been uneven, variegated, and hybrid, and many "non-Western" societies—such as Japan, Argentina, and South Africa—have pursued quite specific paths for lengthy periods of time. Nevertheless, we can legitimately think in terms of a *dispersal of the modernity dialectic,* with all that this implies, both "here" and "there," for conceptions of "the people." For "us" in "the West," the question arising then (a postcolonial question) is: who can, who *may*, speak from "over there"? Respect for cultural difference should not exclude the possibility that one might surprise "others" where they are with an excavation of what is hidden from their gaze. Similarly, the reverse movement might reveal apparently premodern residues "here," strengthened by the effects of that internal colony, the "black Atlantic," but in any case offered a sympathetic home in popular music's permanent longing for carnival, its invitation to the body, its invocation of an excess beyond the purview of the symbolic structures of Western Reason.

Lacanian psychoanalysis has theorized an "object voice"—an impossible, transfinite object of desire, linked to the initial infant cry before the flooding in of culture (interpretation, representation, identification) rendered this forever lost. By analogy, we might posit an equally impossible "object act," linked to a presignifying body, where the organs worked "for themselves," not as extensions of the subject, and where the body existed, with fullness of gesture, as a field rather than discursive property. Just as the silenced object voice can nevertheless be invoked (albeit partially, stutteringly) in the voices we actually hear, so the object act can be enacted (acted, acted out) through fractures and windows in the putative coherence of actual performances. This stakes out ground where the apparently conflicting interests of universalism (still alive in such disparate narratives as Marxism and psychoanalysis) and cultural–historical difference can meet; where "masters" and "slaves" can negotiate new phases in a dialectic that from its beginning marked "the people" as irrevocably split; and where, through a metaphorical unbinding of the "mob" (the *mobile vulgus*—the people on the move), we might pursue the tantalizing if impossible task of bringing culture and politics, discourse and practice, into alignment.

Further Reading

Adorno, Theodor W. 1991. *The culture industry*. London: Routledge.

Bennett, Tony. 1986. The politics of the "popular" and popular culture. Pp. 6–21 in *Popular culture and social relations*. Edited by Tony Bennett, Colin Mercer, and Janet Woollacott. Milton Keynes, U.K.: Open Univ. Press.

Born, Georgina, and David Hesmondhalgh, eds. 2000. *Western music and its others: Difference, representation and appropriation in music*. Berkeley: Univ. of California Press.

Bourdieu, Pierre. 1984. *Distinction: A social critique of the judgement of taste.* Translated by Richard Nice. London: Routledge.

Gilroy, Paul. 1993. *The black Atlantic: Modernity and double consciousness.* London: Verso.

Levine, Lawrence. 1988. *Highbrow/lowbrow: The emergence of cultural hierarchy in America.* New Haven, Conn.: Yale Univ. Press.

Middleton, Richard. 1995. The "problem" of popular music. Pp. 27–38 in *The twentieth century, The Blackwell history of music in Britain.* Vol. six. Edited by Stephen Banfield. Oxford: Blackwell.

———. 2001. Who may speak? From a politics of popular music to a popular politics of music. *Repercussions* 7(8): 77–103.

Stallybrass, Peter, and Allon White. 1986. *The politics and poetics of transgression.* London: Methuen.

Williams, Raymond. 1983. *Keywords: A vocabulary of culture and society.* Rev. ed. London: Fontana.

CHAPTER 22

Music Education, Cultural Capital, and Social Group Identity

LUCY GREEN

A society without music has never been discovered. But although music making is a universal feature of human society, it is by no means universally undertaken by every individual within a society. The more highly specialized is the division of labor generally, the more likely it is that music will also become a specialized sphere of action: listened to and enjoyed by many, but practiced by only a few. In Europe five hundred years ago, not only the church and court, but also the ordinary home, the street, the field, and the tavern all represented places where music was actively created by almost everyone, and in many non-Western societies music making has always been a normal part of everyday life. Nowadays, while technological developments have increased the availability of music for the listener, only a relatively small percentage of the adult population is engaged in active music making.

Over the last hundred and fifty years, there has been a gradual expansion in the sophistication, availability, and state funding of formal music education in schools, colleges and universities in many parts of the world. The decline of music making has occurred in tandem with the expansion of music education. Whether this complementary process is a matter of mere irony, whether music education has developed as a response to falling participation levels in music making, or whether it has been a contributory factor in causing that fall is not possible to demonstrate, at least not in a single chapter. But what is open to examination here is the role of music education in the production and reproduction of certain ideological assumptions and material conditions, which together contribute to overall patterns of musical life in the wider society. I focus on two linked areas: ideologies, particularly those relating to processes of canonization and the split between classical and popular musics; and social groups, specifically those defined by class, gender, and ethnicity. The discussion considers changes in ideologies of musical value and competence, and their part in the production and reproduction of social groups through formal music education in schools over the last forty years of the twentieth century. Many of the examples and illustrations relate specifically to Britain, while I also refer to research in a variety of other countries, and raise issues affecting formal music education globally.

The concept of ideology refers to ideas, values, and assumptions that are neither "true" nor "false," but that, rather, render the world intelligible and legitimate. Even though different ideologies can come into direct conflict, such as in war and revolution, ideologies normally help to maintain social values and relations, either in the forms in which these values and relations already exist, or in the least destabilizing ways possible. Thus ideologies tend to benefit those social groups that are already in relatively beneficent positions. Until recently, musical ideologies have suggested that classical music lays claim to the greatest value, by possessing transcendent qualities such as universality, complexity, originality, or autonomy. Such qualities operate not only as markers for ascertaining musical value in itself, but also provide various means of distinguishing classical music from other musics. The case of popular music provides a clear example, insofar as it is understood, by contrast to classical music, as ephemeral, trivial, derivative, or commercial. But what makes the assumption of the superiority of classical music ideological is not that it is necessarily "wrong." Rather, it tends to perpetuate the values of particular, interested social groups at the expense of others while at the same time appearing to be "objective" or disinterested (Green 1988, 1999).

Schooling helps to perpetuate existing ideologies, assimilate ideological challenges, and produce new ideologies in line with changing economic and social conditions. Formal education imbues children with self-images, expectations, and achievement orientations that correspond in various ways to their existing social situations, guiding them toward adult values and roles that, although often involving overt resistance along the way, are ultimately adaptable to the current economic and social climate, and at the same time largely similar to those that derive from their parents.

This process does not take the form of overt discrimination, since a vital ideological aspect of education in a liberal democracy is precisely to offer equal opportunities to all children. However, whereas real equality of opportunity presupposes equality in values and incentives at the starting post, those children who come to school already sharing the values and incentives propagated and rewarded by the school stand more chance of succeeding. As Bourdieu famously put it, the school "demands of everyone alike that they already have what it does not provide" (1973, 80).

Music education participates in the construction and perpetuation of ideologies about musical value. For the first seventy years or so of the twentieth century, music in schools was overwhelmingly concerned with Western classical music and settings of folk songs by prestigious composers. While formal music education of various kinds occurs in many parts of the world, where schooling is concerned Western models have been most influential (Campbell 1991), especially in countries that were colonized or where missionaries had set up formal schooling programs often involving hymn singing. Thus, for different reasons and to differing degrees, countries as far apart as Singapore, Ghana, Cyprus, Japan, Brazil, and Hong Kong as well as many others have employed Western models of music education in schools, with mainly Western classical music as the content.

During the 1970s, a small number of music educators, mainly in Britain, Scandinavia, and to some extent North America, began to argue that popular music should be included in the school curriculum (Swanwick 1968; Vulliamy 1977a, b; Tagg 1998; Cutietta 1991; Volk 1998). However, reception of such ideas was often lukewarm, and even when the ideas were accepted, this did not necessarily indicate any fundamental changes in musical ideologies. This was partly because many educators assumed that if popular music was valuable, then it must share the qualities of classical music. So, for example, popular music was argued to have "universal" appeal; much popular music was said to be "complex" or "original"; or a distinction was drawn between different kinds of popular music, some of which was assumed to be "autonomous" (such as progressive rock), as distinct from other types that were assumed to be "commercial" (such as chart pop) (Green 1988, 1999a).

Despite some commentators assuming that classical and popular music shared such qualities, when it came to classroom practice, teachers often approached the two musics rather differently from each other. Research in Britain (Swanwick 1968; Vulliamy 1977b; Green 1988) suggested that the treatment of classical music generally focused upon singing and "musical appreciation," based on the assumption of the music's transcendent value. For older children and those taking instrumental lessons, teaching also tackled the intramusical forms and processes: in other words the notes and how they fit together, or how they are to be executed in performance. By contrast, when teachers began to include popular music in the classroom, the aim was not so much to instill appreciation of the music's transcendent value as to encourage an appreciation of its relative value, or in other words its inferiority; to appeal to pupils' existing taste as a stepping-stone toward improving upon it; or to keep pupils entertained (especially those who were liable to be "disruptive"). Furthermore, rather than intramusical processes (the "notes"), teachers tended to concentrate on extramusical associations related to the social circumstances of the music's production and reception, such as the social functions or effects of the music, the dress of the performers, or the lyrics (Green 1988).

Therefore not only explicit but also implicit messages about the value of classical and popular music were conveyed, as a result of the emphasis of study upon a particular *aspect* of music. For if teachers present music only or largely in terms of its intramusical contents, the suggestion is that the significant aspects of the music are not tied to any specific social situation and are therefore autonomous and universal, that they involve complexity, and that they make possible the development of originality. Contrastingly, if teachers draw attention only or mainly to extramusical associations, this suggests that the "music itself" is a servant of its social context, which bolsters the appearance that it cannot be universal or autonomous, resulting in a lack of attention to the music's level of complexity, and this in turn affirms the unlikelihood of its ever affording any means for creative originality.

The treatment of classical and popular music in British schools was thus ideological, both in a parallel, and in a contradictory manner. On the one hand, when teachers, curricula, syllabi, or books *theoretically supported* the value of popular music, they tended to do so by appealing to the very same qualities of universality, complexity, originality, or autonomy upon which the value of classical music rested. But this approach was not necessarily pertinent to understanding or evaluating popular music, as has since been demonstrated by musicologists (e.g., Middleton 1990; Walser 1993; Moore 1993; Brackett 1995). On the other hand, when popular music was *actually used* in the classroom, teachers approached it as if it lacked those very characteristics of universality, complexity, originality, and autonomy purportedly possessed by classical music, and the ultimate superiority of classical music was thus affirmed and legitimated by default. Through such processes, not only in schools but also from the nursery to the university, music education has been a central mechanism in the establishment and maintenance of the classical canon. This canon has developed not as a result of the perpetuation of an arbitrary set of musical values by teachers and lecturers, but as a result of possessing various intra- and extramusical qualities that have marked it for "greatness" according to expert consensus arrived at through music criticism, analysis, and historiography, all of which have been closely tied to processes of educational success and legitimacy.

Just as ideology is reproduced through education, so too are social groups. Here I consider some of the changing processes through which music education and some of its associated ideologies have contributed to the reproduction of three kinds of groups: social class, gender, and ethnicity. This reproduction occurs both at the broad societal level in terms of cultural and economic relations between social groups, and at the level of the individual in terms of personal identity.

Children from all social classes in many countries are generally far more interested in various types of popular music than in classical music, and many children, especially from working-class backgrounds, come from families that do not consider classical music to be especially valuable. Despite or perhaps partly because of this, for the greater part of the twentieth century, Western classical music was accepted as the most valuable and relevant curriculum content for all children in many parts of the world. The ideology of this music's superiority corresponded with the perspectives of a minority of upper- and middle-class children, whereas it deviated from the musical tastes of other children from these classes, and of many working-class children. These latter children came to school already lacking what the school "demanded" in order to achieve music-educational success. Furthermore, since knowledge and skills in Western classical music are often supported by private instrumental lessons, children from families that could not afford to pay the fees missed out on the lessons. Therefore, both for cultural reasons concerning musical value, and for economic reasons concerning access to musical tuition, working-class children were less likely to select music courses, and even when they did select them, they tended to be disadvantaged. They therefore achieved less educational success in music than middle-class children. Through such means, ideologies about musical value participate in the construction of patterns of music-educational success and failure, or success and drop-out rates, and in so doing serve to perpetuate existing cultural and economic relations between social classes.

During the 1980s and nineties, increasing numbers of educators across the globe joined the challenge to the implicit and explicit assumption of Western classical music's canonization and superiority within schooling. This rise in protest was caused partly by broader social movements outside education, including developments in technology, globalization, and localization; the continuing effects of decolonization; changes in demography; and gender, social class, and race relations. The expansion of the music industry made a huge variety of global musical styles available to listeners almost anywhere. At the same time the threat of musical monopolization by the American-dominated popular music industry caused some governments and pressure groups to raise the cultural and educational status of indigenous, local, and national classical, traditional, and popular musics. The relationships of people from differing social groups to music underwent rapid changes: certain styles of music were no longer exclusively associated with certain social classes; women in some parts of the world became less restricted in their musical roles than previously; and particular musics no longer "belonged" primarily to particular ethnic groups.

Today, the music curriculum in many countries reflects these developments in that it includes a mixture of folk, traditional, popular, jazz, and classical musics from all around the world (Volk 1998; Campbell 1991). Not only curriculum content, but also the values and attitudes of many teachers have undergone an apparent transformation. For example, whereas research conducted in England in 1982 suggested that school-teachers regarded classical music as unquestionably the most important, valid, and in many cases the only legitimate music for inclusion in the curriculum, by 1998 a parallel sample of teachers indicated that the most important area of the curriculum was popular music, with classical and "world music" in almost equal second position (Green 2001, 2002).

However, the mere entrance of a wider variety of musical styles into an education system does not simply halt the construction and perpetuation of ideologies of musical value. Rather, value hierarchies and canonization processes continue to operate, only across different styles. Two issues related to popular music can illustrate this. One refers to curriculum content. Precisely by virtue of its entrance into education and the concomitant production of a scholarly literature, popular music develops canons within itself, often based on assumptions that it lays claim to universal, complex, original, or autonomous properties. In this way, it conjoins rather than dismantles the same evaluative axes upon which classical canons are built. The other issue refers to teaching strategies. The majority of popular, folk, and jazz musicians, as well as classical musicians of non-Western music, have largely acquired their skills and knowledge outside, and even in contradistinction to, institutionalized education, employing quite different learning methods to those of Western formal music pedagogy (Green 2001). Yet the assumptions of this pedagogy still inform most music education literature and teaching materials. It is one thing to bring a variety of musics into the classroom, but if the learning methods of the relevant musicians are ignored, a peculiar, classroom version of the music is likely to emerge, stripped of the very methods by which the music has always been created, and therefore bearing little resemblance to its existence in the world outside. So, although covering a wider array of musics, new canons emerge within education, and are positioned in contradistinction to "other" musics that remain beyond the school.

Since the above changes in school curricula, very little research has taken place, to my knowledge, concerning the reproduction of social class by music education. Potential questions might be, for example, to what extent the introduction of popular music into the curriculum is affecting the social class patterning of music-educational success or take-up rates. However, work has been and is being carried out concerning similarly productive and reproductive processes with reference to other social groups. I now briefly examine this area with reference first to gender, then ethnicity.

Schooling helps to perpetuate differences in the musical practices and tastes of boys and girls. Teachers, curriculum planners, and pupils in countries as far apart as Britain, Japan, Spain, the United States, Canada, and Hong Kong, overwhelmingly associate active engagement in popular music, such as playing electric guitars and drums, with boys and masculinity, whereas classical music practices such as singing in the choir and playing the flute are linked with girls and femininity (Green 1997; O'Neill 1997; Koizumi 2002; Riguero 2000; Koza 1992; Hanley 1998; Ho 2001). Perceptions of gender differences are perhaps most subtle in the realm of composition. For example, in research in England, paralleled in Canada (Green 1997; Hanley 1998), many teachers declare that girls possess little ability for composition, tend to compose by "merely" following rules or doing what they are told, and lack imagination and creative spark. Girls themselves declare a lack of confidence and a reliance on teacher direction, and even those who enjoy and value composition often decry their own achievements. These assumptions and self-concepts go hand in hand with the association of girls with classical music as a conformist and conservative cultural sphere. Contrastingly, even though teachers quite explicitly see boys as uninterested, disruptive, and more concerned with peer-group opinion than with teachers' assessments, they nonetheless describe them as "naturally" more adept, spontaneous, and creative, while boys themselves display confidence in their creative compositional abilities. These proclivities are linked to boys' associations with popular music, especially its improvisational qualities, its technology, and its greater potential for symbolizing nonconformity—despite, or perhaps even because of, the presence of some "accepted" (or canonized) popular music in the school.

Not only are different musical instruments, practices and styles associated with girls and boys, but they are also linked to girls' and boys' self-perceptions in terms of musical ability, and to the expectations of teachers. Through labeling and self-fulfilling prophecies, such perceptions and expectations can have a considerable effect on long-term music-educational success (Green 1997). The symbolization of gender through music education thus represents a way in which patterns of musical involvement between the sexes, including educational success and failure in music, are constructed and perpetuated.

While the processes of reproduction through Western classical music tend to reinforce social class and gender differences, the new emphasis upon indigenous classical and traditional musics in the curricula of some countries is explicitly intended to reinforce ethnicities. Such processes occur in Western countries such as Ireland and Wales, and non-Western countries such as Thailand and Hong Kong (McCarthy 1997; Maryprasith 1999; Ho 1999). For example, in Thailand, musical globalization resulted in a two-pronged response during the 1990s: on the one hand, the increased production and purchase of Westernized forms of Thai popular music by the local music industry and consumers; on the other hand, a growing concern by the government, educators, and pressure groups that traditional Thai music was breathing its last breath. The 1997 economic crisis in Thailand then caused a retreat in the production of indigenous popular music, and an increased concentration on British and American popular music by the record industry. At the same time, greater emphasis was placed on traditional Thai music both in schools and the wider society, corresponding with the government's "Amazing Thailand" tourist campaign (Maryprasith 1999). A rather different process of musical nationalization through education has been occurring in Hong Kong. There, formal music education in schools and higher education has operated under the legacy of British imperialism to a large extent. Until recently, courses have been based entirely on Western classical music in a mold derived from British music education. With the end of British sovereignty and the establishment of Hong Kong as an autonomous region of the People's Republic of China in 1997, traditional Chinese music has begun to enter formal music education (Ho 1999). However, young Thai and Hong Kong Chinese students, like students everywhere, generally prefer Western or Westernized, indigenous, mother-tongue popular music, rather than the classical or traditional music of their national heritage (Maryprasith 1999; Ho 1999).

Distinct from moves to reinforce ethnicity by the inclusion of indigenous music in the curriculum, there are at the same time moves toward multiculturalism in music education. Claims are often made that "world music" has the capacity to break down ethnic barriers, particularly in multiracial schools. However, such claims are rarely examined, and when they are, a less optimistic perspective can emerge (Green 1999 [2002]). During research in an inner-city London primary school, Alden (1998) came across a significant degree of reluctance on the part of Hindi-speaking Asian children to reveal their private musical tastes. In discussion with the whole, mixed-ethnicity class, all the pupils gave the impression that they listened entirely to mainstream chart music. But when Alden interviewed the same pupils in small, single-ethnicity groups, he was presented with a very different picture by the Asian children: "although they were familiar with 'pop' music and sometimes listened to *Top of the Pops* they were all very clear that Hindi film music was the substance of their experience at home and they stated that this was their preferred music" (84). He then conducted another whole-class session in which pupils devised a music curriculum for their school. They included only mainstream popular music and its associated instruments, along with some classroom percussion with which they were already familiar. During discussion afterwards, the Asian pupils were silent. "I pointed out that pupils in the school listened to a much wider range of music than those which had been suggested, and asked if this range should be included. Even with such a clear lead, there was no voice strong enough to say 'yes'" (88). Later, he asked the pupils separately why they had not spoken up, and they said it was because of peer pressure (85). Even in a school such as this, with a written antiracist policy, the multicultural curriculum remained unconnected to the musical experiences of many of the children, who appeared to be ashamed of and secretive about their musical tastes. Ethnicity here occurred as a problematic part of musical identity arising from commercial pressures outside, and peer-group pressures inside the school. In such ways, multiculturalism in music education can operate more as an unwitting affirmation rather than a breaking down of ethnic power and status differentials.

Looked at from the perspectives adopted in this chapter, music education appears to affirm preexisting ideologies of musical value, and their corresponding skills and knowledge, thereby reproducing social group differentiation on the basis of, for example, class, gender, and ethnicity. Even radical challenges, such as the explosion in curriculum content and the turnaround in teachers' attitudes described above, seem to be inveigled. Although as individuals it is possible for teachers to step outside of the reproductive effects of the wider social systems to which we all belong, and although many do so in their music classrooms, lecture theaters, and studios every day, overall these social systems are beyond the control of any individual. It is only by taking a critical stance and attempting together to move beyond some of the assumptions and procedures that go to make up our parts in those systems that we can ever come to a deeper understanding of them, and thereby make significant inroads toward improving them. The expansion of the music curriculum to include a more global purview has itself grown out of just such a critical perspective, shared across countries, classes, genders, and ethnicities; and despite the reproductive processes that this expansion involves, it represents a historically necessary recognition of the music, musical tastes, and musical practices of a greater span of humanity than was hitherto represented in education.

Alongside formal music education, informal methods of acquiring musical skills and knowledge have always flourished, leading to the production of most of the world's popular, traditional, classical, and jazz musics throughout history. While schooling has recently incorporated a wider variety of musics as curriculum content, the task now facing music educators, not only in schools but also across the board to higher education, is to make a serious assessment of the very different learning practices by which these "other" musics have been passed down, and a consideration of what light such practices might shed upon our own (Green 2001). Formal music education for all is considered a luxury, by no means available worldwide, and is still sought after by advocates in many countries: but perhaps it has been a mixed blessing. The time is ripe for a complete reassessment of the nature and content of provision.

Further Reading

Bourdieu, Pierre, and Jean Claude Passeron. 1999. *Reproduction in education, society and culture.* Translated by R. Nic. Beverly Hills, Calif.: Sage. (First published as *La réproduction.* 1977.)

Green, Lucy. 1988. *Music on deaf ears: Musical meaning, ideology and education.* New York: Manchester Univ. Press.

———. 1997. *Music, gender, education.* New York: Cambridge Univ. Press.

———. 2001. *How popular musicians learn: A way ahead for music education.* New York: Ashgate Press.

Halsey, A. H., Hugh Lauder, Philip Brown, and Amy Stuart Wells. 1997. *Education: Culture, economy, society.* 2d ed. New York: Oxford Univ. Press.

Hanley, Betty, and Janet Montgomery. 2002. Contemporary curriculum practices and their theoretical bases. Pp. 113–43 in *The new handbook of research on music teaching and learning.* Edited by Richard Colwell and Carol P. Richardson. New York: Oxford Univ. Press.

Small, Christopher. 1980. *Music—Society—Education.* London: John Calder.

Tagg, Philip. 1998. The Göteborg connection: Lessons in the history and politics of popular music education and research. *Popular Music* 17(2): 219–42.

Vulliamy, Graham. 1977a. Music and the mass culture debate. Pp. 179–200 in *Whose music: A sociology of musical language.* Edited by John Shepherd, Paul Virden, Trevor Wishart, and Graham Vulliamy. London: Latimer New Dimensions.

———. 1977b. Music as a case study in the "new sociology of education." Pp. 201–32 in *Whose music: A sociology of musical language.* Edited by John Shepherd, Paul Virden, Trevor Wishart, and Graham Vulliamy. London: Latimer New Dimensions.

CHAPTER 23

The Cultural Study of Musical Instruments

KEVIN DAWE

The sound-producing devices we call musical instruments are firmly embedded in local music cultures worldwide as well as a part of global cultural flows in which they are swept up and relocated (whether in the hands of musicians, tourists, collectors, or museum curators). The forces that move musical instruments around the globe are tied to multifarious systems of social, cultural, economic, and political exchange, their value and meaning negotiated and contested in a variety of cultural arenas. The movement of musical instruments across cultural boundaries is an especially problematic and sensitive issue, as much as "world music" is a thorny and contentious issue. After all, musical instruments are as symbolic and emblematic of peoples and of places as any other musical phenomenon. What I call "world music instruments" are those instruments caught up in the transnational movement of consumer goods, the international trade in "ethnic" crafts, global tourism, and a multimillion dollar music business and musical instrument manufacturing industry. Here, musical instruments are taken into new cultural territories and beyond the range of experience of many of the people who brought them into being. Yet, at the same time musical instruments are still to be found in place in many local contexts throughout the world. When considering the role of musical instruments in the modern world, one quickly enters into a debate about the relationship between objectification and modernity, and how peoples and their artifacts are represented, misrepresented, or not represented at all. Ultimately, any field that defines itself as "the study of musical instruments" has to take all of these matters on board.

I argue here that the study of musical instruments is as much about the study of ethnomusicology, anthropology, and cultural studies as it is about the study of physics, wood science, and biological systematics. It has to be, if we are to gain a better understanding of the affecting presence of musical instruments in human music making and of the ways in which they (and their makers and performers) help to shape societies and cultures, and vice versa. Whether we are considering the place of musical instruments in the cosmological systems of indigenous peoples or the grand classifications of musical instrument specialists in the West, all such schemes are culture-specific in one way or another and are tied to hegemonic systems of one sort or another. Indeed, musical instruments are potent manifestations of such schemes in action. Elsewhere in this book, the reader's attention is drawn to issues relating to cultural difference, and "world music." Here, I discuss these and other issues in relation to the cultural study of musical instruments.

Musical instruments are formed, structured, and carved out of personal and social experience as much as they are built up from a great variety of natural and synthetic materials. They exist at an intersection of material, social, and cultural worlds where they are as much constructed and fashioned by the force of minds, cultures, societies, and histories as axes, saws, drills, chisels, machines, and the ecology of wood.

The making of musical instruments (like the playing of them) requires a range of psychobiological, sociopsychological, and sociocultural skills (whether the maker is Antonio Stradivari, Leo Fender, or one of thousands of others makers, dead or alive). Indeed, musical instruments can provide unique insights into the body–machine interface in their development, construction, and the ways in which they are played. John Baily's work on the plucked lutes of Afghanistan helped to reveal the ways in which "a musical instrument transduces patterns of body movement into patterns of sound" and how "the interaction between the human body and the morphology of the instrument may shape the structure of the music, channelling human creativity in predictable directions" (Baily 1977, 275). At another level, as socially constructed and meaningful, the morphology of musical instruments reveals through their shape, decoration, and iconography features of the body politic, as embodiments of the values, politics, and aesthetics of the community of musicians that they serve. They are at once physical and metaphorical, social constructions and material objects. In fact, as sound producers they are "socially constructed to convey meaning" (Feld 1983, 78) and remain "saturated with meaning" (after Derrida 1978). These approaches can be compatible. Baily's work revealed as much about human motor patterning in musical performance as about the relation between changes in the construction of musical instruments and music made to be meaningful in a multicultural nation-state (Baily 1976).

Debate about the field of "organology" (the study of musical instruments) suggests that there is indeed some effort to combine centuries of scientific work (including classifying and measuring) with new perspectives offered by the cultural study of music (involving ethnography and material culture studies, for instance). Perhaps not surprisingly, the difficulties involved in this process (i.e., the bringing together of both scientific and cultural perspectives) have been encountered to a great extent in organologists' efforts to design classification schemes capable of incorporating all the musical instruments of the world. No wonder then that many have assumed that the field "attends only or primarily to the classification of instruments" (DeVale 1990, 1–2).

One can only applaud the panopticism of some scholars in their efforts to treat musical instruments within the framework of classification systems. At least they have given serious attention to musical instruments outside of the Western world in constructing systems "into which facts can be integrated in order to show their relationships and affinities" (Montagu and Burton 1971, 49). After all, how else does one set about achieving order out of the chaos of such a diverse set of objects? As an ethnomusicologist I would suggest nonetheless that schemes constructed and used by the people who built and played the instruments should be used wherever possible (Zemp 1978; Dawe 2001).

Obviously, objects need some kind of sorting and interpretation, if they are to be displayed to effect in a museum exhibition, form a "collection," and be accessible and retrievable for research and display purposes. There is no doubt that the schemes developed since the late nineteenth century have been useful in providing the means whereby even nonspecialist workers are able to assemble, organize, and maintain museum collections of musical instruments and their catalogues. The schemes apply a basic Eurocentric logic to collections of musical instruments from different parts of the world. After all, instruments from around the world use simi-

lar sound-activating devices (for example, strings, membranes) and res-
onators (for example, the "bodies" or boxes of guitars and other lutes, the
tubes of flutes). These and other recurring features provide some scientifically based criteria with which to sort instruments into groups or types.

The most widely acknowledged classification system (and the one
upon which others are based) is that of Hornbostel and Sachs ([1914]
1961). Based on a system devised by Mahillon, it uses four main taxa:
idiophones, aerophones, chordophones, and membranophones. The criteria used to define groups and types are continuously tested and refined
(creating microgroupings) through an ongoing investigation of material
and acoustic properties, methods of construction, sound qualities, techniques required to produce sounds, and tuning systems, while applying
scientific techniques of preservation, conservation, restoration, measurement, and classification. Usually, a downward classification is employed,
moving from a highly abstract level downward to a more specific level;
for example, idiophones, idiophones struck, struck directly, struck upon,
and so on. The highest classes are broken down into their subclasses until
the individuals that are their members are reached. Downward classification is based on any arbitrary viewpoint that disregards historical factors
(Kartomi 1990).

Such schemes establish an ordering system that shows up particular
aspects of design that the musical instruments in a collection have in
common, and enable them to be placed in an access and retrieval system,
facilitating an overview of the science of musical instruments and their
construction techniques and materials analysis from around the world.

Musical instruments have very different meanings in their cultures of
provenance from those that are invested in them in museums. In other
words, such an object has culture-specific meanings, those meanings
attached to it through entanglement in a web of local cultural relations
that position it within a local musical world. The Australian didjeridu, as
manufactured and played by Aboriginal people (they call themselves
"Yolngu," and in northeast Arnhem Land the instrument is called yidaki
[Neuenfeldt 1997, vii]), is very much a part of a unique cultural heritage.
The instrument is used in ceremonies and ritual practices that are thoroughly shaped by Aboriginal experience, thoughts, skills, needs, and desires,
and it has great importance as an emblem and marker of ethnic and cultural identity. In anthropological terms, this is the emic perspective,
which aims for "the understanding of cultural representations from the

point of view of a native of the culture" (Barfield 1997, 148). It is debatable whether musical instruments can ever have similar cultural resonance, let alone the same meaning, for those who do not have the same experience as the Aboriginal people and without detailed information about their religion, beliefs, ritual practices, social structure, and musical practices.

I want to further illustrate the need for detailed in-the-field study with reference to Alan Merriam's brilliant analysis of drum making in an African village in the late 1960s. Merriam's study must surely be one of the first and finest examples of musical scholarship to show how completely musical instruments are entangled in webs of culture. He brings the complexity of the processes involved in musical instrument making to life in his study of the Bala (Basongye) drum, in an article that epitomizes his approach to the "anthropology of music" (Merriam 1964). He writes:

> [A] substantial number of bits and pieces of culture patterns were revealed, and these included, among others: taboos; children's games; patterns of badinage and boasting; real and ideal behaviour; technological information such as types of woods, the sources of colors, and tool-use patterns; linguistic information, including terms for parts of the drum, tools, woods ... ideas of Europeans; concepts of design; institutional friendships; learning by imitation ... and tricks and jokes. Almost every one of these items requires further research, but all of them were spin-offs from the central procedure being studied. (Merriam 1969, 99)

Merriam's analysis of the role of drum making within Bala society provides a rich and complex model of the ways in which the drum making fits into and even shapes a particular cultural context with "the systematic description of a single contemporary culture ... through ethnographic fieldwork" (Barfield 1997, 157). It is this information that might be fruitfully used to bring the musical instrument displays of the world to life. Another excellent example of musical instrument ethnography at work is Qureshi's wide-ranging and fascinating discussion of the ways in which the North Indian sarangi (an upright, bowed lute) relates to and intersects with many facets of the culture in which it is found. Qureshi notes:

> [T]he complex and intensely affective meanings which were being shared in wide-ranging conversations around the musical, physical, and metaphorical site of the sarangi. I faced a rich palette of responses to that single instrument and its sound: moral depravity as well as emotion, devotion,

feudal domination and servitude, with women who sing for men, and men who play for women. This led me to explore how people experience the sarangi, how players, listeners and patrons negotiate the contradictory, multiply referenced meanings of its music and how the power of music serves the interests of power. (Qureshi 1997, 5–6)

Qureshi's ethnography of what it was like to learn the sarangi as a participant observer provides us with a rich insight into how gender, power, emotion, and feeling are socially and culturally achieved, affected, and built around a musical instrument. I have endeavored to work with this form of analysis in my study of the lyra, a three-stringed, upright, bowed lute found on the island of Crete (and in studies of the guitar in different cultural contexts, see Bennett and Dawe 2001; Dawe 2001). The pear-shaped, fiddlelike features of the lyra suggest both "Western" and "Eastern" influences—it could be Turkish or Venetian, some say Minoan. Indeed, the notion that the lyra has its origins in antiquity suits local constructions of island identity well. Even today there is an extensive folklore that grounds the instrument in a world of pastoralists and mountain villages, up where the air is pure and where Zeus was born.

The lyra-laouto ensemble[1] is a powerful manifestation of the body politic, not only reflecting the values and beliefs of many individuals and communities (urban, village, neighborhood, and family) but also helping to shape them. "The tradition," namely "lyra music," has been significantly updated, reinvented even, in an attempt to make it relevant to contemporary Cretan society—a feat achieved largely through the establishment and the apparatus of a local recording industry. However, the lyra is still regarded as quintessentially Cretan, a man's instrument, its "body," "neck," "eyes," "heart," and "soul" having special symbolic resonance and technical significance. The stylos or "pillar," a device that takes the weight of the bridge and acts as a carrier for the transmission of vibrations between the bridge and the back of the instrument, is said to be the site where the psyche or "soul" of the lyra resides. Indeed, if this pillar is missing, the instrument loses volume and tone—its sound will die, and so too, it is said, will the lyra.

---

1. The *lyra* [lira] (plural = *lyres* [lires]) is a three-stringed, upright, bowed lute; the *laouto* [lauto] (plural = *laouta* [lauta]) is a four-course, plucked, long-necked lute.

The sound of the lyra moves between sweet and bittersweet tones, expressing a range of emotions experienced by sensitive but strong men in the face of what life can throw at them (see Dawe 1996 for a discussion of the interplay among music, poetry, and manhood ideals in Crete). Local musical aesthetics largely revolve around and interpenetrate the instrument itself, as it continues to reinforce long-held ideals that can be seen to make up a poetics of manhood and to form the basis of notions of professional musical performance practice in modern Crete (Dawe 1998, 1999). I argue (Dawe, n.d.) that the Cretan music ensemble, with the lyra as its focal point, belongs to, and subscribes to, what Chris Shilling calls a "body project." To play lyra and laouto, musicians (99.9 percent male) have to subscribe to a grueling regime imposed by "tradition," by teachers, by other authorities, and by those with "the knowledge." They have to learn musical techniques and repertoires, acquire the necessary mental and physical dexterity, stay awake at celebrations lasting up to fifteen hours, and manage an audience of a thousand inebriated guests; in short, a host of skills that require the disciplining of the body and the sharpening of the mind. According to Shilling, "in the affluent West there is a tendency for the body to be seen as an entity which is in the process of becoming; a project which should be worked at and accomplished as part of an individual's self-identity" (1993, 5). I am convinced that a Cretan body project can be similarly identified, which demands that individuals be consciously and actively concerned about the management, maintenance, and appearance of their bodies (whether at celebrations or on CD covers). The Cretan body project is managed in Cretan terms, embodiment is culturally constructed, and the connection to the body (in performance, visual culture, and folklore) bears upon the lyra, especially, as a masculine instrument. The lyra is not only emblematic of cultural difference in Crete, setting it apart from the outside world, it is also engendered, empowered, and is the body politic finely tuned.

Throughout the island, many examples from the iconography of records, posters, and the promotional materials of tourism, as well as displays in music shops and folk-life museums, draw attention to musical instruments and their potential as powerful icons of ethnicity. Indeed, images and displays provide a visual counterpoint to talk about music. They also reveal something about the nature and interaction of the forces that create, sustain, and move musical instruments around. For example, instrument displays in music shops convey much about the types of music popular in the area. In Crete, the fact that lyres are on display with Greek bouzoukis, Turkish baglama (long-necked lutes), and electric guitars speaks volumes about the aspirations of the local musical community, about old and new trends in the local music scene, and about locally held values and beliefs. Musical instrument shops and workshops are therefore microcosms of the greater musical world at large, and have an important and often understated role in the construction of local musical culture.

In trying to build upon the work of scholars like Merriam and Qureshi, I and other researchers interested in musical instruments as cultural objects have used the tools of the field researcher and the ethnographer (Dournon 1981), because, as Clifford and Marcus state with force, "ethnography decodes and recodes, telling the grounds of collective order and diversity, inclusion and exclusion" (Clifford and Marcus 1986, 2–3). How could we set about building information about "didjeridu culture" or the socioeconomics of Bala drum making or the musical culture of the Indian sarangi or the Cretan lyra into the classification schemes offered by scholars in the West? How can we hope to capture, contrast, and compare a small part of a musical and artistic world in isolation—the musical instrument as mere object—without reference to its sound, affect, meaning, and social and economic status?

Throughout the twentieth century, scholars such as Izikowitz, Dräger, Hood, and Ramey tried to develop classification schemes that incorporated clusters of morphological, technomorphic, sociological, and anthropomorphic information as well as noting the performance practice characteristics and the facets determining the sound that an instrument produces (Kartomi 1990). And in an article published in 1986, Dale Olsen even suggested that a classification scheme like the one devised by Hornbostel and Sachs should include a separate category called "corpophones" for "instruments" such as the singing voice that comprise parts of the human body. But can these schemes tell us in detail about a particular musical culture and the role of a musical instrument within it?

The nonfit of imposed cross-cultural classification systems of musical instruments that make assumptions on a global scale from one viewpoint (with sometimes quite small samples) with emergent culture-specific systems (tied to systems of meaning beyond the scientific worldview) is ultimately problematic. However useful, mistranslation, misrepresentation, and incompleteness are clearly possible using such systems, systems that are used to place "old instruments in new contexts" (after Neuenfeldt, 1998). As James Clifford notes:

> Every appropriation of culture, whether by insiders or outsiders, implies a specific temporal position and form of historical narration. Gathering, owning, classifying, and valuing are certainly not restricted to the West; but elsewhere these activities need not be associated with accumulation (rather than redistribution) or with preservation (rather than natural or historical decay). The Western practice of culture collecting has its own genealogy, enmeshed in distinct European notions of temporality and order. (Clifford 1988, 232)

Increasingly, musical instruments are pulled into new social and cultural arenas that are "enmeshed in distinct European notions of temporality and order"—classification is but one arena in which they have become enmeshed. A series of "partial truths" (Clifford and Marcus 1986) may be continuously reflected in as many different ways as there are models of musical instruments in the glass cabinets of museums, the grooves of world-beat records, and the photographic memorabilia of tourism, advertising, and the media.

Building on analyses of the exchange of material goods in both colonial and postcolonial periods throughout the Pacific region, Nicholas Thomas notes that in that context "objects are not what they were made to be but what they have become" (Thomas 1991, 4). In general, we consume objects and give them meaning, and in doing so, reproduce them, so to speak, in our own image—we colonize them. Thomas goes on to say that a view such as this contradicts "a pervasive identification in museum research and material culture studies which stabilises the identity of a thing in its fixed and founded material form" (1991, 4). Whether museum exhibit or "world music" production, the focus is not on studying what musical instruments once might have been but on "what they have become" as "old instruments in new contexts" (after Neuenfeldt 1998). Thomas notes that "creative re-contextualisation and indeed re-authorship may thus follow from the taking, purchase or theft" of material goods. He goes on to say that "since exhibitions or museums of history are no less prominent now than in the epoch of the world's fairs, that is a sort of entanglement that most of us cannot step aside" (Thomas 1991, 5). It is conceivable that musical instruments become so entangled with museum culture and colonization by the "host" that their meaning and exchange value are useful, and function only in relation to, the concepts that make up museum culture. Again, according to James Clifford, this "entanglement" is a means of colonizing, owning, and accumulating the objects of "outsiders," where "collecting has long been a strategy for the deployment of a possessive self, culture, and authenticity" (Clifford 1988, 218; see also Clifford 1992; Vergo 1991).

These are the kinds of questions that organologists will need to continue to ask while attempting to collect and piece together what Margaret Kartomi has called "the broad picture." Indeed, Clifford and Marcus's comment that ethnography "poses questions at the boundaries of civilisations, cultures, classes, races, and genders" (Clifford and Marcus 1986) seems particularly apt here. After all, these boundaries are just the places where we need to ask more and more questions about musical instruments in the cultures and societies of the world.

Further Reading

Appadurai, Arjun, ed. 1986. *The social life of things: Commodities in cultural perspective.* Cambridge, U.K.: Cambridge Univ. Press.

Berliner, Paul. [1978] 1993. *The soul of the Mbira: Music and traditions of the Shona people of Zimbabwe.* Chicago: Univ. of Chicago Press.

Birley, Margaret, Heidrun Eicher, and Arnold Myers. 2000. *Voices for the silenced: Guidelines for interpreting musical instruments in museum collections.* Electronic publication (this update, January 17, 2000). http://www.music.ed. ac.uk/euchmi/cimcim/iwte.html

Bourdieu, Pierre. 1993. *The field of cultural production.* Cambridge, U.K.: Polity Press.

Diamond, Beverley, M. Sam Cronk, and Franziska von Rosen. 1995. *Visions of sound: Musical instruments of first nations communities in northeastern America.* Chicago: Univ. of Chicago Press.

Journal of Material Culture. Vol. 1, no. 1. 1996. Thousand Oaks, Calif.: Sage.

Leppert, Richard. 1988. *Music and image: Domesticity, ideology and socio-cultural formation in eighteenth-century England.* Cambridge, U.K.: Cambridge Univ. Press.

———. 1993 *The sight of sound: Music, representation, and the history of the body.* Berkeley: Univ. of California Press.

Neuenfeldt, Karl. ed. 1997. *The didjeridu: From Arnhem land to internet.* Sydney: John Libbey/ Perfect Beat Publications.

Théberge, Paul. 1998. *Any sound you can imagine: Making music/consuming technology.* Hanover, N.H.: Univ. Press of New England.

Taylor, Timothy. 2002. *Strange sounds: Music, technology and culture.* New York: Routledge.

Waksman, Steve. 1999 *Instruments of desire: The electric guitar and the shaping of musical experience.* Cambridge, Mass.: Harvard Univ. Press.

CHAPTER 24

The Destiny of "Diaspora" in Ethnomusicology

MARK SLOBIN

Starting in the 1970s, the word *diaspora* spilled over its traditional boundaries as designator of the farflung fate of a small number of groups—principally the Jews—outside their homeland. My 1956 *Shorter Oxford English
Dictionary* has a two-word definition, derived from biblical sources: "The
Dispersion." By 1991, my *Random House Webster's College Dictionary* follows the Jews with "any group that has been dispersed outside its traditional homeland." Diaspora's meaning has expanded as part of our ever
greater interest in issues of deterritorialization. With typical Anglo-Saxon
verbal flexibility, it is used as a noun ("in diaspora") or adjective ("a diaspora mentality"), and when a suffix is attached, there is no uniformity,
some liking "diasporan" while others (like myself) prefer "diasporic."

The creation of a learned journal, *Diaspora*, in 1991 was a sign of
recognition of the word's move into prominence. In his opening statement of purpose, the journal's editor summarized the situation:

> We use "diaspora" provisionally to indicate our belief that the term that
> once described Jewish, Greek, and Armenian dispersion now shares mean-
> ings with a larger semantic domain that includes words like immigrant,
> expatriate, refugee, guestworker, exile community, overseas community,
> ethnic community. This is the vocabulary of transnationalism, and any of
> its terms can usefully be considered under more than one of its rubrics.
> (Tololyan 1991, 4)

As suits the world we live in, diaspora studies resemble a tangled thicket of terminology more than a pruned, topiary trope. From the earliest citations of the problem like Tololyan's through today, writers have acknowledged that diaspora is heavily contextual. Not only academics have become addicted, but also key players in the global search for coherence. Nation-states worry increasingly about harboring subcultures with ties abroad, particularly in Europe, but the media view the presence of these subcultures as a matter of optimistic economics. The *Irish Times* (January 22, 2000) urges the Irish government to notice that "diaspora [is] a resource to the labour power of the Celtic Tiger." *USA Today* (January 21, 2000) signals the news that "Hispanics in the USA are the low-hanging fruit for advertisers and entrepreneurs." Governments across Europe rise and fall according to how politicians think their citizens view diasporas, thought of as the strangers in their midst. Many people themselves think they are living away from a homeland, and respond nostalgically or angrily, actively or apathetically to the fact of separation or to the outsider's view that they are potential terrorists, a much-needed labor force, or "low-hanging fruit."

Traditionally, ethnomusicology made little use of the word *diaspora* until into the 1990s. We talked about immigrants, or minorities, or ethnic groups, and much effort went toward figuring out "acculturation." As the academic atmosphere drifted toward a new discourse centered on identity, diaspora crept into usage. By 1994, I made a point of editing a set of essays for *Diaspora* on "Music in Diaspora" (by Gage Averill, Su Zheng, Maria Teresa Velez, Anders Hammarlund, and John Baily; *Diaspora* 3(3), 4(1) for Baily). The aim was to showcase the importance of music to nonmusic diaspora scholars. My framing remarks say that "music offers a richness of methodological possibilities and points of view, opening new windows on diasporic neighborhoods," and ends by hoping that "readers of *Diaspora* can gain some sense of the value of using the filter of music to sort out some of the thorny issues of diasporic studies" (Slobin 1994, 243, 251).

Like all such terms, *diaspora* has been valuable, commonplace, and misplaced in our discourse. It most certainly refuses to be standardized in its reach or its resonance. In this short reflection on the word, I stick to the word's circulation within ethnomusicology, since mapping the whole patterning of the term would be nearly a book-length project at this point. After mapping some paths diaspora has taken as it entered the discipline, I offer a short case study.

First, a short literature review. *Islands in the Global City*, a 1998 anthology on Caribbean music in New York City, would seem to be a natural place to look. Surprisingly, the volume rarely references "diaspora," which pops up only once in the editors' introduction: "Intensive local and comparative study of these scenes will reveal much about the nature of *the diaspora process* and the increasing influence of Caribbean music and culture around the world" (Allen and Wilcken 1998, 5; my italics). What "the diaspora process" might be is left unexplained, but two aspects can be inferred: first, that locally, something methodical and predictable is unfolding, and second, that transnationally, the trend is replicating itself. There's a yawning elliptical space between the sentence's assumptions and its explanatory power. We have to know what a diaspora is before we can turn it into a verblike "process," but there is no definition. The essays that follow detail major differences among New York's "island" populations. Surely U.S.-passport–holding Puerto Ricans of the 1930s diverge distinctively from the marginalized, racialized Haitian immigrants of the 1980s, as the individual studies show. What might the connection actually be between the unidentified "process" and the "increasing" influence of Caribbean music? Increasing since when, and on what terms? Would we group the rhumba, mambo, reggae, and other genres as having greater or lesser impact, and on whom? In cases like this, "diaspora" tells us little, while assuming a lot.

Gage Averill offers an articulate formulation of the word in his essay about a Haitian ensemble, Tabou Combo. The group wrote a song, which became a hit in Paris, "to announce to the world that it was a Haitian band *from New York*. Living in diaspora, posed between cultures, playing in the most ethnically diverse city in the world, group members wanted to show that they were up to the challenge of the global city and the globe" (Averill 1998, 146). Here diaspora, in which they "live," is concisely combined with a multicultural environment and the band's ambition to use a nonhomeland space, New York, as a springboard for transnational expansion of their market. Averill separates the mere fact of diaspora from its cultural potential. Used this way, though, the term still slightly elides the issue of diaspora's nature, since we know from other studies (Guilbault et al. 1993) that a Caribbean band *not* in diaspora (Kassav, in Martinique) also strategized ways to expand a local francophone style to make a splash in Paris. Averill tells us that New York is the engine that drives Tabou Combo to transnationalize, but even if true, we learn little about the broader implications of diasporic "processes" from the example.

Another focused set of papers came out of the 1997 annual confer-ence of the British Forum for Ethnomusicology, for which *diaspora* was the key word presenters were meant to address. Looking at the abstracts, it sometimes seems that the paper writers tried very hard to rationalize their relationship to diaspora.[1] Their strained effort conveniently illus-trates how strangely stretched such a term might become. For example, Anne Ellingsen's "Diaspora in Turkish Arabesk" describes fieldwork on the Black Sea Coast, where middle-aged housewives "express their feel-ings of being in a kind of 'inner exile'" by identifying with Arabesk music and artists, particularly a transvestite artist, Zeki Muren, "who controls himself—like the women themselves try to do—when 'in exile.'" Here both diaspora and its corollary "exile" seem seriously out of place as explanatory headings. The women are at home, but socially alienated along gender lines, a far cry from Haitians in New York or Iranians in Los Angeles (Naficy 1993, to cite an example of diaspora as exile). Another overextended usage occurs in Malcolm Floyd's invocation of an "educational diaspora" when he discusses how the Tanzanian school system imports Western music or how non-Western music flows into European classrooms. This loose application of the word has infiltrated the highest critical circles; for example, Arjun Appadurai's invocation of "a diaspora of terms and images across the world ... a diaspora of key-words" (Appadurai 1996, 36) This anthropomorphization of bodies of information and concepts might lead us away from the physically dis-persed bodies that need our attention so badly.

Another, rather rare, approach in recent writing tries to add an affec-tive charge to the technical term *diaspora* as a way of extending its mean-ing from demographics to consciousness. A prime example here might be George Lipsitz's *Dangerous Crossroads* (Lipsitz 1994). In one four-page section (40–44) he introduces "diasporic consciousness," "diasporic flavor," and "diasporic intimacy." The first comes in a description of how the Nigerian musician Fela Kuti was influenced by a stay in the United States, which "changed his music by informing it with a diasporic con-sciousness." The problem is the vagueness of reference: is this conscious-ness something Fela Kuti encounters or achieves? The artist's own account, which follows immediately, explains that unlike Africans who overvalue

---

1. The abstracts are published in the *British Forum for Ethnomusicology Newsletter* 14: 8–18 (1997).

imports, his travels taught him that what is imported might actually have started first in Africa. This almost implies a reverse diasporic consciousness on his part, as an African whose society feels itself cut off from its sources, which it imports. I am not faulting Lipsitz for ambiguity, but rather am suggesting that the issues he and Fela Kuti raise here are so complex that the term *diasporic* is not all that helpful.

In the next paragraph, Lipsitz describes Fela Kuti's work with American Roy Ayers, and says even before that time, Afro-Cuban jazz had already given music "a diasporic flavor." Again, "diaspora" as terminological rubber band seems stretched to breaking, since Ayers and Fela's work "showed traces of the Afro-Cuban influences on North American jazz as well as of Cuban 'rhumba' bands on African, especially Congolese, music" (40) The full panoply of possibilities of what Paul Gilroy has famously called "the black Atlantic" is being evoked here. Unless "diaspora" is just meant to stand for an all-time, all-space mix, in which case it's simply too much for a term to carry, it is hard to know just what is being referenced.

"Diasporic intimacy" is perhaps the most stimulating of Lipsitz's phrases. He deploys it for situations of oppositionality to "a world coming ever closer together through the machinations of global capital," when small groups huddle with their homeland for warmth in the capitalist chill. Significantly, Lipsitz says that "rooted in egalitarian and democratic visions of the world, diasporic intimacy nonetheless embraces contradiction, change, and growth" (44). This nuanced sense of relationships gives people the agency they so desperately work for. It also concedes that the process of being diasporic is inevitably incomplete, mutable, and messy.

To summarize what I've been saying so far, "diaspora" leads a double life. At its simplest, it merely marks the existence of an identified population that feels that it is away from its homeland, however imagined, however distant in time and space. The subtler meanings of "diaspora" acknowledge that this involves more than just demographics. Some sort of consciousness of a separation, a gap, a disjuncture must be present for the term to move beyond a formalization of census data. Once analysis moves into this territory, the terrain gets very swampy indeed. Whose consciousness? Governments, NGOs, advertisers, packagers, self-proclaimed community leaders, refugees, immigrants, third-generation heritage-seekers—and the list goes on. A phrase like Appadurai's (1996, 10) "diasporic public spheres" can cover too many different types of situations, from Hollywood movies to street protests, to be very helpful. Gilroy's approach is more helpful when he distinguishes between a "spatial focus on the diaspora idea" and issues of "diaspora temporality and historicity, memory and narrativity"

(Gilroy 1993, 191). Gilroy needs the distinction because there are so many black cultures and countercultures to contend with in trying to grapple with a broad concept like his "black Atlantic."

Ingrid Monson sums up the uneasy fit between the general sense of diaspora, which by 2000 has expanded to "dispersion, exile, ethnicity, nationalism, transnationalism, postcolonialism, and globalization," and the specifics of a given diaspora, which for "African" brings in "race and racism ... Pan-Africanism, black nationalism, essentialism, and hybridity" (Monson 2000, 1). Her anthology includes essays that deal only with the cultural dynamics of local African societies, without reference to overseas issues, raising the question of "homeland" studies as part of diaspora, one Monson is eager to answer by insisting that we cannot just study "conditions of dispersion and exile," a stance that stretches the term ever further. Like a rubber band, "diaspora" obligingly extends itself, but one wonders when it will either go slack or simply snap under pressure.

The ethnomusicology of Jewish cultures operates in yet another dimension, since all contemporary communities until the creation of the State of Israel have regarded themselves as being in permanent diaspora. Even in Israel, hardcore Orthodox subcultures deny the validity of a Jewish nation-state being a homeland before the Messiah arrives. So much attention goes to interdiaspora studies. Kay Shelemay quickly confronts her readers with the "multiple diasporas" of Syrian Jews. "The" Jewish diaspora turns out to be much too broad a concept to understand the heritage trail of one subgroup of Jews, who moved from ancient Israel to medieval Spain, migrated to Syria, and from there fanned out to places worldwide where they felt more comfortable (Shelemay 1998, 68). Through songs, each locale and each generation of Syrian Jews finds ways to connect to actual or imagined *pasts*, not *presents*. From this type of study we learn to distinguish *diasporas of remembrance* (a phrase in Shelemay's subtitle) from *diasporas of everyday connection.*

Questioning the unity of any diaspora seems salutary. But the follow-up forces the ethnomusicologist further and further into the thickets of history and aesthetics. Shelemay's Syrians remain dedicated to a model of Arab music that is itself composite; it is not as if they were carrying on a pure strain of music making from their home in Aleppo, Syria. Older community members heard musicians from Damascus, Beirut, and Cairo, and the phonograph allowed them to choose from even wider layers of transnational musics (Shelemay 1998, 106–107). They continue this habit today, keeping up with the latest in Arabic music via recordings. Significantly, New York's Syrian Jews "have had little face-to-face contact with live Arab musicians locally; there is little contact between Jewish, Christian, and Muslim immigrants of Middle Eastern descent" (1998, 113), due partly to interethnic strain. It is precisely in this type of detail that diaspora's meaning lies. Small groups tack with the steering winds to find their way to the communal harbor of their imagination. In so doing, they may refuse to take fellow passengers on board.

My own work (Slobin 2000) on another Jewish diasporic scene, klezmer music, goes off in different directions. Klezmer emerged from diasporic eastern European Jewish life, flourished in another diaspora in the United States from the 1880s through the 1930s, was largely exterminated in Europe by Nazism and Stalinism, made a big comeback in the United States starting in the mid-1970s, and returned to Europe as an American import in the 1990s. In Israel, klezmer was not a known entity. It has only recently appeared there, as an Americanism. The destruction of the European "homeland" meant that the "diaspora" became the music's base. In such a situation, diaspora carries little analytical weight as a term of choice except when intensively redefined. For a musician like Michael Alpert, a Jewish-American from Los Angeles playing eastern European music in Berlin, "homeland" has several meanings, and he can use the experience to write a song that is then put on disc and into circulation to gather more meanings. The music itself becomes a kind of homeland to the musician's compounded sense of diaspora. In liner notes to Brave Old World's album *Beyond the Pale*, Alpert says: "In 1993, Germany is one of the very few countries where you can make a living playing Jewish music. But for whom. . . ." "So play me a sweet Diaspora song, with a longing that's pure," a line from the song "Berlin 1990" that made it to Germany's hit charts (Alpert 1994, 4).

The analyst's problem is to identify the complexity, but not to let it overwhelm the account. The subtitle of Frances Aparicio's provocative book *Listening to Salsa* is: *Gender, Latin Popular Music, and Puerto Rican Cultures*—note the plural. One of her rare uses of *diaspora* is telling. She presents salsa as "a metaphor for race, class, and gender conflicts within the diverse Puerto Rican communities (the island and the diasporas), as well as across Latin America, the United States, and the international scene" (Aparicio 1998, 66). Here Aparicio sets multiple Puerto Rican diasporas into motion, nesting them within giant overlapping geocultural spheres stretching off into an "international scene," which seems too broad to define further. From the vantage point of klezmer studies, I sympathize with her stance, but would like more definition; an endless horizon of musical expansion offers little comfort.

To close this survey, it seems helpful to cite the most comprehensive current attempt to organize musical diaspora studies, Su Zheng's *Claiming Diaspora: Music, Transnationalism, and Cultural Politics in Asian/ Chinese America* (n.d.). Here is her key paragraph of definition:

> In this book, I consider diaspora *as a descriptive term* to illustrate Chinese Americans' past and present social and cultural experiences and their structures of feelings, memories, and imaginations through rich ethnographic treatment; *as an analytical category* to probe the deeper meanings and implications of diasporic conditions of Chinese American expressive cultural forms and practices; *as a mode of awareness* to critique and problematize the pervasive, often Western-centered notion of the bipolar order of the totalizing global system and fragmented local responses, and at the same time, *as a vehicle for oppositional politics* against the oppressive and hegemonic national narratives and cultural formations. (Zheng n.d.; my emphasis)

Zheng ably assembles multiple meanings for diaspora, which she unpacks in subsequent chapters. I would like to isolate one aspect of her work. Zheng suggests a triangulation among the observer, the diasporic insiders, and the outside power structure, all three sharing the same analytical space. Her sense of "descriptive" goes far beyond its usual neutrality to include insiders' states of mind. "Analytical category" seems to be reserved for the observer's assessment. "Mode of awareness" leaves open the question of just who is making the critique of the established order, the diasporic subjects or the analyst, as does the strong insistence on "oppositional politics," and on the idea that politics complements the oppressive narratives of the power structure.

Zheng, a Chinese-born, now Asian-American scholar whose work spans the United States and China, perhaps deliberately diasporizes herself in this way. In any event, her work spotlights the scholar as central agent in the drama of diaspora. A further move in following the trail of musical diaspora studies, then, might lead us back to the ethnomusicologists' houses. The role of diasporic subjects as scholars could use a careful going-over. Often, we either cover our tracks or make too much of a point of a specific "subject position." Either strategy denies the very malleability and multilocality that diaspora implies.

It is this multiplicity that makes it hard to pin down "diaspora." When it combines with the fluidity of definition from inside and outside social groupings at various levels of today's self-conscious societies, the going gets very rough. Take the case of hip-hop, as cogently collected in a recent reader (Mitchell 2001). This pungent and powerful form of expression is globally dispersed. Born as a melange of black Atlantic diaspora sensibilities and practices, hip-hop and rap domesticate differently everywhere, while staying recognizably themselves. Each case study in the volume suggests new shades of meaning for "diaspora." In Germany, for example, clusters of immigrant communities bounce off each other's experiments as they reshape American imported models. Mark Pennay (2001, 120) reports on "a trio of Heidelberg youths of Italian, Ghanaian, and Haitian backgrounds who described in clear German what it was like to possess German citizenship but be treated like a foreigner on the basis of appearance." This statement seems at once to be affirming and denying the group's diasporic status. It also signals the onset of metadiasporas who literally band together. Meanwhile, some "German" rappers explicitly identify themselves with diasporic populations, like Advanced Chemistry's song "Fremd in eigenem Land" ("Foreign in My Own Country"). Rap seems to have a way of bringing diaspora to consciousness. Mir Wermuth (2000, 160) says that in Holland, white rappers try to get around the problem by blithely assuming that official multiculturalism levels the playing field, only to be told off by local black hip-hoppers.

The detailed essays on rap in *Global Noise* bring us to the intersection of diaspora and globalization, not in the commercial, but in the affinity sense of intercultural traffic. Increasingly, people are restive, reaching for dynamic musical movements as they tire of the easy models of official multiculturalism, with their promise of separate but equal artistic expression. A voice from Vancouver spells it out: "Charlie Cho, a radio producer and editor of an Asian-Canadian cultural magazine, Rice Paper, said a confident younger generation in Vancouver could reject the old, earnest credos of multiculturalism: 'At this stage it's all this big exciting thing,' he said, 'in which we're less interested in preserving culture or talking about heritage and all that sort of stuff. What we find really interesting is that contemporary culture is a hybrid'" (Crossette 2001). Here, "hybrid" is more an escape from bureaucracy than a definable practice. Which cultural products are not "hybridized" today, and how could we distinguish "diasporic" hybridity from other varieties?

Whether diaspora is a demographic and socially sustainable fact or anything from a marketing strategy to a state of mind remains an open, exciting question. Looking at a single cultural product might make matters more concrete. The example is a 1986 Tamil film, *Mouna Ragam,* still much appreciated as a fine collaboration between director Mani Rathnam and music director Ilayaraaja.[2] In its plotline, musical choices, and distribution, *Mouna Ragam* builds in multileveled diasporas even as it evokes globalization. It tells the story of a well-to-do Tamil couple who enter a loveless arranged marriage, move from their home city of Chennai in the south to New Delhi, and, through crises and over time, find they can become true partners. A survey of some of the many types of music the film includes can suggest the broad and flexible resources a top creative force like Ilayaraaja can bring to bear on a project. He went into *The Guinness Book of World Records* for the highest number of film scores, but his work is known for its quality, not just quantity, and defined the Tamil movie sound of the 1980s. From a village background, Ilayaraaja was able to combine local vernacular roots with world sources, including a classical music leaning that led him to record with the London Philharmonic.

The film opens with a reworking of "Singin' in the Rain," a classic Hollywood number, repositioned as a frolic of middle-class teenage girls singing and dancing as they go home from private school. They wear outfits that span the range of Western to Indian, and dance in Broadway and MTV style while the main tune riffs on American stylings with an Indianized vocal sound. At one point the lead pauses in an archway that suggests Indianness, perhaps Muslim in quality, while the instruments shift to a more local sound briefly before returning to Western pop. This implicit globalization matches the free-spirited, open-ended fun stage of the heroine's life. When her parents announce the arranged marriage, the music shifts decisively to Indian instruments (sarangi, swaramandala), leading to the nagaswaram and drum clamor of a brief wedding sequence. This segment literally underscores the local as the unchangeable foundation of personal life when it counts.

Relocated in New Delhi, which is signaled by the faint sound of a muezzin in the background, the couple goes to see the sights, accompanied by light synth-based "traveling music" that positions them as modernized, diasporic tourists in their own country. In their upscale house, the housewife pushes a button on her boombox in the high-tech kitchen to

---

2. I am grateful to Vijayashree Mokkapati for insights into *Mouna Ragam* and to graduate students Anuradha Mohan and Joseph Getter for work on Tamil film music.

listen to the Beatles' "Michelle." She imagines her marriage in a more romantic vein by slipping into a daydream fantasy sequence set in the Indian countryside. This features Tamil regional sounds set visually in something like the Kashmiri countryside and costumes. She goes upstairs to flirt with her new husband as he listens to Vivaldi's *Four Seasons* at his desk. She playfully switches off the stereo, initiating an argument, as he accuses her of childishness.

In town, the music continues to be restless. For a restaurant scene, the background sitar music alternates awkwardly with standardized underscoring of the couple's emotions. A melodramatic turning point of the relationship emerges from one of the indispensable street fighting sequences of such films, which is accompanied by a flamenco sound. And so it goes throughout *Mouna Ragam*, which weaves a web of global music strands. The film's success in the Indian diaspora can be charted on the many websites for Tamil film songs, which contain the lyrics and music notation for hundreds of entries, and the easy access to the video version in American— and presumably Singaporean and African—grocery stores or through the Internet. Many such home-movie versions are intercut with ads for investment houses in Hong Kong or Indian cable television services in New Jersey, or can be seen at "Indian nights" locally, as in a strip-mall moviehouse in my Connecticut location.

Mouna Ragam presents an impressive array of diasporic and global sensibilities within a single product. The plot takes on the question of internal diaspora within the huge space of India. The blending and separation of multiple Indian music and dance sources sketch out a society that is both segmented and integrated. The overlay of Western sounds adds layers of meanings that move the discourse toward the global, though from a local perspective: The class orientation of Vivaldi and the Beatles, the randomness of flamenco, the sentimentality of emotional underscoring using both Indian and Western sources, and the knowing parody of "Singin' in the Rain" show off a fluent and virtuoso ability to play with worldwide style sources while staying within a familiar genre model. This efficient eclecticism was apparent from the earliest Indian sound films, and has only accelerated since the 1980s in newer films that leave India to place production numbers on location in venues like Scotland. All of this intentionally targets a global audience that might be Indian or non-Indian. While the movies are literally "diasporic" for many viewers, there is a sense in which the commercial entertainment product creates a diaspora of taste as well as population. As of this writing (early 2002), Indian film, once seen as amusingly peripheral, moves closer to the center under the tutelage of the very powerful Andrew Lloyd Weber. This king of the musical metropole is currently touting a Hindi film nominated for the Oscars while preparing to roll out his own Anglo-Indian production, *Bollywood Dreams.* In the 1990s, music of English-based Indian pop groups swept to the top of the British charts, shifting easy definitions of which entertainment is diasporic or mainstream, subcultural or supercultural. Now the same issues may be coming to the film world as well. Matters of capital, self-representation, and media claim staking will play their parts even as audiences in different time zones vote by long distance.

In conclusion, "diaspora" is here to stay in ethnomusicology even as it threatens to spiral out of control. It arrived somewhat reluctantly, but has now moved from alien to permanent resident status in our scholarly homeland. This essay has only sketched the naturalization process. Like all immigrants, this newcomer is restless, a bit insecure, but working hard to find a niche. Like some émigrés, the term itself seems to have shut the door to its past, and to be content with settling into its new, kinetic surroundings. We are all the richer for the new musics and the new interpretive insights this situation opens.

Further Reading

Diehl, Keila. 2002. *Echoes from Dharamsala: Music in the life of a Tibetan refugee community.* Berkley: Univ. of California Press.

Garland Encyclopedia of World Music. 2001. Vol. 3, *The United States and Canada.* Edited by Ellen Koskoff. New York: Garland.

Glasser, Ruth. 1995. *My music is my flag: Puerto Rican musicians and their New York communities, 1917–40.* Berkeley: Univ. of California Press.

Mitchell, Tony, ed. 2001. *Global noise: Rap and hip hop outside the USA.* Middletown, Conn.: Wesleyan Univ. Press.

Monson, Ingrid, ed. 2000. *African diaspora: A musical perspective.* New York: Garland.

Pettan, Svanibor, Adelaida Reyes, and Masa Komavec, eds. 2001. *Music and minorities.* Ljubljana: Zalozba.

Reyes, Adelaida. 1999. *Songs of the caged, songs of the free: Music and the Vietnamese refugee experience.* Philadelphia: Temple Univ. Press.

Slobin, Mark. 2000. *Fiddler on the move: Exploring the klezmer world.* New York: Oxford Univ. Press.

Veal, Michael. 2000. *Fela: The life and times of an African musical icon.* Philadelphia: Temple Univ. Press.

Velez, Maria Teresa. 2000. *Drumming for the gods: The life and times of Felipe Garcia Villamul, Santero, Palero, and Abakua.* Philadelphia: Temple Univ. Press.

Zheng, Su. n.d. *Claiming diaspora.* New York: Oxford Univ. Press. Forthcoming.

CHAPTER 25

Globalization and the Politics of World Music

MARTIN STOKES

The world music phenomenon tells a simple but resonant story. Suffused with a gentle millennial mysticism as the twentieth century drew to a close, it suggested that something quite new was afoot. A world in which ideas, cultures, and senses of identity were woven snugly and securely into place by the nation-state was unraveling. Previously unimaginable connections were possible, thanks to the increasingly uninhibited circulation of people, ideas, and things. And a previously unimaginable politics was emerging, one capable of addressing truly global issues, ranging from the environment to women's, children's and indigenous people's rights. What better image of this world than the grooving together of cultures remote from one another in music, that perennial source of social warmth in modernity's cold world?

World music is, however, no simple matter. First, the material forces that both enable and constrain the movement of music and musicians about the globe are not always easy to comprehend. To a great extent, we hear what large and powerful corporations enable us to hear, though, as I try to demonstrate, the grasp of these corporations on music making worldwide is by no means total. Much evades them, and their own mechanisms for understanding what is going on are partial and self-interested. Second, the forces that imbue the notion of global musical encounter with such power and persuasion are complex and deeply rooted. We understand world music through profoundly ideological lenses, not easy to do without.

The appropriation of rap and hip-hop in Europe provides a useful critical vantage point, though. Antipathy to American popular culture runs high among the European intelligentsia, while for many migrants and other marginalized people in cities such as London, Berlin and Paris, the link between African-American ghetto experience and their own is powerful and compelling. A younger generation, reared on migrant-oriented genres such as Bhangra, Rai and Arabesk in the 1980s, turned to rap and hip-hop in the 1990s. This not only marked their sense of generational distinction, but also served as a comment upon the rising tide of neo-Nazi hostility to Europe's "blacks." This act of cultural translation has, however, been a turbulent and complex affair.

German-Turkish rappers Cartel appeared in Istanbul in 1995 to a storm of publicity in Turkey. For their supporters among the intelligentsia, here at last was Turkish youth culture taking on the world. People who had once been regarded as a source of cultural embarrassment—Turkish *gastarbeiter* (migrant "guestworkers" in Germany)—became a valued cultural resource overnight. Some Turkish commentators were quick to point out that what was being presented as a total novelty was simply the latest stage in a century-long history of Turkish appropriations from Western popular musical culture. One could draw a straight line, they argued, from the Turkish appropriation of operetta—via tango, chanson, rock, and pop—to Turkish rap and hip-hop. Turks had been successful appropriators over the centuries, but this was not really a criticism. Turkish intellectuals feel that their capacity to absorb and appropriate has been the hallmark of their distinctive cultural style. Those versed in cultural theory added that what sometimes appears to be "mere" mimicry at a casual glance on closer inspection often turns out to be a more complex, dynamic, and creative process. We might learn something important about ourselves, they suggested, by listening closely to what Cartel and other German-Turks were saying.

Cartel also received a warm reception from young Turkish fascists, whose unappealing blend of racialized nationalism and orthodox Islam had been engineered by Alparslan Türkeş in the 1960s, and had resurfaced in the liberal political climate of the late 1980s. Their indignation at the humiliating situation of Turks in Germany had been inflamed by a spate of neo-Nazi outrages, culminating in an arson attack in Sollingen in 1995 that claimed a large number of *gastarbeiter* lives. Here at last were people fighting back, waving a Turkish flag, their gang uniforms and insignia displaying a prominent Islamic crescent. In their opinion, the *dazlaks* (neo-Nazi skinheads) were getting their long overdue come-uppance. The liberal press in Turkey responded anxiously. The intelligentsia, previously enthusiastic, back-pedaled. Attentive to the sensibilities of its CD-buying middle-class clientele, their record company, Raks-Polygram, seemed to lose confidence. Concerts were canceled. The album became increasingly difficult to find. About nine months after its release, I had difficulty finding it, though I eventually managed to buy a copy in one of Raks's suburban outlets. It had to be dug out of a shoebox under the counter, as I remember. The only places in which I would see it displayed were in the stalls of itinerant cassette vendors at the main transport terminals for outlying squatter-town districts. The CD and cassette markets were, by then, worlds apart, and Cartel appeared to have slipped between them.

The members of Cartel were profoundly upset by their reception in Turkey. Their progressive credentials had not, after all, been in doubt in Germany. Like many other Turkish and Turkish-Kurdish rappers, Cartel had emerged in the context of the wider youth movement against neo-Nazism in the early 1990s. Flaunting a Turkish flag and Islamist insignia in Berlin was an explicit and identifiable comment on the failings of social democracy in Germany, which stressed the assimilation of *gastarbeiter* but refused to countenance citizenship. In Cartel's opinion, this gesture in Germany had little if anything to do with those waving Turkish flags and Islamist insignia in Turkey at the same time. Turkish rap and hip-hop continue to thrive in Germany, and also in Holland, but they made little lasting impact in Turkey, where they have remained almost exclusively the preserve of an extreme right-wing subculture. The much-anticipated explosion of hip-hop and the regeneration of a radical music scene in Turkey failed to happen. Musicians and cultural commentators looking anxiously for ways of attaching Turkish musical content to "global" forms came slowly but surely to the conclusion that rap and hip-hop were not the way to go.

There are a number of actors in this particular drama, which one might think of, in less individuated terms, as sites of agency. These are the recording industry, migrant culture, and the nation-state. I deal with them in turn, in each case moving back and forth between general issues and our specific example. The recording industry is important and an appropriate starting point. Transnational companies, in particular Time-Warner, Thorn-EMI, Bertelsmann, Sony, PolyGram, and Matsushita—henceforth "the majors"—have consolidated their grasp on the music industry both through "horizontal" (aiming for synergy with related entertainment industries) and through "vertical" (aiming to connect companies further up and down the production–consumption chain) mergers and acquisitions strategies. In recent years, the challenges of vertical integration have been complicated by MP3s and the circulation of prerecorded music on the Web. The transnationals, represented by the International Federation for Phonographic Industries (IFPI), have been quick to identify web circulation as a form of piracy.

Outside the "developed" markets in the industrial world, the majors have devoted considerable efforts to controlling cassette and radio piracy, and elbowing their rivals, particularly local cassette producers, out of the market. In many respects, the Turkish experience has been typical. The circulation of music via cassettes and radio had been largely a national affair—extending, of course, to Turkish and Kurdish *gastarbeiter* in Europe. Political and economic liberalization at the end of the 1980s introduced CDs, FM radio, and satellite music channels. Music production and consumption began to assume global dimensions. CDs were increasingly assembled at state-of-the-art facilities in various locations around the world, and the fact was much publicized. A "global" audience was often evoked as the ultimate arbiter of success and cultural worth. The point of this rhetoric of globalization in the Turkish recording industry was largely local. It not only validated the self-image of bourgeois Turkish consumers, but also drove a wedge between down-market local cassette production and the glamorous, cosmopolitan world of Turkish pop and rock CDs. One company grasped the nature of the moment, and acted promptly: Raks. By the mid-1990s, Raks had signed up nearly every major pop and rock star, created a tier of elite production articulated by "global" production values, and advertised its products through costly media campaigns. Their lobbying for European copyright law harmonization, as a tool in the battle against cassette piracy, was less successful, but highly publicized. Their efforts in this direction quickly landed a significant prize: a licensing agreement with the PolyGram label. One of the early products of this agreement was Raks's Turkish distribution rights for Mercury, the PolyGram subsidiary in Germany that produced and distributed Cartel.

The Cartel case thus tells, on the face of it, the familiar tale of the movement of the major recording industries into "less-developed" music markets in the third world, their absorption of local industries, and the concomitant spread of Western musical styles. The process might readily be understood in terms of the so-called "cultural imperialism hypothesis." The arguments seem compelling. The IFPI estimates that the multinationals control approximately 80 to 90 percent of sales of (legally) recorded music worldwide. There are few countries in the world in which it is impossible to find recordings by Madonna, Michael Jackson, or George Michael. There are also few parts of the world that have not produced local genres of rock, rap, and hip-hop. But the "cultural imperialism hypothesis" is profoundly misleading. There are four main counterarguments, three of which I mention in passing, and the fourth of which I discuss in more detail.

First, there is no simple correlation between the more or less global spread of African-American musics and the activities of the multinationals, only one of which, Time-Warner, is actually American based.

Second, the circulation of genres such as rock and rap cannot be entirely reduced to the circulation of sound recordings. Live music scenes thrive where recordings are hard to come by (viz. the world of Eastern-European rock). Listeners, as we saw in the case of Cartel, often do with recorded music as they please, and not necessarily to the advantage of recording companies themselves.

Third, the question of "world music" cannot entirely be reduced to the cultural-imperialism formula. The majors have, since the 1980s, been actively involved in promoting "local" musics with a stress on cultural crossovers, and in efforts to refashion or reinvent "the local" in ways that might appeal to metropolitan audiences. The transnationals have not been entirely successful in controlling this market or the music produced within it, which continues to be shaped to a significant extent by small independent labels in Paris, New York, and London. It also continues to provide space for music industries in the Third World, notably the Caribbean, though the extent of their dependence on First World markets and inequities in the distribution of rights certainly give cause for concern. However one weighs the advantages and disadvantages, one can no longer talk in simple terms about "the West" imposing itself culturally on the "third world," or the "center" imposing itself on the "periphery." It is far from clear where and what these might now be, and who is imposing what on whom.

Fourth, the cultural imperialism hypothesis shares with some arguments about globalization the assumption that "the global" is abstract, placeless, and at some conceptual remove from the particularities of place, history, and culture—the things, in short, that one associates with the local. Agents of cultural imperialism such as the majors thus appear so abstracted, in this view of things, as to defy comprehension. Alternative cultural strategies thus become hard to conceptualize. Yet the majors are located in particular places, and have histories and commercial cultures that are extremely relevant to the ways in which global sounds circulate. Thorn-EMI inherited the Columbia and Gramophone lists in 1931, both of which companies had promoted and exploited significant markets for local recorded music in the colonial world early in the twentieth century. Thorn-EMI, alone among the majors, has devoted significant resources to cultivating and exploiting the huge market for recorded music in East Asia. To come back to our case study, Raks linked up with PolyGram to promote Cartel for identifiable reasons. PolyGram came into existence as a result of a merger between Dutch-owned Phonogram and German-owned Polydor in 1972. PolyGram immediately launched an aggressive campaign to buy out a large number of independents across Europe, purchasing French-owned Barcley in 1978. Barcley had signed Algerian Rai singer Khaled, whose 1992 album *Didi* sold in huge numbers to a large European world-music audience, to French-resident North Africans, and across the Middle East. Experience with these complex interlocking markets, and the proximity of large Turkish *gastarbeiter* communities in Germany and Holland, undoubtedly made the promotion of Cartel and partnership with Raks an attractive proposition. This suggests that the former colonizers continue to exert significant cultural and economic control over their ex- and neocolonies, a fact that might appear to confirm the central thrust of the cultural imperialism hypothesis. But it also suggests that this control is historically and culturally contingent. It is neither abstract, nor total, nor inevitable, as the cultural imperialism hypothesis often suggests.

Discussions of globalization focus heavily on the circulation of commodities and capital. The circulation of people in the context of globalization is either ignored or treated with ambivalence. The reasons for this are not hard to imagine. Transnational corporations benefit from the free movement of commodities and capital, but require stable markets and stable pools of exploitable labor. Yet one of the major effects of globalization has been precisely to make markets and labor pools less stable, and populations more mobile. Trade links between first and third worlds, colonial pasts, and neocolonial presents all serve to create well-trod paths to the metropolitan centers of North America, Western Europe, Australia, and Japan. For many, treading these routes is no longer simply a possibility, but an imperative. From a first-world perspective, there are certain benefits. They include the supply of cheap and disposable labor to first-world service sectors, and the presence of immigrant neighborhoods, with their cuisine, music, and fashion as entertainment and distraction for the affluent middle classes. In a less directly material sense, they also include the comforting liberal illusion of multiculturalism in societies that continue to reap benefits from profound global inequalities. The anxieties are palpable, too. Yet the global movements of migrant underclasses are as vital to the creation and transmission of "global" cultures as is the movement of commodities. This is as true in a musical context as it is anywhere else. This brings us to our second site of agency: migrant culture.

Academic commentators have paid increasing attention to the global dimensions of migrant culture over the last two decades. The emergence of "hyphenated identities" (Turkish-German, British-Asian, and so forth) has been hailed as a force undermining the oppressive identity-producing apparatus of the nation-state, and putting into play new, inclusive, and open-ended notions of belonging. The role that African-American musical forms have played in challenging hegemonic local identities, and establishing new kinds of cultural alliances between the marginalized and dispossessed in widely separated societies has been much discussed. No longer can one safely assume that globalization produces cultural homogenization or acquiescence to the political status quo, as proponents of the cultural imperialism hypothesis once argued. However, this hard-won insight is not entirely unproblematic, as the Cartel case shows.

In the first instance Cartel claimed to speak for the German–Turkish *gastarbeiter* community in its totality. This claim was, at best, naïve, and at worst, complicit with the very forces that marginalize Turks in German society. These too are inclined to frame German–Turkish experience as a unitary category, labeled "Middle Eastern/Muslim." Practically all Turks in Germany are Muslim, but not all identify themselves in religious terms. Those born in Turkey, after all, have been brought up in a strongly secular state. Those who do identify themselves in religious terms experience little kinship with the kind of black American Islam that animates the world of rap. Matters of ethnicity also intervene in this claim. Kurds and Turks mix in Germany, and have often worked together to protest against neo-Nazism and to further common interests in Germany. Equally often they have had cause to separate. The war between the Turkish army and the Kurdish separatist PKK in the 1990s created major rifts in immigrant neighborhoods across Germany. Cartel's tactic of bringing together the emblems of Turkish nationalism and African-American Islam was bound to be misinterpreted by those who saw an *essential*, rather than strategic and provisional, connection between Turkishness and Islam, whether in Germany or Turkey.

One might identify a more subtle kind of complicity with currents of liberal multiculturalism in German society. Cartel's popularity coincided with an enthusiasm for migrant chic in Germany in the mid-1990s, cultivated by a slew of articles in *Der Spiegel, Die Zeit-Punkte*, and other up-market magazines on German–Turkish fashion, cinema, jewelry, food, drink, and the attractions of migrant neighborhoods (viewed from a safe distance). Hyphenated identities became extremely hip, an image of empowerment and cosmopolitanism. This is, of course, not necessarily a bad thing. But one might also argue that the thinking-class cultivation of migrant chic fails to address the real roots of discrimination against Turks in German society, and if anything inflames neo-Nazi antagonism further. A single blow struck against Turks now counts twice: once against hated foreigners and once against the hated liberal elite. In addition, the idealization of migrant lives assumes a normative force, and comes to constitute an inflexible standard against which migrant civility is judged. In this sense, hyphenated identities are every bit as controlling as the nonhyphenated variety to which they are routinely opposed. The single category "German–Turkish" lumps together a diverse group of people whose lives have little in common, and whose interests are not necessarily served by being considered in this homogenizing light.

The language of easygoing inclusiveness is misleading, too, on the subject of gender and sexuality. Cartel's macho posturing can certainly be interpreted, and to a measure excused, by the strategic musical connections it was attempting to forge between black American and European migrant experience. But it tells another story, of the gendered and sexualized anxieties that accompany the process of globalization. While the world celebrated the collapse of the Berlin wall, Turks were being squeezed from all directions. Cheap East German labor was rapidly displacing cheap Turkish labor. The collapse of the Berlin wall turned previously marginal immigrant neighborhoods in Berlin, notably Kreuzberg, into valuable real estate, subject to spiraling rents and the kinds of corporate pressure on downtown areas familiar in other "global cities." The service industries' preference for female labor assumed a fixed quality in a general business climate of downsizing, casualization, and outsourcing. In many *gastarbeiter* households, women became the regular breadwinners, and men became more and more superfluous to an increasingly pinched domestic economy. The sexualized tone of Cartel's rhetoric of empowerment thus might be seen as mediating a situation in which people—men in particular—are experiencing processes of disempowerment in direct and intensifying forms, with predictable stresses between men and women.

Theories of globalization have often considered the nation-state to be on the wane. As globalization progresses, the capacity of the nation-state to organize political, economic, and cultural experience is held to diminish. This ignores the fact that nation-states have been actively working in tandem with transnational corporations, creating industrial, business, and entertainment zones in their major cities to facilitate the needs of these corporations. The effects of this process are instantly recognizable in New York, London, Berlin, Bombay, Tokyo, Istanbul, São Paulo, and elsewhere, and are usually signaled by a great deal of local civic pride in attaining the status of "global city." Istanbul's "global" status was much on people's lips when the city hosted the Habitat II conference in 1996, by which time the city's managers had comprehensively cleared the central business area of its slums, bars, and famous brothels—including a street that served as a major center for transsexual prostitution. A vast network of new bridges and roads connected relocated and increasingly dispersed industries, business centers, suburban enclaves, and squatter towns. Here as elsewhere the state has been actively involved in creating a context in which the global can "happen"; it is far from being a passive victim of it. This brings us to our final site of agency: the nation-state.

The nation-state continues to shape cultural experience across the world in direct and important ways. National broadcasting systems continue to be significant in generating local music industries—the BBC and Brit-pop being a case in point. Quota systems have been the traditional means by which nation-states protect local industries from global forces, and these remain effective in a number of European states. Satellite broadcasting and the Web pose a challenge, but these, too, have been subject to inventive legislation on the part of a number of states in recent years. These range from, for example, criminalizing the possession of satellite dishes in Iran to forbidding the sale of Nazi memorabilia on the Web in France. The effects of media industries' expansionism, and protectionist strategies on the part of nation-states, can, however, be complex and unpredictable, as the Cartel case, again, illustrates. At the height of its campaign against the PKK, the Turkish government was able to put pressure on the BBC to close down the satellite from which MED-TV, a London-based Turkish-Kurdish channel, was broadcasting in Turkey. This satellite also beamed MTV to Turkish audiences. The effect of closing down the one was to close down the other. MTV did not pursue the matter (I have no idea why). By this time, however, a market for MTV-style music programming had emerged in Turkey. Kral, a Turkish satellite company, was quick to occupy the vacant space, and devised a program that combined MTV-style formatting with Turkish music content. By 1996 Kral was the main shop window for upmarket companies such as Raks; a repeatedly shown video was a costly but vital adjunct to the publicity campaign for any new act or recording. A great deal of the publicity that surrounded Cartel's appearance in Istanbul was generated by their video, shown repeatedly on Kral TV. The circulation of music on the global media thus still owes a surprisingly large amount to consequences of nation-state intervention, both intended *and* unintended

If the state remains significant in a global world, what then of the nation? The circulation of hybrid cultural forms sometimes has the effect of strengthening rather than weakening a sense of national belonging, contrary to what is usually suggested. The form recordings take does not entirely define people's responses to them, as I have already noted. Cartel's rhetoric of Turkish–Islamic empowerment could be, and was, misread. For German liberals, the tone of anger was neutralized in the context of migrant chic. For conservatives and neo-Nazi racists, it confirmed the alien and unassimilable qualities of *gastarbeiter* culture. In Turkey this same message was read differently again. Ironic samples of Turkish folk culture could be read as a mark of approval of the state's role in preserving national culture. The combination of Turkish and Islamic imagery at a moment when the entire legacy of Atatürk's secular state seemed to be in the balance, and when an Islamist government had just been elected, was explosive. Cartel's rough language and macho posturing also seemed to address the class formations emerging in the wake of two decades of adaptation to the dictates of transnational business in Turkey ("structural adjustment" to its critics, "globalization" to its celebrants). Those excluded from its benefits had much to feel angry about, and Cartel gave them a sense of their own power to instill anxiety in the liberal elites so avidly promoting Turkey's new "global" status. Extreme nationalism here, as in many parts of Europe, has thrived in an atmosphere of disquiet at what globalization has entailed for the have-nots.

Shifts in technology and production, the movements of populations, and sudden extensions in the circulation of commodities have produced millennial hopes and anxieties in various parts of the world for a long time. "Globalization," in this sense, might best be understood as the most recent turn in a long history in which modern institutions have both justified and marveled at the expansion of their power over vast tracts of territory. In this sense, too, there is little "new" about "World Music." Music has always traveled along the grain of political and economic power, establishing lasting dialogues between communities so linked. These dialogues have persisted, in the case of the movement of music between Africa and the New World, for example, for centuries. The problem that "World Music" poses as discourse is in some respects related to that posed by globalization as discourse. It is almost entirely ignorant of its own past, blind to the material conditions of its own existence, and oblivious to the history of power differentials among the various partners in cultural exchange in world history. A critical understanding of the contemporary conditions of global music circulation may, in response to these shortcomings, disperse some of the more vaporous and naively optimistic myths of musical others that surround the "World Music" phenomenon. It might also help us to think of and put into practice more enduring and democratic ways of relating to others through music.

Further Reading

Broughton, Simon, Mark Ellingham, and Richard Trillo, eds. 1999–2000. *World music: The rough guide*. Vol. 1. Africa, Europe and the Middle East. Vol. 2. Latin and North America, Caribbean, India, Asia and Pacific. London: The Rough Guides.

Burnett, Robert. 1996. *The global jukebox: The international music industry*. London: Routledge.

Erlmann, Veit. 1996. Aesthetics of the global imagination: Reflections on world music in the 1990s. *Public Culture* 8(3): 467–88.

Feld, Steven. 1994. From schizophonia to schismogenesis: On the discourses and commodification practices of "world music" and "world beat." Pp. 257–89 in *Music grooves*. Edited by Charles Keil and Steven Feld. Chicago: Univ. of Chicago Press.

Frith, Simon, 2000. The discourse of world music. Pp. 305–22 in *Western music and its others: Difference, representation and appropriation in music*. Edited by Georgina Born and David Hesmondhalgh. Berkeley: Univ. of California Press.

Guilbault, Jocelyne, with Gage Averill, Édouard Benoit, and Gregory Rabess. 1993. *Zouk: World music in the West Indies*. Chicago: Univ. of Chicago Press.

Laing, Dave. 1986. The music industry and the "cultural imperialism" thesis. *Media, Culture and Society* 8: 331–41.

Lipsitz, George. 1994. *Dangerous crossroads: Popular music, postmodernism and the poetics of place*. London: Verso.

Slobin, Mark. 1993. *Subcultural sounds: Micromusics of the West*. Hanover, N.H.: Univ. Press of New England.

Taylor, Timothy. 1997. *Global pop: World music, world markets*. London: Routledge.

CHAPTER 26

Music and the Market
The Economics of Music in the Modern World

DAVE LAING

> [W]ho would think seriously of minimising the role of the market?
> Even in an elementary form, it is the favoured terrain of supply and
> demand, of that appeal to other people without which there would
> be no economy in the ordinary sense of the word. . . . The market
> spells liberation, openness, access to another world. It means com-
> ing up for air.
>
> —Fernand Braudel

This chapter is concerned with the various ways in which the idea of the
market can be used to help us understand how music works as a business.
It begins with a consideration of markets as actual geographical spaces
where goods and services are exchanged, and then discusses some different concepts of what, borrowing from Anderson (1991), I call "imagined markets." Such music markets can involve consumers of musical
goods and services, employers of musicians' labor power, and/or busi-
nesses that use music. Here, ideas such as market failure, public goods,
and intellectual property are introduced. Finally, the chapter briefly deals
with new ways in which music is being consumed online and with the
limits of the market idea.

The Market as Basic Place of Exchange

In his book *The Wheels of Commerce*, the eminent social historian
Fernand Braudel reminds us that "exchange is as old as human history"

(Braudel 1982, 225). The simplest modes of exchange are those involving no or few intermediaries between producer and consumer, and these are modes where supply and demand for goods or services fluctuate little. Exchange may take a variety of forms including the bartering of goods or services without the intermediation of money, but for some centuries the predominant sites of exchange have been various forms of market. Some musical examples are performances at fairs or street markets ("the elementary form" mentioned by Braudel in the epigraph to this chapter), over many centuries to the present day, in all parts of the world, and the sale there of musical commodities in the form of instruments, cassettes, or CDs.

Popular music has had a presence at markets for centuries. In England in 1595, a writer complained that, at every market, ballad singers were "singing their wares" (Clark 1983, 185), while cassette sellers are found in the markets of most, if not all, African, Asian, and Latin American cities today. In contemporary Africa, Sandaga market in Dakar is a center of legitimate cassette production, and in Kankan (Guinea), cassette stalls are set up near the Grand Marché. Chris Waterman's classic study of jùjú music in Nigeria in the 1980s also discussed the role of markets in the dissemination of recordings (Waterman 1990, 152–53).

As far as music is concerned, the most important role of contemporary street markets is as venues for the sale of pirate discs and tapes. In his study of street markets in Mexico City, John C. Cross points out that such "informal economic activity" is more complex than the standard definition of it as "the pursuit of legal ends with illegal means." Cross says that while the sale of unauthorized music cassettes "violates a number of laws" (i.e., laws regulating intellectual property) apart from laws concerning selling in the street, "enforcement rarely reaches the retail level ... [and] ... vendors selling these articles behave in the same way as those selling legal goods" (Cross 1998, 85). Elsewhere in Latin America, the main street market of Lima has become a target for music industry antipiracy teams. More than two million recordable (CD-R) discs were seized in a raid by over five hundred police officers on three hundred stalls at the El Hueco market in June 2001 (IFPI 2001). Even in Europe, music is sold in street markets from Sarajevo (where the biggest market is a major outlet for pirate CDs) to London, whose large weekend market in Camden Town is famous (or notorious) for the sale of bootleg tapes and CDs of concerts by David Bowie, Bob Dylan, and dozens of other performers.

Diawara (1998) and Bohlman (1988) have stressed the continuing strategic significance of street markets in separate ways. Diawara powerfully evokes and analyzes the antiglobalization role of such markets in West African life: "By producing disorder through pricing, pirating, smuggling and counterfeiting African markets participate in the resistance to multinational control of the national economy and culture" (Diawara 1998, 151). In his description of the "bazaar" in North Africa, Bohlman emphasizes its condition as a space of "cultural simultaneity" where musics of different styles, commodity forms, and technologies interact and overlap. He also points up the historical continuity of such musical melanges: "the cultural simultaneity that obtains . . . is not a recent phenomenon. . . . Marketplaces whether in pre-Islam middle east, mediaeval Europe, or 19th century American Midwest have been a locus for diversity" (Bohlman 1988, 123).

Market as Concept in Classical Economics

In the eighteenth century, Western economic theory elaborated the term *market* into a concept denoting an abstract space where supply and demand meet and find equilibrium through the pricing of commodities or services. When demand exceeds supply, prices rise, and where supply is in excess of demand, prices tend to fall. This theory, in its extreme form, claims that distortion by alien forces such as governments or monopolistic practices compromises the operation of a "free" market in providing equilibrium between supply (the producers) and demand (the consumers). At this point, the "market" becomes an autonomous, almost mystical force—Robert Nelson has written of the "religion of economics" (Nelson 2001)—epitomized in Adam Smith's famous phrase from his *The Wealth of Nations*, "the invisible hand" that leads the merchant "to promote an end that was no part of his intention" (A. Smith [1776] 1910, IV, ii, 9).

In practice, the free market concept developed by Smith and later "neoclassical" economists remained an ideal type rather than a precise description of observable markets. Instead of an equilibrium deriving from the possession by producer and consumer of the same information, disequilibrium and asymmetry beset each specific market. In the case of music markets, disequilibrium is most frequently produced when the greater power of the suppliers (the record companies and retailers) determines the recordings to be made available and the prices to be charged. The monopoly status conferred by copyright ownership plays a role here too. On the demand side, disequilibrium is created when the participants (notably the potential audience) do not act as rational economic beings whose behavior can be reliably influenced by such factors as pricing and publicity.

By the mid–twentieth century, the concept of a free market had spilled over from purely economic discourse to become central to much conservative and even social democratic political ideology. It was counterposed to the planned economies of state socialism where the supply of recorded music was controlled by a state monopoly such as Amiga in the German Democratic Republic. Amiga's decision to issue an album was not primarily determined by perceived demand but as "evidence of the official recognition of the artist." Consequently, "(a)s the print run of the record was fixed in advance and second editions rarely appeared, musicians had no (economic) interest in record production, only a chance to gain a reputation" (Maas and Reszel 1998, 269).

If the abstraction of the market in neoclassical orthodoxy remains an ideal type, it nevertheless underlines the fact that in many contemporary economies the face-to-face character of exchange in street markets has generally been supplanted by "imagined markets" where the relationship between producer and consumer is highly mediated. The term *imagined markets* is adapted from Benedict Anderson's description of nation-states as "imagined communities" produced by the action of print media and other forms that connect individuals who can never meet face-to-face (Anderson 1991).

Authors who stress the exceptional character of the culture industries have challenged the idealization and homogenization of the market idea by neoclassical economics. Miège (1989) and Garnham (2000) have commented on the special characteristics of markets for cultural commodities, in particular the unpredictability of consumer demand for such items as songs, books, and films. This unpredictability is a sign that consumer (and often producer) behavior in markets for cultural goods and services frequently deviates from the neoclassical theorists' presentation of these subjects as "homo economicus," concerned only with their own economic welfare. In his important study of large record companies, Negus brings together the motifs of the imagined market and the uncertainty of demand by emphasizing the *construction* of markets and consumers by such companies. He writes that "(m)arkets are not simply out there in the world, forming as members of the public gravitate towards certain recordings and not others. Markets have to be carefully constructed and maintained . . . " (Negus 1999, 32).

Three strategies for the construction of markets where demand can be managed can be identified. First, Miège and Negus (and other authors) emphasize what the latter calls the "portfolio" approach, whereby a large record company will promote a wide range of recordings in the expectation that at least some of them will prove to be successful. According to Miège, in order to reduce the risks of failure, cultural producers such as record companies and film studios bring to the market a "catalog" of a large number of different items in the expectation that profits from the small number of hits will compensate for the losses incurred by unsuccessful titles.

The second strategy is systematically to gather information about consumer preferences and behavior. Here record companies, especially in the United States, are increasingly using the tools and methods of contemporary market research. Negus (1999, 53) describes the Soundata system based on an interview panel of twelve hundred U.S. consumers, and Anand and Peterson argue that information about the market "is the prime source by which producers in competitive fields make sense of their actions and those of consumers, rivals and suppliers that make up the field" (2000, 271). They point out that while some producers can undertake private research such as public opinion surveys, the provision of a generalized "market information regime" by an independent research firm is generally the most important source of such data. In the music industry, the crucial feature of the regime is of course the chart of weekly or monthly soundcarrier sales or radio airplay.

A third strategy is to influence the various gatekeepers or intermediaries perceived to be influential in consumer decisions. These include broadcasting executives, disc jockeys, and journalists. The methods used have often been controversial and unlawful, as the term *payola* testifies (Segrave 1994; Dannen 1990). Since the early 1990s, a more radical version of such marketing has been targeted at supposed opinion formers or tastemakers within the audience itself. This is the use of "street teams" that, according to a record company executive interviewed by Negus, are "going to places where consumers are and hitting them where they live" (Negus 1999, 97).

The only actors with the resources to deploy such strategies consistently in order to limit their exposure to uncertain demand are, of course, large corporations. At the start of the twenty-first century, five major companies—BMG, EMI, Warner, Sony, and Universal—controlled the global distribution of over 80 percent of (nonpirate) CDs and cassettes. This situation has given rise to numerous claims and complaints that these companies operate a de facto cartel that keeps prices high and denies smaller companies the opportunity to compete in the market on equal terms. In the sphere of market regulation, notably in North America and Europe, the oligopolistic tendencies of the record industry have led government agencies to prohibit mergers in the sector, and to outlaw certain marketing practices. Additionally, researchers analyzing the provenance of hit records have argued that the dominance of the major companies inhibits innovation in music markets (Peterson and Berger 1990; Rothenbuhler and Dimmick 1982; Lopes 1992; Christianen 1995).

Musical Labor Markets

In the past, hiring fairs for musicians could be found in specific parts of cities, such as Archer Street in central London. Today the distribution of musical labor is carried out by imagined markets where the "uncertainty" or "unpredictability" that characterizes consumer markets is echoed in the oversupply of musicians and singers for the available work and income opportunities. A study of the British market for classical singers by Towse (1993) found that the market was "distorted" because the supply of labor was far greater than the demand from opera companies, choirs and so on. According to mainstream economic theory, such a disequilibrium should be corrected by the surplus workers moving to other industries where labor is in short supply. Towse concluded that the singers were motivated more by the aesthetic attraction of music than their economic self-interest.

Discussion of the general market for opera and classical music performances has been dominated by the so-called cost disease first diagnosed in the 1960s by the American economist William Baumol. This "disease" is intended to explain the need for subsidy or sponsorship of arts performances. Baumol asked his readers to

> [c]ompare what has happened to the cost of producing a watch with the cost of a musical performance over the centuries. There has been vast, labour-saving technical progress in watchmaking, which is still continuing. But live violin playing benefits from no labour (or capital)-saving innovations—it is still done the old-fashioned way, *as we want it to be....*
>
> This is another way of saying that cost per attendee or per performance must rise faster than the average price of other things: arts budgets therefore must rise faster than the economy's rate of inflation, which is simply

the average increase in the prices of all the economy's outputs. (Baumol and Bowen [1966] 1997, 214; my emphasis)

Baumol's theory has become widely accepted among economists of the arts but it is open to some major criticisms. First, it ignores the fact that many sectors of the music business *have* been restructured by "labor-saving technical progress." For example, the introduction of amplification permitted bands to play to larger audiences (and thereby cut the cost per attendee), while innovation in instrument design enabled the size of bands to be reduced as synthesizers and drum machines have replaced performers. Perhaps more crucially, Baumol ignores the role of "technical progress" in recording and broadcasting, two media that have provided many participants in the labor-intensive performance-based sector with additional income.

A second criticism of the Baumol thesis is that it ignores an important source of cost inflation in classical performance: the escalating payments to star conductors and soloists in the contemporary classical music industry. In his analysis of the industry, Norman Lebrecht (1996) shows that a cartel of agents and administrators has increased the fees of star musicians at a rate far greater than any increase in the salaries of orchestral musicians and opera choruses. Lebrecht's data emphasize the degree to which the contemporary classical music market is characterized by a complex mixed economy of public subsidy and oligopolistic commercialism.

Music and Market Failure

Economists use the concept of "market failure" to describe situations where suppliers are unable or unwilling to provide certain commodities or services for which there is a demand. Examples of remedies for market failure in the music industry include subsidies for performances through state funding or private sponsorship to remedy the cost disease in order to make tickets affordable, and the production and distribution of low-priced soundcarriers when the previously available copies are priced too highly for some consumers. A graphic example is the success of the Naxos record company, which since its formation in 1987 has become a leading firm in classical music by selling newly made recordings at about one-third of the price charged for new releases by other labels.

Another remedy for market failure is the sale of pirate or unauthorized copies of recordings, notably in developing countries where "legitimate" copies of certain music on CDs or cassettes are unaffordable for most of the population or are simply unavailable because no company holds the rights in a particular country. This situation is graphically portrayed in Waterman's study of jùjú music in Ibadan, Nigeria. Waterman reproduces newspaper reports of the clash between bandleaders and cassette sellers over the propriety of this mode of exchange. While a musician complains that piracy robs musicians of income, a market trader is quoted as saying that the common people cannot afford to buy the vinyl discs made by the bandleaders and their record companies:

> Fuji musician Ayinde Barrister has these [*sic*] to say: "The record pirates make all the money leaving little for us and nothing for the government. It is ridiculous that in a country of over 80 million people, a successful musician cannot boast that his record would sell over one million."
>
> Mr. Lanre Lawal . . . cassette seller at Ogunpa says: "music should not be for only the rich men alone, poor people should also enjoy good music. . . . We offer recording services for people who cannot afford to buy records and this, to my mind, is a kind of promotion for the musicians themselves." (Waterman 1990, 152–53)

Despite the authoritarian rigidity ascribed to state socialist "unfree" markets, they were as much subject to the condition of market failure as were free markets. In the words of Verdery, "the socialist economy needed the black market to fulfil its shortcomings" (1991, 423) and "audiences and performers experimented in the interstices of official culture" (Silverman 1996, 239). Unofficial performances and cassette recordings constituted a "second market" for popular music throughout the socialist bloc, providing audiences with music excluded from the official repertoire, both locally created and foreign. The extent to which the second market was tolerated by the official institutions varied considerably according to the overall political and economic stresses and policies of each country at any particular time. In the Bulgarian case, the growth of the second market for music was associated with the relaxation of state controls on the "petty form of private enterprise" in rural areas, and farmers benefiting from such enterprise could afford to pay for the "wedding music" of such performers as the clarinetist Ivo Papazov (Rice 1996, 182–84).

Public Goods and Copyright

A public good is defined by economists as one whose consumption by an individual does not preclude its consumption by others. While a loaf of bread is a private good (if I consume it, you are prevented from doing so), a free-to-air radio or television broadcast has the status of a public good. The public good idea has been applied to cultural production in contrasting ways by Baumol and Garnham.

In a somewhat tortuous justification of state funding for the high arts, the former seeks to define performances of drama, opera, and classical music as public goods insofar as their existence has value for society in general in addition to the small minority that actually attends such performances. He writes that "Government must provide funds only where the market has no way to charge for all the benefits offered by an activity" (Baumol and Bowen 1997, 260). The difficulty with this formulation is that it provides no systematic way to determine these "benefits," which are mostly potential in the sense that they remain available to a larger audience should that audience one day materialize. Garnham emphasizes a different aspect by linking the concept of a "public good" to a discussion of the "free rider." He begins by asserting that in dealing with "media or information," "the market model of provision has serious problems" (Garnham 2000, 57). The most fundamental of these is the lack of scarcity of cultural products and services (market economics holds that the price of a commodity is determined by its availability: a scarce "out of season" fruit will cost more than a fruit plentifully available). But when a free-to-air broadcast is available to all or a digitized recording can be easily copied or cloned, there is no automatic or internalized pricing mechanism. The "free rider" is the consumer (or competing producer), who thereby can acquire the commodity free of cost. Garnham goes on to list three ways in which the market is adapted to "solve" this problem and to ensure that the producer recovers the cost of production. One (adopted by commercial broadcasters) is through selling audiences to advertisers; another is to erect box office barriers such as pay-per-view television broadcasts; the third, and the most significant for music economics, is through the granting by governments of a legal right to intellectual property, notably the copyright. This last is in many cases the overdetermining factor in music market structures, introducing "a monopoly and the producers' right to a monopoly rent" (p. 57).

Rental is an idea familiar from markets for housing and other expensive goods such as video recorders or automobiles. Its application to music is less obvious but is based on the legal status of a song or recording as the inalienable property of an individual or company. A useful economist's explanation of the application of "rent" to the music business can be found in Andersen and James (2000). As intellectual property, the song or recording cannot pass wholly into the ownership of another (although the physical object embodying it can), and any subsequent user of the music is liable in law to pay a "rent" in the form of a royalty until the duration of its property status has expired. Currently the expiration date for compositions is seventy years following the death of the author, and for recordings is fifty years after a track's first release. A royalty is the customary form of payment in business-to-business markets, such as those linking recording artist and record company or broadcaster and composer. The latter market involves an important intermediary, the authors' collection society. Examples are the Performing Right Society in Britain or the competing groups ASCAP and BMI in the United States.

The "free rider" problem has reached crisis point with the advent of the Internet and the most prevalent form of online music exchange, the numerous P2P (peer-to-peer) file-sharing networks whose best-known example is Napster. Within such networks, any music tracks stored on the computer of any participant can be copied by any other participant and held on the latter's computer (see Alderman 2001). The music industry considers such behavior to be both unethical and illegal since no money is paid to copyright owners when such copies are made. In legal terms, the practice of P2P is a version of "private copying," a term invented to describe the use of audiotape cassettes by consumers to make copies of recordings, a practice that became widespread in the 1980s. At that time, a legal remedy was found by legislators in the "blank tape levy," a fee paid by manufacturers of tapes that was used to pay "compensation" to composers and record companies. This solution is not possible in the case of P2P since it involves no tangible copying product apart from the computer itself.

There is, however, another perspective from which to view the practice of P2P—the notion of the "gift economy." This concept was introduced into Western thought by the anthropologist Marcel Mauss, whose book *The Gift* (1954) was a study of the economics of gift-giving in precapitalist societies. This alternative economy has drawn much interest from philosophers and political scientists in recent years. For some of these, the gift economy is important for its diametrical opposition to the logic of the conventional economy of exchange. In the words of Derrida, "for there to be a gift there must be no reciprocity, return, exchange, countergift or debt" (Derrida 1992, 12). The significance for the music market of this resistance to the logic of exchange among music consumers is not yet clear. For the present, P2P activity coexists on the Internet with the efforts of the music industry to establish an exchange economy there. Some experts believe that coexistence is a form of symbiosis: "the gift economy and the commercial sector can only expand through mutual collaboration within cyberspace" (Barbrook 1998).

Limits of the Market

This chapter has sought to show the usefulness of the idea of the market in understanding music as a business. But this process has its limits, which are twofold.

First, even in an era whose dominant economic mode is capitalist globalization, many musical activities have no connection, or only a tenuous connection, to markets. These include religious practices, military bands, ceremonial music, work songs, and music for political causes. Bohlman notes of such music making that music "articulates the organisation of society" through its "role in ritual" and through "transforming labour into a communal activity" (1988, 1). Second, there is much evidence to show that there is an important aspect of the music economy that is surplus to, or exterior to, the market relation. For example, considering the supply of music, Toynbee discusses "proto-markets" that "bring together performer and audience in arenas which are not fully commodified. Examples include local rock scenes, dance music networks or jazz performance by players taking time out from regular session work" (Toynbee 2000, 27). And echoing Towse's comments on classical singers, he concludes that in such contexts, "the level of activity cannot be explained by economic factors alone" since the financial rewards are minimal or nonexistent.

From the aspect of consumption, the previously noted features of unpredictability and irrationality are symptoms of what Jacques Attali has called "the extra-market production of demand . . . " (Attali 1985, 42). They also underlie Toynbee's proposition that "in order for culture to be sold it must be shown to be (partially) external to the economic system" (Toynbee 2000, 3). In other words, market forces can never be autonomous, only "themselves." They are always in flux, vulnerable to the impact of an aestheticomusical unconscious that overflows the economic and problematizes exchange relations.

Further Reading

Baumol, William J., and William G. Bowen. [1966] 1997. On the rationale of public support. Pp. 243–60 in *Baumol's cost disease. The arts and other victims.* Edited by Ruth Towse. Cheltenham, U.K.: Edward Elgar.

Garnham, Nicholas. 2000. *Emancipation, the media and modernity: Arguments about the media and social theory.* New York: Oxford Univ. Press.

Laing, Dave. 1993. The international copyright system. Pp. 25–36 in *Music and copyright.* Edited by Simon Frith. Edinburgh: Edinburgh Univ. Press.

———. 2002. Copyright as a component of the music industry. Pp. 171–94 in *The business of music.* Edited by Michael Talbot. Liverpool: Liverpool Univ. Press.

Lebrecht, Norman. 1996. *When the music stops . . . Managers, maestros and corporate murder of classical music.* London: Simon and Schuster.

Manuel, Peter. 1993. *Cassette culture. Popular music and technology in North India.* Chicago: Univ. of Chicago Press.

Miège, Bernard. 1989. *The capitalization of cultural production.* New York: International General.

Negus, Keith. 1999. *Music genres and corporate cultures.* London: Routledge.

Peterson, Richard and David Berger. [1975] 1990. Cycles in symbol production: The case of popular music. Pp. 140–59 in *On record: Rock, pop and the written word.* Edited by Simon Frith and Andrew Goodwin. London: Routledge.

Stamm, Brad K. 2000. *Music industry economics. A global demand model for pre-recorded music.* New York: Edwin Mellen Press.

Wallis, Roger, and Krister Malm. 1984. *Big sounds from small peoples: The music industry in small countries.* London: Constable.

References

Adler, Guido. 1885. Umfang, Methode und Ziel der Musikwissenschaft. *Viertel-jahrsschrift für Musikwissenschaft* 1: 5–20.

Adler, M. 1985. Stardom and talent. *American Economic Review* 75(1): 208–12.

Adorno, Theodor Wiesengrund. [1938] 1991. On the fetish character in music and the regression of listening. Pp. 26–52 in *The culture industry. Selected essays on mass culture.* Edited by J. M. Bernstein. London: Routledge.

———. 1973. *Philosophy of modern music.* Translated by Anne G Mitchell and Wesley V. Bloomster. London: Sheed and Ward.

———. 1976. *Introduction to the sociology of music.* New York: Seabury Press.

———. 1984. *Aesthetic theory.* Edited by Gretel Adorno and Rolf Tiedemann. Translated by C. Lenhardt. New York: Routledge and Kegan Paul.

———. 1990. On popular music. Pp. 301–14 in *On record: Rock, pop and the written word.* Edited by Simon Frith and Andrew Goodwin. London: Routledge.

Agawu, V. Kofi. 1991. *Playing with signs: A semiotic interpretation of classic music.* Princeton, N.J.: Princeton Univ. Press.

Alden, Andrew. 1998. What does it all mean? The national curriculum for music in a multi-cultural society. MA thesis. London Univ. Institute of Education.

Alderman, John. 2001. *Sonic boom: Napster, P2P and the battle for the future of music.* London: Fourth Estate.

Allanbrook, Wye Jamison, ed. 1998. *The late eighteenth century.* Vol. 5 of *Strunk's source readings in music history,* rev. ed. Edited by Leo Treitler. New York: Norton.

Allen, Ray, and Lois Wilcken. 1998. *Island sounds in the global city.* Brooklyn, N.Y.: Brooklyn College.

Alpert, Michael. 1994. Liner notes to *Brave old world: Beyond the pale.* Rounder Records CD 3135.

Anand, N., and Richard A. Peterson. 2000. When market information constitutes fields: Sensemaking of markets in the commercial music industry. *Organization Science* 11(3): 270–84.

Andersen, Birgitte, and Vanus James. 2000. *Copyrights and competition. Towards policy implications for music business development.* Manchester, U.K.: ESRC Centre for Research on Innovation and Competition.

Anderson, Benedict. [1983] 1991. *Imagined communities: Reflections on the origins and spread of nationalism.* 2d ed. New York: Verso.

Aparicio, Frances R. 1998. *Listening to salsa: Gender, Latin popular music, and Puerto Rican cultures.* Hanover N.H.: University Press of New England.

Appadurai, Arjun. 1990. Disjuncture and difference in the global economy. Pp. 1–24 in *Global culture: Nationalism, globalization and modernity.* Edited by Mike Featherstone. London: Sage.

———. 1996. Modernity at large: Cultural dimensions of globalization. Minneapolis: Univ. of Minnesota Press.

Aracena, Beth K. 1999. Singing salvation: Jesuit musics in colonial Chile, 1600–1767. Ph.D. thesis, Univ. of Chicago.

Arendt, Hannah. 1966. *The origins of totalitarianism.* London: Allen and Unwin.

Arnold, John H. 2000. *History: A very short introduction.* New York: Oxford Univ. Press.

Arnold, Matthew. 1963. Culture and anarchy. Edited by J. Dover Wilson. Cambridge, U.K.: Cambridge Univ. Press.

Aston, Elaine, and George Savona. 1991. *Theatre as sign-system: A semiotics of text and performance.* London: Routledge.

Attali, Jacques. 1985. *Noise: The political economy of music.* Translated by Brian Massumi. Minneapolis: Univ. of Minnesota Press.

Averill, Gage. 1998. "Moving the Big Apple": Tambou Combo's diasporic dreams. Pp. 138–61 in *Island sounds in the global city.* Edited by Ray Allen and Lois Wilcken. Brooklyn, N.Y.: Brooklyn College.

Back, Les. 1996. X amount of Sat Siri Akal! Apache Indian, Reggae music, and the cultural intermezzo. *New Formations* 27: 128–47.

Baily, John. 1976. Recent changes in the dutar of Herat. *Asian Music* 8(1): 26–64.

———. 1977. Movement patterns in playing the Herati dutar. Pp. 275–330 in *The anthropology of the body.* Edited by John Blacking. London: Academic Press.

————, ed. 1995. *Working with Blacking: The Belfast years.* [Special issue] *The World of Music* 37(2).

————. 1996. Using tests of sound perception in fieldwork. *Yearbook for Traditional Music* 28: 147–73.

Bakhtin, Mikhail M. 1981. *The dialogic imagination. Four essays.* Edited by Michael Holquist. Translated by Caryl Emerson and Michael Holquist. Austin: Univ. of Texas Press.

Baraka, Amiri. 1967. *Black music.* New York: William Morrow.

Barbrook, Richard. 1998. The hi-tech gift economy. http://firstmonday.dk/issues/issue3_12/barbrook/index.html (accessed August 6, 2002).

Barfield, Thomas, ed. 1997. *The dictionary of anthropology.* Oxford: Blackwell.

Barnes, Ken. 1988. Top 40 radio: A fragment of the imagination. Pp. 8–50 in *Facing the music.* Edited by Simon Frith. New York: Pantheon. .

Barthes, Roland. 1977. The death of the author. Pp. 142–48 in *Image/Music/Text.* London: Fontana.

————. 1986. *The responsibility of forms: Critical essays on music, art, and representation.* Translated by Richard Howard. Oxford: Blackwell.

Barz, Gregory F., and Timothy J. Cooley. 1997. *Shadows in the field. New perspectives for fieldwork in ethnomusicology.* New York: Oxford Univ. Press.

Baumol, William J., and Hilda Baumol. [1985] 1997. On the cost disease and its true policy implications for the arts. Pp. 213–24 in *Baumol's cost disease. The arts and other victims.* Edited by Ruth Towse. Cheltenham, U.K.: Edward Elgar.

Baumol, William J., and William G. Bowen. [1966] 1997. On the rationale of public support. Pp. 243–60 in *Baumol's cost disease. The arts and other victims.* Edited by Ruth Towse. Cheltenham, U.K.: Edward Elgar.

Baxandall, Michael. 1972. *Painting and experience in fifteenth century Italy, a primer in the social history of pictorial style.* Oxford: Oxford Univ. Press.

Becker, Howard S. 1982. *Art worlds.* Berkeley: Univ. of California Press.

Beckwith, John. 1982. Kolinski: An appreciation and list of works. Pp. xvii–xxiv in *Cross-cultural perspectives on music (Essays in memory of Mieczyslaw Kolinski from his students, colleagues, and friends).* Edited by Robert Falck and Timothy Rice. Toronto: Univ. of Toronto Press.

Bendelow, Gillian, and Simon J. Williams, eds. 1998. *Emotions in social life. Critical themes and contemporary issues.* London: Routledge.

Benjamin, Walter. [1970] 1973. The work of art in the age of mechanical reproduction. Pp. 217–51 in *Illuminations.* Edited by Hannah Arendt. Translated by Harry Zohn. London: Collins/Fontana Books.

Bennett, Andy, and Kevin Dawe, eds. 2001. *Guitar cultures.* New York: Berg.

Berger, Peter L., and Thomas Luckmann. 1966. *The social construction of reality.* London: Allen Lane.

Bergeron, Katherine, and Philip V. Bohlman, eds. 1992. *Disciplining music: Musicology and its canons.* Chicago: Univ. of Chicago Press.

Bernstein, Charles, ed. 1998. *Close listening: Poetry and the performed word.* New York: Oxford Univ. Press.

Bernstein, Jay M. 1992. *The fate of art: Aesthetic alienation from Kant to Derrida and Adorno.* Cambridge, U.K.: Polity Press.

Besseler, Heinrich. 1931. *Die Musik des Mittelalters und der Renaissance.* Potsdam, Germany: Akademische Verlagsgesellschaft Athenaion.

Bhabha, Homi. 1994. *The location of culture.* New York: Routledge.

Birley, Margaret, Heidrun Eicher, and Arnold Myers. 2000. *Voices for the silenced: Guidelines for interpreting musical instruments in museum collections.* Electronic publication (this update, January 17, 2000). http://www.music.ed. ac.uk/euchmi/cimcim/iwte.html.

Björk. 2001. *Björk.* London: Little-i.

Blacking, John. 1973. *How musical is man?* Seattle: Univ. of Washington Press.

———, ed. 1977. *The anthropology of the body.* New York: Academic Press.

———. 1987. *"A commonsense view of all music." Reflections on Percy Grainger's contribution to ethnomusicology and music education.* Cambridge, U.K.: Cambridge Univ. Press.

———. 1995. *Music, culture, and experience: Selected papers of John Blacking.* Chicago: Univ. of Chicago Press.

Blackmore, Susan J. 1999 *The meme machine.* Oxford: Oxford Univ. Press.

Bloomfield, Terry. 1993. Resisting songs: Negative dialectics in pop. *Popular Music* 12(1): 13–31.

Blum, Stephen. 1991. European musical terminology and the music of Africa. Pp. 3–36 in *Comparative musicology and anthropology of music: Essays in the history of ethnomusicology.* Edited by Bruno Nettl and Philip V. Bohlman. Chicago: Univ. of Chicago Press.

Boa, Elizabeth. 1996. *Kafka: Gender, class, and race in the letters and fictions.* Oxford: Clarendon Press.

Bohlman, Philip V. 1988. *The study of folk music in the modern world.* Bloomington: Indiana Univ. Press.

———. 1999 Ontologies of music. Pp. 17–34 in *Rethinking music.* Edited by Nicholas Cook and Mark Everist. Oxford: Oxford Univ. Press.

———. 2000. The Remembrance of things past: Music, race, and the end of history in modern Europe. Pp. 644–76 in *Music and the racial imagination.* Edited by Ronald Radano and Philip V. Bohlman. Chicago: Univ. of Chicago Press.

―――. 2002.a Landscape-region-nation-reich: German folk song in the nexus of national identity. Pp. 104–27 in *Music and German national identity*. Edited by Celia Applegate and Pamela M. Potter. Chicago: Univ. of Chicago Press.

―――. 2002b. World music at the "end of history." *Ethnomusicology* 46(1): 1–32.

Bonds, Mark Evan. 1997. Idealism and the aesthetic of instrumental music at the turn of the nineteenth century. *Journal of the American Musicological Society*, 50(2–3): 387–420.

Boretz, Benjamin. 1992. Experiences with no names. *Perspectives of New Music* 30: 272–83.

Born, Georgina. 1995. *Rationalizing culture. IRCAM, modernism and post modernism: The anthropology of the musical avant-garde*. Berkeley: Univ. of California Press.

―――. 2000. Musical modernism, postmodernism, and others. Pp. 12–21 in Introduction to *Western music and its others*. Edited by Georgina Born and David Hesmondhalgh. Berkeley: Univ. of California Press.

Born, Georgina, and David Hesmondhalgh, eds. 2000. *Western music and its others. Difference, representation, and appropriation in music*. Berkeley: Univ. of California Press.

Bourdieu, Pierre. 1973. Cultural reproduction and social reproduction. Pp. 71–112 in *Knowledge, education and cultural change*. Edited by Richard K. Brown. London: Tavistock.

―――. 1977. *Outline of a theory of practice*. Cambridge U.K.: Cambridge Univ. Press.

―――. 1984. *Distinction: A social critique of the judgment of taste*. Cambridge, Mass.: Harvard Univ. Press.

―――. 1990. *In other words: Essays towards a reflexive sociology*. Cambridge, U.K.: Polity.

―――. 1993a. Public opinion does not exist. Pp. 149–57 in *Sociology in question*. Translated by Richard Nice. London: Sage.

―――. 1993b. *The field of cultural production: Essays on art and literature*. Edited by R. Johnson. Cambridge, U.K.: Polity Press.

Bourdieu, Pierre, and Jean Claude Passeron. [1977] 1999. *Reproduction in education, society and culture*. Translated by Richard Nice. Beverly Hills, Calif.: Sage.

Brackett, David. 1994. The practice and politics of crossover in American popular music, 1963–65. *Musical Quarterly* 78(4): 774–97.

―――. 1995. *Interpreting popular music*. Cambridge, U.K.: Cambridge Univ. Press.

————. 2002. (In search of) musical meaning: Genres, categories, and cross-over. Pp. 65–83 in *Popular music studies*. Edited by David Hesmondhalgh and Keith Negus. London: Arnold.

Brake, Mike. 1980. *The sociology of youth cultures and youth subcultures*. New York: Routledge and Kegan Paul.

Braudel, Fernand. 1982. *The wheels of commerce*. London: Collins.

Brett, Philip, Elizabeth Wood, and Gary C. Thomas. 1994. *Queering the pitch: The new gay and lesbian musicology*. New York: Routledge.

Broughton, Simon, Mark Ellingham, David Muddyman, and Richard Trillo. 1994. *The rough guide to world music*. 1st ed. London: Penguin.

Broughton, Simon, Mark Ellingham, and Richard Trillo, eds. 1999–2000. *World music: The rough guide*. 2d ed. Vol. 1, *Africa, Europe and the Middle East*. Vol. 2, *Latin and North America, Caribbean, India, Asia and Pacific*. London: The Rough Guides.

Bürger, Peter. 1984. *Theory of the avant-garde*, 2d ed. Translated by Michael Shaw. Minneapolis: Univ. of Minnesota Press.

Burke, Peter. 1987. *The historical anthropology of early modern Italy: Essays on perception and communication*. Cambridge, U.K.: Cambridge Univ. Press.

Burnett, Robert. 1996. *The global jukebox: The international music industry*. London: Routledge.

Burnham, Scott. 2001. How music matters: Poetic context revisited. Pp. 193–216 in *Rethinking music*. Edited by Nicholas Cook and Mark Everist. Oxford: Oxford Univ. Press.

Butler, Gillian, and Freda McManus. 1998. *Psychology: A very short introduction*. Oxford: Oxford Univ. Press.

Butler, Judith. 1990. *Gender trouble: Feminism and the subversion of identity*. New York: Routledge.

Campbell, Patricia Shehan. 1991. *Lessons from the world: A cross-cultural guide to music teaching and learning*. New York: Schirmer Books.

Caplan, Patricia. 1989. *The cultural construction of sexuality*. New York: Routledge.

Carr, Edward H. 1961. *What is history?* New York: St Martin's Press.

Cavicchi, Daniel. 1998. *Tramps like us: Music and meaning among Springsteen fans*. New York: Oxford Univ. Press.

Chakrabarty, Dipesh. 2000. *Provincializing Europe: Postcolonial thought and historical difference*. Princeton, N.J.: Princeton Univ. Press.

Chanan, Michael. 1995. *Repeated takes: A short history of recording and its effects on music*. London: Verso.

Chernoff, John Miller. 1997. "Hearing" in West African idioms. *The World of Music* 39(2): 19–25.

Chester, Andrew. [1970] 1990. Second thoughts on a rock aesthetic: The band. Pp. 301–19 in *On record: Rock, pop, and the written word.* Edited by Simon Frith and Andrew Goodwin. New York: Pantheon.

Christianen, Michael. 1995. Cycles in symbol production? A new model to explain concentration, diversity and innovation in the music industry. *Popular Music* 14(1): 55–93.

Christiansen, Anna Sofie. 2001. Mechanical music in Weimar Germany: "Absolute music" as performance paradigm. Paper presented at Second Biennial International Conference on 20th-century music, Goldsmiths College, U.K.

Chua, Daniel K. L. 1999. *Absolute music and the construction of meaning.* Cambridge, U.K.: Cambridge Univ. Press.

Cixous, Hélène. 1980. Sorties. Pp. 90–98 in *New French feminisms.* Edited by Elaine Marks and Isabelle de Courtivron. New York: Schocken.

———. 1990. *Reading with Clarice Lispector.* Edited by Verena Andermatt Conley. Minneapolis: Univ. of Minnesota Press.

Clark, Peter. 1983. *The English alehouse: A social history, 1200–1830.* New York: Longman.

Clarke, David. 1996a. Language games: Is music like language? *The Musical Times* 137(1835): 5–10.

———. 1996b. Speaking for itself: How does music become autonomous? *The Musical Times* 137(1836): 14–18.

Clarke, Eric F. 1999. Subject-position and the specification of invariants in music by Frank Zappa and P. J. Harvey. *Music Analysis* 18: 347–74.

———. 2001. Meaning and the specification of motion in music. *Musicae Scientiae* 5: 213–34.

Clarke, Eric, and Jane Davidson. 1998. The body in performance. Pp. 74–92 in *Composition-performance-reception: Studies in the creative process in music.* Edited by Wyndham Thomas. Aldershot: Ashgate.

Clayton, Martin R. L. 2000. *Time in Indian music. Rhythm, metre and form in North Indian rāg performance.* Oxford: Clarendon Press.

Clifford, James. 1988. *The predicament of culture. Twentieth-century ethnography, literature, and art.* Cambridge, Mass.: Harvard Univ. Press.

———. 1992 Travelling cultures. Pp. 96–116 in *Cultural studies.* Edited by Lawrence Grossberg, Cary Nelson, and Paula A. Treichler. New York: Routledge.

Clifford, James, and George E. Marcus, eds. 1986. *Writing culture. The poetics and politics of ethnography.* Berkeley: Univ. of California Press.

Cohen, Sara. 1991. *Rock culture in Liverpool: Popular music in the making.* Oxford: Clarendon Press.

Collins, John. 1992. *West African pop roots.* Philadelphia: Temple Univ. Press.

Comaroff, Jean, and John Comaroff. 1992. *Ethnography and the historical imagination*. Boulder, Colo.: Westview Press.

Cook, Nicholas. 1990. *Music, imagination and culture*. Oxford: Clarendon Press.

———. 1994. Perception: A perspective from music theory. Pp. 64–95 in *Musical perceptions*. Edited by Rita Aiello and John A. Sloboda. Oxford: Oxford Univ. Press.

———. 2001. On qualifying relativism. *Musicae Scientiae, Discussion Forum* 2: 167–89.

Cook, Nicholas, and Mark Everist, eds. 1999. *Rethinking music*. Oxford: Oxford Univ. Press.

Cooke, Deryck. 1959. *The language of music*. Oxford: Oxford Univ. Press.

Cooke, Peter. 1999. Was Ssempeke just being kind? Listening to instrumental music in Africa south of the Sahara. *The World of Music* 41(1): 73–83.

Crafts, Susan D., Daniel Cavicchi, and Charles Keil. 1993. *My music*. Hanover, N.H.: Wesleyan Univ. Press.

Crapanzano, Vincent. 1994. Réflexions sur une anthropologie des émotions. *Terrain: carnets du patrimoine ethnologique* 22: 109–17.

Crofton, Ian, and Donald Fraser, eds. 1985. *A dictionary of musical quotations*. New York: Schirmer.

Cross, Ian. 1998. Music analysis and music perception. *Music Analysis* 17(1): 3–20.

———. 1999. Is music the most important thing we ever did? Music, development and evolution. Pp. 10–39 in *Music, mind and science*. Edited by Suk Won Yi. Seoul: Seoul National Univ. Press. (see: http://www.mus.cam.ac.uk/~cross/MMS/) accessed August 6, 2002.

———. 2001. Music, cognition, culture and evolution. *Annals of the New York Academy of Sciences*. 930: 28–42.

Cross, John C. 1998. *Informal politics. Street vendors and the state in Mexico City*. Stanford, Calif.: Stanford Univ. Press.

Crossette, Barbara. 2001. Canada's global city (not Toronto). *New York Times*, November 26, A6.

Currid, Brian. 1998. The acoustics of national publicity: Music in German mass culture, 1924–1945. Ph.D. thesis, Univ. of Chicago.

Cutietta, Robert. 1991. Popular music: An ongoing challenge. *Music Educators Journal* 77(8): 26–29.

Dahlhaus, Carl. 1989a. *The idea of absolute music*. Translated by Roger Lustig. Chicago: Univ. of Chicago Press.

———. 1989b. The metaphysic of instrumental music. Pp. 88–96 in *Nineteenth-century music*. Translated by J. Bradford Robinson. Berkeley: Univ. of California Press.

Dannen, Fredric. 1990. *Hit men: Power brokers and fast money inside the music industry.* New York: Times Books.

Davies, Martin L. 1989. History as narcissism. *Journal of European Studies* 19: 265–91.

Dawe, Kevin. 1996. The engendered lyra: Music, poetry and manhood in Crete. *British Journal of Ethnomusicology* 5: 93–112.

———. 1998. Bandleaders in Crete: Musicians and entrepreneurs in a Greek island economy. *British Journal of Ethnomusicology* 7: 23–44.

———. 1999. Minotaurs or musonauts? Cretan music and world music. *Popular Music* 18(2): 209–25.

———. 2001. People, objects, meaning: Recent work on the study and collection of musical instruments. *The Galpin Society Journal* 54: 219–32.

———. n.d. Lyres and the body politic: Studying musical instruments in the Cretan musical landscape. In *Popular music and society,* Special Issue: *Reading the instrument: Techniques and technologies in popular music.* Edited by S. Waksman. Forthcoming.

Dawe, Kevin, with Moira Dawe. 2001. Handmade in Spain: The culture of guitar making. Pp. 63–87 in *Guitar cultures.* Edited by Andy Bennett and Kevin Dawe. New York: Berg.

de Certeau, Michel. 1988. Ethno-graphy: Speech, or the space of the other: Jean de Léry. Pp. 209–43 in *The writing of history.* Translated by Tom Conley. New York: Columbia Univ. Press.

de Léry, Jean. 1578. *Histoire d'un voyage faict en la terre du Brésil.* La Rochelle, France: Antoine Chuppin.

DeNora, Tia. 1995, *Beethoven and the construction of genius. Musical politics in Vienna, 1792–1803.* Berkeley: Univ. of California Press.

———. 1999. Music as a technology of the self. *Poetics* 26: 1–26.

———. 2000. *Music in everyday life.* Cambridge, U.K.: Cambridge Univ. Press.

Derrida, Jacques. 1978. *Writing and difference.* Translated by Alan Bass. Chicago: Univ. of Chicago Press.

———. [1975] 1987. Le facteur de la vérité. Pp. 411–96 in *The post card: From Socrates to Freud and beyond.* Translated by Alan Bass. Chicago: Univ. of Chicago Press.

———. 1992. *Given time 1: Counterfeit money.* Translated by Peggy Kamuf. Chicago: Univ. of Chicago Press.

Desan, S. 1989. Crowds, community and ritual in the work of E. P. Thompson and Natalie Davis. Pp. 47–71 in *The new cultural history.* Edited by Lynn A. Hunt. Berkeley: Univ. of California Press.

Deutsch, Diana, ed. [1982] 1999. *The psychology of music.* 2d ed. New York: Academic Press.

DeVale, Sue Carole. 1990. Organizing organology. Pp. 1–34 in *Issues in organology*. Edited by Sue Carole DeVale. *Selected Reports in Ethnomusicology* 8.

DeVeaux, Scott. 1997. *The birth of bebop: A social and musical history*. Berkeley: Univ. of California Press.

Diamond, Beverley, M. Sam Cronk, and Franziska von Rosen. 1995. *Visions of sound: Musical instruments of first nations communities in Northeastern America*. Chicago: Univ. of Chicago Press.

Diawara, Manthia. 1998. *In search of Africa*. Cambridge, Mass.: Harvard Univ. Press.

Dibango, Manu (with Danielle Rouard). 1994. *Three kilos of coffee: An autobiography*. Chicago: Chicago Univ. Press.

Dibben, Nicola. 2001. What do we hear when we hear music? Musical material and the perception of meaning. *Musicae Scientiae* 5(2): 161–94.

DiMaggio, Paul. 1987. Classification in art. *American Sociological Review* 52: 440–55.

Dissanayake, Ellen. 2000. Antecedents of the temporal arts in early mother-infant interactions. Pp. 389–407 in *The origins of music*. Edited by Nils Wallin, Björn Merker, and Steven Brown. Cambridge, Mass.: MIT Press.

Dournon, Geneviève. 1981 *Guide for the collection of traditional musical instruments*. Paris: Unesco Press.

Durkheim, Emile. 1912. *Les formes élémentaires de la vie religieuse: Le système totémique en Australie*. Paris: Presses universitaires de France.

Eagleton, Terry. 1983. *Literary theory: An introduction*. Minneapolis: Univ. of Minnesota Press.

———. 2000. *The idea of culture*. Oxford: Blackwell.

Eco, Umberto. 1976. *A theory of semiotics*. Bloomington: Indiana Univ. Press.

Ehrlich, Cyril. 1985. *The music profession in Britain since the eighteenth century*. Oxford: Clarendon Press.

———. 1990. *The piano: A history*. rev. ed. Oxford: Clarendon Press.

Elias, Norbert. 1993. *Mozart: Portrait of a genius*. Cambridge, U.K.: Polity.

Eliot, T. S. 1963. *Collected poems 1909–1962*. New York: Harcourt, Brace and World.

Ellison, Ralph. 1964. *Shadow and act*. New York: Random House.

Elton, Geoffrey R. 1967. *The practice of history*. London: Methuen.

Erlmann, Veit. 1996. *Nightsong: Performance, power and practice in South Africa*. Chicago: Univ. of Chicago Press.

Esslin, Martin. 1959. *Brecht, a choice of evils: A critical study of the man, his work and his opinions*. London: Heinemann.

Ethnomusicology. 1992. Vol. 36, no. 3. Special issue on *Music and the Public Interest*.

Evans, Richard J. 1997. *In defence of history*. London: Granta Books.

Eze, Emmanuel Chukwudi. 1997. *Race and the enlightenment: A reader.* Oxford: Blackwell.

Fabbri, Franco. 1982. A theory of musical genres: Two applications. Pp. 52–81 in *Popular music perspectives: Papers from the first international conference on popular music research, Amsterdam, June 1981.* Edited by David Horn and Philip Tagg. Göteborg: IASPM.

Fanon, Franz. 1967. *The wretched of the Earth.* Translated by C. Farrington. Harmondsworth, U.K.; Penguin.

Faultline. 1999. *Closer Colder* [CD]. Leaf: bay 12cd.

Fauquet, Joël-Marie, and Antoine Hennion. 2000. *La grandeur de Bach. L'amour de la musique en France au XIXe siècle.* Paris: Fayard.

Feld, Steven. 1983. Sound as a symbolic system: The Kaluli drum. *Bikmaus* 4(3): 78–89.

———. 1990. *Sound and sentiment. Birds, weeping, poetics and song in Kaluli experience.* 2d ed. Philadelphia: Univ. of Pennsylvania Press.

———. 1994. From schizophonia to schismogenesis: On the discourses and commodification practices of "world music" and "world beat." Pp. 257–89 in *Music grooves.* Edited by Charles Keil and Steven Feld. Chicago: Univ. of Chicago Press.

———. 2000. The poetics and politics of Pygmy pop. Pp. 254–79 in *Western music and its others.* Edited by Georgina Born and David Hesmondhalgh. Berkeley: Univ. of California Press.

Finnegan, Ruth. 1989. *The hidden musicians: Music-making in an English town.* Cambridge, U.K.: Cambridge Univ. Press.

Floyd, Samuel A., Jr. 1991. Ring shout! Literary studies, historical studies, and black music inquiry. *Black Music Research Journal* 11(2): 265–88.

———. 1995. *The power of black music: Interpreting its history from Africa to the United States.* New York: Oxford Univ. Press.

Fodor, J. 1998. Look! Review of *Consilience: The unity of knowledge* by Edward O. Wilson. *London Review of Books* 20–21: 3–6.

Foley, Robert. 1995. *Humans before humanity.* Oxford: Blackwell.

Ford, Charles. 1991. *Così: Sexual politics in Mozart's operas.* Manchester, U.K.: Manchester Univ. Press.

Forkel, Johann Nicolaus. 1967. *Allgemeine Geschichte der Musik* (Leipzig, 1788). Facsimile ed. Edited by Othmar Wessely. Graz, Austria: Akademische Druck- und Verlagsanstalt.

Foucault, Michel. 1969. Qu'est-ce qu'un auteur? *Bulletin de la Société Française de Philosophie* 69(3): 73–104.

———. 1970. *The order of things: An archaeology of the human sciences.* London: Tavistock.

————. 1972. *The archaeology of knowledge.* Translated by Alan Sheridan. New York: Pantheon.

————. 1978. *The history of sexuality.* Vol. 1. Translated by Robert Hurley. New York: Pantheon.

————. 1979. Pp. 195–230 in *Discipline and punish: The birth of the prison.* Translated by Alan Sheridan. New York: Random House.

Francès, Robert. 1988. *The perception of music.* Translated by W. Jay Dowling. Hillsdale, N.J.: Erlbaum.

Frank, Thomas. 2002. *One market under God: Extreme capitalism, market populism and the end of economic democracy.* London: Vintage.

Franklin, Peter. 1991. *Mahler: Symphony No. 3.* Cambridge music handbooks. Cambridge, U.K.: Cambridge Univ. Press.

Freud, Sigmund. [1900] 1955. *The interpretation of dreams.* Vols. 4 and 5 of the *Standard edition of the complete psychological writings of Sigmund Freud.* London: Hogarth Press/Institute of Psycho-Analysis.

————. [1905] 1977. *On sexuality: Three essays on sexuality and other works.* Vol. 7 of *The Penguin Freud library.* New York: Penguin Books.

Frith, Simon. 1978. *The sociology of rock.* London: Constable.

————. 1981. *Sound effects: Youth, leisure and the politics of rock 'n' roll.* London: Constable.

————. 1998. *Performing rites: On the value of popular music.* Cambridge, Mass.: Harvard Univ. Press.

————. 2000. The discourse of world music. Pp. 305–22 in *Western music and its others.* Edited by Georgina Born and David Hesmondhalgh. Berkeley: Univ. of California Press.

Frith, Simon, and Andrew Goodwin, eds. 1990. *On record: Rock, pop, and the written word.* New York: Pantheon Books.

Frow, John. 1995. *Cultural studies and cultural values.* Oxford: Clarendon Press.

Fukuyama, Francis. 1992. *The end of history and the last man.* New York: Free Press.

Fulcher, Jane F. 1987. *The nation's image. French grand opera as politics and politicized art.* New York: Cambridge Univ. Press.

Fuss, Diana, ed. 1991. *Inside out: Lesbian theories, gay theories.* New York: Routledge.

Gadamer, Hans Georg. 1975. *Truth and method.* Edited and translated by Garrett Bardon and John Cumming. New York: Seabury Press.

Garnham, Nicholas. 2000. *Emancipation, the media and modernity: Arguments about the media and social theory.* Oxford: Oxford Univ. Press.

Gates, Henry Louis III. 1986. *"Race," writing, and difference.* Chicago: Univ. of Chicago Press.

———. 1988. *The signifying monkey: A theory of African-American literary criticism.* New York: Oxford Univ. Press.

Gaver, William. W. 1993. What in the world do we hear? An ecological approach to auditory event perception. *Ecological Psychology* 5(1): 1–29.

Geertz, Clifford. [1972] 1973. Deep play: Notes on the Balinese cockfight. Pp. 412–53 in *The interpretation of cultures.* New York: Basic Books.

———. 1973. Thick description: Toward an interpretive theory of culture. Pp. 3–30 in *The interpretation of cultures.* New York: Basic Books.

———. [1974] 1977. "From the native's point of view": On the nature of anthropological understanding. Pp. 480–92 in *Symbolic anthropology: A reader.* Edited by Janet L. Dolgin, David S. Kemnitzer, and David Murray Schneider. New York: Columbia Univ. Press.

———. [1980] 1983. Blurred genres. Pp. 19–35 in *Local knowledge: Further essays in interpretive anthropology.* New York: Basic Books.

———. 1988. *Works and lives.* Stanford, Calif.: Stanford Univ. Press.

George, Nelson. 1985. *Where did our love go? The rise and fall of the Motown sound.* London: Omnibus Press.

Gibson, James J. 1966. *The senses considered as perceptual systems.* Boston: Houghton Mifflin.

———. [1979] 1986. *The ecological approach to visual perception.* Hillsdale, N.J.: Erlbaum.

Gilroy, Paul. 1993. *The black Atlantic: Modernity and double consciousness.* Cambridge, Mass.: Harvard Univ. Press.

Ginzburg, Carlo. 1980. *The cheese and the worms: The cosmos of a sixteenth-century miller.* Translated by John and Anne Tedeschi. Baltimore: Johns Hopkins Univ. Press.

———. 1985. *The night battles: Witchcraft and agrarian cults in the sixteenth and seventeenth centuries.* Translated by John and Anne Tedeschi. New York: Penguin.

Gjerdingen, Robert. 1999. An experimental music theory? Pp. 161–70 in *Rethinking music.* Edited by Nicholas Cook and Mark Everist. Oxford: Oxford Univ. Press.

Godlovitch, Stan. 1998. *Musical performance: A philosophical study.* London: Routledge.

Goehr, Lydia. 1992. *The imaginary museum of musical works: An essay in the philosophy of music.* Oxford: Clarendon Press.

———. 1993. "Music has no meaning to speak of": On the politics of musical interpretation. Pp. 177–90 in *The interpretation of music: Philosophical essays.* Edited by Michael Krausz. Oxford: Clarendon Press.

———. 2000. "On the problems of dating" or "looking backward and forward with Strohm." Pp. 231–46 in *The musical work: Reality or invention?* Edited by Michael Talbot. Liverpool: Liverpool Univ. Press.

Gomart, Emilie, and Antoine Hennion. 1998. A sociology of attachment: Music lovers, drug addicts. Pp. 220–47 in *Actor network theory and after.* Edited by John Law and John Hassard. Oxford: Blackwell.

Goodman, Elaine. 2000. Analysing the ensemble in music rehearsal and performance: The nature and effects of interaction in cello–piano duos. Ph.D. thesis, Royal Holloway (University of London).

Gordon, Steven. 1990. Social structural effects on emotions. Pp. 145–79 in *Research agendas in the sociology of emotions.* Edited by Theodore Kemper. Albany: State Univ. of New York Press.

Gramsci, Antonio. 1971. *Selections from the prison notebooks.* Edited and translated by Quintin Hoare and Geoffrey Nowell-Smith. London: Lawrence and Wishart.

Gratier, M. 1999. Expressions of belonging: The effect of acculturation on the rhythm and harmony of mother-infant interaction. *Musicae Scientiae,* Special Issue. 93–122.

Green, Lucy. 1988. *Music on deaf ears: Musical meaning, ideology and education.* New York: Manchester Univ. Press.

———. 1997. *Music, gender, education.* New York: Cambridge Univ. Press.

———. 1999. Ideology. Pp. 5–17 in *Key terms for popular music and culture.* Edited by Bruce Horner and Thomas Swiss. New York: Basil Blackwell.

———. 2001. *How popular musicians learn: A way ahead for music education.* New York: Ashgate Press.

———. [1999] 2002. Research in the sociology of music education: Some fundamental concepts. In *Teaching music in secondary schools: A reader.* Edited by Gary Spruce. New York: RoutledgeFalmer.

———. 2002. From the Western classics to the world: Secondary teachers' changing perceptions, 1982 and 1998. *British Journal of Music Education* 19(1): 5–30.

Greenblatt, Stephen. 1991. *Marvelous possessions: The wonders of the new world.* Chicago: Univ. of Chicago Press.

Griffiths, Paul. 1978. *Modern music: A concise history from Debussy to Boulez.* London: Thames and Hudson.

Gross, Joan, David McMurray, and Ted Swedenburg. 1997. Arab noise and Ramadan nights: Rai, Rap, and Franco-Maghrebi identity. *Diaspora* 3(1): 3–39.

Guilbault, Jocelyne. 1997. Interpreting world music: A challenge in theory and practice. *Popular Music* 16(1): 31–44.

Guilbault, Jocelyne, with Gage Averill, Édouard Benoit, and Gregory Rabess. 1993. *Zouk: World music in the West Indies.* Chicago: Univ. of Chicago Press.

Habermas, Jürgen. 1977. A review of Gadamer's Truth and Method. Pp. 335–63 in *Understanding social inquiry.* Edited by Fred R. Dallmayr and Thomas A. McCarthy. Notre Dame, Ind.: Notre Dame Univ. Press.

Hall, Stuart. 1980. Cultural studies: Two paradigms. *Media, Culture and Society* 2: 57–72.

———. 1981. Notes on deconstructing "the popular". Pp. 227–40 in *People's history and socialist theory.* Edited by Raphael Samuel. London: Routledge.

Hallam, Susan. 2001. *The power of music.* London: The Performing Right Society.

Hamm, Charles. 1979. *Yesterdays: Popular song in America.* New York: Norton.

Handel, Stephen. 1989. *Listening: An introduction to the perception of auditory events.* Cambridge, Mass.: MIT Press.

Hanley, Betty. 1998. Gender in secondary music education in British Columbia. *British Journal of Music Education* 15: 51–69.

Hanslick, Eduard. [1885] 1974. *The beautiful in music: A contribution to the revisal of musical aesthetics.* 7th ed. Translated by Gustav Cohen. New York: Da Capo Press.

Haraway, Donna. 1991. *Simians, cyborgs, and women: The reinvention of nature.* London: Free Association.

Harker, Dave. 1997. The wonderful world of IFPI: Music industry rhetoric, the critics and the classical Marxist critique. *Popular Music* 16(1): 45–80.

Haskell, Francis. 1976. *Rediscoveries in art. Some aspects of taste, fashion and collecting in England and France.* Oxford: Phaidon Press.

Haskell, Francis, and Nicholas Penny. 1981. *Taste and the antique. The lure of classical sculpture 1500–1900.* New Haven, Conn.: Yale Univ. Press.

Hebdige, Dick. 1979. *Subculture: The meaning of style.* London: Methuen.

Heelas, Paul. 1996. Emotion talk across cultures. Pp. 171–99 in *The emotions. Social, cultural and biological dimensions.* Edited by Rom Harré and W. Gerrod Parrott. London: Sage.

Hegel, Georg Wilhelm Friedrich. [1807] 1910. *The phenomenology of mind.* Translated by J. B. Baillie. London: Allen and Unwin.

———. [1822–88] 1975. *Lectures on the philosophy of world history.* Translated by H. B. Nisbet. Cambridge, U.K.: Cambridge Univ. Press.

Hennion, Antoine. 1989. An intermediary between production and consumption: The producer of popular music. *Science, Technology and Human Values* 14(4): 400–24.

————. 1993. *La passion musicale. Une sociologie de la médiation.* Paris: Métailié.

————. 1997. Baroque and rock: Music, mediators and musical taste. *Poetics* 24: 415–35.

————. 2001. Music lovers. Taste as performance. *Theory, Culture, Society* 18(5): 1–22.

Hennion, Antoine, and Joël-Marie Fauquet. 2001. Authority as performance. The love of Bach in nineteenth-century France. *Poetics* 29: 75–88.

Hennion, Antoine, Sophie Maisonneuve, and Emilie Gomart. 2000. *Figures de l'amateur. Formes, objets et pratiques de l'amour de la musique aujourd'hui.* Paris: La Documentation Française.

Henrotte, Gayle. 1985. Music as language: A semiotic paradigm? Pp. 163–70 in *Semiotics 1984.* Edited by John Deely. Lanham, Md.: Univ. Press of America.

Herder, Johann Gottfried. 1778–1779. *Stimmen der Völker in Liedern* and *Volkslieder.* 2 vols. Leipzig, Germany: Weygandsche Buchhandlung.

————. 1968. *Sämtliche Werke,* vol. 25. Edited by Bernhard Suphan. Hildesheim, Germany: G. Olms.

Hesmondhalgh, David. 2000. International times: Fusions, exoticism and anti-racism in electronic dance music. Pp. 280–304 in *Western music and its others.* Edited by Georgina Born and David Hesmondhalgh. Berkeley: Univ. of California Press.

Ho, Wai-chung. 1999. The sociopolitical transformation and Hong Kong secondary music education: Politicization, culturalization, and marketization. *Bulletin of the Council for Research in Music Education* 140: 41–56.

————. 2001. Musical learning: Differences between boys and girls in Hong Kong Chinese co-educational secondary schools. *British Journal of Music Education* 18(1): 41–54.

Hochschild, Arlie. 1983. *The managed heart; The commercialization of human feeling.* Berkeley: Univ. of California Press.

Hoffmann, E. T. A. [1810] 1989. Review of Beethoven's fifth symphony. Pp. 234–51 in *E. T. A. Hoffmann's musical writings: Kreisleriana, the poet and the composer, music criticism.* Edited by David Charlton. Translated by Martyn Clarke. Cambridge, U.K.: Cambridge Univ. Press.

hooks, bell. 1992. *Black looks: Race and representation.* Boston, Mass.: South End Press.

Horn, David. 2000. Some thoughts on the work in popular music. Pp. 14–34 in *The musical work: Reality or invention?* Edited by Michael Talbot. Liverpool: Liverpool Univ. Press.

Hornbostel, Erich Moritz von. [1905] 1975. The problems of comparative musicology. Translated by Richard Campbell. Pp. 247–70 in *Hornbostel opera omnia,* vol. 1. Edited by Klaus P. Wachsmann, Dieter Christensen, and Hans-Peter Reinecke.

———. 1928. African Negro music. *Africa* 1(1): 30–62.

Hornbostel, Erich Moritz von, and Curt Sachs. [1914] 1961. A classification of musical instruments. *Galpin Society Journal* 14: 3–29.

Hornby, Nick. [1995] 2000. *High fidelity.* London: Penguin Books.

Huneker, James. [1909] 1927. *Chopin: The man and his music.* New York: Scribner.

Hunt, Lynn A., ed. 1989. *The new cultural history.* Berkeley: Univ. of California Press.

Huyssen, Andreas. 1986. *After the great divide: Modernism, mass culture, postmodernism.* Bloomington: Indiana Univ. Press.

IFPI. 2001. Peru raids net 2m CD-Rs. *IFPI network* 8 (October): 3.

Irigaray, Luce. 1985. *Speculum of the other woman.* Translated by Gillian C. Gill. Ithaca, N.Y.: Cornell Univ. Press.

Ivy, Marilyn. 1995. *Discourses of the vanishing: Modernity, phantasm, Japan.* Chicago: Univ. of Chicago Press.

James, William. 1890. *The principles of psychology.* New York: Holt.

Jameson, Fredric. 1988. The politics of theory: Ideological positions in the postmodernist debate. Pp. 372–83 in *Modern criticism and theory: A reader.* Edited by David Lodge. New York: Longman.

Jarvis, Simon. 1998. *Adorno: A critical introduction.* Cambridge, U.K.: Polity Press.

Jenkins, Keith. 1995. *On "What is history?": From Carr and Elton to Rorty and White.* New York: Routledge.

Johnson, James H. 1995. *Listening in Paris: A cultural history.* Berkeley: Univ. of California Press.

Jones, Arthur Morris. 1959. *Studies in African music.* 2 vols. Oxford: Oxford Univ. Press.

Kafka, Franz. [1922] 1993a. Investigations of a dog. Pp. 420–59 in *Franz Kafka: Selected stories.* Translated by Willa and Edwin Muir. Edited by Gabriel Josipovici. London: David Campbell.

———. [1922] 1993b. Josephine the singer or the mouse folk. Pp. 233–50 in *Franz Kafka: Selected stories.* Translated by Willa and Edwin Muir. Edited by Gabriel Josipovici. London: David Campbell.

Kallberg, Jeffrey. 1994. Small fairy voices: Sex, history and meaning in Chopin. In *Chopin studies. vol.* 2. Edited by John Rink and Jim Samson. Cambridge, U.K.: Cambridge Univ. Press.

Kant, Immanuel. [1790] 1952. *The critique of judgement.* Translated by James Creed Meredith. Oxford: Clarendon Press.

———. [1790] 2000. *Critique of judgment.* Translated by John Henry Bernard. New York: Prometheus.

Kartomi, Margaret. 1990. *Concepts and classifications of musical instruments.* Chicago: Univ. of Chicago Press.

Kaye, Nick. 1994. *Postmodernism and performance.* London: Macmillan.

Kearns, Katherine. 1997. *Psychoanalysis, historiography, and feminist theory: The search for critical method.* Cambridge, U.K.: Cambridge Univ. Press.

Keightley, Keir. 2001. Reconsidering rock. Pp. 109–42 in *The Cambridge companion to pop and rock.* Edited by Simon Frith, Will Straw, and John Street. Cambridge, U.K.: Cambridge Univ. Press.

Keil, Charles. 1979. *Tiv song.* Chicago: Univ. of Chicago Press.

Keil, Frank C. 1994. The birth and nurturance of concepts by domains: The origins of concepts of living things. Pp. 234–54 in *Mapping the mind: Domain specificity in cognition and culture.* Edited by Lawrence A. Hirschfeld and Susan A. Gelman. Cambridge, U.K.: Cambridge Univ. Press.

Kerman, Joseph. 1985. *Musicology.* London: Fontana.

Kershaw, Baz. 1992. *The politics of performance: Radical theatre as cultural intervention.* London: Routledge.

Kisliuk, Michelle. 1997. (Un)doing fieldwork: Sharing songs, sharing lives. Pp. 23–44 in *Shadows in the field: New perspectives for fieldwork in ethnomusicology.* Edited by Gregory F. Barz and Timothy J. Cooley. New York: Oxford Univ. Press.

———. 1998. *Seize the dance! BaAka musical life and the ethnography of performance.* New York: Oxford Univ. Press.

Kittler, Friedrich. 1985. *Discourse networks 1800/1900.* Translated by Michael Metteer with Chris Cullens. Foreword by David E. Wellbery. Stanford, Calif.: Stanford Univ. Press.

———. 1990. *Gramophone, film, typewriter.* Translated with introduction by Geoffrey Winthrop-Young and Michael Wutz. Stanford, Calif.: Stanford Univ. Press.

Koestler, Arthur. 1975. *The act of creation.* 2d ed. London: Picador.

Koizumi, Kyoko. 2002. Popular music, gender and high school pupils in Japan: Personal music in school and leisure sites. *Popular Music* 21(1): 107–25.

Korsyn, Kevin. 1999. Beyond privileged contexts: Intertextuality, influence, and dialogue. Pp. 55–72 in *Rethinking music.* Edited by Nicholas Cook and Mark Everist. Oxford: Oxford Univ. Press.

Kotthoff, Helga. 2001. Aesthetic dimensions of Georgian grief rituals: On the artful display of emotions in lamentation. Pp. 167–94 in *Verbal art across cultures. The aesthetics and proto-aesthetics of communication.* Edited by Hubert Knoblauch and Helga Kotthoff. Tübingen, Germany: Narr.

Koza, Julia Eklund. 1992. Picture this: Sex equity in textbook illustrations. *Music Educators' Journal* 78(7): 28–33.

Kramer, Lawrence. 1990. *Music as cultural practice, 1800–1900.* Berkeley: Univ. of California Press.

———. 1993. Music criticism and the postmodern turn: In contrary motion with Gary Tomlinson. *Current Musicology* 53: 25–35.

———. 1995. *Classical music and postmodern knowledge.* Berkeley: Univ. of California Press.

———. 1998. Primitive encounters: Beethoven's "Tempest" sonata, musical meaning, and enlightenment anthropology. Pp. 31–66 in *Beethoven forum.* Vol. 6. Edited by Glenn Stanle. Lincoln: Univ. of Nebraskra Press.

———. 2001. *Musical meaning: Toward a critical history.* Berkeley: Univ. of California Press.

Krims, Adam. 2000. *Rap music and the poetics of identity.* Cambridge, U.K.: Cambridge Univ. Press.

Kristeva, Julia. 1987. Narcissus: The new insanity. Pp. 103–21 in *Tales of love.* Translated by Leon S. Roudiez. New York: Columbia Univ. Press.

Krumhansl, Carol L. 1990. *Cognitive foundations of musical pitch.* New York: Oxford Univ. Press.

———. 1991. Music psychology: Tonal structures in perception and memory. *Annual Review of Psychology* 42: 277–303.

———. 1998. Topic in music: An empirical study of memorability, openness, and emotion in Mozart's string quintet in C major and Beethoven's string quartet in A minor. *Music Perception* 16(1): 119–34.

———. 2000. Music and affect: Empirical and theoretical contributions from experimental psychology. Pp. 88–99 in *Musicology and sister disciplines Past, present, future.* Edited by David Greer. Oxford: Oxford Univ. Press.

Kubik, Gerhard. 1979. Pattern perception and recognition in African music. Pp. 221–49 in *The performing arts.* Edited by John Blacking and Joann W. Kealiinohomoku. The Hague Amsterdam: Mouton.

Kuhn, Thomas S. 1962. *The structure of scientific revolutions.* Chicago: Univ. of Chicago Press.

Kuper, Adam. 1999. *Culture: The anthropologists' account.* Cambridge, Mass.: Harvard Univ. Press.

Lacan, Jacques. [1953] 1977. The function and field of speech and language in psychoanalysis. Translated by Alan Sheridan. Pp. 30–113 in *Écrits: A selection.* London: Tavistock.

———. [1955] 1977. The Freudian thing. Translated by Alan Sheridan. Pp. 114–45 in *Écrits: A selection.* London: Tavistock.

————. [1964] 1979. *The four fundamental concepts of psycho-analysis.* Translated by Alan Sheridan. New York: Penguin.

Laing, Dave. 1985. *One chords wonders: Power and meaning in punk rock.* Milton Keynes, U.K.: Open Univ. Press.

————. 1986. The music industry and the "cultural imperialism" thesis. *Media, Culture and Society* 8: 331–41.

Lakoff, George, and Mark Johnson. 1980. *Metaphors we live by.* Chicago: Univ. of Chicago Press.

Lamont, Michèle, and Marcel Fournier, eds. 1992. *Cultivating differences: Symbolic boundaries and the making of inequality.* Chicago: Univ. of Chicago Press.

Langlois, Tony. 1996. The local and global in North African popular music. *Popular Music* 15(3): 259–73.

La Rochelle, Réal. 1987. *Callas, la diva et le vinyle: la popularisation de l'opéra par l'industrie du disque.* Montréal: Triptyque.

Lebrecht, Norman. 1996. *When the music stops: Managers, maestros and corporate murder of classical music.* London: Simon and Schuster.

Le Huray, Peter, and James Day, eds. 1981. *Music aesthetics in the eighteenth and early-nineteenth centuries.* Cambridge, U.K.: Cambridge Univ. Press.

Leman, Marc. 1995. *Music and schema theory. Cognitive foundations of systematic musicology.* New York: Springer.

Leppert, Richard. 1993. *The sight of sound: Music, representation, and the history of the body.* Berkeley: Univ. of California Press.

Leppert, Richard, and Susan McClary. 1987. *Music and society: The politics of composition, performance and reception.* Cambridge, U.K.: Cambridge Univ. Press.

Lerdahl, Fred, and Ray Jackendoff. 1983. *A generative theory of tonal music.* Cambridge, Mass.: MIT Press.

Levin, Theodore Craig. 1996. *The hundred thousand fools of God: Musical travels in Central Asia (and Queens, New York).* Bloomington: Indiana Univ. Press.

Levine, Lawrence W. 1988. *Highbrow/lowbrow: The emergence of cultural hierarchy in America.* Cambridge, Mass.: Harvard Univ. Press.

Levinson, Jerrold. 1997. *Music in the moment.* Ithaca, N.Y.: Cornell Univ. Press.

Leyshon, Andrew, David Matliss, and George Revill, eds. 1998. *The place of music.* New York: Guilford.

Lhamon, W. T. 1998. *Raising Cain: Blackface performance from Jim Crow to hip-hop.* Cambridge, Mass.: Harvard Univ. Press.

Ligota, Christopher R. 1982. "This story is not true": Fact and fiction in antiquity. *Journal of the Warburg and Courtauld Institutes* 45: 1–13.

Lipsitz, George. 1994. *Dangerous crossroads: Popular music, postmodernism, and the poetics of place.* London: Verso.

Lomax, Alan. 1968. *Folk song style and culture.* Washington, D.C.: American Association for the Advancement of Science.

Lomax, Alan, and Norman Berkowitz. 1972. The evolutionary taxonomy of culture. *Science* 177: 228–39.

Lomax, Alan, Roswell Rudd, Victor Grauer, Norman Berkowitz, Bess Lomax Hawes, and Carol Kulig. 1978. *Cantometrics: An approach to the anthropology of music: audiocassettes and a handbook.* Berkeley: Univ. of California Extension Media Center.

Longinovic, Tomislav. 2000. Music wars: Blood and song at the end of Yugoslavia. Pp. 622–43 in *Music and the racial imagination.* Edited by Ronald Radano and Philip V. Bohlman. Chicago: Univ. of Chicago Press.

Lopes, Paul D. 1992. Innovation and diversity in the popular music industry 1969 to 1990. *American Sociological Review.* 57(1): 56–71.

Lott, Eric. 1993. *Love and theft: Blackface minstrelsy and the American working class.* New York: Oxford Univ. Press.

Lupton, Deborah. 1998. *The emotional self.* London: Sage.

Lutz, Catherine, and Geoffrey M. White. 1986. The anthropology of emotions. *Annual Review of Anthropology* 15: 405–36.

Lutz, Catherine, and Lila Abu-Lughod, eds. 1990. *Language and the politics of emotion.* Cambridge, U.K.: Cambridge Univ. Press.

Lyotard, Jean-François. 1991. *The inhuman: Reflections on time.* Translated by Geoffrey Bennington and Rachel Bowlby. Oxford: Basil Blackwell.

Maas, Georg, and Hartmult Reszel. 1998. Whatever happened to ? . . . The decline and renaissance of rock in the former GDR. *Popular Music* 17(3): 267–78.

MacDonald, Ian. 1995. *Revolution in the head: The Beatles' records and the sixties.* London: Pimlico.

Manuel, Peter. 1988. *Popular musics of the non-Western world: An introductory survey.* New York: Oxford Univ. Press.

———. 2000. The construction of a diasporic tradition: Indo-Caribbean "Local classical music." *Ethnomusicology* 44(1): 97–119.

Marcus, George E., and Michael M. J. Fisher. 1986. *Anthropology as cultural critique: An experimental moment in the human sciences.* Chicago: Univ. of Chicago Press.

Marcus, Greil. [1976] 1982. *Mystery train: Images of America in rock 'n' roll music.* New York: Dutton.

Martin, Peter. 1995. *Sounds and society: Themes in the sociology of music.* Manchester, U.K.: Manchester Univ. Press.

Maryprasith, Primrose. 1999. The effects of globalisation and localisation on the status of music in Thailand. Ph.D. thesis, London University Institute of Education.

Mauss, Marcel. 1954. *The gift: Forms and functions of exchange in archaic societies.* Glencoe, Ill.: Free Press.

McCarthy, Maree. 1997. Irish music education and Irish identity: A concept revisited. *Oideas* 45: 5–22. Dublin: Department of Education and Science.

McClary, Susan. 1991. *Feminine endings.* Minneapolis: Univ. of Minnesota Press.

———. 1994. Constructions of subjectivity in Schubert's music. Pp. 205–34 in *Queering the pitch: The new gay and lesbian musicology.* Edited by Philip Brett, Elizabeth Wood, and Gary C. Thomas. New York: Routledge.

McClary, Susan, and Robert Walser. 1990. Start making sense! Musicology wrestles with rock. Pp. 277–92 in *On record: Rock, pop and the written word.* Edited by Simon Frith and Andrew Goodwin. London: Routledge.

McGuigan, Jim. 1992. *Cultural populism.* London: Routledge.

Melrose, Susan. 1994. *A semiotics of the dramatic text.* London: Macmillan.

Merriam, Alan P. 1964. *The anthropology of music.* Evanston, Ill.: Northwestern Univ. Press.

———. 1969. The ethnographic experience: Drum-making among the Bala (Basongye). *Ethnomusicology* 13: 74–100.

Metzler, Fritz. 1938. Dur, Moll und "Kirchentöne" als musikalischer Rassenausdruck. Pp. 1–27 in *Zur Tonalität des deutschen Volksliedes.* Edited by Guido Waldmann. Wolfenbüttel, Germany: Kallmeyer.

Meyer, Leonard B. 1956. *Emotion and meaning in music.* Chicago: Univ. of Chicago Press.

———. 1973. *Explaining music: Essays and explorations.* Berkeley: Univ. of California Press.

Middleton, Richard. 1990. *Studying popular music.* Milton Keynes, U.K.: Open Univ. Press.

———. 2000. Work-in-(g) practice: Configuration of the popular music intertext. Pp. 59–87 in *The musical work: Reality or invention?* Edited by Michael Talbot. Liverpool: Liverpool Univ. Press.

Miège, Bernard. 1989. *The capitalization of cultural production.* New York: International General.

Miller, Geoffrey. 2000. Evolution of human music through sexual selection. Pp. 329–60 in *The origins of music.* Edited by Nils Wallin, Björn Merker, and Steven Brown. Cambridge, Mass.: MIT Press.

Mingus, Charles. 1995. *Beneath the underdog.* Edinburgh: Payback Press.

Mitchell, Tony. 1996. *Popular music and local identity.* London: Wesleyan Univ. Press.

———, ed. 2001. *Global noise: Rap and hip-hop outside the USA*. Middletown, Conn.: Wesleyan Univ. Press.

Mithen, Steven J. 1996. *The prehistory of the mind*. London: Thames and Hudson.

Modleski, Tania. 1986. Femininity as mas(s)querade: A feminist approach to mass culture. Pp. 37–52 in *High theory, low culture: Analysing popular television and film*. Edited by Colin McCabe. Manchester, U.K.: Manchester Univ. Press.

Monson, Ingrid. 1996. *Saying something: Jazz improvisation and interaction*. Chicago: Univ. of Chicago Press.

———, ed. 2000. *African diaspora: A musical perspective*. New York: Garland.

Montagu, Jeremy, and John Burton. 1971. A proposed new classification system for musical instruments. *Ethnomusicology* 15(1): 49–70.

Montaigne, Michel Eyquem de. [1580] 1952. *Essais*. Paris: Editions Garnier Frères.

Moore, Allan. 1993. *Rock: The primary text*. Milton Keynes, U.K.: Open Univ. Press.

Morley, David, and Kuan-Hsing Chen, eds. 1996. *Stuart Hall: Critical dialogues in cultural studies*. London: Routledge.

Morrow, Mary Sue. 1989. *Concert life in Haydn's Vienna: Aspects of a developing musical and social institution*. Stuyvesant, N.Y.: Pendragon Press.

Mugglestone, Erica. 1981. Guido Adler's "The scope, method and aim of musicology" (1885): An English translation with an historico-analytical commentary. *Yearbook for Traditional Music* 13: 1–21.

Muir, Edward, and Guido Ruggiero, eds. 1991. *Microhistory and the lost peoples of Europe*. Translated by Eren Branch. Baltimore: Johns Hopkins Univ. Press.

Mulhern, Francis. 2000. *Culture/Metaculture*. New York: Routledge.

Naficy, Hamid. 1993. *The making of exile communities*. Minneapolis: Univ. of Minnesota Press.

Negus, Keith. 1999. *Music genres and corporate cultures*. London: Routledge.

Negus, Keith, and Michael Pickering. 2000. Creativity and cultural production. *Cultural Policy* 6(2): 259–82.

Nelson, Richard. 2001. *Economics as religion*. Philadelphia: Pennsylvania State Press.

Nettl, Bruno. [1973] 1992. Comparison and comparative method in ethnomusicology. *Yearbook for Inter-American Musical Research* 9: 148–61.

———. 1987. *The Radif of Persian music: Studies of structure and cultural significance*. Champaign, Ill.: Elephant & Cat.

Nettl, Bruno, Ruth M. Stone, James Porter, and Timothy Rice, eds. 1998–2002. *The Garland encyclopedia of world music*. 10 volumes. New York: Garland.

Neuenfeldt, Karl, ed. 1997. *The Didjeridu: From Arnhem Land to Internet.* Sydney: John Libbey/Perfect Beat.

——, ed. 1998. Old instruments in new contexts. Special Edition of *The World of Music* 40(2).

Newlin, Dika. 1980. *Schoenberg remembered: Diaries and recollections (1938–76).* New York: Pendragon Press.

Nietzsche, Friedrich. [1901] 1969. *The will to power.* Edited by Walter A. Kaufmann. Translated by Walter A. Kaufmann and R. J. Hollingdale. New York: Random House.

Olsen, Dale. 1986. Note on "corpophone." *Newsletter of the Society for Ethnomusicology* 20(4): 5.

O'Neill, Susan. 1997. Gender and music. Pp. 46–63 in *The social psychology of music.* Edited by David J. Hargreaves and Adrian C. North. New York: Oxford Univ. Press.

Ottenberg, Simon. 1996. *Seeing with music: The lives of three blind African musicians.* Seattle: Univ. of Washington Press.

Ovid. 1986. *Metamorphoses.* Translated by A. D. Melville. Oxford: Oxford Univ. Press.

Paddison, Max. 1996. *Adorno, modernism and mass culture. Essays on critical theory and music.* London: Kahn and Averill.

Pagden, Anthony. 1993. *European encounters with the New World: From Renaissance to Romanticism.* New Haven, Conn.: Yale Univ. Press.

Paine, Thomas. [1791–92] 1969. *Rights of man.* Edited by Henry Collins. Harmondsworth, U.K.: Penguin.

Papousek, Hanus. 1996. Musicality in infancy research: Biological and cultural origins of early musicality. Pp. 37–55 in *Musical beginnings. Origins and development of musical competence.* Edited by Irène Deliège and John A. Sloboda. Oxford: Oxford Univ. Press.

Papousek, Mechthild. 1996. Intuitive parenting: A hidden source of musical stimulation in infancy. Pp. 88–112 in *Musical beginnings. Origins and development of musical competence.* Edited by Irène Deliège and John A. Sloboda. Oxford: Oxford Univ. Press.

Parry, Hubert. 1896. *The evolution of the art of music.* New York: D. Appleton.

Pennay, Mark. 2001. The birth of a genre. Pp. 111–33 in *Global noise: Rap and hip-hop outside the USA.* Edited by Tony Mitchell. Middletown, Conn.: Wesleyan Univ. Press.

Peterson, Richard A. 1997. *Creating country-music: Fabricating authenticity.* Berkeley: Univ. of California Press.

Peterson, Richard A., and David Berger. [1975] 1990. Cycles in symbol production: The case of popular music. In *On record: Rock, pop and the written word*. Edited by Simon Frith and Andrew Goodwin. London: Routledge.

Philip, Robert. 1992. *Early recordings and musical style: Changing tastes in instrumental performance, 1900–1950*. Cambridge, U.K.: Cambridge Univ. Press.

Pinker, Steven. 1994. *The language instinct*. London: Allen Lane.

———. 1997. *How the mind works*. London: Allen Lane.

Pöppel, Ernst, and Marc Wittmann. 1999. Time in the mind. Pp. 841–43 in *MIT encyclopedia of cognitive sciences*. Edited by Robert A. Wilson and Frank C. Keil. Cambridge, Mass.: MIT Press.

Potter, John. 1998. *Vocal authority: Singing style and ideology*. Cambridge, U.K.: Cambridge Univ. Press.

Potter, Pamela M. 1998. *Most German of the arts: Musicology and society from the Weimar Republic to the end of Hitler's Reich*. New Haven, Conn.: Yale Univ. Press.

Qureshi, Regula B. 1997. The Indian sarangi: Sound of affect, site of contest. *Yearbook for Traditional Music* 29: 1–38.

Radano, Ronald, and Philip V. Bohlman, eds. 2000. *Music and the racial imagination*. Chicago: Univ. of Chicago Press.

Ratner, Leonard G. 1977. *Music. The listener's art*. New York: McGraw-Hill.

Raynor, Henry. 1972. *A social history of music*. New York: Taplinger.

Regev, Motti. 1997. Rock aesthetics and musics of the world. *Theory, Culture and Society* 14(3): 125–42.

Reynolds, Simon. 1997. Rave culture: Living dream or living death? Pp. 84–93 in *The club cultures reader*. Edited by Steve Redhead. Oxford: Blackwell.

Rice, Timothy. 1994. *May it fill your soul: Experiencing Bulgarian music*. Chicago: Univ. of Chicago Press.

———. 1996. The dialectic of economics and aesthetics in Bulgarian music. Pp. 176–99 in *Retuning culture. Musical changes in central and eastern Europe*. Edited by Mark Slobin. Durham, N.C.: Duke Univ. Press.

Rich, Adrienne. 1986. Compulsory heterosexuality and lesbian existence. Pp. 23–75 in *Blood, bread and poetry: Selected prose 1979–1985*. New York: Norton.

Riguero, Patricia Digon. 2000. An analysis of gender in a Spanish music text book. *Music Education Research* 2(1): 57–73.

Robins, Kevin, and David Morley. 1996. Almanci, Yabanci. *Cultural Studies* 10(2): 248–54.

Rosaldo, Michelle Z. 1984. Toward an anthropology of self and feeling. Pp. 137–57 in *Culture theory. Essays on mind, self and emotion*. Edited by Richard A. Shweder and Robert A. LeVine. Cambridge, U.K.: Cambridge Univ. Press.

Rose, Tricia. 1994. *Black noise: Rap music and black culture in contemporary America*. Hanover, N.H.: Univ. Press of New England.

Rosen, Charles. 1994a. *The frontiers of meaning: Three informal lectures on music.* New York: Hill and Wang.

———. 1994b. Music à la mode. *New York Review of Books,* June 23, 1994. 55–62.

Rosenwald, Lawrence. 1993. Theory, text-setting, and performance. *Journal of Musicology* 11: 52–65.

Rosselli, John. 1984. *The opera industry in Italy from Cimarosa to Verdi: The role of the impresario.* Cambridge, U.K.: Cambridge Univ. Press.

———. 1991. *Music and musicians in nineteenth-century Italy.* Portland, Ore.: Amadeus Press.

Rothenbuhler, Eric W., and John Dimmick. 1982. Popular music: Concentration and diversity in the industry, 1974–1980. *Journal of Communication* 32(1): 143–49.

Rothstein, William. 1995. Analysis and the act of performance. Pp. 217–40 in *The practice of performance: Studies in musical interpretation.* Edited by John Rink. Cambridge, U.K.: Cambridge Univ. Press.

Rumph, Stephen. 1995. A kingdom not of this world: The political context of E. T. A. Hoffmann's Beethoven criticism. *19th Century Music* 19(1): 50–67.

Sahlins, Marshall. 1985. *Islands of history.* Chicago: Univ. of Chicago Press.

Said, Edward W. 1992. *Musical elaborations.* London: Vintage.

Sassen, Saskia. 1998. *Globalization and its discontents: Essays on the new mobility of people and money.* New York: New Press.

Schama, Simon. 1995. *Landscape and memory.* New York: Alfred A. Knopf.

Schechner, Richard. 1998. *Performance theory.* rev. ed. New York: Routledge.

Schonberg, Harold C. 1963. *The great pianists.* New York: Simon and Schuster.

Schott, Rüdiger. 1968. Das Geschichtsbewusstsein schriftloser Völker. *Archiv für Begriffsgeschichte.* 12: 166–205.

Schumann, Robert. [1840] 1946. *On music and musicians.* Translated by Konrad Wolff. Edited by Paul Rosenfeld. New York: Pantheon.

Schutz, A. 1951. Making music together: A study in social relationship. *Social Research* 18: 76–97.

Schwartz, Theodore, Geoffrey White, and Catherine A. Lutz. 1992. *New directions in psychological anthropology.* Cambridge, U.K.: Cambridge Univ. Press.

Schwarz, David. 1997. Oi: Music, politics and violence. Pp. 100–32 in *Listening subjects: Music, psychoanalysis, culture.* Durham, N.C.: Duke Univ. Press.

Scott, Derek B. 1994. The sexual politics of Victorian music aesthetics. *Journal of the Royal Musical Association* 119(1): 91–114.

Scruton, Roger. 1983. *The aesthetic understanding.* London: Methuen.

Sedgwick, Eve Kosofsky. 1985. *Between men: English literature and male homosocial desire.* New York: Columbia Univ. Press.

—. 1990. *Epistemology of the closet.* New York: Penguin Books.

Seeger, Charles. 1977. *Studies in musicology 1935–1975.* Berkeley: Univ. of California Press.

Segrave, Kerry. 1994. *Payola in the music industry: A history 1880–1991.* London: McFarland.

Serafine, Mary Louise. 1988. *Music as cognition. The development of thought in sound.* New York: Columbia Univ. Press.

Sharma, Sanjay, John Hutnyk, and Ashwani Sharma. 1996. *Dis-orienting rhythms: The politics of the new Asian dance music.* London: Zed Books.

Shelemay, Kay Kaufman. 1998. *Let jasmine rain down. Song and remembrance among Syrian Jews.* Chicago: Univ. of Chicago Press.

Shepherd, John. 1977. The musical coding of ideologies. Pp. 69–124 in *Whose music? A sociology of musical languages.* Edited by John Shepherd, Phil Virden, Graham Vulliamy, and Trevor Wishart. London: Latimer New Dimensions.

—. 1982. A theoretical model for the sociomusicological analysis of popular musics. *Popular Music* 2: 145–77.

—. 1987. Music and male hegemony. Pp. 151–72 in *Music and society: The politics of composition, performance and reception.* Edited by Richard Leppert and Susan McClary. New York: Cambridge Univ. Press.

—. 1991. *Music as social text.* Cambridge, U.K.: Polity.

Shilling, Chris. 1993 *The body and social theory.* Thousand Oaks, Calif.: Sage.

Silverman, Carol. 1996. Music and marginality: Roma (Gypsies) of Bulgaria and Macedonia. Pp. 231–53 in *Retuning culture. Musical changes in central and eastern Europe.* Edited by Mark Slobin. Durham, N.C.: Duke Univ. Press.

Slobin, Mark. 1982. *Tenement songs: The popular music of the Jewish immigrants.* Urbana, Ill.: Univ. of Illinois Press.

—. 1989. *Chosen voices: The story of the American cantorate.* Urbana, Ill.: Univ. of Illinois Press.

—. 1993. *Subcultural sounds: Micromusics of the West.* Hanover, N.H.: Univ. Press of New England.

—. 1994. Music in diaspora: The view from Euro-America. *Diaspora* 3(3): 243–52.

—. 2000. *Fiddler on the move: Exploring the klezmer world.* New York: Oxford Univ. Press.

Sloboda, John A., and Susan O'Neill. 2001. Emotions in everyday listening to music. *Music and emotion. Theory and research.* Edited by Patrik N. Juslin and John A. Sloboda. Oxford: Oxford Univ. Press.

Small, Christopher. 1987. Performance as ritual: Sketch for an enquiry into the true nature of a symphony concert. Pp. 6–32 in *Lost in music: Culture, style and the musical event.* Edited by Avron Levine White. London: Routledge and Kegan Paul.

———. 1998. *Musicking: The meanings of performing and listening.* Hanover, N.H.: Univ. Press of New England.

Smith, Adam. [1776] 1910. *An enquiry into the nature and causes of the wealth of nations.* London: Everyman.

Smith, Chris. 1998. Miles Davis and the semiotics of improvised performance. Pp. 261–89 in *In the course of performance: Studies in the world of musical improvisation.* Edited by Bruno Nettl with Melinda Russell. Chicago: Univ. of Chicago Press.

Sober, Elliott, and David S. Wilson. 1998. *Unto others: The evolution and psychology of unselfish behavior.* Cambridge, Mass.: Harvard Univ. Press.

Solie, Ruth, ed. 1993. *Musicology and difference: Gender and sexuality in music scholarship.* Berkeley: Univ. of California Press.

Spelke, E. 1999. Infant cognition. Pp. 402–404 in *MIT encyclopedia of cognitive sciences.* Edited by Robert A. Wilson and Frank C. Keil. Cambridge, Mass.: MIT Press.

Sperber, D. 1999. Culture, cognition and evolution. Pp. cxi–cxxxii in *MIT encyclopedia of cognitive sciences.* Edited by Robert A. Wilson and Frank C. Keil. Cambridge, Mass.: MIT Press.

Spivak, Gayatri Chakravorty, with Ellen Rooney. 1989. In a word [Interview]. *Differences* 1(2): 124–56.

St. Augustine. 1991. *Confessions.* Translated by Henry Chadwick. Oxford: Oxford Univ. Press.

Steiner, George. 2001. *Grammars of creation.* London: Faber.

Sterne, Jonathan. 2001. A machine to hear for them: On the very possibility of sound's reproduction. *Cultural Studies* 15(2): 259–94.

Stevens, Wallace. [1945] 1954. *The collected poems.* New York: Alfred A. Knopf.

Stobart, Henry, and Ian Cross. 2000. The Andean anacrusis? Rhythmic structure and perception in Easter songs of Northern Potosí, Bolivia. *British Journal of Ethnomusicology* 9(2): 63–94.

Stockfelt, Ola. 1994. Cars, buildings and soundscapes. Pp. 19–38 in *Soundscapes: Essays on vroom and moo.* Edited by Helmi Järviluoma. Tampere, Finland: Department of Folk Tradition Univ. of Tampere and Institute of Rhythm Music Seinäjoki.

Stokes, Martin. 1992. *The Arabesk debate: Music and musicians in modern Turkey.* Oxford: Clarendon Press.

————, ed. 1994. *Ethnicity, identity and music. The musical construction of place.* Oxford: Berg.

————. 2001. Ethnomusicology IV/2, Contemporary theoretical issues. Pp. 386–95 in *The new Grove dictionary of music* vol. 8. rev. ed. Edited by Stanley Sadie. London: Macmillan.

————. n.d. Turkish rock and pop. *Garland encyclopaedia of world music, Middle East.* Forthcoming.

Stratton, Jon. 1982. Reconciling contradictions: The role of artist and repertoire in the British record industry. *Popular Music and Society* 8(2): 90–100.

Straw, Will. 1991. Systems of articulation, logics of change: Communities and scenes in popular music. *Cultural Studies* 5(3): 368–88.

Strohm, Reihhard. 2000. Looking back at ourselves: The problem with the musical work-concept. Pp. 128–52 in *The musical work: Reality or invention?* Edited by Michael Talbot. Liverpool: Liverpool Univ. Press.

Stumpf, Carl. 1911. *Die anfänge der Musik.* Leipzig, Germany: Barth.

Subotnik, Rose Rosengard. 1976. Adorno's diagnosis of Beethoven's late style. *Journal of the American Musicological Society* 29: 242–75.

————. 1991. The challenge of contemporary music. Pp. 265–93 in *Developing variations: Style and ideology in Western music.* Minneapolis: Univ. of Minnesota Press.

Swanwick, Keith. 1968. *Popular music and the teacher.* Oxford: Pergamon Press.

Tagg, Philip. 1982. Analysing popular music: Music theory, method and practice. *Popular Music* 2: 37–69.

————. 1998. The Göteborg connection: Lessons in the history and politics of popular music education and research. *Popular Music* 17(2): 219–42.

Taiwo, Olufemi. n.d. Exorcising Hegel's ghost: Africa's challenge to philosophy. http://web.africa.ufl.edu/asq/v1/4/2.htm (accessed August 6, 2002).

Talbot, Michael, ed. 2000. *The musical work: Reality or invention?* Liverpool: Liverpool Univ. Press.

Taruskin, Richard. 1995. *Text and act: Essays on music and performance.* New York: Oxford Univ. Press.

————. 1997. *Defining Russia musically: Historical and hermeneutical essays.* Princeton, N.J.: Princeton Univ. Press.

Taylor, Charles. 1994. *Multiculturalism: Examining the politics of recognition.* Edited by Amy Gutman. Princeton, N.J.: Princeton Univ. Press.

Taylor, Timothy. 1997. *Global pop: World music, world markets.* London: Routledge.

————. 2002. *Strange sounds: Music, technology and culture.* New York: Routledge.

Tchaikovsky, P. [1878] 1970. Letter: Florence, 17 February, 1878. Pp. 57–60 in

Creativity: Selected readings. Edited by Philip E. Vernon. Harmondsworth, U.K.: Penguin Books.

Théberge, Paul. 1998. *Any sound you can imagine: Making music/consuming technology.* Hanover, N.H.: Univ. Press of New England.

Thomas, Nicholas. 1991 *Entangled objects: Exchange, material culture, and colonialism in the Pacific.* Cambridge, Mass.: Harvard Univ. Press.

Thompson, Edward P. [1963] 1968. *The making of the English working class.* London: Victor Gollancz. rev. ed. London: Pelican.

Titon, Jeff Todd. 1988. *Powerhouse for God.* Austin: Univ. of Texas Press.

———. 1991. *The Clyde Davenport HyperCard stack.* Providence, R.I.: the author. http://www.stg.brown.edu/projects/davenport/CLYDE_DAVENPORT.html (accessed August 6, 2002).

———. 1995a. Bi-musicality as metaphor. *Journal of American Folklore* 108: 287–97.

———. 1995b. Text. *Journal of American Folklore* 108: 432–48.

———. 1997. Knowing fieldwork. Pp. 87–100 in *Shadows in the field: New perspectives for fieldwork in ethnomusicology.* Edited by Gregory F. Barz and Timothy J. Cooley. New York: Oxford Univ. Press.

Titon, Jeff Todd, Elwood Cornett, and John Wallhausser. 1997. *Songs of the old regular Baptists.* Washington, D.C.: Smithsonian Folkways CD 40106.

Tocqueville, Alexis de. [1835] 1956. *Democracy in America.* Edited and abridged by Richard D. Heffner. New York: Mentor Books.

Tololyan, Khachig. 1991. The nation-state and its others: In lieu of a preface. *Diaspora* 1(1): 3–7.

Tomlinson, Gary. 1993. Musical pasts and postmodern musicologies: A response to Lawrence Kramer. *Current Musicology* 53: 18–24.

———. 1995. Ideologies of Aztec song. *Journal of the American Musicological Society* 48: 343–79.

———. 1999. *Metaphysical song: An essay on opera.* Princeton, N.J.: Princeton Univ. Press.

Tomlinson, John. 1991. *Cultural imperialism.* London: Pinter.

Toop, David. 1994. Sleevenotes to [Various artists], *Artificial Intelligence II.* Warp, LP23.

Towse, Ruth. 1993. *Singers in the marketplace: The economics of the singing profession.* Oxford: Clarendon Press.

———, ed. 1997. *Baumol's cost disease. The arts and other victims.* Cheltenham, U.K.: Edward Elgar.

Toynbee, Jason. 2000. *Making popular music: Musicians, creativity, institutions.* London: Arnold.

————. 2002. Mainstreaming: Hegemony, market and the aesthetics of the centre in popular music. Pp. 149–63 in *Popular music studies*. Edited by David Hesmondhalgh and Keith Negus. London: Arnold.

Tracey, Hugh. 1954. The state of folk music in Bantu Africa. *African Music* 1(1): 8–11.

Trehub, Sandra E., E. Glenn Schellenberg, and D. Hill. 1997. The origins of music perception and cognition: A developmental perspective. Pp. 103–28 in *Perception and cognition of music*. Edited by Irène Deliège and John A. Sloboda. Hove, U.K.: The Psychology Press.

Trevarthen, Colwyn. 1999. Musicality and the intrinsic motive pulse: evidence from human psychobiology and infant communication. *Musicae Scientiae* [Special Issue] 155–215.

Trumpener, Katie. 1996. Imperial marches and mouse singers: Nationalist mythology in central European modernity. Pp. 67–90 in *Text and nation: Cross-disciplinary essays on cultural and national identities*. Edited by Laura García-Moreno and Peter C. Pfeiffer. Rochester, N.Y.: Camden House.

Turner, Victor, and Edward Bruner, eds. 1986. *The anthropology of experience*. Urbana: Univ. of Illinois Press.

Tylor, Edward Burnett. 1871. *Primitive culture*. London: John Murray.

Van Leeuwen, Theo. 1999. *Speech, music, sound*. Basingstoke, U.K.: Macmillan.

Venturi, Robert, Denise Scott Brown, and Steven Izenour. 1977. *Learning from Las Vegas: The forgotten symbolism of architecture*. rev. ed. Cambridge, Mass.: MIT Press.

Verdery, Katherine. 1991. Theorising socialism: A prologue to the transition. *American Ethnologist* 18(3): 419–39.

Vergo, Peter, ed. 1991. *The new museology*. London: Reaktion Books.

Vico, Gianbattista. 1968. *The new science of Gianbattista Vico*. Translated by Thomas Guddard Bergin and Max Harold Fisch. Ithaca, N.Y.: Cornell Univ. Press.

Virolle, Marie. 1995. *La Chanson Rai: De l'Algerie profonde à la scene internationale*. Paris: Karthala.

Volk, Therese. 1998. *Music, education, and multiculturalism: Foundations and principles*. New York: Oxford Univ. Press.

Vulliamy, Graham. 1977a. Music and the mass culture debate. Pp. 179–200 in *Whose music: A sociology of musical language*. Edited by John Shepherd, Paul Virden, Trevor Wishart, and Graham Vulliamy. London: Latimer New Dimensions.

————. 1977b. Music as a case study in the "new sociology of education." Pp. 201–32 in *Whose music: A sociology of musical language*. Edited by John

Shepherd, Paul Virden, Trevor Wishart, and Graham Vulliamy. London: Latimer New Dimensions.

Waksman, Steve. 1999 *Instruments of desire: The electric guitar and the shaping of musical experience.* Cambridge, Mass.: Harvard Univ. Press.

Wallis, Roger, and Krister Malm. 1984. Big sounds from small peoples. World music in the 1990s. *Public Culture* 8(3): 467–88.

Walser, Robert. 1993. *Running with the devil: Power, gender and madness in heavy metal music.* Hanover, N.H.: Univ. Press of New England.

Waterman, Christopher. 1990. *Jùjú. A social history and ethnography of an African popular music.* Chicago: Chicago Univ. Press.

———. 1991. The uneven development of Africanist ethnomusicology: Three issues and a critique. Pp. 169–83 in *Comparative musicology and anthropology of music.* Edited by Bruno Nettl and Philip V. Bohlman. Chicago: Univ. of Chicago Press.

Watson, John B. 1919. *Psychology from the standpoint of a behaviorist.* 2d ed. Philadelphia: J. B. Lippincott.

Weber, Max. [1921] 1958. *The rational and social foundations of music.* Carbondale, Ill.: Southern Illinois Univ. Press.

Weber, William. 1975. *Music and the middle class. The social structure of concert life in London, Paris and Vienna between 1830 and 1848.* London: Croom Helm.

———. 1992. *The rise of the musical classics in eighteenth-century England: A study in canon, ritual and ideology.* Oxford: Clarendon Press.

Weinstein. Deena. 1991. *Heavy metal: A cultural sociology.* New York: Lexington.

Wenner, Jann. 1972. *Lennon remembers: The Rolling Stone interviews.* Harmondsworth, U.K.: Penguin.

Wermuth, Mir. 2001. Global dichotomies on a national scale. Pp. 149–70 in *Global noise: Rap and hip-hop outside the USA.* Edited by Tony Mitchell. Middletown, Conn.: Wesleyan Univ. Press.

White, Hayden V. 1973. *Metahistory: The historical imagination in nineteenth-century Europe.* Baltimore: Johns Hopkins Univ. Press.

Wicke, Peter. 1990. *Rock music: Culture, aesthetics, and sociology.* Cambridge, U.K.: Cambridge Univ. Press.

Williams, Raymond. 1961. *Culture and society 1780–1950.* Harmondsworth, U.K.: Penguin.

———. 1965. *The long revolution.* Harmondsworth, U.K.: Penguin.

———. 1981. *Culture.* London: Fontana.

———. 1983. *Keywords: A vocabulary of culture and society.* rev. ed. London: Fontana.

Williams, Simon. 2001. *Emotion and social theory. Corporeal reflections on the (ir)rational.* London: Sage.

Willis, Paul E. 1978. *Profane culture.* London: Routledge and Kegan Paul.

———. 1990. *Common culture: Symbolic work at play in the everyday cultures of the young.* Milton Keynes, U.K.: Open Univ. Press.

Wilson, Olly. 1974. The significance of the relationship between Afro-American music and west African music. *The Black Perspective in Music* 2 (Spring). 3–22.

Windsor, W. Luke. 2000. Through and around the acousmatic: The interpretation of electroacoustic sounds. Pp. 7–35 in *Music, electronic media and culture.* Edited by Simon Emmerson. Aldershot, U.K.: Ashgate Press.

Yonnet, Paul. 1985. *Jeux, modes et masses. La société francaise et le moderne, 1945–1985.* Paris: Gallimard.

Zaslaw, Neal. 1989. *Mozart's symphonies: Context, performance practice, reception.* Oxford: Clarendon Press.

Zbikowski, Lawrence M. 2002. *Conceptualising music: Cognitive structure, theory, and analysis.* New York: Oxford Univ. Press.

Zemp, Hugo. 1978. 'Are'are classification of musical types and instruments. *Ethnomusicology* 22(1): 37–68.

Zheng, Su. n.d. *Claiming diaspora: Music, transnationalism, and cultural politics in Asian/Chinese America.* New York: Oxford Univ. Press. Forthcoming.

Zolberg, Vera L. 1990. *Constructing a sociology of the arts.* Cambridge, U.K.: Cambridge Univ. Press.

Notes on Contributors

Kofi Agawu is Professor of Music at Princeton University and Visiting Scholar at the University of Ghana, Legon. He is the author of *African Rhythm: A Northern Ewe Perspective* (Cambridge, 1995). Contact: kagawu@princeton.edu.

Ian Biddle lectures in Music and Cultural Theory at the Department of Music, University of Newcastle upon Tyne. He has published widely on music, gender, and sexuality, and his book, *Listening to Men: Music, Masculinity and the Austro-German Tradition 1789–1914* (University of California Press) is due out in December 2003. His research interests also include popular music, nationalism, Czech music (especially opera) and the "traditional" musics of Spain.

Philip V. Bohlman is Professor of Music and Jewish Studies at the University of Chicago. His recent publications include *World Music: A Very Short Introduction* (Oxford), *Music, Nationalism, and the Making of Modern Europe* (ABC-CLIO), and *Music and the Racial Imagination* (coedited with Ronald Radano; Chicago). Among his current projects are books on Johann Gottfried Herder's writings about music and nationalism, and on the music for the stage in the concentration camp at Terezín.

David Brackett teaches in the Department of Music at SUNY Binghamton. His publications include *Interpreting Popular Music* (Berkeley: University of California Press [1995], 2000) and numerous articles on contemporary music. He served as President of the United States branch of the International Association for the Study of Popular Music (US-IASPM) from 1998 to 2000, and is currently completing a popular music reader for Oxford University Press.

David Clarke is Reader in Music at the University of Newcastle upon Tyne. He is a music theorist who has also written extensively on the music of Michael Tippett, including, most recently, *The Music and Thought of Michael Tippett: Modern Times and Metaphysics* (Cambridge University Press, 2001). Contact: D.I.Clarke@ncl.ac.uk.

Eric F. Clarke went to Sussex University to read for a degree in neurobiology, and graduated with a degree in music in 1977. He is Professor of Music at the University of Sheffield, having worked previously in the Music Department at City University in London. His principal research is in the psychology of music, with particular interests in musical meaning, performance, and the study of time and rhythm. He is coeditor (with Nicholas Cook) of *Empirical Musicology* (Oxford University Press, 2002), and is currently writing a book on listening (also for Oxford).

Martin Clayton works in the Music Department of the Open University, where he is also Chair of the Musics and Cultures Research Group. He served (with Suzel Ana Reily) as Editor of the *British Journal of Ethnomusicology* from 1998 to 2001. His recent publications include *Time in Indian Music: Rhythm, Metre and Form in North Indian Rāg Performance* (Oxford University Press, 2000). Contact: m.r.l.clayton @open.ac.uk. Web page: www.open.ac.uk/arts/music/mclayton.htm

Nicholas Cook is Research Professor of Music at the University of Southampton, having previously taught at the Universities of Hong Kong and Sydney. His books include *A Guide to Musical Analysis; Music, Imagination, and Culture; Beethoven: Symphony No. 9; Analysis through Composition; Analysing Musical Multimedia;* and *Music: A Very Short Introduction.* Coeditor (with Mark Everist) of *Rethinking Music,* and Editor of the *Journal of the Royal Musical Association.* He was elected a

Fellow of the British Academy in 2001. Contact: ncook@soton.ac.uk. Web page: http://www.soton.ac.uk/~ncook/

Ian Cross teaches and researches in Music and Science at the University of Cambridge, where he is a University Lecturer and Fellow of Wolfson College. He has published numerous papers and book chapters as well as two co-edited books on music cognition. Contact: ic108@cus.cam.ac.uk. Web page: www.mus.cam.ac.uk/~cross.

Kevin Dawe is Lecturer in Ethnomusicology in the School of Music at the University of Leeds, U.K. He has worked as a professional musician, ethnomusicologist, organologist and scientific researcher in a variety of cultural contexts, including zoological gardens, museums, and recording studios in Greece, Spain, and Papua New Guinea. Contact: k.n.dawe @leeds.ac.uk

Nicola Dibben is a Lecturer in Music at the University of Sheffield. She has published on music perception, gender identity and music, and popular music, and is currently working on projects on emotion and music and analysis of popular music.

Ruth Finnegan is Emeritus Professor/Visiting Research Professor at Open University; Honorary Fellow of Somerville College Oxford; and Fellow of the British Academy. Her books include *Oral Literature in Africa; Oral Poetry; Literacy and Orality; The Hidden Musicians: Music-Making in an English Town; Oral Traditions and the Verbal Arts; Tales of the City: A Study of Narrative and Urban Life;* and *Communicating: The Multiple Modes of Human Interconnection.* Contact: Faculty of Social Sciences, Open University, Milton Keynes MK7 6AA, U.K.

Simon Frith is Professor of Film and Media at the University of Stirling, author of *Performing Rites. On the Value of Popular Music,* and chairs the judges of the Mercury Music Prize. Contact: s.w.frith@stir.ac.uk

Lucy Green is Reader of Music Education at the Institute of Education, London University, where she lectures in music education and the aesthetics and sociology of music. She is the author of *Music on Deaf Ears: Musical Meaning, Ideology and Education* (1988), *Music, Gender, Education* (1997), and *How Popular Musicians Learn: A Way Ahead For Music*

Education (2001). She has contributed articles and chapters on music education and the sociology of music to a number of journals and books.

Antoine Hennion is the Director of the Centre de Sociologie de l'Innovation, Ecole des Mines de Paris. He has written extensively on the sociology of music, and on the sociology of innovation, media, and cultural industries. His main fieldworks include studies on disc, music, radio, design, and advertising. His present work deals with different kinds of "amateurisms," passions, addictions, and attachments. Contact: antoine.hennion@ensmp.fr Web page: http://www.ensmp.fr/Fr/CSI/

Trevor Herbert is Professor of Music at the Open University. He has written extensively on the history, idioms, and culture of brass instruments and on Welsh music.

Lawrence Kramer is Professor of English and Music at Fordham University, New York, and coeditor of *19th-Century Music*. He is the author of numerous articles and books on the intersection of music and culture; recent books include *Musical Meaning: Toward a Critical History* (2001) and *Franz Schubert: Sexuality, Subjectivity, Song* (1998).

Dave Laing is Reader in the School of Communication and Creative Industries at the University of Westminster. His books include *The Sound of Our Time* (1969) and *One Chord Wonders: Power and Meaning in Punk Rock* (1985).

Richard Middleton is Professor of Music at the University of Newcastle upon Tyne, England. He is the author of *Pop Music and the Blues* (1972), *Studying Popular Music* (1990), and *Reading Pop* (2000), and was a founding editor of the journal *Popular Music*.

John Shepherd is Associate Dean (Research and Development) in the Faculty of Arts and Social Sciences at Carleton University, Ottawa, Canada, where he is also Professor of Music and Sociology. He has published widely in the area of the sociology and aesthetics of music and popular music studies. Dr. Shepherd is Chair of the Editorial Board and Managing Editor of *The Encyclopedia of Popular Music of the World*, and was elected a Fellow of the Royal Society of Canada in 2000.

Mark Slobin is Professor of Music at Wesleyan University and the author of numerous works on the musics of Afghanistan, eastern European Jews in the United States, and the theory of musical subcultures. Contact: mslobin@mail.wesleyan.edu

Martin Stokes received a Ph.D. in Social Anthropology at the University of Oxford in 1989. He currently teaches in the Music Department at the University of Chicago, where he is also a member of the Committee for the History of Culture, The Centre for Middle East Studies, and an affiliated member of the Department of Anthropology. He is the author of *The Arabesk Debate: Music and Musicians in Modern Turkey* (Clarendon, 1992) and the editor of *Ethnicity, Identity and Music: The Musical Construction of Place* (Berg, 1994).

Jeff Todd Titon is Professor of Music and Director of the Ph.D. Program in Music at Brown University. A Fellow of the American Folklore Society, his books include *Powerhouse for God* (1988), *Give Me This Mountain* (1989), *Early Downhome Blues* (2d ed., 1995), *Old-Time Kentucky Fiddle Tunes* (2001), and *Worlds of Music* (4th ed., 2002). From 1990 to 1995 he served as editor of *Ethnomusicology*, the Journal of the Society for Ethnomusicology. Contact: Jeff_Titon@brown.edu

Gary Tomlinson is Annenberg Professor in the Humanities and Chair of the Department of Music at the University of Pennsylvania. His books include *Monteverdi and the End of the Renaissance* (University of California Press, 1987), *Music in Renaissance Magic* (University of Chicago Press, 1993), and *Metaphysical Song: An Essay on Opera* (Princeton University Press, 1999). His essays published in journals and anthologies explore topics ranging from Aztec song to Miles Davis.

Jason Toynbee is Senior Lecturer in Communication, Culture and Media at Coventry University. His current research is on the relationship between the individual auteur and the creative network in popular music scenes. Contact: J.Toynbee@coventry.ac.uk

Rob C. Wegman teaches at Princeton University. His research interests include Josquin des Prez, Alexander Agricola, and the history of musical aesthetics.

Index